Anetso, the Cherokee Ball Game

FIRST PEOPLES
New Directions in Indigenous Studies

THE UNIVERSITY OF
NORTH CAROLINA PRESS
Chapel Hill

Anetso, the Cherokee Ball Game

At the Center of Ceremony and Identity

MICHAEL J. ZOGRY

Publication of this book was made possible, in part, with a grant from the Andrew W. Mellon Foundation.

© 2010 THE UNIVERSITY OF NORTH CAROLINA PRESS

All rights reserved. Designed by Kimberly Bryant and set in Scala and Scala Sans by Tseng Information Systems, Inc. Manufactured in the United States of America

The University of North Carolina Press has been a member of the Green Press Initiative since 2003.

Library of Congress Cataloging-in-Publication Data
Zogry, Michael J., 1966–
Anetso, the Cherokee ball game : at the center of ceremony and identity / Michael J. Zogry. — 1st ed.
p. cm.
Includes bibliographical references and index.
ISBN 978-0-8078-3360-5 (cloth : alk. paper)
1. Cherokee Indians—Games. 2. Anetso. 3. Cherokee Indians—Sports. 4. Cherokee Indians—Ethnic identity. I. Title.
E99.C5Z64 2010
305.897′557—dc22

2010003402

14 13 12 11 10   5 4 3 2 1

Contents

Acknowledgments *ix*

INTRODUCTION *Taladu quo!* (It is still 12!) *1*

1 *Tadatse anetsodui* (Go and play ball with them):
   Anetso in the Cherokee Narrative Tradition *33*

2 *Hani!* (Here!):
   Anetso as an Enduring Symbol of Cultural Identity
   in an Era of Great Change (1799–1838) *67*

3 *Ahaquo!* (Still there!):
   The Anetso Ceremonial Complex *107*

4 *Tseduga!* (Pass it to me!):
   Performing the Cherokee Ball Game in the
   Twentieth Century *147*

5 *Woye!* (Foul!):
   Theory and the Meaning of Anetso *185*

CONCLUSION *Taladu ogisquodiga*
   (12, we finished) *227*

Notes *237*
Bibliography *287*
Index *305*

Figures

1.1 "Wolftown Ball Game Team, with Feather Charms in Hair, Holding Rackets 1888" *8*
1.2 Wolftown team picture, Cherokee Fall Festival, 2004 *8*
1.3 "Men Playing Ballgame 1900" *14*
1.4 Wolftown players wrestle during an exhibition game, Cherokee Fall Festival, 2005 *14*
3.1 "Ceremony, Pre–Ball Game Dance 1888" *124*
3.2 "Pre–Ball Game Dance, 1946" *124*
3.3 "Ball Game n.d." *128*
3.4 Scarifier *128*
3.5 "Players Going to Water" *135*
4.1 "A Draught of the Cherokee Country" *156*
4.2 "The players before taking places on grounds for playing game of 'La Crosse'" *166*
4.3 "The 'Indian Ball' Teams" *168*
4.4 "Wolftown 1939 Ball Team" *177*
5.1 Pair of ball sticks *197*
5.2 Ball sticks, ball, and case *197*
5.3 Ball dress pants *199*
5.4 War dance mask representing human and rattlesnake *199*

Acknowledgments

The research and publication of this book were supported by an American Academy of Religion Individual Research Grant, three University of Kansas General Research Fund Awards, and a Friends of the Hall Center for the Humanities Book Publication Award.

For their friendship, as well as thoughtful engagement with and support of my work over the years, thanks in particular to Frank M. Chapman, Vincent J. Cornell, Sam D. Gill, James B. Jeffries, Joel S. Kaminsky, James M. McLachlan, Carrie McLachlan, Michael McNally, Craig Prentiss, Anne F. Rogers, and Daniel B. Stevenson. I also thank Vine Deloria Jr., Raymond D. Fogelson, John D. Loftin, Charles H. Long, Dwight F. Reynolds, Jonathan Z. Smith, and Inés M. Talamantez for their critiques, guidance, and suggestions regarding earlier formulations of ideas that made their way into this book. Thanks as well to the two anonymous readers for their keen critiques and constructive suggestions. For excellent conversation and an even better critical reading of the manuscript, I again thank my colleague Dan Stevenson here at the University of Kansas. Finally, I thank Elaine Maisner, my editor at the University of North Carolina Press, for her support, editorial advice, and patience.

I was aided immeasurably in my archival research by staff members at the following institutions: the Smithsonian Institution's National Museum of Natural History Department of Anthropology, the National Anthropological Archives, and the National Museum of the American Indian, Washington, D.C., and Suitland, Md.; the National Archives, Washington, D.C.; the Museum of the Cherokee Indian Archives, Cherokee, N.C.; the American Philosophical Society Library, Philadelphia, Pa.; the National Archives regional depositories in Morrow, Ga., and Kansas City, Mo.; the Newberry Library, Chicago, Ill.; the Moravian Archives, Winston-Salem, N.C.; the North Carolina Collection, University of North Carolina, Chapel Hill; and the Manuscript Collections, Duke University, N.C. Of great assistance in particular were past and present archivists at the Museum of the Cherokee Indian Archives, Joan Greene and James "Bo" Taylor.

On the Qualla Boundary in North Carolina, many individuals and institutions aided me in the completion of this book. First, I would like to thank the Eastern Band of Cherokee Indians Tribal Council for their formal approval of my research projects. Thanks to the staff at the Museum of the

Cherokee Indian, Cherokee, N.C., for their collegiality. In particular, I would like to thank Ken Blankenship, director of the museum, and Barry Hipps, former director of the Cherokee Historical Association, for their assistance and support. I want to extend a special thank you as well to the staff, "lunchtime crowd," and residents of Tsali Manor, the Eastern Band of Cherokee Indians Senior Citizens Center, who always made me feel welcome. Particular thanks are due to Deborah West, director of the center.

A number of friends, consultants, and interview participants who live on the Qualla Boundary have educated me immeasurably; others who did the same have passed away. Many individuals who have shared a great deal of their knowledge with me will not appear by name or by any other identifying characteristic in this book. I do, however, want to take this opportunity to thank all of them for sharing their time, experiences, and viewpoints with me, for the welcome that they gave me, as well as for their patience and, at times, bluntness.

For their longtime support I acknowledge my mother, Sharon Davis, and my brothers, Kenneth and Eric. I also acknowledge my father, Arnold Zogry, and my stepfather, Robert Davis, both of whom have passed away. Wherever they are, I hope there is a library. To my children, Sophia and Daniel, Daddy's finally done with his book! I look forward to watching you both grow up and make your own marks and remarks on the world. Finally, to my wife, Sally Monahan Zogry, I'm finally done with the book! I couldn't have done it without you. Well, even if I could have, as I will no doubt say when my time in this world is through, I wouldn't have wanted to.

INTRODUCTION

Taladu quo!
(It is still 12!)

Throughout the first decade of the twenty-first century, certain members of the Eastern Band of Cherokee Indians have continued a centuries-long practice by engaging in *anetso*, what has, in English parlance, come to be called the "Cherokee ball game." Anetso, as an event, is itself the focus and hub of an extended series of distinct activities. This series of actions can and has been identified as a ceremonial complex (or cycle), because historically it has featured virtually every activity that Cherokee people and non-Cherokee observers have identified as elemental of Cherokee "religion" or "ritual." However, interpreted as "game" within a broader framing of "religion," anetso simultaneously resists and problematizes such classifications.

Ostensibly an athletic contest that at one time pitted teams from the local community against one another in a regular seasonal schedule of games, it is a vigorous, sometimes violent activity that rewards speed, strength, and agility. Spirited wagering by community members on the outcome of the regular seasonal games was de rigueur until the first decades of the twentieth century. For centuries anetso also has been a staple of public performances for the benefit of visitors. As such it can be interpreted as a marker of Cherokee cultural identity that Cherokee people perform or self-present to both community members as well as other onlookers.

At the present time, typically two or three games of anetso are played each fall during the annual Cherokee Indian Fair, attended by Cherokee people from the local area and a number of tourists. Thus the players perform selected aspects of their cultural identity for a diverse crowd of spectators. A typical crowd might include community members who are invested deeply, mildly, or not at all in the activity, as well as tourists who possess varying levels of familiarity with anetso, including some with little or no understanding of what they are watching at all.

Anetso, like several other single- and double-racket ball games played by First Nations or Native American peoples, is a precursor to the game of lacrosse. People were playing it long before 1867, when the rules of lacrosse were standardized. Anetso appears in foundational Cherokee cultural narratives that have the same significance as those found in the Hebrew Bible, New Testament, Qur'an, Bhagavad-Gita, or any other texts considered to be key components of particular religious systems. In this sense it has an analogue in the ball games that are featured in the Popol Vuh. Beginning as early as 1714, non-Cherokee missionaries, ethnographers, and other itinerant travelers have described, discussed, and written about anetso regularly for almost three hundred years.

The Cherokee term for the ball game gives immediate insight into the cultural ubiquity of the practice. Spelled in Cherokee with three syllabary characters, "anetso" means "they are playing it" or "that which they play."[1] The word "ball" ("a-lhsgalhdi") is not in the term, presumably because it is not necessary for identification.[2] Based on my own conversations with Cherokee consultants, the preferred English translations are "Cherokee Indian ball" or some variation of that term, in addition to "Cherokee ball game."[3] Variations of these two terms have been favored by scholars as well.

Because anetso also is the center of a ceremonial complex, it defies simple classification. To expand on my characterization above ("an extended series of distinct activities"), by "ceremonial complex" I mean a group or cycle of individual ritual activities performed in a standardized sequence as parts of a single ritual event. Several scholars have employed something akin to this term to mark clusters of Cherokee ritual activities. Stanley Tambiah's discussion of "ritual complexes," based on his research in a Thai village, also has been quite influential. Tambiah assigned this term to four distinct groups of ritual activities, each as well as all four together being "a collectivity of rituals seen as a system in its own right (in terms of the arrangement of categories and symbols and officiants)."[4] To this designation I append the capability of a complex to incorporate a small number of other activities that are conducted in a prescribed manner, even if they are not isolatable ritual activities.

This is a useful concept in that it provides greater specific detail than simply defining the whole lot as a "ritual," while simultaneously illuminating the multifaceted structure of the overall event or "system." I choose "ceremonial" rather than "ritual" because it connotes this systemic quality more clearly, and for me points out an interpretive divide that is a key issue in the study of ritual. I will address the thorny issue of the definition of ritual below, but common definitions of both terms as nouns illustrate this divide: a ceremonial is a "*system* of rites," while a ritual is a "prescribed *order* of performing rites."[5] The emphasis of the first is the collectivity itself, while the emphasis of the second is rules about enacting the collectivity.

Through observation of ceremonial complexes, which may stretch over a series of days and include a variety of activities, various levels of interrelation become visible. Beyond the connections among activities themselves, a latticework of meaning is constructed that encompasses not only ritual but narrative and belief as well. In certain complexes the individual activities are all directed at a broader concern or goal, while in others attention is focused on one particular activity that is the nexus or hub of the complex.

This is the case with the Cherokee anetso complex. Bedrock Cherokee ceremonial activities constitute the majority of the complex, and this constellation of activities will be discussed in depth, including the proper Cherokee linguistic terminology. The activities include retention of a religious specialist who aids the team by performing a number of actions to affect individual players and the outcome of the game ("conjuring"), bathing or laving in running water ("going to water" and being "taken to water"), divination, use of formulas (ritual combinatory speech acts, later written down), scarification (scratching), ingestion and application of medicine, dietary and contact proscriptions, and dancing. Gambling and marching are two additional activities that are part of the cycle as well. While they are not discrete ritual elements per se, they are performed in a prescribed manner during the complex.

Considered as a unit, the anetso ceremonial complex incorporates a variety of activities that complicate standard scholarly distinctions such as ritual vs. game, public display vs. private performance, and tradition vs. innovation. Over centuries the ceremonial complex has undergone alteration, yet a ritual history of anetso reveals that the activity itself, as well as several of the constituent activities of the complex, has shown remarkable persistence, disputing the trajectory of decline and degeneration plotted even in the recent past by many scholars of First Nations cultures. For certain participants and observers alike it has remained vital as a series of practices as well as a symbolic link to a shared history, a distinctly emic vehicle of cultural identity and sometimes even a packaged response to the objectifications of cultural outsiders.

This vitality is clear in historical documents as well as in the larger context of scholarship about Cherokee people, in which the voices of Cherokee actors in history often are silent. As I detail in the book, historical evidence of anetso and its persistence in the face of condemnation by missionaries and government officials provides a type of historical "voice" for Cherokee people in those contexts. Why has anetso persisted in the face of serious and difficult circumstances in which participation in Cherokee cultural activities has lessened or ceased due to forcible suppression, coercion, pragmatism, or choice? Theorizing about the anetso ceremonial complex in a manner that recognizes the factor of diachronic change while highlighting the notion of persistence allows one to illustrate how it can feature discrete primary meanings in specific historical moments.

Finally, I also am keen to understand why the Cherokee ball game defies standard scholarly characterization as either solely a ritual or "simply" a game. The "game" of anetso is at the center of a series, cycle, or complex of "rituals" or "ceremonies"; at least these are the terms that often have been employed by most scholars as well as Cherokee people when discussing these isolatable, constituent activities occurring in repeatable sequences. Why is the phrase "it's only a game" so prevalent in discourse, and the phrase "it's only a ritual" is not? What assumptions underlie these categories, including assumptions about their mutual exclusivity?

No scholar working in the academic study of religions has conducted an in-depth study of the Cherokee game or the complex that it anchors. For that matter, there are very few sustained book-length treatments in any discipline of First Nations "games," in isolation or in combination with other activities that have so typically been portrayed as "rituals." There are several possible explanations for this lack of attention, but my primary contention is that it is due in part to the received categories of "ritual," "game," and "sport" (again, typically considered as a subset of game). Traditionally, at least in the United States and Europe, the realms of game and ritual have been considered distinct if not mutually exclusive in common parlance. This also has been the case in most scholarly discourse on the two categories, particularly after Claude Lévi-Strauss addressed the issue in *The Savage Mind* (1966 [1962]).[6]

Thus most scholars have not considered the possible conceptualization of the ball game *itself* as a ritual. Conversely, research suggests that for Cherokee people, realms of ritual, game, and sport traditionally have interfaced. In this book I will biopsy this pervasive dichotomy and, from a perspective in the academic study of religions, attempt to situate anetso in the contemporary scholarly discourse about ritual.

For all the reasons that I have outlined above, anetso is a perfect model to test the limits of received categories and definitional boundaries in order to provide more clarity of description regarding human activity, particularly with regard to these concepts of ritual, game, and sport. Examination of anetso and the complex it anchors provides a striking opportunity for rethinking approaches to the study of ritual and performance, as well as their relationship to cultural identity. In addition it will provide readers with a carefully researched, up-to-date, and much-needed reappraisal of scholarly discourse on the Cherokee religious system, with particular focus on the Eastern Band of Cherokee Nation.

Apprehending Anetso

We used to laugh about people coming to the boundary and wanting to do a book on Indians. They could come one day at eight and leave at four and write a full history. Others could come and stay for years and look back and say man I don't even know where to begin this book.
—Gil Jackson, "Fading Voices," Cherokee oral history documentary transcripts, 1987

On a brisk, sunny day in October 1997 I stepped on to the fairgrounds in Cherokee, North Carolina, during the 85th annual Cherokee Indian Fair. I had come as a bright- (or rather, bleary-) eyed Ph.D. candidate to watch anetso for the first time. The town of Cherokee, or *Elowadi* (Yellowhill), is located on the Qualla Boundary in western North Carolina. It is the seat of government for the Eastern Band of Cherokee Indians (ECBI), a federally recognized First Nation comprised of *Anitsalagi* (*Tsalagi*, Cherokee) people, whose name for themselves is *Aniyvwiya* (Principal People, Real People). The Boundary, home to the majority of the approximately 13,400 enrolled members of the Eastern Band, is a portion of what once was a vast homeland, but it is not a reservation.[7] The Eastern Band owns the land, with Cherokee individuals holding title to about 80 percent, and the federal government holds the land in trust.[8]

The Boundary proper is divided into five communities, also referred to as townships: Wolftown, Painttown, Birdtown, Big Cove, and Yellowhill. Each community has two representatives on the Cherokee Tribal Council. There are other smaller tracts of Cherokee-owned land around the perimeter of the Qualla Boundary, including the 3200-Acre Tract. The small Cherokee community called Snowbird, some sixty miles away in Robbinsville, North Carolina (Graham County), is a township as well. It splits its two representatives on the tribal council with the residents of the Tomotla community (Cherokee County).

The Qualla Boundary is a beautiful area of old-growth forests, mountains, rivers, streams, valleys, and coves. In fact, some of its forests are among the oldest in the world. As it was that day in 1997, today the Cherokee Indian Fair Grounds, which many local residents refer to as the Ceremonial Grounds, are located on a large rectangular lot in the center of town. The Museum of the Cherokee Indian flanks one short side of the lot, while the council house and offices of the Eastern Band of Cherokee Indians span the other.

The fairgrounds face Highway 441 North, with the Oconaluftee River situated across the two-lane road behind a strip of tourist shops and a motel. River and road wind together through town until they part ways on the outskirts, the river heading into a section of the Great Smoky Mountains National Park that contains a segment of the Blue Ridge Parkway, and the road continuing straight into the park and on to Gatlinburg, Tennessee. According to the National Park Service's website, the Great Smoky Mountains National Park, which straddles the border between North Carolina and Tennessee, is "America's most visited national park."[9] The Blue Ridge Parkway runs north over 450 miles to the Shenandoah National Park in Virginia; it routinely ranks first and the park third on the National Park Service's list of most visited units, with a combined total of approximately 23.35 million visitors in 2008.[10]

Highway 441 North extends to the opposite end of town where it intersects with Highway 19, leading to another major tourist attraction of decidedly more recent vintage. Harrah's Cherokee Casino opened in November 1997, and three years later it was one of the top attractions in the Southeast, with one newspaper report anointing it "the most visited private tourist spot in North Carolina."[11] In July 2008, despite the economic downturn in the United States, the casino indicated that it planned to continue a $650 million expansion.[12] In January 2009 the casino eliminated one hundred jobs, 5 percent of its workforce, citing a 15 percent decrease in visitors, but plans for the expansion remained in effect.[13]

The town of Cherokee has changed a great deal physically since 1997, but a visitor still would recognize the basic features of the Ceremonial Grounds, albeit with differences. On the back side of the grounds is a hill with inset stone bleachers that date back to the 1940s when the lot served as the football field for the Bureau of Indian Affairs school. Today a large soundstage faces the bleachers, but in 1997 there was a much smaller temporary wooden stage that did not obscure the view of the field. At that time the bleachers provided seating for various events on the grass-and-dirt playing field, including the Cherokee ball game.

From that vantage point in October 1997 a spectator gazing across the field would have seen a small midway, with children and teenagers crowded around stalls that offered games of chance and amusement rides. The fair was in full swing, and the town was brimming with tourists and locals alike. The imminent opening of the casino was a main topic of conversation, with residents expressing mixed views.

Vendors sold artwork, clothing, books, and music. Facing the road beyond the midway lay a 1970s-era colonnade; above and beyond it in the distance rose the lush green mountains that are so distinctive to the area, arranged like a hand of playing cards. To the left of the midway stood an exhibition building, and to the immediate left, lining the short end of the field, ran a set of temporary wooden food booths. Hungry fairgoers packed the tables beneath a large tent next to the food booths, their plates piled with hamburgers, "Indian tacos," and a local favorite, bean bread. To the right, at the other short end of the field sat an old scoreboard, and a chain link fence ringed the entire grounds.

As I made my way through the crowd that day in October 1997, I moved past the area of whizzing and spinning carnival rides and over to the field. I noted that a crowd of spectators, both local residents and tourists, was massing on either side of the field to form human sidelines, and the bleachers were filling up as well. At that moment a rush of anticipation and excitement came over me. Finally I was going to see a Cherokee ball game.

At the time, I was enamored with the idea of identifying ritual or religious practices that were athletic in nature, having been introduced to anetso while taking a course with Raymond Fogelson. Fogelson had written his 1962 dissertation on the ball game but had not published a book-length work on the topic. My initial research questions were quite straightforward: 1) Did anetso presently (thirty years after Fogelson's study) or at some point in the past function as a ritual? In other words, were people in fact praying, worshiping, or engaging in other activities typically characterized as "religious" by playing this game? 2) How often did Cherokee people still play this game, and how did they interpret what they were doing?

My angle was to study anetso from an academic study of religions perspective, more specifically with a particular theoretical interest in ritual as a defining religious activity. Other people had studied dance, theater, singing, even gambling games, and had made interesting claims about their religious natures. There also were scattered scholarly sources from a variety of disciplinary perspectives that discussed relationships between sports, games, performance, and ritual. In my mind many of the conclusions ventured in these sources were uneven.

As I began to research the history of and cumulative scholarship on anetso I found it to be the axis or hub of an extended complex or cycle of related activities. For example, early on I read James Mooney's 1890 article in the *American Anthropologist* entitled "The Cherokee Ball Play." According to the author, he spent "several field seasons" studying the "mythology and ceremonial" of the ball play, as he referred to it.[14] Mooney chose the last game he witnessed, in September 1889, to illustrate the features of the activity. He was puzzled that previous authors, when mentioning anetso, seemed "completely unaware of the secret ceremonies and incantations—the fasting,

FIGURE I.1. "Wolftown Ball Game Team, with Feather Charms in Hair, Holding Rackets 1888." Wolftown Ball Team, October 1888, on the banks of a river, probably the Oconaluftee, before going to water. Back row, left to right: Eldridge Crow, Joe Crow, Kuwana ("Duck"), Twister (Captain), Jin Johnson (Danaiski), Sawanuka, Luyisi (Lewis Hornbuckle). Front row: Joe Standing Deer (Ahawi-kataga), Peter Crow (Kagu-Ayeltiski "Crow Mocker"). (National Anthropological Archives, Smithsonian Institution, Negative #1041, Inventory #06217800; photograph by James Mooney.)

FIGURE I.2. Wolftown team picture, Unity Field, Cherokee Fall Festival, 2004. (Photograph by author.)

bathing, and other mystic rites—which for days and weeks preceded the play and attend every step of the game."[15]

In a period review of the article, the anonymous reviewer noted that Mooney brought out "in the most emphatic way the close connection between religious life and the customs of ordinary life among primitive men."[16] The reviewer noted that there was a "myth" connected to the game, and continued, "The players are trained, but have at the same time to go through certain performances of a religious character, abstaining from certain food and certain occupations, ceremonial bathing and bleeding. The night preceding the game a dance is held by the whole tribe in which men and women take part and which has evidently a religious significance."[17]

Therefore I quickly realized that in order to understand the game, I would need to understand the complex that it anchored: the activities done before, during, or after it. These "performances of a religious character," these "secret ceremonies" or "mystic rites . . . which for days and weeks preceded the play and attend every step of the game" were clearly manifold. Five were mentioned in the article and the review: "incantations," "abstaining from certain food and occupations," "ceremonial bathing and bleeding," and a community dance the night before the game with "religious significance." Moreover, as the above quotations illustrate, scholars had dubbed several of these activities "rites," "ceremonies," or "religious" activities either by means of their own received categories or based on research with Cherokee people. The initial assumption that emerged from my first perusal of the material was that anetso anchored a ceremonial complex (or cycle) featuring virtually every activity that Cherokee people and non-Cherokee observers have identified as being religious. On the other hand, anetso itself most often was identified as a game, and Claude Lévi-Strauss's classic distinction between game and ritual, which I read for the first time, supported this interpretation.[18]

As I continued to research the topic of "Cherokee religion" systematically, to my dismay I found that despite the availability of an enormous amount of Cherokee studies scholarship, there was no published book-length scholarly treatment available on the subject of anetso and its role in Cherokee religion and culture, let alone one focused on the Eastern Band of Cherokee Nation's religious system. Though plentiful, the Cherokee studies scholarship on the whole was uneven. Additionally, much to my surprise, the two standard works on anetso remained the anthropologist James Mooney's 1890 article and Raymond Fogelson's unpublished 1962 doctoral dissertation. Even more surprising was the fact that Mooney and Fogelson were two of the most careful scholars of the Cherokee religious system.

Now here I was, in 1997, on the sideline, preparing to see a live game, four years after first embarking on the project. I had conferred with Cherokee consultants, or in prevalent terminology, "conducted ethnographic research." I had interviewed elderly individuals about what the game was like "back in the day," and I had spoken with current participants. I had read several Cherokee cultural narratives about ball games, including one about birds and animals who played anetso before humans inhabited the earth. There also were other narratives in which the Little Men, who were the sons of *Kanati,* the first hunter, and *Selu,* who gave corn to the Cherokee people, played anetso. I had read countless accounts of the game written in the eighteenth, nineteenth, and twentieth centuries by anthropologists, missionaries, and other itinerant travelers. In addition, I had read widely in the areas of religious studies and related disciplines, devouring works on ritual in particular. For all these reasons, I considered myself learned.

At the time I was working concurrently on an oral history video project, Enduring Voices, in collaboration with the Museum of the Cherokee Indian. I had conceived the project, written the grant proposal, and taken the role of principal investigator in order to financially support and conduct my cultural consultation, or fieldwork, in what I felt was a responsible and ethical manner. In December 1996 the Eastern Band of Cherokee Indians Tribal Council formally granted permission to proceed with both my dissertation fieldwork and the documentary project. The immediate objective of the project was to interview elderly Cherokee people, who were encouraged to share what information and reminiscences they might like to preserve for future generations in that format. All participants received financial compensation for their time and videotape copies of their interviews. Whenever possible, community members were involved in every phase of the project.[19]

Now, standing on the edge of the field, I held a video camera provided by the museum at the ready. Completely absorbed in my task, I stationed myself near midfield at the front of the crowd and checked the camera for angle and focus. A nearby spectator suggested that I back up, explaining that with no actual sidelines the game often spilled into the crowd. I smiled and politely thanked him, but stood my ground. After all, I thought to myself, I am here as a documentarian and a scholar, and I am willing to take risks for the footage.

Though many questions raced through my mind as I awaited the start of the game, one persisted as if on a loop: What interpretive theoretical framework would best apprehend and categorize this activity? I scrolled through a mental rolodex of names and theories. Would this "cultural performance," as Milton Singer would term it, conform to Claude Lévi-Strauss's distinction between game and ritual and reveal itself as one or the other, or rather would it conform to Stewart Culin's view that all First Nations games were once religious? Would I agree with Victor Turner's description of the event as a transformative "sacred game" with a "liminoid" character, or would I see evidence of deep play and cultural identity as text, as Clifford Geertz had with the Balinese cockfight? Would the event be more of a complex performance type, as John MacAloon might argue, presenting elements of ritual and spectacle in combination with carnivalesque elements, per Mikhail Bakhtin?[20]

Would it illustrate Pierre Bourdieu's notion of *habitus*, thereby informing Catherine Bell's notion of "ritualization," or would Ronald Grimes's notion of "ritualizing" be more apt? Alternatively, would I see that anetso really was its own telos, that it was self-referential or autotelic, thus supporting theories of such scholars as Don Handelman? If this proved to be the case, would Frits Staal's theory of the "meaninglessness" of ritual in the sense of reference to other functions or interpretations in fact mean that it was autotelic?

Having additionally immersed myself in Cherokee studies, would I see evidence of anthropologist James Mooney's 1900 assessment that the ball play, as he referred to it, was on its last legs, just ten years after he wrote the first scholarly article on the activity? Would my observations verify Leonard Broom's assertion in 1937 that anetso preserved an entire body of cultural knowledge that otherwise would have disappeared? Perhaps I would see what Raymond Fogelson did; he felt that the complex was no longer as integral to Cherokee culture as it once was and eventually would disappear. Surprised by the continued survival of many of the activities that Mooney had described, Fogelson attributed this to their role in the presentation of the ball game to tourists. Would my analysis resonate with Fogelson's insights, or those of any of the many other anthropologists who studied and engaged in fieldwork among the Eastern Cherokee before me?

Finally, what if the activity did not conform to any of the categories, descriptions, or interpretations that I had studied? Would the "seriously playful" approach that Sam Gill has advocated, knowingly asserting a stance while simultaneously recognizing its arbitrary and absurd nature, be the way to go? I was sure that once I saw the game for myself, it would hit me like a flash of light—the event would come clearly into focus and fall into meaningful place. Abruptly I snapped out of my hermeneutical (and hermetic) reverie and surveyed my surroundings—the game was about to begin.

The crowd now was quite substantial, and I noticed that there were tree saplings placed into the ground at diagonal opposite corners of the field, roughly where the two end zones would have been. Then I saw the two opposing teams, each with ten players, enter from opposite ends of the field, walking single-file. They then lined up across either end of the field, facing in the other team's direction. Each player held in his hands two wooden sticks with webbed cups at the ends. They wore no shirts, shoes, headgear, or other padding—only short pants.

A signal was given, and with a series of synchronized movements and loud calls, the two teams moved in line formation toward the center of the field. One designated player would call out, and his entire team would respond in unison as they moved forward while holding the line. Then they would stop, and the other team would do the same. They continued this procedure a prescribed number of times until they met at the center of the field. Then, standing in their two lines facing each other, they laid their sticks down on the ground in front of them, pointed at the other team.

One man clearly was the official appointed to oversee the game. Several of the players shifted anxiously from one foot to the other as he walked between the two lines. Two men accompanied him, each carrying a long thin tree branch. The official matched up each player against a player on the other team of comparable ability, size, and experience. They remained paired for the duration of the game, guarding each other much like a man-to-man defense in basketball. The official then reviewed the rules. Finally, all was ready.

The players broke ranks and gathered around him in the middle of the field, and the official called out *"Taladu quo!* (It is still 12!)" as he tossed a small golf-sized ball up into the air, much like a jump ball at the beginning of a basketball game. Sticks and bodies crashed together as players fought for the ball, and the struggle continued as players tried to pick the ball up with their sticks. The pace was fast and the play was furious.

Though forbidden from picking up the ball with their hands, players could touch it once they had lifted it a certain predetermined distance off the ground with their sticks. Once a player had possession of the ball, he could either race toward his own home goal in hopes of scoring, or throw the ball, handing it off to a team member. The ball seemed tiny to me, and I found it difficult to follow the action, even more so through the camera's eye. Confused by players running in different directions, I did not know what to film; I slung the camera wildly this way and that in an attempt to catch the chaotic action.

Oftentimes it seemed to me that some players were more interested in one-on-one wrestling matches with their individual opponents than chasing the ball. At one point, the group was near midfield, and suddenly a player burst from the scrum and raced away. As the rest of the players made chase, two players squared off and began grappling. Suddenly, one of the two players grabbed the other in a headlock, and in a swift motion bent the other player backwards and flipped him on to the ground. The crowd responded with a combination of cheers and gasps, and the players continued to struggle for a minute or two until the player who had gained the advantage, confident that he had delayed his opponent long enough, released his hold. The players shoved each other as they were getting up from the ground, and then ran to rejoin the rest of the action.

All of a sudden I realized that the mass of bodies was hurtling toward me. But where was the ball? I remember thinking to myself, "I'll just hop out of the way at the last second if I need to, but surely they won't just bowl people over. Especially not me, since I am here in an official capacity to document this cultural activity for posterity. *But where is the ball? They're still running full tilt. They're really* not going to sto—!"

I do not remember what happened in the next few seconds, but the video footage recorded the sights and sounds for posterity: players headed in my direction, people in the crowd cheering and shouting, a sudden impact and grunt from me, and then . . . the sky. I was knocked flat on my back, lying on the ground with the camera pointed skyward. For a moment, my mind was clear of questions; I certainly had ceased to think about the theoretical implications of the ball game. It was a brief respite. As I lay there on the ground, I wondered if this is what Jonathan Z. Smith meant when he said that situational incongruity gives rise to thought. I gathered myself together, and, ever the intrepid ethnographer, I managed to hop up, refocus the camera, and catch sight of a player running down the edge of the field toward one of the goals.

After the game was over, I trailed behind the players as they made their way out of the fairgrounds, across the street, and down the short incline to the Oconaluftee River. This game had been an exhibition between two squads of the Wolftown township's team because no other community had fielded a team that year. Once on the riverbank the players lined up as they had on the field, and the team manager, positioned between them and the water, walked up and down the line, talking to them. I could not hear what he was saying, because I had instinctively decided to stop at the bottom of the incline, out of earshot. I did not feel it was appropriate to film either. When he had finished his remarks, the manager stepped aside.

The man who had led the call-and-response sequences on the field called out once again, and the team responded in unison, once again a prescribed number of times. Then the players laid their sticks on the ground and waded out into the water. At first it seemed like they were just taking a swim, perhaps to cool off after the game. They were laughing, joking, and splashing each other.

FIGURE 1.3. "Men Playing Ballgame 1900." Two players wrestle while the game continues apace down the field. There are cross designs on one of the player's shorts. (National Anthropological Archives, Smithsonian Institution, Negative #1038-37, Inventory #01766200; photograph by James Mooney.)

FIGURE 1.4. Wolftown players wrestle during an exhibition game, Cherokee Fall Festival, 2005. (Photograph by author.)

But then I noticed that some of the players were rubbing each other's backs with water, and in the midst of all the activity each player at some point went underneath the water several times. This is an activity known in English as "going to water." I will discuss it in detail in an upcoming chapter, but here I will note that historically and presently, the general consensus among both Cherokee people and those who study their culture has been that it *is* a ritual.

When the players began emerging from the water and heading up the hill I joined them and walked across the street, talking about the game. A few players could barely contain their laughter as they asked me about being knocked down. In the hours, days, and weeks after the game, I did not really understand why so many coworkers and consultants in the community thought that what had happened to me was so funny. But I was teased quite a bit about it and heard the episode referenced with amusement many times. It also was quite surprising that so many people knew what had happened to me even before I told them.

When I brought the video to a team gathering a week later, several team members felt that they had to rewind that portion of the tape where I was knocked down. They watched it over and over again, laughing all the while. Well, at least my colleagues at the museum were concerned, or so I thought: several approached me with worried looks on their faces to ask if the video camera was all right, only to break into laughter when I replied crankily that, yes, the camera was fine.

At the time, this seemed to be an innocuous event, a passing incident. Yes, it was a source of great amusement for people who knew me (and likely those who did not) in the community. In addition, the fact that eventually I was able to laugh about it, and at myself, was helpful as I bumbled around the Qualla Boundary, over time ever slightly less awkwardly so. However, at the time, I imbued the event with no lasting significance.

Since then, however, it has continued to reassert itself as a strong memory. I now think of it as a metaphor for describing my process of grappling with the relevant issues, and frankly, the limitations of my scholarly perspective to apprehend even this bit of culture in anything but a fleeting way. Seeing anetso for the first time I was struck (literally) by the fact that the experience was different than I had expected. Other than getting knocked down, it was not that something unexpected had happened, and it was certainly not that I was disappointed. Instead, watching anetso firsthand had raised more questions than it had answered.

What I was sure of at that time was that anetso, whether considered as game or ritual, just did not fit either rubric. The following year, 1998, I asked for and received permission to film the team going to water after their last game of the fair. An unselfconscious entry from my October 11th fieldwork notes encapsulated both the conceptual impasse and the intensity of that day's game: "Later, filmed Wolftown and after, gtw [going to water]. Those guys knocked the crap out of each other."[21]

I maintain the same viewpoint today; either anetso skewers received categories or those categories are skewed, I'm not sure which. In any case the available theoretical frameworks have the wrong-shaped holes for this Cherokee peg. Sixteen years after my first visit to the Qualla Boundary, try as I might to keep up with the action and interpret it, I am perpetually flat on my back on the ground, digitally recording the sky. The players are already past me, the game is continuing apace, and I'm thinking to myself, "Man, I don't even know where to begin this book."

Bodies of Knowledge

I think that sport is, with dance, one of the terrains in which is posed with the maximum acuteness the problem of the relations between theory and practice, and also between language and the body.
—Pierre Bourdieu, "Programme for a Sociology of Sport," 1990

In 2007, Sam Gill wrote that "prayer, Native American religions, ritual, and dancing . . . share an odd commonality, and that is that they all seem religiously ignored, or less dramatically, underappreciated by the academic study of religion."[22] I would add game and sport to this list. Gill observed that "for an academic study heavily centered in North America to all but ignore the indigenous traditions that are meshed with American identity seems likewise confounding."[23] He further observed that "the paucity of attention given to ritual really needs no argument."[24]

In an earlier essay, entitled "Embodied Theology," Gill argued that notions of the body from European Christianity continue to dominate interpretive frameworks of scholars, hampering the discussion of ritual.[25] He proposed that the academic study of religion, as a subset of the "Western academy," is itself a form of embodied theology, a position he reiterated in the 2007 article.[26] Though at present I am not prepared to grant this notion the universal application that Gill suggests, his point of view is provocative.

Related to the question of why there is not more attention to ritual is the question of how to write about it. As Gill once said to me in an email conversation regarding this issue, "I do think that one of these days we need to know how to actually foreground action when action is our subject."[27] In a similar vein Catherine Bell has stated, with regard to Pierre Bourdieu's commentary on the subject (which she rightly characterized as somewhat vague), that "habitus is an awkward but explicit formulation of the real insight within Bourdieu's work on practice, namely the need 'to confront the act itself.'"[28] Both qualities Bell attributed to the notion are on display in the most often-quoted definition of *habitus*, itself a 106-word sentence. It does, however, contain the key phrase "systems of durable, transposable *dispositions*, structured structures predisposed to function as structuring structures."[29]

Bourdieu himself said in his article "Programme for a Sociology of Sport" that sport was "an element of the system of dispositions (of the habitus)"; later in the article he elaborated on the subject:[30]

> There is a way of understanding which is altogether particular, and often forgotten in theories of intelligence: that which consists of understanding with one's body. There are heaps of things that we understand only with our bodies, outside conscious awareness, without being able to put our understanding into words. The silence of sportspeople . . . stems partly from the fact that, when you are not a professional analyst, there are certain things you can't say, and sporting practices are practices in which understanding is bodily. Very often, all you can do is say: "Look, do what I'm doing."[31]

Strategies to foreground action, to confront the act itself, and to write about it remain elusive.

Bourdieu argued that sport's "dominant meaning, that is, the social meaning attached to it by its dominant social users (numerically or socially speaking) may change: indeed, it is frequent that at one and the same time—and this is true of a philosophical work too—a sport may be given two very different meanings."[32] He further argued that the "objective polysemia" and "partial indeterminancy" of sport make it "available for different uses."[33]

He continued: "A sport, at a given moment, is rather like a musical work: it is both the musical score (the rules of the game, etc.), and also the various competing interpretations (and a whole set of sedimented interpretations from the past); and each new interpreter is confronted by this, more unconsciously than consciously, when he proposes 'his' interpretation. We would need to analyse in accordance with this logic the 'returns' (to Kant, to period instruments, to French boxing, etc.)."[34]

That anetso fits this description is no surprise. However it is my contention that these attributes—polysemia, indeterminancy, and the characteristic of being at once the game as it has been, or is "supposed to be," along with an active tradition of competitive reinterpretation—also are shared by ritual. While generally speaking I ascribe to the contemporary scholarly trend of highlighting difference rather than affinity, I will argue in Chapter 5 that in this case reasserting affinities between the cultural frames of game, sport (as a subset of game), and ritual is not counterproductive. This is because, as I will demonstrate, in *The Savage Mind* Claude Lévi-Strauss inaccurately rendered what has become a classic differentiation of game and ritual that continues to inform contemporary scholarship. I am not arguing that one cannot differentiate between the two categories of activity, but that they cannot be differentiated universally in the manner that Lévi-Strauss argued. Anetso is but one First Nations activity that complicates this game/ritual distinction, and in Chapter 5 I will present several selected examples in the process of arguing for a corrective to this standard distinction.

The following 1997 quotation from Catherine Bell, perhaps the foremost historian of scholarship on ritual, reflects the fact that there is a generally held notion about this binary opposition or conceptual dyad of game and ritual:

> Although European and American societies are apt to describe table etiquette, sports, theater productions, and political rallies as ritual-like, there is still a general consensus that they are not the best examples of what we usually mean by ritual. No matter how ritual-like sports and theater might appear to be at times, we are not apt to consider them the same thing as a church wedding ceremony. We have found it appropriate to see some basic distinctions among these ways of acting even if we occasionally note how blurred those distinctions can become.[35]

The quotation lends credence to my point, particularly Bell's use of the "royal we" in such a general sense along with her value judgment about "best examples." Bell went on to say that "other cultures also draw and blur distinctions," and that investigating these "can reveal interesting aspects of the ways in which people in that culture are likely to experience and interpret the world."[36]

Scholars being purveyors of "distinction" par excellence, one must be careful to separate such actions on the part of those being studied from those of the researcher. In the context of his discussion of the development of religion as an anthropological concept in the sixteenth century, Jonathan Z. Smith made the point that it was "not a first person term of self-characterization . . . [but a] category imposed from the outside on some aspect of native culture."[37] The concept was imbued with "implicit universality . . . [and] thought to be a ubiquitous human phenomenon" with this important caveat: its "characteristics [were] those that appear[ed] natural to the other."[38] Many people simply do not have analogous notions of religion in their own cultures. I submit that such perspectives outlined by Bell and Smith obtain today.

The Meaninglessness of Ritual Definition

The search for the definition of ritual has been a lost cause from the outset.
— Bruce Kapferer, "Ritual Dynamics and Virtual Practice:
Beyond Representation and Meaning"

In the course of researching and writing about the anetso ceremonial complex, I have found it necessary to characterize certain contours of "Cherokee religion" or "the Cherokee religious system," and then attempt to place anetso in relationship to these self-conscious constructions. To reiterate my contention from above, the anetso complex incorporates the great majority of activities designated by the received category "religious."

Thus the study of the anetso ceremonial complex, in addition to fruitfully problematizing standard notions of "ritual" and "game/play," provides an excellent introduction to the Cherokee religious system and larger questions surrounding its historical study. As with the term "ritual," I use the phrase "religious system" advisedly; I cite, among other such discussions of terminology, Robert Ford Campany's recent incisive critique of "isms," the terms "religious traditions" and "religious systems," and his concurrent alternatives "imagined communities" and "religious repertoires."[39] Although I will problematize these terms in the course of the present work, for the time being I will define a religious system, or "repertoire," tautologically and simply as "a constructed group, set or relationship of a number of cultural elements, all of which have been designated by the received category 'religious,' either by adherents or scholars."[40] The group or set can expand or contract, and relationships need not be permanent.

Additionally, in employing this term "religious," I do not suggest any sort of truth value with respect to an essential, universal "nature" of religion and religiosity; nor do I adhere to Geertz's "system of symbols."[41] While my formulation does belie an affinity for the conceptualization of religion as a cultural construct akin to Geertz's "system of symbols," since this position is inherently grounded in culturally specific truth-value judgments I stop short of making this claim.[42] In turn, I provisionally define a ritual as an activity that is part of a religious system, or "repertoire," having been designated as such by the received category "religious," either by adherents or scholars, and subject to the same conditions as the system or repertoire.

I am of course mindful of committing the cardinal sin of the tautologic definition. Obviously as such these definitions are nothing more than heuristic devices that allow me to engage with relevant scholarship, provide a framework for interpretation of cultural consultant's viewpoints and archival documents, and construct a platform from which to theorize about the issues at hand. They are useless beyond these and one additional function. These definitions also underscore the inherent polysemia of the terminology and subject matter itself in academic discourse as well as common parlance.

Bruce Kapferer has argued that "ritual is one of the most used, perhaps overused, sociological categories and one of the most resistant to adequate definition."[43] He commented further that, "even though, it seems, that anthropologists can recognize a ritual when they seen one, they have very diverse criteria for labeling what they see to be ritual."[44] I see the problem in this way: Everybody seems to think that they know what a ritual is, but no one seems to be able to come up with a definition that satisfies anyone else.

As evidence of his contention, Kapferer cited a laundry list of approaches marshaled to address the issue of definition, including "representational, linguistic, and literary approaches," "psychiatry and psychoanalysis," and "philosophy of numerous varieties, but in particular neo-Kantian and phenomenological existential perspectives."[45] Kapferer argued that other scholars "have borrowed freely from linguistic philosophy (e.g., the application of the Austinian concept of performatives by Rappaport 1999), from drama and performance theory (e.g. Bell 1992), [and] from cybernetics and systems theory (e.g., Shore 1999)." He contended that these interpretations, while "insightful," nevertheless "subordinate ritual to the logic and rationale of practices that are not necessarily those of ritual."[46] Thus, for him they ultimately produced "limited and all too frequently overly ethnocentric and occasionally mystical results."[47] I could not agree with him more.

Despite Gill's comment about the "paucity of attention given to ritual," the world does not need another taxonomy of theories about ritual, least of all one constructed by me. Therefore I will invoke only those selected theories about ritual that inform my project most directly. In "The Meaningless of Ritual," Frits Staal openly wondered why it had "proved so difficult to define the meaning, goals and aims of ritual," as well as why there existed "so many different answers and theories, not only often contradictory between themselves, but of such disparate character that it is difficult to even compare them with each other."[48] His answer was succinct: "ritual has no meaning, goal or aim."[49] Elaborating on the point, he said that ritual "is pure activity," and continued, "to say that ritual is for its own sake is to say that it is meaningless, without function, aim, or goal, or also that it constitutes its own aim or goal. It does not follow that it has no value: but whatever value it has is intrinsic value."[50]

Contrasting ritual with "our ordinary, everyday life," he stated that "in ritual activity, the rules count, but not the result. In ordinary activity it is the other way around. What is essential in the ceremony is the precise and faultless execution, in accordance with rules, of numerous rites and recitations. The result is important, but it has only ritual use and can only be reached in the ritually prescribed manner."[51] One might say the same about game. Staal of course has his critics, one of the most vocal being Hans Penner, but his question and answer about ritual still resonate today.[52]

In his introduction to a 2005 edited volume on ritual, Don Handelman reiterated his opposition "to the value of any universal, overarching definition or conception of ritual."[53] While he agreed that "ritual does not have meaning within itself, for its own sake, since meaning indexes representation," he objected to Staal's "speaking for 'ritual' as a general category" as well as his use of any one ritual as "paradigmatic of all ritual."[54] He proposed "phenomenological" and "hermeneutical" steps designed to "illumine whether—and if so, how—the ritual can be said to have its own interior integrity, and therefore whether it exists more as a representation of sociocultural order or more through its own autonomy forms such order.... without necessarily slipping into an inherently functionalist understanding."[55] While unlike Handelman I do not regard the phenomenological move as essential, I do agree with the call for consideration of the activity as an entity unto itself.

Handelman defined ritual, "however loosely, . . . as a class of phenomena whose forms, in greatly differing kind and degree, are characterized by interior complexity, self-integrity, and irreducibility to agent and environment."[56] He highlighted the notion of "self-organization," and noted that "whatever is being organized is self-referential or self-reflexive."[57] Handelman favored the term "autopoiesis" to name this attribute ("self-making") and stated that the "phrasing" of his introduction "addresses ritual as a curving towards self-closure and self-organization."[58]

In a like manner I employ the term "autotelic," as Victor Turner did, drawing in turn from the work of John MacAloon and Mihaly Czikszentmihalyi. Turner remarked of a certain experience that it was, "'autotelic,' i.e., *it seems to need no goals or rewards outside itself.*"[59] Kapferer cited Victor Turner's scholarship as formative to his own thinking because "his is the main route, within anthropology, for a discussion of ritual dynamics that is grounded in the phenomenon of ritual action itself."[60] Handelman's notion of autopoesis, Staal's idea of the meaning of ritual being intrinsic, and Turner, Czikszentmihalyi, and MacAloon's use of "autotelic" all speak to this point.

Another scholar deeply involved in the study of ritual and also influenced by Victor Turner is Ronald Grimes. In a 1982 article, Grimes described "ritualizing" as what "transpires as animated persons enact formative gestures in the face of receptivity during crucial times in founded places."[61] More recently Grimes has continued to use the term "ritualizing," as well as employing the term "ritualization." His definition of the former is "the act of deliberately cultivating or constructing a new rite."[62] The latter is, with regard to humans, "activities not normally viewed as rites but treated as if they were or might be, for instance, giving birth, house cleaning, canoeing, and TV watching—all have been regarded as ritual."[63] The difference for Grimes between a rite and a ritual is that the former are "sequences of action rendered special by virtue of their condensation, elevation, or stylization . . . [a] distinct, socially recognized set of procedures."[64] The latter is a "general idea of actions characterized by a certain 'family' of qualities."[65]

In the essay "Putting Space in Its Place," Ronald Grimes offered a critique of well-known assertions about ritual put forth by Jonathan Z. Smith in his article "The Bare Facts of Ritual" and his book *To Take Place: Toward Theory in Ritual*.[66] Grimes began the piece with objections to "some of Smith's assumptions and with the uncritical way that his arguments are appropriated by others."[67] He asserted that "both Smith and I theorize about ritual, but he privileges space, and I do not. If I privilege anything, it is action."[68] Grimes presented his theory as a van Gennep-Turner-inspired position of action and juxtaposed this with his characterization of Smith's anti-Eliadian position as being place-based, due to the fact that Smith was in essence caught in Eliadian theory's gravitational pull.[69] To be fair to Smith, at least in the earlier work his task was more of a response to Eliade than an assertion of a position; as he noted elsewhere, "I tend not to speak my mind, but to speak my mind in relation to another mind."[70] Nevertheless, Grimes did effectively draw a useful line of emphasis between this discourse and others regarding ritual.

Employing a time-honored strategy, I locate myself right on the line between place and agency and once again argue for the primacy of the actions themselves. Of course people have to engage in the actions, but I still agree with Handelman's provisional definition of ritual discussed above, in which he stipulated the following characteristics: "interior complexity, self-integrity, and irreducibility to agent and environment." Grimes's understanding of ritualizing highlights the characteristic of action or agency just as Bourdieu's *habitus*, and by extension, Catherine Bell's notion of ritualization.

Bell explained her "preliminary sense" of ritualization in the following manner: "ritualization is a matter of various culturally specific strategies for setting some activities off from others, for creating and privileging a qualitative distinction between the 'sacred' and the 'profane,' and for ascribing such distinctions to realities thought to transcend the powers of human actors."[71] She went on to say that, "confronting the ritual act itself . . . would involve asking how ritual activities, in their doing, generate distinctions between what is or is not acceptable ritual," rather than constructing a "theory or model of ritual practice."[72]

I think that the primary utility of Bell's notion of ritualization is that rather than defining what a ritual is, to repeat my comment from above, she located the importance or interpretation in the agency of the individual, the one who "ritualizes" a particular action or event. This is the final characteristic of the four she suggested, and it "can be evoked through the concept of 'redemptive hegemony,' which is a synthesis of Kenelm Burridge's notion of the 'redemptive process' and Antonio Gramsci's notion of 'hegemony.'"[73] This "is not an explicit ideology or a single and bounded *doxa* that defines a culture's sense of reality. It is a strategic and practical orientation for acting, a framework possibly only insofar as it is embedded in the act itself."[74] Therefore it "does not reflect reality more or less effectively; it creates it more or less effectively."[75] Such a focus on ritualization results in the conclusion that "what is ritual is always contingent, provisional, and defined by difference."[76]

I understand her use of "hegemony," but question the inclusion of "redemption." Granted the term does not have to be interpreted theologically, but to my mind there is some sort of value system in operation. In this sense I agree with Kapferer's assessment above that Bell and other theorists "subordinate ritual to the logic and rationale" of other practices, which can produce limited, "ethnocentric and occasionally mystical results." However I do agree with Bell's summation of ritual as "strategic and practical orientation . . . embedded in the act itself," and "always contingent, provisional and defined by difference." The point that ritual functions in such a way as to create reality is perhaps too influenced by Geertz's definition of religion, but ritual as the source and not as the reflection of belief, text, and action is right on the mark.

Bell, like Bourdieu, described the contours of the debate, but as with habitus, ritualization is so general a concept that its explanatory capacity is limited at best. What is so important about both concepts, however, is their recognition of the ways in which people mark or differentiate their actions. Of course recognizing this pattern is one thing and attempting to systematically delineate examples of it is quite another.

Bell demurred with regard to the creation of a new theory of ritual because such a task would require her to "imply or designate some independently existing object, named ritual, with a set of defining features that characterize all instances of ritual."[77] Such a theory also would need to "distinguish ritual from ceremony and ceremony from magic and social etiquette, and so on."[78] In addition, she wished to "free this analysis from the required format of demonstrating the originality, systematicity, and general applicability that a claim for a new theory would warrant."⁷⁹ Rather, Bell saw her work "as an exploration of ways of *not* thinking about ritual as well as ways of rethinking the idea and the data."⁸⁰ My method is similar, and I add to this task consideration of ways *not* to think about the division between ritual and game.

Since I will address this division in depth in the last chapter of the book, the remaining relevant concepts to consider here are "game" (again, with sport being a subset) and "play." Most serious discussions of games and play will invoke the names of two scholars: Johan Huizinga and Roger Callois. A Dutch historian, Huizinga is best known for his *Homo Ludens: A Study of the Play Element in Culture* (1950 [1938]).⁸¹ In this work he wondered "if ritual proves to be formally indistinguishable from play the question remains whether this resemblance goes further than the purely formal."⁸² He was surprised that "anthropology and comparative religion have paid so little attention to the problem of how far such sacred activities as proceed within the forms of play also proceed in the attitude and mood of play."⁸³

He drew support for his thesis from what he called the "Platonic identification of play and holiness."⁸⁴ According to Huizinga, play is "a free activity standing quite consciously outside 'ordinary' life as being 'not serious,' but at the same time absorbing the player intensely and utterly."⁸⁵ His definition of game was that it, like play, is "time-bound ... has no contact with any reality outside itself, and its performance is its own end."⁸⁶

Huizinga further remarked that "there is no distinction whatever between marking out a space for a sacred purpose and marking it out for purposes of sheer play," leading to the surprising conclusion that the "turf, tennis-court, the chessboard and pavement-hopscotch cannot formally be distinguished from the temple or magic circle."⁸⁷

Huizinga summed up his position with a grand pronouncement: "The great competitions in archaic cultures had always formed part of the sacred festivals and were indispensable as health and happiness-bringing activities. This ritual tie has now been completely severed; sport has become profane, 'unholy' in every way and has no organic connection whatever with the structure of society."⁸⁸ As we shall see, though later scholars challenged aspects of his theory, Huizinga's speculative assumptions about the nature of the religious activities of "primitive" or "archaic" societies, and the concomitant notion of degeneration, were widespread both before and after the publication of his book. Yet this self-referential, or autotelic quality he remarked upon is significant for its specific applicability with regard to the Cherokee ball game.

John MacAloon (whose work I will engage in Chapter 5) characterized

Huizinga as the "boldest" of those scholars who, having found the "appearance of game forms in the religious mythologies and cults of various peoples . . . have gone on to find in the ludic process a mode of transcendence and, therefore, an essential aspect of the religious imagination itself."[89] He questioned Huizinga's interpretation of Plato's identification of "'play and holiness,'" and sided with classicists who "have found reason to doubt the 'for-their-own-sake' character Huizinga believed crucial to 'true play and games' was really present or developed in classical Greek ideology."[90] Yet as Frits Staal has noted, this work remains foundational: "The importance of Huizinga's *Homo ludens* is that he characterized play precisely and enumerated a number of its features, including the circumstance that it is generally engaged in for its own sake. He included ritual in this characterization."[91] Since Huizinga's influential but overreaching study addressed the relationship between ritual, play, and games, other noteworthy scholars have offered more nuanced takes on this relationship, and I will discuss selected examples in Chapter 5.

Two works by the French sociologist of religion Roger Callois, the book *Man, Play, and Games* and his article "The Structure and Classification of Games," also have been influential in the study of play and games.[92] Turning again to John MacAloon for a succinct summary and critique, Callois classified games into four categories: *agon* (competition), *alea* (chance), *mimicry* (simulation), and *ilinx* (vertigo). These were located along a continuum from *paidia*, or "relatively unstructured, spontaneous, labile forms," to *ludus*, or "more conventionalized, jural and elaborated forms."[93] MacAloon concluded that Callois's categorization of games was "helpful in parsing the religious functions associated with types of games: cosmological, eschatological, moral contests; divination; imitative magic and ceremonial; altered states of consciousness."[94] However, such theory has "generated little insight of a truly comparative nature," because, in MacAloon's opinion, all games are "combinations of these aspects," and "all religions accommodate these functions."[95]

One final theoretical consideration is the issue of gambling. For centuries intense gambling on ball games was a regular, widespread activity. Broadly speaking, the relationships between gambling, ritual, and religion across cultures are manifold and worthy of a separate monograph.[96]

In terms of gambling, ritual and otherwise, among First Nations communities, there is ethnographic data and scholarship available, though by and large this topic suffers from a lack of scholarly attention.[97] However, as is the case with anetso, such categorical associations need to be contextualized and circumscribed carefully. My view is that gambling is one of the few activities in the complex that is not a discrete element of the Cherokee religious system, though it was undertaken in a prescribed manner and is featured in certain Cherokee cultural narratives.

I do think that the presence of gambling at ball games, along with the sometimes violent nature of the games themselves, have militated against interpretations of anetso as a ritual. Generally speaking, to paraphrase Bell, European and American societies are apt *not* to consider gambling and violence as part of rituals, at least not their own. Moreover, it is reasonable to conclude that some spectators and players may have been more interested in ball games because they had a vested interest in the outcome, or because the games served some sort of redistributive economic function at some point in time, as some scholars have postulated. The argument could be made that such stakes might even produce the interest necessary to create and sustain the ceremonial complex. In my view none of these scenarios is complete, and though these significant matters of economic concerns and the notion of violence certainly warrant treatment, in the interest of immediate concerns I will touch upon them in context and leave full consideration of them to a future project.

In the end, the goal of this book is not to "prove" whether or not anetso is a Cherokee ritual. Beyond the perspectives cited above, to paraphrase something that I heard Jonathan Z. Smith say years ago, "If we ever do determine what religion is, then we might as well pack up and go home, because our work is done."[98] Therefore I do not presume to assert a comprehensive definition of "Cherokee religion" either. What I shall argue in this book is that historically Cherokee people have employed anetso in service of several cultural meanings; or to put it another way, there are several possible functions that one might suggest it has performed. Reduction of the manifold cultural implications of anetso to one interpretation simply does not do justice to the character of the activity.

Obviously one watchword of academia, especially with regard to the study of First Nations, is change. For too many years and in too many contexts peoples were described as either stuck in the past like insects in amber or floating in the ether of some sort of timeless ethnographic present. Quite obviously and unquestionably peoples and cultures change. But the qualities of continuity and perseverance that typically are accorded to elements of many "mainstream" religious systems often are ignored or downplayed with regard to many elements of First Nations systems, perhaps for fear of replicating interpretive sins of the past. And in my view, not reflecting the reality of the hardiness of many traditions and activities is a simple substitution of one transgression for another.

For nearly three centuries, a varied and diverse group of commentators has chosen to make mention of the Cherokee ball game. They have done so in government reports, travel logs, mission records, trade reports, minutes of trade meetings, military transmissions, personal letters, newspaper articles, and ethnographic documentation. What impresses me again and again about accounts of the ball game that I read is consistency. I have been struck by the similarities between what I have observed in recent years and accounts from fifty, seventy, a hundred, even two hundred years ago. The accounts consistently report anetso ceremonial complex activities, and they are consistent in what they report.

Anetso also is featured in a number of Cherokee cultural narratives, such as "Kana´tĭ and Selu" (to be discussed in the first chapter); individuals in these narratives either played the game or employed the concept of it as a figure of speech. This dual usage carried over into early non-Cherokee historical documents, such as the testimony of a witness in a 1714 hearing published in the *Journals of the Commissioners of the Indian Trade* of South Carolina. A man named Clea swore that there was a Cherokee plan to raid the Yuchi village of Chestowe, and in his opinion, "ye Cherikees designed to invite the Euchees to a ball play in order to cut them off."[99] Interpreters have viewed this passage both as evidence of the ball game as a literal event designed to lure the Yuchi into a confrontation, and also as a figurative declaration of intent to engage in confrontation.

In the aftermath of the French and Indian and Revolutionary Wars, warfare between the Cherokee and other groups essentially halted. Thus meanings of the ball game bound up with actual warfare receded, and other valences became more pronounced.

In the eighteenth and nineteenth centuries, the ball game was a popular and widespread event, as I discuss in Chapter 2. During the first four decades of the nineteenth century, a number of different missionaries mentioned the ball game several times, and most, if not all disapproved of the event. For example, in 1827, the missionary Isaac Proctor referred to the "Ball plays" that he witnessed as "purely heathenish sports."[100] However, most missionaries seemed more concerned with the heavy gambling, drinking, and rowdy behavior that accompanied the event rather than anetso itself. Since the game itself seemed to be the occasion for such public behavior, the missionaries disapproved. It is likely that they were unaware of the extent of the private elements of the ceremonial complex.

Missionaries did not need to ascertain exactly what anetso was to lobby against it; any Cherokee practice that retained traditional non-Christian ways or reliance on conjurers (traditional Cherokee religious and medical practitioners) was to be stopped. Therefore, missionaries preached against anetso, and converts were censured for attending matches.[101] Yet even though the activity itself was identified as a heathenish practice, throughout the nineteenth century the Cherokee ball game continued; and for many it was an occasion for the expression of Cherokee identity in the face of the missionaries' disapproval. Presently anetso continues to be an occasion for expression of identity, particularly since it is played only one week of the year, on the decidedly public stage of the Cherokee Indian Fair.

Cherokee people seem to have had a passion for anetso for centuries. Accounts from the eighteenth, nineteenth and early twentieth centuries also reveal that Cherokee people continued to gamble passionately on the outcome of regular intertown Cherokee ball games until perhaps the 1940s. Certainly gambling was associated with ball games at least as early as 1774, and there are accounts of money, wagons, oxen, clothing, even land having been wagered. This provoked strong reactions from government officials as well as missionaries.

Though they were definitively opposed to the attendant gambling, in the last two hundred years government officials have been less definitive in their responses to the ball game itself. All agreed that it represented retention of "old ways," but some government officials recognized and encouraged the activity, while others worked to halt it or replace it with other activities. For example, one Indian agent at the turn of the twentieth century remarked ruefully that Cherokee people were reviving the ball game to protest being stripped of voting rights.[102]

One scholar reported that the Cherokee Indian Agency even banned anetso, yet there is no clear-cut evidence that the activity had ever abated.[103] Only ten years earlier the anthropologist James Mooney had found it actively being pursued. In his opinion, however, it was withering on the vine.[104] As we shall see, though there were alterations, reports of the ball game's complete demise were greatly exaggerated.

On the other hand, some Indian agents in the 1920s and 1930s facilitated exhibitions of the contest around the country.[105] This function or cultural meaning of the ball game as a tourist spectacle had emerged previously. For example, in the late eighteenth century a game was played for a French prince, and there are several accounts of tourists from the eighteenth century onward attending the contest.[106]

Throughout the twentieth century and into the twenty-first, as noted above, anetso has remained a staple of the annual Cherokee Indian Fair. I argue that anetso has persisted because people are committed to its preservation. This process has been aided because of its form as a "game"; it is a tradition in the hands of many people. It is in the hands of individuals who do not necessarily hold positions of power in the community, and those who are not necessarily perceived by non-Cherokee people as traditionalists or cultural elites. Though it was actively suppressed during certain times in Cherokee history, it escaped sustained overt suppression because many government agents, missionaries, and observers separated the activity itself from other accompanying activities, in their own minds choosing to focus on those as ills rather than on the "thing" itself.

Given all that I have said above about definitions, in order to appreciate the main arguments of this book one must possess at least a basic understanding of each relevant individual element of the complex as well as the place of each in my putative "Cherokee religious system." I do not assume such knowledge on the part of the reader, and the situation I described above regarding the dearth of up-to-date scholarly sources still obtained at the time that this book was going to press. Contemporary scholarship on any aspect of "Cherokee religion" among members of the Eastern Band of Cherokee Nation is limited to scattered scholarly journal articles, again of uneven quality, and the situation with regard to the Cherokee Nation of Oklahoma is not much different.[107]

The work of Mooney and Fogelson, along with the more recent work of a very few scholars, continues to dominate contemporary interpretations of Cherokee religious system data, no matter what time period is under consideration. While there is no question that these two scholars provide an excellent foundation for any additional research, as with all scholarly discourse, theirs are not the last words. Therefore in context throughout the book I will present skeletal summaries of the most basic information necessary for orientation to my subject matter.

Every chapter but one, Chapter 4, contains such information. The subject of Chapter 1 is twofold: cultural narratives that feature anetso and the ritual transmission of cultural narratives. In this context I will include a discussion of core cultural narratives, basic cosmology, and significant other-than-human persons. Chapter 2 is an examination of anetso as an expression of Cherokee identity during the period between 1799 and 1838, beginning with the entrance of Christian missionaries into the Cherokee Nation and concluding with the forced removal known as the Trail of Tears. I will use written accounts from the period, primarily by missionaries, to gauge the significance of anetso as an important cultural activity. In this context, in addition to introductory material about several denominational missions, I will present brief discussions of two events, the so-called "religious revivals" of 1811–13 and what is known as "White Path's rebellion," from 1824 to 1827.

The heart of Chapter 3 is a summary of every element of the ceremonial complex, with a focus on one particular element, going to water. Making use of received scholarship and data from my cultural consultation, I assess change and persistence in the complex. In the main I juxtapose the observations of three ethnographers in order to accomplish this task: James Mooney's at the turn of the twentieth century, Raymond Fogelson's from the late 1950s to 1962, and my own from the late 1990s to 2007. This chapter will begin with a summation of a watershed event in Cherokee history, the shift from a hereditary caste of priests to a system of individual practitioners. I then will present an annotated list of the ritual actions included in the ceremonial complex. The chapter also will include an assessment of the "religious landscape" on the Qualla Boundary at the turn of the twenty-first century.

Chapter 4 departs from this strategy in order to focus on the utilization of anetso as a cultural presentation of identity. It also treats the prevalent notion of cultural degeneration that in the past has been endemic to scholars of First Nations cultures. Though the focus is on events in the first several decades of the twentieth century, I do contextualize events in this time period with selected examples that span several hundred years.

In the final chapter, I consider two main points: 1) What are the "meanings" of anetso, according to cultural consultation and scholarly investigation; and 2) what is the history of scholarship regarding the game/ritual divide? Here I interrogate the work of Stewart Culin and Claude Lévi-Strauss, along with scholars who have followed in their considerable wakes. As I will reiterate throughout the book, there is much work to be done in the study of the Cherokee religious system. While I cannot pretend to offer a definitive account of anetso either as a key site of Cherokee cultural production, or as a topos for genesis of a new set of definitions regarding "ritual" and "game," nonetheless I will conclude with some reflections on both my particular and more general observations, and where they might lead in future investigations.

Fieldwork

Discussions with cultural consultants as well as my own observations over the past sixteen years aided immeasurably in the construction of my argument. Therefore it is imperative that I explain my method of cultural consultation, or fieldwork. I began my research consultation activity with a weeklong visit to the Qualla Boundary in July 1993, and I have continued to visit the Qualla Boundary regularly since that time. As I noted earlier in the Introduction, in December 1996 I asked the Tribal Council of the Eastern Band of Cherokee Indians for formal permission to conduct my dissertation fieldwork and the video documentary. The Tribal Council approved both projects. The Enduring Voices Project began in September 1997 and was completed in September 1999.[108]

The most concentrated span of time I spent in western North Carolina was from 1997 to 1999. I lived on the Qualla Boundary from September to December 1997 and in nearby Cullowhee, N.C., visiting and working on the Qualla Boundary virtually every day, for parts of two summers (ten weeks in 1998, six weeks in 1999). During these summers I taught a session of summer school at Western Carolina University, and in 1999 I taught a university satellite course on the Qualla Boundary. In addition, a schedule of weeklong visits during university breaks and shorter visits, typically several days each, occurred during the period 1997–2001. Finally, I attended the Cherokee Indian Fair and watched ball games during the years 1997–2001, 2004–5, and 2007.

Certain Cherokee consultants and I have become friends, and I have been told in no uncertain terms that while they are happy to provide certain information and identify it as appropriate for inclusion in my academic work, our friendships would be irretrievably ruined if they themselves were to be identified in my academic work. Therefore in order to respect the wishes of many of my consultants who desire to remain anonymous, I will not cite any individual names. In most cases I will not quote people directly, but paraphrase their comments. Certain citations give the year and month of a particular statement, and others give a range of years. In these cases several different consultants corroborated the same information. In addition, many times a consultant has referred back to a previous conversation or pointed out something to me, in some cases with an interval of several years.

I recognize that this strategy creates distance between the people themselves and the reader, but it is a distance that I need to maintain. I liken it to my inclination to stay back on the hill when I first watched a team go to water. Issues of cultural propriety and privacy are paramount. After all, I am not Cherokee, do not speak for Cherokee people, and do not want anyone to get the impression that I am doing so.

A decade ago someone said to me, "So, you will publish this [book], and some idiot will read it and think you are the expert on Cherokee religion because you've studied it so much and have spent some time here. Then they'll come to the rez and go around telling people they're not Indians because they don't do what the book says."[109] This wonderfully succinct statement rings in my ears to this day, echoing a similar statement made by Vine Deloria Jr. in *Custer Died for Your Sins*.[110] If, after reading this book the reader wants to know what a Cherokee person thinks about all of this, then go ask a Cherokee person. I do, however, claim full responsibility for the quotations, assessments, characterizations, and any inferences herein.

Over such a period of time as I have visited the Qualla Boundary, circumstances for discussion of relevant issues have varied widely. Thus I have chosen the umbrella phrase "personal communication" to represent the variety of conversational situations, ranging from brief comments to mealtime conversations to more formal interviews. I have included selected references to Enduring Voices Project interviews and, with permission, a small number of quotations, but per the contributors' requests these too have been rendered anonymous and exact dates of interviews removed. Researchers could track down the specific passages in individual interviews if they so desired, but I urge them to respect the privacy of contributors and implore them to acknowledge the contributors' intellectual property rights to material in the Enduring Voices Collection.

Tadatse anetsodui
(Go and play ball with them)
Anetso in the Cherokee Narrative Tradition

The inclusion of anetso in several Cherokee cultural narratives of different genres is one facet of its cultural cachet among members of the Eastern Band of Cherokee Nation.¹ Key Cherokee narratives include the ball game, either literally or as a figure of speech to indicate a contest or battle of some kind. Review of the received scholarly classification of narratives along with explication of the Cherokee mode of oral transmission of knowledge helps to illustrate this embedded importance.

Situating these narratives in their given order as designated by Mooney and contextualizing them by presenting summaries of selected other salient narratives provides the framework for a brief but necessary overview of fundamental aspects of the "Cherokee religious system," including cosmology and significant other-than-human persons.² Certain other-than-human persons played the ball game or employed the figure of speech "to play ball against." This linguistic turn of phrase also has surfaced in early historical records written by non-Cherokees reporting interchanges with Cherokee people.

Even stripped of all theoretical window dressing, the fact that Cherokee people continue today to perform an action described in a number of their cultural narratives is noteworthy. Imagine for a moment reading a Hebrew Bible narrative in which the Israelites, wandering through the desert, stayed fit for battle, tested their physical skills, or even alleviated their boredom by kicking or throwing a ball around. The activity might include the whole community, either as participants or spectators, and display various aspects of the culture. Dancing, singing, special foods, clothing, and preparations all might be included, not to mention other ceremonial or religious activities. In another biblical narrative, mention of this well-known activity might be used as a figure of speech to refer to battle or engagement of some kind—"let's play ball with the so-and-sos." Future generations also might choose to commemorate certain events or to represent ideals important to the community by performing this activity.

Next imagine an important biblical figure taking part in the activity. For example, instead of Jacob wrestling with God, the two might play lacrosse.[3] This is an apt comparison, because in fact this wrestling match is a signal event in the Genesis narrative. As a result, Jacob is renamed "Israel," or "The one who strives with God," and "the community of Israel, as descendants of this god-wrestler, is depicted as a group that successfully strives with God and humans."[4] Now consider what significance this activity would have if people were still participating in it today, accompanied by other actions that both Cherokee people and non-Cherokee scholars have identified as ritual practices. This analogy begins to describe the enduring cultural significance of anetso, the ball game, and how it is grounded in the Cherokee narrative tradition.

Classification of Cherokee Narratives

Published Cherokee narratives abound, yet scholarly analysis of Cherokee narratives is slim. The only attempted typology that I have located is James Mooney's, and his collection of narratives is the most comprehensive. Thus sources for my study begin with Mooney's *Myths of the Cherokee*, which includes 125 narratives, and continue with his handwritten notes for the publication housed in the National Anthropological Archives.[5]

Mooney stated that "Cherokee myths may be roughly classified as sacred myths, animal stories, local legends, and historical traditions."[6] He furthered subdivided them as follows: "Cosmogonic Myths"; "Quadruped Myths"; "Bird Myths"; "Snake, fish, and insect Myths"; "Wonder Stories"; "Historical Traditions"; and "Miscellaneous Myths and Legends."[7] Overall, there is some confusion to Mooney's organization, and he never satisfactorily explained his divisions. Keith Basso's delineation of the major categories of Western Apache speech, including the category "'to tell of holiness,'" may be helpful in formulating a theory of Cherokee speech acts, but that is beyond the scope of this study.[8]

Because this is the most comprehensive account of the Cherokee narrative schema extant, and the order of the narrative cycle and the typological classifications are both Mooney's, any speculation about these details is of limited value. However, perhaps an analogue to this situation is that of James R. Walker's collection of Lakota narratives; possibly Mooney had an idealized mythology that he was arbitrarily reconstructing, in the same way Walker molded a Lakota corpus to fit a preconceived framework based on Greek and Roman mythology.[9] On the other hand, it may have been simply a matter of Mooney ordering and classifying on the basis of a normative order. The anthropologist William H. Gilbert remarked that Mooney's classification of narratives was "based on the formal subject matter of the myths rather than on the story themes contained in them."[10] In a 1943 publication Gilbert provided a table of nineteen narratives he had collected, citing thematic elements such as "kinship," "revenge," and "explanatory," and arguing that "killing and revenge for killing, clan sanctioned, are basic themes."[11]

Mooney believed that missionary activity affected the narrative tradition, but not in the way one might think: "It might perhaps be thought that missionary influence would be evident in the genesis tradition, but such is not the case. The Bible story kills the Indian tradition, and there is no amalgamation.... The whole primitive pantheon of the Cherokee is still preserved in their sacred formulas."[12]

To Mooney, what he collected were mere fragments of a lost complete narration, including a long migration narrative.[13] He remarked that the myths of the Cherokee "are too far broken down ever to be woven together again into any long-connected origin legend," although "a few still exhibit a certain sequence which indicates that they once formed component parts of a cycle."[14] According to Mooney, certain conceptions, "could only be the outgrowth of a special cosmogonic theology, though now indeed broken and degraded, and it is probable that many myths told now only for amusement are really worn down fragments of ancient sacred traditions."[15] Other scholars have suggested similar scenarios, but these opinions may reflect the prevalent notion of degeneration, which I treat in depth in an upcoming chapter. There are several viewpoints on the origin of the Cherokee people in their present location, with most scholars citing a lack of clear origin narratives, but the matter merits further study.[16]

Mooney's collected narratives, and the general characterizations he made about individuals and events in them, will provide a base point from which to discern, to paraphrase him, how these stories might be fragments of a unified whole. What Mooney meant was a linked set of narratives, including a complete migration episode. In my terms, it means attempting to discern internal consistencies, or relationships, among elements of the Cherokee religious system.

In the introduction to the narratives themselves, Mooney said of this category: "To the first class belong the genesis stories, dealing with the creation of the world, the nature of the heavenly bodies and elemental forces, the origin of life and death, the spirit world and the invisible beings, the ancient monsters, and the hero-gods."[17]

In Mooney's typology, the second group of narratives he delineated was of a more general nature than the cosmogonic myths. They concerned animals, and were in wider circulation among the general public: "To the second class belong the shorter animal myths, which have lost whatever sacred character they may once have had, and are told now merely as humorous explanations of certain animal peculiarities."[18] As I will demonstrate below, the ball game appears in examples from both narrative classes.

Transmission of Cherokee Narratives

Mooney distinguished between the different classes of narratives in two additional ways, in terms of influence and transmission: "While the sacred myths have a constant bearing upon formulistic prayers and observances, it is only in rare instances that any rite or custom is based upon an animal myth. Moreover, the sacred myths are known as a rule only to the professional priests or conjurers, while the shorter animal stories are more or less familiar to nearly everyone and are found in almost identical form among Cherokee, Creeks, and other southern tribes."[19]

Though I do not agree with Mooney's generalization, he did point out the clear relationship between Cherokee narrative and ritual action. Concurring with Mooney, Gilbert went so far as to say in 1937 that "the magical familiarity of the formulas, linking up with the familiarity of actual social life (the latter as we have seen, being an integral part of preferential mating), is linked with a familiarity counterpart in the myths."[20] In a later publication he said that the "dramatis personae of the myths are involved in frequent quarrels with each other and with man, and the struggle for power between the various conjurers is reflected in the myths in various ways."[21]

Leaving aside the "chicken and egg" question of which influenced which, the fact that they are so interrelated warrants future study. It remains the case that virtually all activities that continue today, save going to water, have correlate animal activity in narratives, including clans, councils, dances, and ball games. Particular individuals may understand the narratives metaphorically or literally as with, for example, Bible stories, but there is explanatory rationale for clans, disease, and healing in these narratives.[22] In the case of anetso, whether or not the ball game is "based upon an animal myth," humans and other-than-human persons, including animals, have played it.

Two points from Mooney's quote above merit reiteration: "the sacred myths have a constant bearing upon formulistic prayers and observances"; and "the sacred myths are known as a rule only to the professional priests or conjurers." It is notable that Mooney stated that the "sacred myths" (by which he apparently meant the "cosmogonic myths") "were not for every one, but only those might hear who observed the proper form and ceremony."[23] In a *Journal of American Folklore* article published over a decade before *Myths*, Mooney focused attention on one of these narratives in particular, "Kana'tĭ and Selu: Origin of Corn and Game":

> The first is one of the best known of the Cherokee myths of a sacred character, and in the old times any one who heard it, with all the explanation, was obliged to "go to water" after the recital; that is, to bathe in the running stream at daybreak, before eating, while the medicine-man went through his mystic ceremonies on the bank. I heard the story in its entirety from two of the best story-tellers, one of whom is a medicine-man, and the other is supposed to be skilled in all their hunting secrets. Neither of them speak English. In addition, so many beliefs and customs turn upon this story of Kanati that I probably heard each of the principal incidents at least half a dozen times.[24]

This quote clearly illustrates the significance of this particular narrative, and I will discuss the narrative in some detail below. First, however, I want to draw attention to two equally significant issues: the importance of ritualized transmission for the maintenance of the oral tradition, and the fact that this process delineates a differentiated class of narratives for the participants as well as alert observers.

These "myths of a sacred character" were stories held in trust and passed down through generations by recognized individuals which required performance of certain ritual activity with their retelling. Several of Mooney's sources, including John Ax ("Ităgû′năhĭ"), related that when they were boys, "now some eighty years ago" (before 1887–90, when Mooney was collecting data), these were told only at night inside the *osi* (a "low-built log sleeping house"), a multifunctional structure.[25] Mooney commented that, "with some tribes the winter season and the night are the time for telling stories, but to the Cherokee all times are alike."[26] Further, as the lengthy quote that follows illustrates, narrative transmission was one of a class of ritual activities that required a morning ritual immersion in a running stream, or going to water, at the conclusion of the session:[27]

> At times those who desired instructions from an adept in the sacred lore of the tribe met him by appointment in the âsĭ, where they sat up all night talking, with only the light of a small fire burning in the middle of the floor. At daybreak the whole party went down to the running stream, where the pupils or hearers of the myths stripped themselves, and were scratched upon their naked skin with a bone-tooth comb in the hands of the priest, after which they waded out, facing the rising sun, and dipped

seven times under the water, while the priest recited prayers upon the bank. This purificatory rite, observed more than a century ago by Adair, is also a part of the ceremonial of the ballplay, the Green-corn dance, and, in fact, every important ritual performance.[28]

In addition to both the ball game and narrative transmission, Mooney listed the Green Corn Dance in his statement that "every important ritual performance" required two ritual activities, scarification and going to water. Obviously the fact that Mooney classed them together speaks to the significance of all of these activities.[29]

Mooney stated that during his time the osi was "now nearly obsolete," and Frans Olbrechts, who visited the Qualla Boundary between 1926 and 1927, agreed that it was "but a dim memory."[30] Olbrechts was told that a man wanting to learn medicine would go to a recognized specialist and ask to be tutored; at that time relation of narratives was "no longer the appanage of priests and elders."[31] Both Olbrechts's and Ax's comments only referred to men, but since the narratives continued to be transmitted, in several cases by women, clearly there were other modes of transmission.

There is further evidence from the John Howard Payne Papers, dated fifty years before Mooney's first visit, that in fact women were conservators and transmitters of cultural traditions commonly ascribed to men. Lee Irwin has noted that though men were the majority of missionary Daniel S. Butrick's informants, the "comments of Cherokee women show that these elder women also had a knowledge of many rituals, the ceremonial prayers, purification and childbearing rites, traditional dress, and mourning customs."[32]

Certain consultants did speak about the method of passing on knowledge Mooney and Olbrechts described, but clearly there were other ways to learn the narratives as well, including the ever-increasing availability of the narratives in print form. Most elderly consultants of mine, both male and female, recalled times when they were young when elderly people would gather in homes and talk late into the night. A number of people recalled adults "shooing" them outside during the times the old people would talk. They were told to go out and play until bedtime and not to disturb the conversation. Additionally, several consultants recalled hearing snippets of conversations, and one recounted hiding and listening to the conversation. Conversely, sometimes during dances when the children attended they stayed inside a nearby home during parts of the evening.[33]

Mooney also reported a linguistic device that signaled to the informed listener that the presenter had received the information in the culturally prescribed way. I want to highlight this device, a prefatory statement, in order to support further my contention that the performance of cultural narratives was and is ritualized action. Mooney reported, "As our grandmothers begin, 'Once upon a time,' so the Cherokee story-teller introduces his narrative by saying: 'This is what the old men told me when I was a boy.'"[34]

Despite his comment about the widespread use of the phrase, Mooney himself attached this introduction to only two of the 125 narratives he collected in *Myths*. In the first, "Kana'tĭ and Selu," it ran, "When I was a boy this is what the old men told me they had heard when they were boys."[35] In the second, "Nûñ'yunu'wĭ," it ran, "This is what the old men told me when I was a boy."[36] Perhaps it may reflect what his sources said (or be a simple case of omission), but this sparse usage of the phrase in his own collected examples is somewhat odd given the generality of his above statement.

The version of the comment that I have heard most often is "when I was a boy this is what the old men told me that the old men had told them when they were boys." This is much like the preface in Mooney's published account of Kanati and Selu cited above. Female consultants often made the same comment with appropriate gender substitution.[37] Male or female, this was especially the case among particular consultants who considered themselves to be conservative culturally as well as physically (some of whom refer to themselves as "real Indians," "fullbloods," or "bloods").[38] In specific cases, these consultants also began with the preface before they related other cultural information, such as a conjurer's feats that they had not witnessed themselves, or a foretelling of the future they had heard.[39]

Sometimes consultants prefaced their discussion of certain information in the context of a formal interview session with this statement, but the majority of instances in which consultants employed the device were not formal sessions. Over the years I can recall a number of situations in which I was part of a discussion, either one-on-one or in a group, in which individuals inserted such information into other conversation. We could be talking about a grandchild's school basketball team, the weather, really anything at all and suddenly an individual would seamlessly insert the preface. What followed might be a brief comment or a longer story, and when it was complete the person would move on to the next topic. Thus the action was not a dramatic oratory flourish, but something integrated into conversation that attentive individuals would recognize.[40] To reiterate my point from above, what I find particularly interesting is that this verbal signal is available to the alert visitor as well as to community members.

In my experience, this prefatory statement is more than a stylistic convention. Certain consultants who spoke with me did not fail to repeat these exact words, or some reasonable facsimile, before relating a narrative of some particular significance. I fully recognize the possibility that certain individuals who did not in fact receive the information in this way may have been aware of the significance of the preface, heard other people use it, and employed it themselves in order to attach cachet to their account. What I am saying here is that in my opinion there are people who have employed and continue to employ the phrase because that in fact is how they received the information.

Furthermore these consultants did not begin with this preface all the time, for everything we discussed. By beginning with the phrase, consciously employing it as an introduction, such individuals in my view demarcate the information, announcing it as a specially differentiated speech act.[41] Thus the preface itself is evidence of culturally prescribed, ritualized transmission. The introduction is the verbal signal to the listener that the storyteller has acquired the information in a culturally prescribed fashion.

The "Cosmogonic Myths"

A contemporary exposition of the narrative corpus, while beyond the scope of the present work, would surely be a worthwhile endeavor. My present focus being the ball game, I will highlight several narratives in which the ball game figures either literally or as a figure of speech. However, as with my review of selected ritual actions, it is useful to provide similar context for the narratives by providing brief introductions to additional narratives of relevance.

Before I discuss the narratives themselves, I should explain my research approach with regard to the "collection" of narratives. As a non-Cherokee researcher, though I would sometimes initiate discussion of narratives with consultants, after my first few visits I never asked to hear a particular narrative unless the speaker first offered.[42] I felt that plenty of people had conducted interviews in this way in the past, and some were still doing so. People knew of my interests, narratives came up in conversation, and I left it up to the individual if they wanted to relate a narrative to me. More often a consultant would be discussing a certain topic and I would allude to what I felt was a relevant individual or event from a narrative, and the individual might incorporate that into the conversation. In addition to the oral accounts, I have assembled multiple versions of both narratives from archives or published works.[43]

There are fourteen narratives in the first section, "Cosmogonic Myths."[44] They include narratives detailing the creation of the world and the origins of disease and medicine, the first fire, death, fish and frogs, and strawberries. Also in this category are narratives describing the origins of hunting game and raising corn (the narrative of Kanati and Selu) as well as the bringing of tobacco, a deluge narrative, and five narratives dealing with the sun, moon, stars, Thunders, Milky Way, Pleiades, and the pine tree. In what follows I will summarize briefly the first and second narratives as Mooney presented them, then provide a more detailed discussion of the third, and finally summarize briefly the fourth and fifth narratives.

"How the World Was Made"[45]

This narrative, the first Mooney presented, described a universe segmented into different worlds or planes, including a world humans now inhabit, an underworld, and a world above the sky. The middle world was described as an island floating on water, suspended by cords at the four cardinal points from a stone sky vault. The stone sky vault arches and tilts daily to allow entities or other-than-human persons such as the sun to pass between worlds; and one day the cords will break and the earth will fall back into the ocean.[46] The name of the world above the sky vault is conventionally rendered as *Galvladi* ("Gălûñ´lătĭ"; *galvlati*, "above") in a tiered series of planes.[47] It is home to various entities such as thunder and the sun, as well as archetypal animals. These animals, "like the traditional hero-gods, were larger and of more perfect type than their present representatives."[48]

The narrative described how the animals living in Galvladi felt crowded, so they sent "Dâyuni´sĭ" the water beetle to search for a place to live below the sky vault, where all was water. The water beetle retrieved mud from the bottom of the water and brought it to the surface, where it expanded to its present size. It then was fastened to the sky vault with four cords, one at each cardinal direction. As the mud of the earth was still drying, the animals sent the Buzzard down, and the flapping of his great wings created the present-day mountains and valleys of the Cherokee homeland. The sun was placed too close to the earth, so conjurers moved it up successive hand-breadths until it reached its present position just beneath the sky vault in the seventh height.[49]

The narrative also explained the existence of a world like earth beneath this one in which everything was the same save for the seasons, and to which one could pass if certain circumstances prevailed. The nocturnal quality of animals and the evergreen quality of trees were explained, as was the propagation of humans. The narrative began with a brother and sister, and the brother "struck her with a fish and told her to multiply."[50]

"The First Fire"[51]

In this narrative, "Ani´-Hyûñ´tikwălâ´skĭ," the Thunders, sent a lightning bolt down to hit the bottom of a hollow sycamore tree growing on an island. The animals then held a council to determine how to retrieve the bolt, and after several male animals failed and were scarred permanently in the process, "Kănăane′skĭ Amai′yĕhĭ" the Water Spider succeeded in bringing back a coal in her *tu′sti* bowl.⁵²

"Kana′tĭ and Selu: Origin of Corn and Game"⁵³

This narrative is the third Mooney placed under the heading "Cosmogonic Myths," and the first that contains a reference to the ball game. I have been told portions of the narrative and have discussed it in some depth with consultants. It should be noted that even though Mooney placed this narrative after the previous one, the Thunders are not constituted as a group until the end of this narrative.

The narrative introduces Kanati (literally, in "third person habitual verbal form," "he is lucky, or successful, in hunting") and Selu (literally, "corn"), as well as their two sons, who along with their father will become known as "the Thunders."⁵⁴ This narrative explained the origin of the cultivation of corn and the origin of hunting, two major subsistence activities. One son was the product of the parents' union, while the second brother, the reader learns, formed from hunted animals' blood that Selu washed off in the river. Subsequently the second boy would emerge from the water, play with the first boy, and then return to the water at the end of the day.⁵⁵

Elderly people would hear the boys playing and laughing, but they never caught a glimpse of the second boy. The first boy told his parents about his playmate, who called himself the other's "elder brother" and said "his mother was cruel to him and threw him in the river." Eventually, after some time Kanati instructed the first boy to challenge the other to a wrestling match, which he did. As soon as they began wrestling, the boy called for his father, and the parents came running. The second boy, who Mooney called the "Wild Boy" at this point, cried, "'Let me go; you threw me away.'"⁵⁶

The parents were able to capture the second boy, keep him in the house, and "tame" him, but, the narrative continued, "he was always wild and artful in his disposition, and was the leader of his brother in every mischief. It was not long until the old people discovered that he had magic powers, and called him I′năge-utăsûñ′hĭ (He-who-grew-up-wild)."⁵⁷ As the narrative progressed, the Wild Boy coerced his brother into mischievous behavior with disastrous results.

The two brothers were determined to uncover the secrets of their parents: how their father procured game and how their mother produced corn and beans. Upon learning their mother's secret, they resolved to kill her, which they did by beheading her. Knowing that she was going to die, she instructed them in how to use her body to produce corn. Their father, upon learning of their deed, left them and attempted to have them killed by the Wolf people (I discuss this event in more detail below).[58]

They escaped this trap, and soon after people came to them asking for corn grain. They gave the people seven grains, instructing them to follow certain directions, which the people failed to do, resulting in corn now taking half a year to mature, when before it did so overnight. The boys next determined to search for their parents. They chased after their father, who warned them of two upcoming trials, which they survived. The boys were finally reunited with their parents on the other side of the sky, and their slain mother was reheaded and bore no grudge. However, the boys were allowed only a brief visit before being instructed to take up their station to the west in the Darkening Land as the Thunders.[59]

According to Mooney, several individuals related this narrative to him; he heard it "in nearly the same form from Swimmer and John Ax (east) and from Wafford (west), and a version is also given in the Wahnenauhi manuscript."[60] Mooney also had the following to say about this particular cultural narrative: "So much of belief and custom depend upon the myth of Kana'tĭ that references to the principal incidents are constant in the songs and formulas. It is one of those myths held so sacred that in the old days one who wished to hear it from the priest of the tradition must first purify himself by 'going to water,' i.e. bathing in the running stream before daylight when still fasting, while the priest performed his mystic ceremonies upon the bank."[61]

This quotation is a reformulation (with less detail) of a passage from Mooney's *Journal of American Folklore* article presented above.[62] To reiterate, in the above quote Mooney said the narrative was "of a sacred character" and that he had heard it "from two of the best story-tellers, one of whom was a medicine-man, while the other was supposed to be skilled in all their hunting secrets." Mooney remarked that neither of the men spoke English, and included the additional detail of not eating before going to water. He concluded that he had heard "each of the principal incidents at least half a dozen times." In fact, Mooney commented that several times "before beginning one of the stories of the sacred class the informant would sometimes suggest jokingly that the author first submit to being scratched and 'go to water.'"[63]

The Relevant Passage

In the narrative, the sons first discovered the secret of their father's hunting success: all the animals lived in a cave closed up with a boulder, and he let them loose as he needed them for food. Soon after the boys unwittingly allowed all the animals to escape, Kanati discovered them and unleashed upon them a variety of vermin kept in jars in the cave as punishment. He then sent his sons home to their mother while he headed into the woods to hunt.[64]

When they arrived home they spied on their mother, who always mysteriously produced baskets of corn and beans from a storehouse. Observing her producing beans and corn from her body by rubbing her stomach and armpits, and determining that she was a witch, they resolved to kill her.[65] Selu knew of her fate, yet let her sons kill her. Before they did so she instructed them how to produce corn using her decapitated body, but they only followed some (but not all) of the directions that she had given them for what to do with her body. Their lack of attention to detail had etiological ramifications: 1) corn grows only in certain areas of the world, instead of everywhere; and 2) corn grows at such a rate that farmers can only grow two crops in a single season, instead of even faster.[66] In fact, corn or maize does grow at this rate in North Carolina.

Kanati arrived in the morning after a long night of hunting and looked for his wife. His sons showed her to him and told him what they had done and why. Angered by his sons' murder of their mother, Kanati left them, traveled to the Wolf people, and asked them to attack his sons: "When the Wolf chief asked him his business, he said: 'I have two bad boys at home, and I want you to go in seven days from now and play ball against them.' Although Kana'tĭ spoke as though he wanted them to play a game of ball, the Wolves knew that he meant for them to go and kill the two boys."[67] In the endnote accompanying this passage Mooney reported that "play ball against them . . . is a Cherokee figurative expression for a contest of any kind, more particularly a battle."[68] It seems that the ball game was a familiar cultural concept known so well by the characters and by the listening audience that it needed no explanation, but the narration did pause to explain the figurative sense of the phrase.

The National Anthropological Archives has three handwritten versions of this narrative in Mooney's own hand, and one in particular, "Origin of Game and Vegetables, 2nd Version," seems to approximate most closely the published version. In this version, written in shorthand, Kanati said, "I hv 2 bad boys, go & play tm (ta'tátsanetsătû'ĭ) in 7 days—Sd as if play bal, bt ment fight, attack & klm."[69] Rendered fully, the second half of this sentence is, "said as if play ball, but meant fight, attack and kill them." It seems as if this explanation was part of the narrative as told to Mooney, but one cannot know for sure.

The boys managed to escape from the wolves, and an additional two trials awaited them. In the course of the second, the power of lightning was unleashed against the boys' enemies, the "Anada´dûñtăskĭ," or "Roasters."[70] As

I will discuss below, lightning is a relative of the Thunders. After surviving the challenges, the boys managed to catch up with Kanati, who outdistanced them as they headed for the end of the world. Though he was out of sight, the boys continued on and passed through an area where the sky went up and down, and climbed up on the other side to find their parents.

Although they bore no ill will or permanent injury, a reheaded Selu and Kanati welcomed their sons for a visit but informed them they must forever reside elsewhere in the firmament. The boys visited with their parents and then left to take up their station as the Thunders. As Mooney related the narrative, their parents were happy to see them but told them they could only stay a little while, and "then they must go to live where the sun goes down. The boys stayed with their parents seven days and then went on toward the Darkening land, where they are now. We call them Anisga'ya Tsunsdĭ' (The Little Men), and when they talk to each other we hear low rolling thunder in the west."[71]

Thus the reader learned that Kanati's sons are called "The Little Men," and thunder is the sound of their voices. Mooney ended by noting that "the Thunder Boys," as apparently he dubbed them, taught the Cherokee seven songs to call the deer: "It all happened so long ago that the songs are forgotten—all but two, which the hunters still sing whenever they go after deer."[72] In the other published versions of "Kanati and Selu" the narratives end somewhat more abruptly, typically with a description of how Selu's body produced corn and the explanation of current harvesting practices.[73]

"Origin of Disease and Medicine"[74]

The next narrative illustrates how, in terms of the internal cohesion of a postulated Cherokee belief system (at least among members of the Eastern Band), the relationships between animals, plants, humans, and other beings have been accentuated in discourse as well as practice to a much greater degree than in, for example, Jewish and Christian biblical traditions.[75] Mooney stated that men and animals are essentially the same: "In the primal genesis period they seem to be completely undifferentiated, and we find all creatures alike living and working together in harmony and mutual helpfulness until man, by his aggressiveness and disregard for the rights of others, provokes their hostility, when insects, birds, fishes, reptiles, and fourfooted beasts join forces against him."[76]

After a series of heated council meetings in which several groups of animals stated their grievances against man, they decided to inflict disease upon man in any way imaginable. The plants heard of the animals' plan but, because they were friendly to humankind, "determined to defeat the [animals']

Tadatse anetsodui 45

evil designs." Each agreed to furnish a cure for a disease, and each said, "'I shall appear to help Man when he calls upon me in his need.'" Every single plant, even weeds, "has its use if we only knew it," Mooney related. This narrative ended with the following line: "When the doctor does not know what medicine to use for a sick man the spirit of the plant tells him."[77] At least two ritual and medicinal specialists with whom I spoke stated that a particular plant makes itself known when they are out hunting in the woods, be it among a patch of several other plants or alone in an unexpected place.[78]

"The Daughter of the Sun: Origin of Death"[79]

Mooney termed this narrative, fifth in the cosmogonic myths, "one of the principal myths of the Cherokee."[80] In the narrative, the Sun plotted to kill all humans because she became jealous of her brother the Moon. Every day as the Sun moved across the sky she visited her daughter who lived "in the middle of the sky, directly above the earth." She noticed that the humans were unable to look her in the face, but they enjoyed gazing at her brother the Moon. She bombarded the humans with "such sultry rays that there was a great fever and the people died by the hundreds."[81]

While Mooney followed Swimmer's version in most of the details, he inserted one element of the John Ax version, the Little Men, whereas in other versions it is a conjurer or chief who came to the humans' aid. In the John Ax version, the people went to the Little Men for help, and the Sun herself was killed. In the other versions, it is the daughter of the Sun who was killed.[82]

In the version Mooney related, the Little Men "made medicine" and transformed two men into snakes, "Copperhead" and "Spreading-adder," but they were unable to complete the task. The people came back a second time, when the Little Men performed the same operation to create "the great Uktena" and "Rattlesnake." The over-eager Rattlesnake killed the daughter of the Sun but forgot to wait for the mother, heading back to the people with the angry Uktena following behind. The narrative continued: "Since then we pray to the rattlesnake and do not kill him, because he is kind and never tries to bite if we do not disturb him. The Uktena grew angrier all the time and very dangerous, so that if he even looked at a man, that man's family would die. After a long time the people held a council and decided that he was too dangerous to be with them, so they sent him up to Gălûñ´lătĭ, and he is there now. The Spreading-adder, the copperhead, the Rattlesnake, and the Uktena were all men."[83]

After this the Sun would not come out due to her grief, and the Little Men explained that the humans must travel to the "Tsûsginâ´ĭ, the Ghost country, in Usûñhi´yĭ, the Darkening land in the west" to bring back the daughter of the Sun. The Little Men proscribed a particular method for the humans to find her at a dance and capture her in a box, which they were not to open until they had returned. Despite the daughter's pleas, they followed instructions until they were almost home, when they raised the lid because she said she was smothering. She flew out, having become the Redbird. Had the people done as instructed, "we could bring back our other friends also from the Ghost country, but now when they die we can never bring them back."[84] Additional narratives featuring both the Little Men and rattlesnakes will be treated below, but next I will discuss the activity of birds and animals in one of the best-known Cherokee narratives.

"The Ball Game of the Birds and Animals"[85]

This narrative comes from the second group of narratives Mooney delineated, the "animal myths," and is set in the time before humans inhabited the earth. The narrative of a ball game between the birds and animals has been, and continues to be, one of the most widely told Cherokee narratives; many Cherokee consultants told me they first heard it when they were children.[86] There even is a stone mural in the Harrah's Casino that has a scene from this narrative, based on schoolchildren's drawings.

The narrative began with the animals challenging the birds to a ball game and described their subsequent preparations, including holding ball dances the night before the contest. In the morning, as the two teams made final preparations to meet, a field mouse and a squirrel approached the Eagle, the captain of the birds. These two small animals climbed the tree where the Eagle was perched and asked to join his team. Noticing that they were four-legged creatures, he asked them why they were not playing on the animals' team. They answered that they were deemed too small by the animals, and were ridiculed and driven away by them.

The Eagle told them they could play with the birds, but first wings had to be fashioned for them. Excess leather (groundhog skin) from a drumhead was cut into wing shapes, stretched with cane splints, and fastened onto the mouse, transforming it into "Tla′mehă," the Bat. However, no leather remained for wings for the squirrel. Two large birds took hold of the squirrel and stretched the skin on both sides between his fore and hind legs. Thus it became "Tewa," the Flying Squirrel. These flying animals then proved themselves in the game, and the birds carried the day, with the Bat scoring the winning point.[87]

Some versions of the narrative do not contain references to Tewa. Fogelson recorded a version of this narrative in 1960 from Lloyd Runningwolf Sequoyah, and it omits the reference to the flying squirrel as well.[88] A short

Tadatse anetsodui 47

epilogue describing a traditional victory dance also is included, in which the Rabbit schemed to set the "flying animals" against each other to gain revenge for losing the bet and game.[89] There are several published versions of this narrative, and I have recorded or heard several more.[90]

In addition, a consultant offered two new details concerning the narrative. First, the reason the wings of bats are almost transparent is that the leather was taken from the drumhead itself, which had been worn with use. This individual also added the detail that the reason the bat flies as it does, darting back and forth and never flying straight, is that it is still getting used to its new wings.[91] This consultant made a point of including both animals, *Tsameha* and *Tewa*, in the narrative, as well as offering the traditional prefatory statement that this was what elders had told this person as a child, and their elders had done the same when they were children.[92]

This narrative provides a link with tradition for Cherokee people, who today still can watch the ball game, even if they do not have family participating or are not playing themselves. Although it is not part of Mooney's postulated special category of cosmogonic cultural narratives, the narrative has cultural relevance for the lessons about inclusiveness, adaptability as proscription for social behavior, and boastful behavior it teaches, particularly to young children.

Other Narratives Featuring the Thunders

Based on the narratives presented to this point, the significance of the Thunders should be apparent. Another cosmogonic narrative, "The Moon and the Thunders," gathered together information about the Moon, the Sun, the Thunders, and the ball game.[93] This short selection is an account of the sun and moon, as sister and brother, involved in an incestuous affair. Grafted to the end of this story were four additional paragraphs of information.

In the first, the moon was said to be stuck in the sky as a result of a player in the ball game picking up the ball with his hand just as the other team was about to win. This account went on to say that when the moon is small and pale that means someone has handled the ball unfairly, and it remains in the sky to remind players not to cheat. This is why "they formally played only at the time of a full moon."[94] After two paragraphs concerning eclipses and names of heavenly bodies, the last paragraph provided information on the Thunders. Coincidence or not, again the ball game and the Thunders were mentioned in the same context.[95]

"Ûñtsaiyĭ´, the Gambler"[96]

Even though both this narrative and the next feature the Thunders, they appear in Mooney's category of "Wonder Stories," presumably because they do not explain the genesis of anything. It also does not link seamlessly with the Kanati and Selu narrative.

In this narrative, Thunder, who lived in the west, had apparently borne a son on one of his frequent trips east.[97] As the son, who had been left behind with his mother, grew up, he became covered with scrofula sores. Seeking relief, he was advised by his mother to seek his father, Thunder, a great doctor, to cure him.

On the way to the west the boy met *Vtsayi*, or "Brass" as he is sometimes called. Vtsayi was a great gambler, and he played the wheel-and-stick gambling game known as *gatayûstĭ* whenever he had the chance.[98] When the boy came by looking for his father, Vtsayi tried to entice him into playing the game, but the boy said he must find his father first. Vtsayi informed the boy that Thunder lived next door, where he could be heard grumbling all the time.[99]

After the boy proved to Thunder that he was indeed his son by sitting on the thorns of a honey locust tree without injury, Thunder agreed to help him, and put the boy in a large pot of boiling water filled with roots. Thunder's wife (not the boy's mother) assisted, and after a while Thunder instructed her to dump the pot, boy and all, into the river. She did so, and the boy clung to the roots of a service tree on the banks. She helped him up and noticed his skin was now clean. As they walked back to the house, she told him that when they returned his father would dress him in new clothes, tell him to pick ornaments from a special box, and then send for his sons to play ball against him. She instructed him to pick his ornaments from the bottom of the box and told him to strike a favorite tree of his father's when he began to tire during the ball game, and Thunder would stop the contest.[100]

As Thunder's wife had predicted, Thunder dressed his son in a suit of buckskin and then opened a box for him to pick out necklaces and bracelets. The son peered inside and saw several different kinds of snakes swarming around, but he was not afraid and reached down to the bottom where he drew out a great rattlesnake. This he used as a necklace; and he then grabbed four copperheads for wrist and ankle bracelets. His father handed him a war club and said:

'Now you must play a ball game with your two elder brothers. They live beyond here in the Darkening land, and I have sent for them.' He said a ball game, but he meant that the boy must fight for his life. The young

Tadatse anetsodui

men came, and they were both older and stronger than the boy, but he was not afraid and fought against them. The thunder rolled and the lightning flashed at every stroke, for they were the young Thunders, and the boy himself was Lightning. At last he was tired from defending himself alone against two, and pretended to aim a blow at the honey-locust tree. Then his father stopped the fight, because he was afraid the lightning would split the tree, and he saw that the boy was brave and strong.[101]

Though Thunder's wife spoke to the boy as if he would actually play ball, this is another good example of the usage of the figure of speech "to play ball" in a cultural narrative featuring significant other-than-human persons.

Lightning figured prominently in one episode in "Kanati and Selu." It is reckoned to have properties attributed to the Thunders, and like them is almost always a friend of the Cherokee people. The lightning boy went on, with the aid of his father, to defeat Vtsayi in the gatayusti gambling game. He and his brothers chased, finally caught, and imprisoned Vtsayi when he tried to escape them after gambling away all his possessions, his wife, and finally his life.[102]

Mooney reported that while the father and two sons "seem to be Kana'tĭ and the Thunder Boys," no informant "would positively assert this, while the boy hero, who has no other name, is said to be the lightning."[103] I will consider this point in detail below, but I will say here that I believe this to be the case, based on my research. The rejoining of Lightning with his family, the Thunder family, is an interesting story development. It mirrors the struggle of the Thunder Boys to rejoin their father in "Kanati and Selu," and the figure of speech "to play ball" is employed in both narratives as well.

In a written manuscript version of this narrative, the boy seemed to play anetso with the brothers. In shorthand, Mooney wrote that Thunder told the boy to go to the sunset and "find his (2) oldr brothrs (tsetsanili) & chlng to ball play—Boy go, find brothrs & begin BP—thundr roll wn play & T know at play—aftr while T think playd enuf & tel com home."[104] This is an interesting variant, one that is similar to the next narrative I will present. Either way, the ball game is the test of courage that allows the third boy to reunite with his family.

The Man who Married the Thunders' Sister[105]

In several of his published articles, the anthropologist John Witthoft included narratives conveyed to him by certain Cherokee individuals. Moses Owl of Birdtown (Qualla Boundary) was the source of a version of "Kanati and Selu" as well as the narrative I will discuss next. A caveat regarding these accounts: Witthoft presented them as the words of the people and did not provide any qualifying footnoting of any kind. Until further proof about Witthoft's method comes to light, then, one can assume they do reflect editing, but this may never be known for sure. Owl began, "Once a young man fell in love with a strange girl at a dance and followed her home. He caught up with her and she agreed to marry him. They went a long way up into the mountains to her house, and were welcomed by her mother."[106]

The next day the man was told that the girl's two brothers were expected; later the Thunders came roaring up mounted on huge rattlesnakes. Though they were happy to have another man to help them with their work, they complained of the unpleasant smell of human in the house. Owl continued, "However, they assured him that he would quickly lose his human scent, and invited him to play ball with them the next day. They asked him to stable their 'horses' for them in order to try his courage. He was very frightened, but he managed to lead the snakes off and put them away without showing fear."

The following day proved more harrowing than the last:

Early the next morning they told him to get onto a third snake and come with them. He was terribly frightened but he climbed on and rode a long way with them until they came to a ball-ground. Here they got out their sticks and began a ball-stick game. This was his third trial for they used a human skull as a ball. When he saw it come flying at him with its jaws agape, he was afraid, but he thought of his wife and played well. So he proved his courage and became the third Thunder. He can be heard sometimes traveling across the sky with his brother-Thunders, who make a louder noise than he does.[107]

The third trial was playing the game; notice the outcome was not mentioned. He proved his courage, and the last test was the ball game. He played with the brothers and was accepted into the family. Together with the detail of using a human skull, the comment that he would lose his human scent suggests a metamorphosis to another kind of being or at least to an anomalous state.[108] This resemblance to the "Vtsayi, the Gambler" narrative is clear.

The similarities between this narrative collected by Mooney and the one told by Moses Owl are the test of courage to prove oneself, the presence of rattlesnakes, and the Thunder brothers. For Moses Owl, the boy became the third Thunder after demonstrating his courage, while in Mooney's narrative he actualized himself as Lightning. Rattlesnakes are mounts in one narrative and jewelry in another. The ball game was played in Owl's narrative, while there seems to be a discrepancy between the published and handwritten

Tadatse anetsodui 51

versions of the one collected by Mooney. To reiterate from above, the usage of "to play ball" as a figure of speech, as in the Kanati and Selu narrative, is operative in the published version of the Vtsayi narrative; yet Mooney's handwritten version of the narrative seems to suggest they actually played.

Interpretation of the Narratives

While several of my Cherokee consultants are familiar with the Kanati and Selu narrative, in my experience the narrative of the ball game between the birds and the animals is the one that Cherokee people typically associate with the ball game, having learned it as children. The "When I was a young child . . ." preface is not invoked before people relate the narrative, and I have not had a Cherokee consultant ruminate on deeper philosophical issues with regard to it. Here I offer a few brief observations on the narratives featuring anetso and concentrate on the links between ritual and narrative. As for further analysis, a proper consideration of the Cherokee cultural narrative tradition deserves a dedicated treatment of its own.

The narratives of Kanati and Selu, the ball game between the birds and animals, Vtsayi, and the man who married the Thunders' sister all relate trials that an individual must overcome either to rejoin one's family or to belong in a group. The themes of overcoming hardship and struggle are presented as inherent parts of life, and the transformations undergone by characters in the narratives reflect the ideal that in the moment of truth, the Cherokee person will persevere, whether alone or with the aid of others. An important point again and again seems to be not being afraid to participate, win or lose. Participation in the ball game seems to be a preferred method of testing the mettle of young males, be they human or other than human, including animals. Such an observation leads one to consider the relationship then, between this activity and preparation for warfare, which I will do in Chapter Five.

In three of these four narratives, the boys were able to pass the tests they had to face. In the fourth, their "family" actually rejected certain animals; only when transformed into other beings were they able to join another "family" or group. Thus the themes of coming of age (particularly young men becoming adults), agon, and overcoming great odds to succeed all could be applied to these narratives. Other-than-human persons as well as humans participate in anetso in order to win bets, win for the sake of winning, compete against other communities for bragging rights, carry on a tradition, and represent their communities.

There is a clear link between the relevant narratives and the physical activity of anetso. Richard King has noted, regarding the Latin term *religio*, from which the term "religion" derives, that "in the pre-Christian era Cicero provides an etymology of the term relating it to *relegere*—to re-trace or re-read. Thus, *religio* involves the retracing of 'the lore of the ritual' of one's ancestors."[109] I think this idea of "retracing the lore of the ritual" is quite suggestive, and is one way of thinking about the relationship between cultural narratives and ritual.

It puts me in mind of a suggestion that Raymond Fogelson offered but did not develop in his dissertation: the idea that the ball game "can be conceptualized" as "a kind of ritual drama periodically performed as an enactment of premises implicit in the myth-dream."[110] Here he invoked Kenelm Burridge's notion, then quite contemporary, of a cultural narrative that exerts influence in a community by virtue of its meaning to the group as a whole.[111] By casting the ball game in this light, Fogelson recognized the possibility of the activity being a ritual drama, even if he did not offer any formal definitions of the categories or develop the argument. While nearly fifty years later I do not find Fogelson's invocation of Burridge's idea of the myth-dream convincing, in this context, as with King's quote, it is suggestive insofar as it draws attention to the broader issue of the relationship between cultural action and cultural text.

Cherokee Beliefs in Other-than-Human Persons

As even the few selected examples above illustrate, Cherokee cultural narratives are populated by a variety of other-than-human persons. Prominent among them are Kanati and his sons, referred to ceremonially as the Red Man and the Little Red Men, respectively, who hold equally prominent positions in any account of what Fogelson has called a "Cherokee pantheon."[112] In addition to their appearance in cultural narratives both "cosmogonic" and otherwise, they have been beseeched by Cherokee people for assistance in various contexts. Though the acceptance of Christianity has lessened their overt importance for many Cherokee people over time, their presence is continued, clear, and identifiable for some members of the Eastern Band of Cherokee Nation.[113]

Raymond Fogelson is the only scholar to attempt systematic classification of the range of Cherokee other-than-human persons, so in addition to consulting his work I plowed back through the relevant scholarship, tracking the Thunder Beings in the context of the range of Cherokee other-than-human persons.

Supreme Beings

Historically, members of the Eastern Band of Cherokee have expressed belief in a Supreme or Creator Being, whether or not they have couched it in Judeo-Christian terminology by calling it "God." I have met several individuals who continue to do so, often referring to "the Creator" in discussion, but this other-than-human person is known by at least one other name as well.[114] A number of scholarly sources support my position. As Alan Kilpatrick has noted: "The Creator is most often referred to, in religious tracts as well as in the magico-medical spells, as *une:hlanv':hi* 'the one who provides' (Kilpatrick and Kilpatrick 1964:27; Kilpatrick and Kilpatrick 1965b:34; Kilpatrick and Kilpatrick 1968:33; and Kilpatrick and Kilpatrick 1970:102–105, 116, and 118)."[115] As he explained in a footnote, Kilpatrick differed with Mooney in his translation of this word. Mooney, and Olbrechts after him, translated the word as "apportioner"; Kilpatrick presumed this was due to Mooney's belief that the Cherokee supreme deity was the sun.[116]

Frans Olbrechts stated that the sun was always referred to "in the ritualistic language" by two names; he translated the first as "'He has apportioned, allotted, divided into equal parts,'" and was less sure about the second, suggesting "'woman . . . very important'" and "'woman . . . par excellence.'"[117] Because the second term clearly includes the stem for "woman," Olbrechts stated that it was "clear that a feminine person is meant."[118] This is despite the first term being masculine and Olbrechts's own habit of referring to this other-than-human person as "he."

Olbrechts further noted that because this other-than-human person "has always been looked upon as their most powerful spirit by the Cherokee, the missionaries have read into his name the meaning of 'Great Spirit,' 'Creator'"; Cherokee people "who have been missionized to some extent identify this spirit with the God of the Christians." Only "a very few of the older people" seemed to know much about this being; most were not aware that it was the sun or knew its sex.[119] In fact the word *Unehlanvhi* is used for "God" in Cherokee translations of the bible.[120]

Olbrechts continued:

> Although this spirit was not considered responsible for the origin of things (see Mooney, Myths, pp. 239, 248), yet he must once have had the reputation of a most eminent spirit, if not the preeminent deity. When such very important tribal or ritualistic events take place as the ball game, or the search for medicine, he is always invoked in a very humble and propitiating way. He and the Fire (they are still by a few of the oldest informants felt to be one and the same person) are the only spirits to which prayers, in

the true meaning of the term, are ever offered; of them things are asked, while other spirits are merely commanded to do things.[121]

Mooney included an example of this invocation in "The Cherokee Ball Play." After pregame activities were completed, and the lines of opposing players faced each other in the middle of the field, an elderly man addressed them, telling them that "Une.lanu.hi, 'the Apportioner'—the sun—is looking down upon them, urging them to acquit themselves in the game as their fathers have done before them; but above all to keep their tempers, so that none may have it to say that they got angry or quarreled, and that after it is over each one may return in peace along the white trail to rest in his white house."[122]

William H. Gilbert related a narrative he called "The Story of the Creation of Man," in which he began, "At first there was a Great Spirit or 'apportioner' living in this world called by a name which means 'He has prepared.' This name came about because of the fact that he had already prepared or created the sun, the moon, and the earth."[123] On the page before Gilbert had listed twelve other beings, "who may help or hinder human purposes depending upon the magic power wielded by the human being." These included: "The Man of the Whirlwind who stirs up tornadoes and dangerous winds"; "the Cloud People who often come to visit and commune with humans"; "the Red Man of Lightning"; and "the Thunder Men who make known their presence during the storm."[124] The sun and moon were not mentioned.

Historical sources coincide with the basic details described above. In the Payne-Butrick Manuscript (1830s), the author cited "*A, ke, yv, ku - Squa, ne, lv, nv, hi*—Sun, my Creator" as an address found in many "prayers."[125] The author noted that "it is plain that the Sun was generally considered the superior in their devotions."[126]

The trader Alexander Longe reported in 1725 that one of the Cherokee "Indian priests" referred to "the great emperor that being above" as "the Grate ouga Calaster the vola."[127] Elsewhere he noted their "opinion of the divine power, they own one supreme power that is above the fermement [sic] and that power they say was he that made the heavens and the earth and all things that is therein and governs all according to his will and pleasure." This "great king" had four messengers, one at each cardinal direction, "to attend the 4 seasons of the year, which we call the 4 quarters of the year and to mind the moving of the sun and moon and stars."[128]

In *Early History of the Cherokees* (1917), Cherokee historian Emmet Starr ranked beings in the following order: "The sun, their superior deity, was called 'The Apportioner.'" This being was responsible for "dividing time into day and night, giving the four seasons, besides being the traditional giver of the 'divine fire' of their ancestors." He ranked the "'Long man'" second, and the "'Red man' (the name derivative, possibly, from the rising moon) the representative of the east," third. He also made mention of the "'Little man,' who lived in the thunder" and the "'Little people,' fairies who dwelt in the rock cliffs." In addition, he noted that there were red (east), white (south), blue (north), and black (west) gods; while brown, "like a cloud, obscured all, but was propitious, as after clouds we expect sunshine." The red god "bestowed triumph and happiness"; the blue god, "defeat and trouble"; the white god, "peace and happiness"; and the black god, death.[129]

So what conclusion does this source material support? The sources seem to agree on a concept of a singular other-than-human person or being, the Apportioner or Provider, as supreme. Several consultants with whom I spoke, across generations, have supported this conclusion. One college-age individual commented that this person's grandparents had said that the Cherokee always believed in God before the Christians came; they just used a different term to refer to this being. An elderly Cherokee minister told me much the same thing.[130] In addition to many Christians, there are members of the Eastern Band of Cherokee Nation who continue to express belief in a Supreme or Creator Being but do not couch it in Judeo-Christian terminology by calling it "God." It is not the sun, river, Red Man, or the Thunders.

The Thunders

The position ascribed to the Thunder Beings by members of the Eastern Band of Cherokee Nation has been expressed in formulas, cultural narratives, popular belief, and ritual activity. Several accounts, by elderly consultants and in the written record, have discussed incidents of weather control, or averting negative weather conditions by proper ritual behavior. Certain of these comments provide the rationale for ritual behavior when eating the first corn of the year.[131]

Alexander Longe made what were perhaps the earliest recorded written comments about thunder in the same 1725 document cited above. Longe was told that "the thunder and lightning is god's great guns."[132] The John Howard Payne Papers (1830s) contain relevant information on this subject as well. There is a reference to the "Red man" as the "first, and the original of all" of the four "vice-regents of the Great Supreme."[133] The author also made the following comments: "Thunder was adored; or rather, thunders, for there was supposed to be many, stationed, or dwelling, in different places, each charged with a specific duty. A very exemplary Cherokee, after having fasted seven days, it is said, went to the top of a stupendously high mountain, while it was thundering, and there saw the Beings whence the thunders came."[134]

Mooney provided a good general statement on the Thunders in the glossary to *Myths of the Cherokee*:

> Anisga'ya Tsunsdi'—Abbreviated from Anisga'ya Tsunsdi'ga, "Little Men." These two sons of Kana'tĭ, who are sometimes called Thunder Boys and who live in Usûñhi'yĭ above the sky vault, must not be confounded with the Yûñwĭ Tsunsdi', or "Little People," who are also Thunderers, but who live in caves of the rocks and cause the short, sharp claps of thunder. There is also the Great Thunderer, the thunder of the whirlwind and the hurricane, who seems to be identical with Kana'tĭ himself.[135]

Mooney also offered this information about the Thunders: "The great Thunder and his sons, the two Thunder boys, live far in the west above the sky vault. The lightning and the rainbow are their beautiful dress. The priests pray to the Thunder and call him the Red Man, because that is the brightest color of his dress. The great Thunders above the sky are kind and helpful. . . . One must not point at the rainbow, or one's finger will swell at the lower joint."[136] In fact, Mooney entitled one handwritten version of the narrative of Kanati and Selu located in the Smithsonian, "The Thunder Family."[137]

Elsewhere, Mooney remarked that the Red Man was "one of the greatest of the gods, being repeatedly called upon in formulas of all kinds, and is hardly subordinate to the Fire, the Water, or the Sun. His identity is as yet uncertain, but he seems to be intimately connected with the Thunder family."[138] On the following page he said the Red Man "is the spirit of power, triumph, and success" and is invoked by the "shaman . . . to the assistance of his client."[139]

Frans Olbrechts noted in 1932 that "the Thunder's rôle is that of a disease expeller rather than that of a disease causer. He and his two sons are the enemies of the Black Man and of anything and anybody having his abode in the 'Black Land,' in the 'Evening Land,' in the 'Dark Land,' or in the West."[140] Olbrechts also noted that the "Cherokee pretend that Thunder is the friend of all Indians, and that he never kills one."[141] Then, as now, some Cherokee people will say that lightning will not strike them but will hit trees and European Americans.[142]

In narratives recorded by John Witthoft about fifty years after those collected by Mooney, Will West Long and Molly Sequoyah of the Big Cove community on the Qualla Boundary related further details of the Thunder beings and added to the opinions concerning both their identities and their dwelling places.[143] Witthoft concurred with the information reported by Mooney, that the Little Red Men live above the sky vault, are "invoked in several of the conjuror's formulae, and are 'beneficent and powerful.'"[144] Witthoft himself distinguished them from other beings, referring to them as "anisgaya tsundi, the Thunder Boys."[145] As quoted by John Witthoft, the two individuals stated the following: "According to Will West Long of Big Cove, the thunders are known as nayɔhi unehí. They live in the rock cliffs and go up into the sky to play ball, which causes a thunder storm. They will listen to you if you invoke them properly, and some conjurors are said to be able to control thunderstorms. According to Molly Sequoyah of Big Cove, a ball made of red string is used in the Indian Ball game as played in the Big Cove, since that is like the ball used by the Thunders."[146] Current consultants have told me about a red ball being used by the Big Cove team, though not all agree the ball was made of string. Although Witthoft, quoting Mooney, said these Thunders live above the sky vault, Long's comment seems to suggest a residence in the rock cliffs (or this worldly realm).

As is so often the case with regard to matters of the Cherokee religious system, Raymond Fogelson has made a careful study of what he refers to as the "Thunderers." In one article Fogelson aligned different beings along continuums based upon size, noise, beneficence to mankind, and power.[147] In all cases the Thunderers are the culmination; as he noted: "Finally, except perhaps for their aloof father, Kanati, whose agents they are, the Thunderers are the most powerful beings in the Cherokee pantheon."[148] He stated that Mooney "is correct in noting that the Thunderers are among the most potent spiritual beings in Cherokee theology, ritual magic, and that they have important cosmogonic significance." Noting that they "control thunder and lightning and reside in the western skies beyond the celestial firmament," Fogelson continued: "Mankind enjoys an abiding friendship with the Thunderers, for according to several myth fragments, humans once rendered support and assistance in a battle for cosmic supremacy when the Thunderers defeated their arch-enemy, the evil, dragon-like Uktena. Ever since, Cherokees have petitioned the Thunderers for a wide variety of boons, including victory in war or the ballgame, success in love, gambling luck, and prevention of and relief from illness."[149]

He went on to remark,

> The Thunderers are considered to be very dangerous and powerful. In some of the scales of spiritual power that are evoked in ritual, the Thunder Spirits outrank even the Sun (cf. Kilpatrick and Kilpatrick 1965:81–2). They are responsible for the deep, resonant, rumbling thunder; lightning bolts are sometimes interpreted as being caused by clashes of the Thun-

derers when they play ball against one another. These powerful beings honor their friendship with the Cherokees, who, in turn, regard them as beneficent culture heroes.¹⁵⁰

To support these comments he highlighted the narrative "The Red Man and the Uktena," collected by Mooney, in which the humans aided the Thunderers in their defeat of the Uktena, "their arch-enemy."¹⁵¹ Also influential were narratives collected or edited by the Kilpatricks; presumably the "myth fragments" Fogelson mentioned in the first quote.¹⁵²

To repeat my question from above, what is one to conclude regarding this material? I found that among the Eastern Band of Cherokee, the Thunder Beings have held a secondary, though important, position, to a Creator being. Interestingly, at one time among at least some members of the Western Nation, the Thunder Beings seem to have assumed a primary role.¹⁵³ Whatever the numerical rank, as I have displayed in this section, in the context of a posited "Cherokee theology" there is ample evidence to support the theological significance of the Thunderers. There also is ample evidence of their involvement with anetso, both in terms of playing it themselves and in aiding human ball teams.

One last point is that some people only reference the Thunder Beings obliquely, as I mentioned above. Several consultants have made it clear that the Cherokee term is not to be uttered in everyday conversation.¹⁵⁴ It is only after several years of fieldwork in the community that certain consultants have deigned to relay even that point to me.¹⁵⁵ The Thunders are never referred to explicitly by name.¹⁵⁶

Frans Olbrechts noted this when he stated that one risked angering Thunder by referring to him as Red instead of White in everyday speech.¹⁵⁷ As for his sons, the "Two Little Red Men," Olbrechts reported that "the Cherokee never explicitly call them 'Thunder Boys.'"¹⁵⁸ The fact that this attitude still persists is evidence enough that some amount of traditional belief continues with reference to these beings.

In my opinion, this term is similar to the Hebrew covenant name for the God of Israel that is considered too sacred to be pronounced. Traditionally the name (YHVH) is not pronounced when it appears in the text, and the Hebrew term for "my Lord" is substituted for it.¹⁵⁹ One difference between the two traditions is that Cherokee individuals may verbalize such a term in ritual conditions, but depending upon the occasion entire passages might be chanted, spoken inaudibly, or spoken only in the conjurer's mind, i.e., spoken to oneself.¹⁶⁰

Tadatse anetsodui 59

Rattlesnakes

There is one last category of other-than-human persons to consider. Rattlesnakes, as evidenced above in several narratives, often were in the company of the Little Men, serving variously as their necklaces, mounts, or agents. Mooney noted that snakes "are all regarded as *anida´wehĭ*, "supernaturals," having an intimate connection with the rain and thunder gods, and possessing a certain influence over the other animal and plant tribes. . . . The feeling toward snakes is one of mingled fear and reverence, and every precaution is taken to avoid killing or offending one, especially the rattlesnake."[161]

According to Mooney, "the rattlesnake is called *utsa´nătĭ*, which may be rendered, 'he has a bell,' alluding to the rattle."[162] Mooney noted the presence of the rattlesnake in the narratives involving the daughter of the sun and Vtsayi (see above), and continued, "By the old men he is also spoken of as 'the Thunder's necklace' . . . and to kill one is to destroy one of the most prized ornaments of the thunder god. In one of the formulas addressed to the Little Men, the sons of the Thunder, they are implored to take the disease snake to themselves, because 'it is just what you adorn yourselves with.' For obvious reasons the rattlesnake is regarded as the chief of the snake tribe and is feared and respected accordingly."[163] Fogelson concurred, noting that "snakes, particularly rattlesnakes, occupy an important status as transformation symbols in the Cherokee world view."[164] He continued: "In common with many native peoples around the world, the Cherokee apperceive an identity between snakes and lightning. The powerful Sons of Thunder, the Little Red Men, are frequently associated with snakes in Cherokee myths and ritual formulae, particularly those dealing with war and the ballgame."[165]

I will return to considerations of these relationships between the Thunders and Cherokee people in Chapter Five, where I will argue that both the Little Men and their agents the rattlesnakes historically have remained intimately connected with the playing of anetso both physically and symbolically. These interconnections also help one to understand why anetso has been such a hardy tradition, and why it survived through periods of immense change.

The Figure of Speech "to play ball against" in British Legal and Military Discourse: The Incident at Chestowe

The earliest non-Cherokee written reference to the ball game located thus far is from 1714. It is contained in the *Journals of the Commissioners of the Indian Trade September 20, 1710–August 29, 1718* of South Carolina.[166] At the beginning of the eighteenth century in the Carolinas, trade between colonists and "Indians" was so unregulated that a commission was created to try to regulate the expanding market in the colonies. One of the duties of the commissioners of the Board of Indian Trade was to bring to trial and discipline traders who were acting illegally.

In this case the trader was Alexander Longe, who a decade later would produce the account cited above. Longe and his accomplice Eleazer Wiggan were accused of inciting Cherokee warriors from a particular group of settlements (either the Middle or Overhill towns, sources differ as to which) to attack the Yuchi town of Chestowe and capture its people for slaves.[167] Longe and Wiggan operated a trading store at Chestowe. They had induced the townspeople of Yuchi to accumulate debt they could not repay, and then began demanding payments.

During one encounter between Longe and townspeople in 1711 or 1712, an individual "knocked him down and ripped off a strip of his scalp."[168] Determined to get revenge, in 1713 Longe convinced two town leaders, or headmen, Caesar and Flint, to raise a force to destroy Chestowe, for which he would give them half of the people captured to sell as slaves.[169] Though the Yuchi were longtime foes, apparently there was some opposition to the raid by a Lower town headman by the name of Partridge.[170] Cherokee headmen, although they often united against non-Cherokee foes, were nevertheless autonomous commanders.

After surrounding the Yuchi town during the night, Caesar and Flint's Cherokee force ambushed at dawn, totally surprising the Yuchi. The Yuchi retreated into their town house, where the group seems to have decided to die rather than live a life of slavery. The men cut the throats of their families and then killed each other. Only six Yuchi people remained alive to take back to Charles Town: one woman and five children.[171]

As John Phillip Reid has noted, the "raid turned into a tragedy and then became a scandal."[172] The commission investigated the incident, citing the instruction to traders that "no Indian shall be deemed a Slave and bought as such unless taken in War."[173] The mass suicide scandalized the region, and the trail of carnage led straight back to a British trader.

The *Journals* preserved the testimony of witnesses in this case, given before the commission. One witness's comments recorded in an entry dated May 4, 1714, were as follows: "Mr. Benja. Clea being sworn said he heard Capt. Card say there was a Design among the Cherikees to cut off Chestowee 10 Dayes before the said Town was cut off, and that the Cherikees designed to invite the Euchees to a Ball Play in order to cut them of. That he heard from Mr. Dillon that the Indians gave an Account of some white People that pretended the Governor's Order for cutting off Chestowee. That Mr. Long had some Difference with an Euche Indian who had puled of sum of his Hair."[174]

Tadatse anetsodui

What this is saying is that the witness, a trader by the name of Benjamin Clea, reported Captain Card, another trader, as saying there was a "Design" among the Cherokees to "cut off" Chestowe; they "designed to invite" the Yuchis to a "Ball Play" in order to do so.

Based on knowledge of what events transpired in this situation, it should be clear that "cut off" is a figure of speech meaning to attack and decimate in defeat.[175] To "design to invite" suggests people were hatching a plot. The witness reported a Mr. Dillon hearing Cherokees saying other "white People" had presented them with what they said were orders from the governor to attack Chestowe. Clearly the witness offered this comment in defense of the Cherokee position, suggesting that they never would have done such a thing if they had known that it was not the governor's orders. According to this scenario, Longe would not be denied; he had been partially scalped and deceived people to facilitate his revenge.

As for interpretations of the ball game in the account, Fogelson found a truncated version of this reference in a secondary work on Cherokee history by Henry T. Malone. Malone quoted a portion of the above *Journals* entry and noted the "use of the ball-play as a stratagem in warfare."[176] Fogelson agreed with Malone's assessment, commenting that it appeared "to be a ruse to achieve certain military objectives."[177] Theda Perdue, in her discussion of the "Indian slave trade" in the colonies, attributed such warfare to the incitement of traders, and quoted trader James Adair to that effect.[178]

Were the Cherokees using the occasion of the ball game as an excuse to entrap as many people of Chestowe as possible? This seems to be the suggestion of the evidence. Were they using the figure of speech "to play ball against" to announce intentions of going to war? It seems unlikely in this case, at least at first, as the witness reported on the "designs" of the Cherokee. However, it is possible that the witness did not understand the cultural contextual use of the figure of speech, and in fact the Middle townspeople were discussing the attack.[179] In other words, Cherokee people amongst themselves *could have been* using the figure of speech in context to refer to the impending warfare; but it seems the trader thought they *were* using the occasion of the ball game as a military ruse.

One wishes a Cherokee or Yuchi account of the situation had survived. Partridge, a Cherokee headman who was called as a witness in the case, spoke only of the plan to raid, his opposition, and his alibi.[180] My interpretation is that neither Clea, the witness, nor Card, the man who reported what was "literally said," understood the usage of this figure of speech.

No further mention of the ball game was made in the *Journal* entries dealing with this case, and no explanation was given when it was mentioned, so it is reasonable to assume that the activity was well-enough known such that it did not require explanation. Evidently at least some colonists were familiar with selected Cherokee customs and activities other than the ball game at this time; later in Clea's testimony he made mention of another Cherokee activity. Remarking on the timing of the impending attack, "an Indian told Mr. Wiggen that Mr. Long said the Euchee shoold be cut off before green Corne Time."[181] He was referring to the harvest of green corn, which was accompanied by a number of ceremonial activities often glossed by scholars as "Green Corn ceremonialism."[182]

Just as Kanati told the Wolf people to play ball against his boys when he meant for the Wolf people to kill them, perhaps the Overhill Cherokee warriors employed the figure of speech in planning the attack on Chestowe. It is a coincidence, if nothing more; but it does neatly link the first mention in written history of the ball game (based on current research) to Cherokee cultural narratives. However, there is another report of this figure of speech a half-century later, lending further credence to the conclusion that the Cherokee phrase, in active usage at the time, was misunderstood.

The Treaty at Augusta

In military correspondence to Colonel Henry Bouquet, dated November 7, 1763, the British Colonel Adam Stephen remarked, "I understand that the Cherokee refuse coming to the treaty at Augusta and that the Creeks have been soliciting them to join in a Game at Ball, which they have a mind to play with the English."[183]

This paragraph is the last in a letter dealing with other military matters that appear to have no direct connection to this statement. Again, as was the case with the witness Clea's statement, the author did not explain the ball game, which suggests that it was not necessary to do so. Stephen was referring to the event of November 10, 1763, when the British and a council of southern First Nations concluded a "treaty of mutual peace and friendship" at Augusta, Georgia.[184] In attendance was Captain John Stuart, the British crown's superintendent for the southern tribes in America, along with the governors of four southern colonies, who "explained fully to the Indians the new condition of affairs."[185]

Three days before this summit some faction of the Muskogees (Creeks) were soliciting the Cherokees to do something. This could be a report of an attempt of an alliance or an allusion to an attack; another interpretation is that the Muskogees were using the invitation in an attempt to deceive the Cherokees. I base this interpretation on a report from Captain Stuart.

In a letter to the Earl of Egremont dated December 5, 1763, Stuart commented that his presence in Augusta had the advantage of allowing private conferences with all tribal leaders. He reported on the anger on the part of the Cherokees for the dubious dealings of the Creeks. From what Stuart related, one thing becomes apparent. The Cherokees blamed the Creeks for deception that led to the Cherokee War and the current situation they faced. In a letter to Stuart, Stephen suggested that the Creeks had recently plotted to entice the Cherokee to attack the English and then double-cross them. Stuart said that the Cherokees expressed apprehension about coming to Augusta and made clear their feelings about the Creeks:

> The Cherokees at this time have an Inveterate Hatred to the Creeks, which does not only proceed from the late murder of Two of their People by Them; but also from a Remembrance of their having by their Machinations, Messages and Promises of Assistance decoyed them into a War with us, and left them [?] exposed to our resentment and a most Severe Chastisement, which they still feel. The Cherokees used all their Art, during the Congress, to inspire us with the same Sentiment of the Creeks which they entertained and they earnestly wish for an Opportunity of retaliating the Usage they have received from them.[186]

So according to Stuart, the Cherokees did not want to come to Augusta because of their distrust of the Creeks.

It is true the Cherokees may have been playing both sides of this situation, but my point still rests on the report of a European military source's usage of a Cherokee figure of speech. He heard it, reported it, and perhaps understood and conveyed the intent of the comment. Again, Stephen did not explain what the ball game was, and since it was a military report it was not a document to contain trifling matters or matters that did not relate to the military situations at hand. He reported it because it was significant. Though Stuart did not mention the most recent deceit suggested by Stephen, it is not too far-fetched to conclude that the deception took the form of the invitation to "play ball." The Creeks would entice the Cherokees to boycott the summit, ostensibly either to play ball or to plot against or attack the English, and then would double-cross them.

In both quoted statements presented above, the Cherokee figure of speech "to play ball against" fits the situations. By means of this figure of speech, Cherokee people potentially were suggesting to each other, and Creek people were suggesting to Cherokee people, to move militarily against an enemy. Cherokee leaders in the early and mid-eighteenth century were using the same language that was in their cultural narratives to express ideas in their interactions with the English and other First Nations, though it seems that the English individuals doing the reporting did not understand completely what Cherokee people were saying.

Threatened by ever-increasing challenges to both their sovereignty and identity, the Cherokee people were about to enter what was perhaps the most tumultuous period in their history. During the first thirty-eight years of the nineteenth century the Cherokee nation experienced great upheaval, and it was also during this period that Christian missionary activity flourished, with mixed results. This upheaval became physical and literal with the advent of the forced removal to Oklahoma, the Trail of Tears. It was also during this time that anetso was in essence the Cherokee national pastime.

Hani!
(Here!)

Anetso as an Enduring Symbol of Cultural Identity in an Era of Great Change (1799–1838)

One could endlessly enumerate the values given body, made body, by the hidden persuasion of an implicit pedagogy which can instill a whole cosmology, through injunctions as insignificant as "sit up straight" or "don't hold your knife in your left hand," and inscribe the most fundamental principles of the arbitrary content of a culture in seemingly innocuous details of bearing or physical or verbal manners, so putting them beyond the reach of consciousness and explicit statement.
— Pierre Bourdieu, The Logic of Practice

Values Given Body

Two hundred years ago, the Moravian missionaries John and Anna R. Gambold complained about the Cherokee ball game in a mission school report to their bishop, Carl Gotthold Reichel.[1] The passage in the July 1808 report read: "That ball game seems also to have had a bad effect on our Indian children. It seems that they imagined that because of it they were at once accepted into the class of men, and believed they could demand more freedom."[2]

The Gambolds' complaint to their superior is a revealing statement. Participation in the ball game was an assertion of identity for Cherokee boys that signaled a change in their social status according to Cherokee cultural norms. The missionaries themselves provided this information even as they dismissed what the boys "imagined" was now their right to more freedom.

This is but one of many references to the ball game included in journal entries and correspondence of missionaries in the Cherokee nation. As Theda Perdue commented in one work, references to ball games "pepper" mission journals.[3] More often than not they are complaints, whether the missionaries were Moravian, Baptist, or from the American Board of Commissioners for Foreign Missions (ABCFM).

In certain cases, the reports read as if the shaker top was loose and the pepper dumped out on the page. For example, in December 1827, Isaac Proctor, a missionary and teacher at an ABCFM mission school in the Cherokee Nation, wrote a letter to the national corresponding secretary of the organization, Jeremiah Evarts, in which he also complained about the ball game.[4] Proctor was in the midst of reporting on the Cherokee students when, after a passage in which he praised his students' character, he grumbled: "It is truly painful, however, to see young men, sons of professors, who have a good education strolling about whooping & yelling in the most savage manner and yet it is a fact respecting many of them who attended Mr. Hall's school. Some of them the other day assembled in plain sight of the Mission house, stripped themselves entirely naked, and for some time played Ball."[5] Nineteen years after the Gambolds' report, missionaries still were complaining about the ball game, and they would continue to do so until most left the Cherokee Nation in advance of its removal to Oklahoma.

What can one infer from these missionary accounts of students playing the Cherokee ball game, nearly twenty years apart? As far as we know, none of the Cherokee students involved left written comments about what they were doing or why they were doing it. This of course is not uncommon; in historical documents as well as in the context of scholarship about Cherokee people, the voices of Cherokee actors in history often are silent. Thus, in arguing for my interpretation, I maintain that discussion of anetso in nineteenth-century written comments of missionaries provides a type of historical "voice" for Cherokee people. Through passages such as those above and several more below, I contend that we still can hear Cherokee voices loud and clear.

Furthermore I argue that what we hear is a clear message: for the Cherokee boys enrolled in the mission schools, participation in the ball game was an unmistakable statement of identity, the staking of an ontological position. Whether the statement was primarily an assertion of their identity as Cherokee people, or rather as men instead of boys, or both, remains unclear. What is clear, however, is that the students chose to express their identity in a way that the missionaries could not possibly ignore, indeed, in a way that challenged the missionaries to ignore it.

In this context I find provocative Pierre Bourdieu's statement in the epigraph to this chapter regarding "the values given body, made body, by the hidden persuasion of an implicit pedagogy which can instill a whole cosmology." My immediate interest is less about power and controlling bodies through pedagogy (though this is certainly an interesting and worthwhile topic) and more with the notion of "values given body"; the notion of cosmology implicit in bodily movement. In this sense the boys expressed and performed emic Cherokee notions about identity, notions that were inscribed in the physical activity of the ball game.

Of course I am aware that an interpretive exercise such as this involves a healthy dose of speculation. I do not wish to suggest for a moment that twenty-first-century academic theories about identity can or should be applied universally to describe the motivations of these people who lived in the nineteenth century. On the other hand, neither do I want to deny these people the capacity for agency. Instead, I theorize about the ball game as an expression of existence through symbol as well as an "expression of an ontological position"; here I quote from Charles H. Long in his discussion of the "silence of the non-Western world during the period of colonialism."[6]

Drawing upon the work of scholars who have discussed Cherokee identity in the nineteenth century, I contend that historically as well as at present, one can offer an interpretation of anetso as a vehicle for the assertion or expression of identity. In his discussion of the nineteenth-century Cherokee religious system, Lee Irwin acknowledged the "plurality of voices" and "tensions and contradictions" that scholars must navigate as they work with relevant historical source material; as other scholars have noted, this is particularly the case when discussing Cherokee society in the late eighteenth century until the forced removal in 1838.[7] Gregory Dowd, for example, agreed with William McLoughlin's argument that a "new, 'national,' Cherokee identity" had developed by 1810, but he pointed out that this did not eliminate or even mitigate "the strain between nativism and accommodation."[8] In terms of the Cherokee religious system, Irwin contended that "the spiritual dimensions of Cherokee religious identity were constantly informed by personal experience through dreams, visions, and healing rites that worked in conjunction with the sacred word (formulas) and the sacred world."[9] I would add anetso to Irwin's list of "constants in Cherokee religion that helped to maintain viability and consistency throughout the ongoing struggle to determine the significance of traditional values and beliefs."[10]

Jon F. Sensbach, when describing how an African American man by the name of Adam repeatedly rebuffed a Moravian missionary's conversion attempts in 1835, noted that "repudiating Christianity could be as powerful an assertion of identity as embracing it."[11] I think the same point applies to Cherokee people who persistently participated in or attended the ball game, dances, and other activities in the face of missionary opposition. I also think that the notion is relevant for Cherokee children and parents who were part of the missionary system, either as students or converts.

Missionaries to the Cherokee nation struggled to gain and then to retain converts. The ABCFM missionary William Holland included a list in a mission report of what William McLoughlin termed the "most common causes for church censure."[12] Holland listed the following activities: "drunkenness, fornication, sabbath-breaking, gambling in various ways, fighting, conjuring, lying, cheating, faithlessness in fulfilling bargains, ingratitude for favors shown them, and profane swearing."[13] McLoughlin stated that "not included in this particular list" were "the sins of attending ballplays and the customs of infanticide and polygamy."[14]

Though most of Holland's list seems logical, the curious comments about fulfilling bargains and ingratitude suggest Holland's flock was not responding to him in ways he deemed appropriate. McLoughlin's interpretation of Holland's comments was that "the missionaries were unable to make it clear to the converts that Christianity demanded a total abnegation of everything that gave the Cherokees an identity of their own; it left no aspect of their lives unchanged."[15] I think this point was crystal clear to the converts; though they may not have formally repudiated Christianity as in Sensbach's example, these people rejected the idea that their status as converts precluded their involvement in such activities.

Many children and adults simply refused to cease participating in or attending the ball games, apparently whether or not the missionaries considered them, or they considered themselves, to be Christians. Parents came to the schools to take their children to the ball games and children skipped school and risked the missionaries' wrath to attend them. These actions were powerful assertions of identity for Cherokee people, and the missionaries' responses were definitive; in certain cases, Cherokee students were expelled, and converts were censured or even excommunicated for participating in such activities as ball games and dances.

Reading People Back into History, People Talking Back

Anetso was not simply prevalent but *persistent* in this era. Expression or assertion of identity as well as resistance and response take many different forms, whether or not written accounts interpret them in this way. It is as if by the sheer impact of the actions themselves that the people involved demanded that written accounts would record them and that their voices would be heard. Thus I understand these actions as indicative of the strength of identity and "tradition." Recognizing the nature of such events in primary source material *about* Cherokee people gives voice to the Cherokee actors who are mostly silent in the pages of written history.

Such a strategy of, in my own words, "reading people back into history" is emerging in the historical study of First Nations missions, in part due to the wider availability of missionary accounts in published form, such as *The*

Moravian Springplace Mission to the Cherokees (2007). For example, Joel W. Martin has encouraged scholars to look "behind the writings of missionaries and historians who depended too heavily on the missionaries' versions of events and ventriloquize their assumptions."[16] In a review of two earlier relevant works, *Writing Indians: Literacy, Christianity, and Native Community in Early America* (2000) and *The Brainerd Journal: A Mission to the Cherokees, 1817–1823* (1998), Catherine Corman spoke of the "technique of 'reading through' Euro-American documents to recover and interpret Indian voices and experiences."[17] Corman noted that the author of the first book decided to "rely warily" on such an approach, aware of potential pitfalls such as arguing for a "universal, traditional, 'authentic Native voice' speaking to us from the past."[18]

Given the efforts of the missionaries who penned the accounts in the Brainerd Journal to present themselves and their efforts in the most favorable light, Corman observed that the editors of the volume "do not help to clarify these biases when . . . they succumb to the kind of romantic language that obscures missionaries' complicated role in these Christian communities."[19] Nevertheless, Corman pointed out that in certain passages, the "missionaries wrote with sufficient candor to give readers a sense of Indians' own perceptions and motivations." Since Cherokee people comprehended the missionary discourse "and responded in a multiplicity of ways . . . scholars need to accept . . . the messiness of these understandings and work to create a new history of these rich and troubling encounters."[20]

I agree with Martin and Corman that these are complicated encounters, and assessing the accounts themselves is a complicated enterprise as well. Assuming that one has access to original documents, one still must infer information about authorial intent, intended audience, and other factors, not to mention being able to decipher the individual's handwriting properly. In addition, when one is working with edited collections of such accounts, as is often the case, there is another layer of such intent to excavate. When faced with the silence of particular voices in historical accounts, however, the enterprise is certainly worthwhile.

That being said, I want to stress that it certainly is *not* my intention to presume that Cherokee people or any other people for that matter "need" or want to be magnanimously "read back into history"; and those who might certainly do not need my help. Furthermore, though I speculate about how participation in the ball game is an assertion of Cherokee identity, it is not my intention to presume to pronounce the existence of such a static normative category as "authentic Cherokee identity" or to identify any Cherokee people, past or present, as illustrating its contours. Such assertions in any given context would be exceedingly hubristic and paternalistic as well as simply misguided and offensive.

My goals are more modest. To inform my argument that the ball game is a vehicle for identity assertion, I employ Frederick Hoxie's concept of First Nations peoples "talking back to American society": "By talking back to those who considered themselves superior, Indians could show that they rejected the self-serving nationalism they heard from missionaries and bureaucrats. The Natives made it clear that they refused to accept the definitions others had of them—savage, backward, doomed."[21]

In *Talking Back to Civilization* (2001), Hoxie collected documents in English written by First Nations people. He said that those documents "capture a cross section of this Indian 'back talk' in all of its moods: angry, clever, subtle, tenacious even playful."[22] Among other possible examples, one could point to how in the 1960s and 1970s, several of Vine Deloria Jr.'s books asserted this dialectical position, with titles such as *Custer Died for Your Sins* and *We Talk You Listen*.[23] In considering the ball game in this light, I expand Hoxie's concept to include other physical actions, in particular the ball game, which one might interpret in the same way.

As Joel W. Martin has argued, such a stance as Hoxie described can be proactive and offensive as well as reactive and defensive. In speaking about First Nations religious revolts, Martin addressed the "gap in our knowledge," which he argued "results from our discourse in Native American religions which *resists imagining Native American religions in creative contact with history*."[24] Martin further argued that "our scholarship discounts historical movements in which Native American religions demonstrated resiliency, improvisation and/or 'nontraditional' assimilation in contact with Europeans or Africans."[25] In a later work Martin echoed his own point by citing Robert Allen Warrior's "postessentialist" proposition that "Indianness . . . is highly fluid, relational, improvisational, and continually recreated in community and in relation to land and orients people toward survival in the face of colonialism."[26]

Similarly, Theda Perdue has observed that the "'decline' of Native people is embedded in contact history, largely because scholars have focused on military defeat and land loss. There are, however, other indices to culture change."[27] Perdue listed "production, reproduction, religion, and perceptions of self, as well as political and economic institutions" as such indices.[28]

I maintain that the Cherokee ball game, while not a "movement" or an "institution," is a type of cultural index, and not only of change, but of persistence as well. Through this cultural form of long duration certain Cherokee people talked back to history; they asserted their identity, demonstrated resiliency, and creatively improvised responses to changing circumstances. It was evident that students were "back talking" their missionary school teachers in the two accounts cited at the beginning of this chapter; and in the Proctor account, apparently the students were talking with their "backs" as well.

Silence, Symbol, and a Cultural Underground

Despite, or perhaps because of, the fact that there are few Cherokee accounts in this chapter, the silence of Cherokee voices is particularly noteworthy. In his article entitled "Silence and Signification," Charles Long spoke about the "irony of silence," citing Ludwig Wittgenstein's well-known aphorism: "'What can be shown cannot be said.'"[29] Wittgenstein's statement speaks to the relationship between cognition, speech, and language; for my purposes I modify the statement to "what can be shown was not said," at least in terms of the perspectives of events that were recorded. In the case of the ball game, accounts in written documents can be "shown" in the absence of written perspectives from Cherokee people to make the point that anetso was a prevalent and important activity for Cherokees, so much so that it repeatedly brought both Cherokee children and adults into conflict with different missionaries over a period of several decades.

Long used the term "voice of silence" to remind readers that "one must also take account of those peoples who had to undergo the 'creativity' of the Western world—those peoples and cultures who became during this period the 'pawns' of Western cultural creativity."[30] These peoples, Long asserted, "existed as the pauses between words—those pauses which are necessary if speech is to be possible—and in their silence they spoke."[31] Therefore "silence does not mean absence"; Long argued that the "silence of the non-Western world during the period of colonialism ... indicated that the expression of their existence through symbols and myths was at the same time the expression of an ontological position."[32] Thus "silence is a fundamentally ontological position."[33]

I find these notions quite useful, particularly the notion that people expressed their existence through symbols and myths.[34] At least in terms of my (perhaps idiosyncratic) interpretation, Long's concept of silence underlines the agency of actors whose voices are missing from the produced narratives of history of which they were a part. This recognition can prompt consideration of other methods that might begin to illuminate such information.[35]

In this way anetso is a practice, a physical action, that expresses ideas, but it also serves as a symbol of unspoken ideas to Cherokee people and others. As such it was utilized again and again by Cherokee people during

Hani! 73

this period, as it has been since that time. Thus, as I suggested above the task really is not to "read people back into history" but to see the ways in which their imprint is already there. In the missionary accounts at the beginning of this chapter, and with those that now follow, one sees evidence of Cherokee people "talking back" to the missionaries then; now, two hundred years later, the contemporary reader still can hear their voices.

Joel W. Martin has argued for the existence of one additional technique of cultural persistence related to the concept of silence in the first decades of the nineteenth century. While "[a] small and highly visible elite turned toward white ways and became commercial planters and slave owners," a "much larger number pursued alternative paths designed to prevent the extinction of their cultures."[36] The majority of Cherokee people "relied increasingly upon a kind of cultural 'underground,' a hidden set of beliefs and practices that reinforced their identity as Indians and strengthened their will to survive and resist."[37] Moreover, as Martin reiterated in a later work, this majority of "nonelite . . . seem to have used the elite to shield themselves from the intrusive and domineering gaze of American authorities and missionaries . . . by delegating diplomacy and intercultural negotiations to the elite."[38]

Martin argued that even the use of the Sequoyan syllabary and subsequent literacy "nurtured, without betraying, the Cherokee underground."[39] In this regard he highlighted a comment by William McLoughlin that the written language functioned to "'sustain the traditional community *beyond the perception* of the authorities, red or white.'"[40] Martin concluded that "although purposefully hidden by its creators and long overlooked by historians, the southeastern Indians' underground should be unearthed at last and ignored no longer."[41] In a later work he reiterated this call to action, urging scholars to "return to the archives and reinterpret historical Native American movements."[42] This is what I hope to do with regard to the history of anetso.

"That ball game seems also to have had a bad effect":
Anetso in Moravian Diary Accounts

In 1775, when the Cherokee headman Attakullakulla (Little Carpenter) visited Salem, N.C., in the settlement of Wachovia on his way to a treaty negotiation, Moravian Brethren broached the subject of a mission with him. According to the Moravian account, he expressed interest in the creation of a school. In 1783 the Moravian Brother Martin Schneider met with another headman, Tassel, about creating a mission; and in 1799, Brethren Abraham Steiner and Christian Frederic de Schweinitz journeyed to the Cherokee Nation for further discussions. They returned in the fall of 1800 to the Council House at

Tellico to speak with a full council of headmen.⁴³ After a debate "in which the Indians showed considerable difference of opinion, it was decided to open a mission."⁴⁴ Cherokee people only wanted the Moravians to "teach their children English. When the Cherokees learned that the missionaries intended to instruct the Cherokees and their children about the gospel, the leaders made it quite clear that the Christian religion held no interest for them."⁴⁵

Construction work began on a mission in April of 1801; two missionaries, Brethren Abraham Steiner and Gottlieb Byhan, lodged with a Cherokee headman until their quarters were ready.⁴⁶ Impatient with what they perceived as a lagging pace, "the great council at Ustanali sent orders to the missionaries to organize a school within six months or leave the nation."⁴⁷ The mission was located in Springplace, in what is now northwestern Georgia.⁴⁸ This agreement inaugurated a period of sustained activity by several denominations.⁴⁹

In the midst of this activity the United States government also was initiating an acculturation policy that dovetailed nicely with the missionaries' endeavors. In 1789 George Washington's policy for First Nations peoples was implemented, and a July 2, 1791, treaty with the Cherokee nation stipulated one in a series of large land cessions to the United States. One provision of the treaty was that "in order for 'the Cherokee nation [to] be led to a greater degree of civilization and to become herdsmen and cultivators, instead of remaining in a state of hunters, the United States will, from time to time, furnish, gratuitously, the said nation with useful implements of husbandry.'"⁵⁰ In 1792 Congress appropriated funds to be used more broadly for this policy.

According to a government report from 1801, the federal policy that had been implemented by the 1791 treaty was by then "continued and broadened to such an extent" that, "in the Cherokee agency, the wheel, the loom, and the plough is in pretty general use."⁵¹ James Mooney reported that problems developed between the mountain towns, which had refused the implements, and those who accepted and welcomed the changes. He noted further that, "along with other things of civilization . . . negro slavery had been introduced and several of the leading men were now slaveholders."⁵²

Those who supported the assimilation program, termed the "progressives," threatened to secede from the more conservative mountain towns in response to their complaints.⁵³ John Finger has noted that while, "mixed-blood Cherokee elites resided in Georgia, Tennessee, and Alabama," the "North Carolina Indians . . . were predominantly fullbloods, had less wealth, and were more traditional than their brethren."⁵⁴ According to one observer in 1808, they were, "'at least twenty years behind' other Cherokees."⁵⁵

Hani! 75

Secretary of War Henry Knox lobbied for the missionaries to be foot soldiers in the government's assimilation efforts, noting in 1789 that they "should be made the instruments to work on the Indians."[56] As I will discuss below, a Presbyterian mission school was in operation from 1804 to 1810. The American Board of Commissioners for Foreign Missions entered the Cherokee Nation in 1816, and they were joined in turn by the Baptists in 1819 and the Methodists in the winter of 1823–24.[57] In 1819, Congress appropriated funds to support missionary endeavors among First Nations.[58] By this date, the Cherokee Nation land base had been reduced from approximately 40,000 square miles of land over parts of eight present states to a fraction of its size, in contiguous areas of North Carolina, Tennessee, Georgia, and Alabama.

Although McLoughlin stated that the Moravian school opened in November 1804, Rowena McClinton stated that they were instructing two girls in the spring of 1802.[59] In 1804 the school took in an additional four boys who boarded there as well; McLoughlin estimated there were "three or four other children, some of them girls," who boarded elsewhere.[60] Whatever the exact number, it was a fraction of the estimated three to four thousand school-age children; according to McLoughlin, the school had but eight students a year from 1804 to 1810.[61] By this time the Moravians faced competition from a Presbyterian mission school that began with eleven students but soon claimed twenty-five, and then thirty to forty a year until it closed in 1810 due to the unsavory actions of its founder, the Reverend Gideon Blackburn.[62] At least for the time being, this left the Moravians, as the old saying goes, the only game in town.

In 1805 John Gambold and his wife Anna Rosina arrived at Springplace, and they served there until 1821, longer than any other missionaries at that location.[63] In 1810, Margaret Scott Vann, the widow of James Vann, was baptized as their first adult convert; they had only one additional convert over the next eight years.[64] The mixed-blood headman and eventual Second Principal Chief Charles Hicks was one of the few Moravian converts, however, and he vouchsafed their presence in the nation.[65]

The Moravian missionaries carefully recorded their experiences in diaries and letters, the originals of which are located in the Moravian Archives in Winston-Salem, N.C.; all are catalogued as "The Springplace Diary." This correspondence was edited and published as *The Moravian Springplace Mission to the Cherokees* (cited earlier in this chapter).[66] The Gambolds were no exception to this practice, and their diaries and letters do provide useful information to Cherokee studies scholars. Anna Gambold was the primary author of the diary during the Gambolds' tenure, though John Gambold is listed as the author in both the Salem, North Carolina, and Bethlehem, Pennsylvania, archives.[67]

In that same July 1808 letter in which they complained about the ball game generally, the Gambolds reported on the status of a particular student, Rufus King Anderson, who unlike the rest of the students, was European American. Their bishop, Carl Gotthold Reichel, had decided to dismiss the boy from school; the missionaries stated that they would inform the boy's father and spoke of their "grief" regarding the boy.[68] In a comment that displayed these individuals' racially charged views of African Americans, the Moravians seemed resigned to the boy's circumstances, noting "his all-too neglected up-bringing" and "the many bad things which had been impressed on his disposition through the constant contact with Negro children."[69]

A tone of inevitably about the situation pervaded this section of the letter, which continued with an account about an incident involving Anderson and James Vann, an influential, extremely wealthy, and by all accounts mercurial Cherokee trader and headman of the time: "To that was added another unfortunate circumstance. Mr. Vann, who tries all kinds of things to provide diversion for himself, hit upon the idea of inviting our children to have them practice playing ball. (That was May 31 in the afternoon.) As unwillingly as we permitted this, still we could not prevent it, since the thing itself is not bad, and we let them go with much good advice and heavy hearts."[70]

The statement "the thing itself is not bad" is certainly clear and, though it contradicts other statements in the diary, supports the contention documented elsewhere in this chapter that many missionaries were in the end ambivalent about anetso. In some cases it was not the game itself to which they objected, but the potential for exposure to alcohol and unsavory company. Since the boys at the mission school were only going for the afternoon, it seems likely that this was not part of a training regimen for a scheduled game, and thus they were not engaging in any other activities of the complex. It is unclear if the missionaries were aware of the possible range of the ceremonial complex, and their remarks appear to focus on the contest itself. Gambold went on to report that two boys returned home in the evening drunk: "Rufus, however, was so full that he soon began to vomit, and then for several hours he lay there more dead than alive, so that I believe that if he had been in that condition without help, it might have cost him his life."[71]

Apparently this result confirmed the fears of the missionaries, as the letter noted parenthetically that (presumably) John had "spoken with Mr. V. about this and for the future forbidden anything of the sort."[72] Further along in the same letter the quotation with which I opened the chapter appeared, bemoaning the "bad effect" of the ball game—that after playing it the children "believed they could demand more freedom." It is worth noting that the edited diary does not contain an entry for this particular date.[73] Drawing upon and paraphrasing the Gambolds' account, William McLoughlin recounted that Vann had "lured their male students (aged ten to twelve) to his home, encouraged them to indulge in pagan Ball Play (a form of lacrosse) and gave them so much brandy that they all returned intoxicated and were sick for days afterward."[74]

This account, including the phrase "pagan Ball Play," may tell as much about McLoughlin's view of the ball game as it does about the Gambolds' view. The passage quoted above is one of the two original accounts upon which his statements were based, and clearly McLoughlin's opinion here is that the missionaries believed the activity itself to be pagan. However the word "pagan" did not appear in the July 20 passage.[75]

Again, as with all of these accounts, one wishes for a Cherokee perspective. Did Vann want to reassert traditional cultural practices in the children's lives? Was he trying to subvert the missionaries? If he was organizing ball games and providing alcohol before or during the games it seems he was not adhering to traditional prohibitions, though if they drank after the games this would not have been an issue. As I have suggested above, here again perhaps Vann, along with the students, was making a statement with action rather than words. Just a year later, a visitor arrived who had much to say about anetso, and he made quite an impression on the Moravian missionaries as well.

"The Spectators and those who intend to bett were very numerous": Major Norton's Visit

On Sunday, September 3, 1809, the Moravian diary reported the visit of John Norton, an adopted member of the Mohawk Nation, who had come to the nation to "cover the corpse of his father with wampum."[76] Norton visited the Cherokee Nation from April 27, 1809, until the middle of June 1810, and published a 370-page journal account of this and other travels as *The Journal of Major John Norton (Teyoninhokarawen)* (1816).[77] Norton described the scene as, it "being Sunday, we all walked over to visit the worthy Missionaries, who are blest with the feelings of true religion. May the Almighty, bless and prosper the pious labours of these worthy Christians."[78] He was effusive about Christianity and the work of the missionaries, and he quoted a long comment by a missionary concerning the spiritual uplift of souls.[79] The missionaries in turn praised him as "particularly worthy to us" because of his strong Christian faith.[80]

Norton was the son of a Cherokee father and a Scottish mother who was educated in England; upon his return to the United States the Grand River Mohawk community had adopted him.[81] Raymond Fogelson dubbed Norton an "ethno-ethnologist" due to his careful observation and the detailed nature of his travel accounts.[82] Norton made several references to the "Ball-Play" in his journal, and because this account is not in wide circulation, I will quote from several passages.[83]

By this time Norton already had attended several ball games. For example, at the town of "Tanissee" his party had arrived on the scene, temporarily interrupting unnamed pregame preparations.[84] Soon the action began, as Norton reported: "The ball is cast up, and great exertions are made on both sides." According to Norton this activity differed "from the manner of playing ball to the Northward, being a more athletic exercise." Norton would have been familiar with the activity, as it was played among all nations, including the Mohawk, of the Haudenosaunee, or Six Nations Confederacy ("Iroquois"). After the contest, there was an all-night dance inside the "Town House" building, and he described it in detail.[85]

A few pages later in his journal, Norton wrote that he was on his way to another Ball Play, "at a Village up Chicamauga . . . in consequence of a challenge between the Village of Cold-run and another Village, reputed the best players in the nation."[86] Norton's party lodged at the home of a man named Catawgwatihih, "where the players of Cold-run were assembled to prepare themselves by practice and regimen for the violent exertions they had in view." Norton continued, "the rule is, to abstain from spirits, from associating with women, and to dance all night, the dance peculiar to the game. They also have their Conjurors who pry into futurity and predict generally in a vague manner the event of the pending contest for superiority."[87]

Norton continued with a brief description of the Ball Play Dance, and reported that in the next afternoon they split into two groups and began playing. Because they did not finish the game by the end of the day, they danced once again that night, and concluded the game the following day. According to Norton, they danced all night once again, and the very next day headed off to the next game, where they would once again dance all night and play the following day "those with whom they had engaged to contend."[88]

Unfortunately, a heavy rain shower interrupted preparations and one party asked to postpone until the next day; an argument ensued, but there was to be no contest: "The Spectators and those who intend to bett were very numerous, and had collected from more than forty miles distance in every direction. All returned to their respective homes without any apparent discontent at the disappointment; only observing that these boasted players were afraid to come into contact with each other."[89]

Norton saw his next game about two weeks later, and he visited the Moravian missionaries sometime between these two events. The latter ball game was "between the same villages who had made preparations to contend for the superiority before, but who desisted when they came to the Ground; and who now repeated the challenge." The next day, "in the forenoon," his party arrived at "an open wooded, level spot, unincumbered with underwood." He did not name the place, but it seems by his description above to be the same site near Chickamauga, in present-day Tennessee.[90]

Next, Norton provided a precise description of the sticks and the method of play, along with information about that specific contest. He continued: "Great bets had been staked before we arrived; the Ball-players prepared to begin the contest; all were stripped except the lap fastened round the waist, with their belt; they raised their vigorous arms; they advanced to meet each other, with a shout of mutual defiance; they stopped to challenge each other; to bett in confidence of their respective dexterity and strength."

After he provided what amounted to a bit of play-by-play commentary about the contest, Norton concluded: "Twelve constituted the Game. The one party completed the number, whilst the other obtained only five; three were carried out by an active young man Clokeske Kayelli, and one apiece by two others. Much was lost by the vanquished, and by those who had betted in that favour, in horses, money and goods; but not one murmured; they only blamed themselves for having been too negligent in preparing for the contest by practice."[91]

The amount of detail in Norton's descriptions is exceptional. He reported several ceremonial complex elements that are consistent with later accounts, including rules for players, conjuring, dancing before the game, the players' approach to the center ground, and gambling. In addition to these pre- and postgame activities, he reported spectators' and players' opinions and behavior, and even a score and an individual player's name. According to his accounts, in 1809 ball games were frequent and popular public events, with crowds of spectators gathering from as far away as forty miles and gambling heavily.

Norton returned to visit Springplace in April 1810 and left the area in June 1810, having spent additional time in the area with relatives of his father; he apparently never ventured back into Cherokee territory, though he did keep in touch with the Gambolds by mail.[92] His account is a unique source from this era, and provides an important perspective. At this time anetso was a matter of great interest among Cherokee people, and unlike his Moravian friends, Norton clearly shared this sentiment.

"The mother of the nation has left you": The "Religious Revival" of 1811–12

In February 1811 a Cherokee individual named Charlie reported a vision that he and two unnamed women had experienced in which they were told that they should turn back from ongoing assimilation to European American culture and return to traditional Cherokee lifeways.[93] Mooney reported the event, and several historians have written about it; but Michelene Pesantubbee has produced perhaps the most nuanced account of the events themselves, detailing "three separate strands to the events of 1811–12" rather than considering them as one.[94]

According to Mooney, Charlie chose to reveal this vision after a "great medicine dance" at the national capital of "Ustanali" (Oostenally) during a council meeting.[95] Anna Gambold wrote a detailed account of the vision, as retold by "Chief Koychezetel," in a February 10, 1811, diary entry.[96] The entry stated that a group of "Indians" on small black horses appeared to the group, and their leader said to them, "'Do not be afraid; we are your brothers and sisters and are sent from God to speak with you. God is dissatisfied that you so indiscriminately lead the white people onto my land.'"[97]

The leader said the people should buy back the land, give back the "'white people's corn,'" plant "'Indian corn and pound it according to your ancestors' ways.'" He continued, "'The mother of the nation has left you, because all her bones are being broken through the milling. She will return, however, if you get the white people out of the country and return to your former way of life.'" The account concluded with the vague threat that if Charlie and the women told people about the vision and anyone did not believe it, "'know that things will not go well for him.'"[98] Gregory Dowd identified the mother as Selu, and I would tend to agree.[99]

In the first three months of 1812, Anna Gambold recorded additional accounts of prophesied cataclysmic events in the wake of a string of earthquakes that began in December 1811, as well as the sighting of a comet.[100] In the first, a Cherokee man named Big Bear related a story about a father with sick children who had a vision in which a man "clothed completely in tree leaves with a wreath of the same foliage on his head" provided medicine to heal them. According to the account "God" was dissatisfied with the Cherokee practice of selling so much land to the "white people," including "Tugalo," "the *first* place that God created," and where "he put the *first* fire in a hill there."[101] Gambold noted Big Bear's serious countenance as he related what she termed a "cock-and-bull story," and wished that "the miserable Indians really get to know Him."[102]

February 23 brought another report of "dreamers and lying prophets," from David McNair, an Anglo man who was married to a Cherokee woman, along with an account of people hiding in caves to escape forthcoming giant hailstones.[103] When the day had passed uneventfully, "they returned to their homes, ready and willing to believe each new deceiver."[104] The next day brought an early-morning "small earthquake," and Gambold reported yet another prophecy that was causing certain people to head for a particular mountain: someone's "relatives dreamed the whole surface of the earth will be flooded with water and only a certain mountain in this country will remain free."[105]

On March 1 and 8, respectively, two Cherokee women, "Laughing Molly" and "Mother Vann" (James Vann's widow) reported apocalyptic prophecies with certain similar elements.[106] Laughing Molly's account foretold of a lunar eclipse, giant hailstones, and the destruction of cattle and then of the earth.[107] Mother Vann, who made it clear that she did not believe what she was telling the missionaries, stated that the earth would be darkened for three days, during which time "all the white people and also those Indians who had clothing or household items in the style of the white people would be carried away along with their livestock."[108]

In the midst of these events, in an October 11, 1811, entry Gambold remarked that many Cherokee people on the way to and from a ball play stopped at the Gambolds' home, where they fed them, though she wished "they had come in such great numbers for *another* purpose."[109] Visitors' reports of violence against men and horses and horse theft troubled Gambold, who exclaimed, "Oh, it is a quite unholy thing, the ball play here in this country, and the longer the worse! One is just barely over when a new one is arranged. It is very difficult for us when it is held so close to us, because the Indians who gather for it always stop in here and make our children want to attend it as well."[110] It may be that her initial comment reflected other recent events that she interpreted as "quite unholy" as well.

William McLoughlin has argued that this movement died out as the Creek War began in 1813, soon merging with the ongoing War of 1812.[111] Pesantubbee has suggested it was because there was no "unifying theme": "Charlie's prophecy was nativist and restorationist in nature, the father's dream had nativist components but was more closely tied to healing, and the prophecies that appeared in 1812 were apocalyptic and millennial."[112] Mooney reported the end of the "revival" came when the prophet appointed a day for the great destruction and bade followers to seek shelter high in the Great Smoky Mountains, which they did, only to return home disheartened when the event did not transpire.[113]

William McLoughlin interpreted this revival in the context of what he theorized was Cherokee cultural anomie and renascence. McLoughlin argued that the treaty of 1791 was the harbinger of massive cultural upheaval experienced by Cherokee people during the decades before and after the turn of the nineteenth century. In a book chapter entitled "Cherokee Anomie, 1794–1810," McLoughlin portrayed the treaty of 1791 as a watershed event, and this period as one of great cultural decline. He cited the decline of "communal ceremonies," as well as hunting, which led to the decline of attendant dances; according to him "only the Green Corn Dance and the Ball Plays retained any vitality in these years. But even these became increasingly secularized."[114] McLoughlin said that the Green Corn Dance, "originally a harvest ritual, became a plaything of the federal agents," who arranged with headmen to have the celebrations during annuity distributions or treaty negotiations when they could provide "provisions and whiskey."[115]

With regard to the ball plays he argued that consumption of alcohol by players, non-Cherokee spectators, and gambling were evidence of this cultural decline:

> The Ball Plays, instead of communal festivals with religious overtones, became spectacles for white visitors and scenes of wild orgies of gambling, drunkenness, and brawling. Instead of replacing hunting and war as they might have done to enable young men to exhibit skill, strength, endurance and daring, they became a kind of professionalized gambling, a quick way to make money (or to lose it)—a symptom of despair, not of vitality. In better days, and in the more conservative parts of the nation, the Ball Plays were hallowed by sacred prayers, dances, and rituals; players abstained from sexual intercourse prior to playing in order to retain their strength; to be chosen as a player marked one as a person of high integrity and honor. But during the Cherokee nadir, all this was forgotten.[116]

Though McLoughlin did not cite any sources to support his contention about the Green Corn Dances, he did cite one 1792 source that described an occasion in which both teams engaged in heavy drinking. In Chapter 4 I will discuss this account in more detail, but here I will simply say that the evidence is by no means overwhelming. I want to reiterate that I do not for a moment subscribe to the notion that culture is a static entity. Obviously cultures change, and surely it is quite plausible that such changes occurred. After all, McLoughlin is only talking about a sixteen-year period. Nevertheless, I question his theoretical framework of degeneration as well as his specific conclusions based on the available evidence.

In this chapter and elsewhere in the book I cite accounts of ball games throughout the first four decades of the nineteenth century that provide ample evidence of alcohol, gambling, and non-Cherokee spectators, and there is no question that these factors sometimes caused problems. But it is important to stress that these factors, particularly gambling, are not necessarily fundamental signs of decline. The practice of gambling by Cherokee people on the outcomes of games was firmly established by this time, as was the custom of playing the ball game before dignitaries and other tourists, along with the attendant rowdiness on the part of spectators. According to Cherokee consultants and my archival research, there are several accounts of players in the past being barred from playing because they drank during the training period leading up to and including the games. Finally, Norton's descriptions of the anetso complex activities, while including details about non-Cherokee spectators and gambling, do not suggest that he was cognizant of any degeneration of the activities.

To support his claim of a cultural renascence, McLoughlin cited a report by the federal government agent Return Jonathan Meigs on March 19, 1812, eleven days after the last Springplace diary account. Meigs reported that Cherokee people "have revived their religious dances of ancient origin with as much apparent solemnity as ever was seen in worship in our churches. They then repair to the water, go in and wash."[117] This account included the important detail about the people engaging in the ritual of going to water in conjunction with the dances.

However, contrary to McLoughlin, Gregory Dowd cited 1801 and 1805 accounts by Meigs in which he remarked on the solemnity of the Green Corn Ceremony, in Dowd's words, "despite the claims of some historians that the ceremony had lost its meaning."[118] Meigs commented in the earlier account that the event "'suggests the Idea of a religious dance.'"[119] Oddly, Meigs apparently thought there was a revival, or at least an increase in activity, even though he had made the second of two comments only seven years before. If it was a revival, any postulated "nadir" would have to have been even shorter than McLoughlin speculated.

Dowd argued that the "revival is better understood as a fully religious expression of social and political conflict than . . . as the cathartic reformation of Cherokee culture in the face of psychic stress."[120] In an endnote he cited his departure "from William McLoughlin's interpretation of Cherokee religion and politics, which ties the Cherokee revival to rising Cherokee nationalism, both against a background of religious and cultural decline." Dowd's opinion was that the "strongest defenders of the traditional religion did not oppose change," but that the revival was "a revolt, expressed in religious rhetoric, against the influence of Americans in Cherokee affairs." Critics of the revolt included "accomodationists," as Dowd referred to them, who were neither "federal tools" nor assimilationists. These people opposed the idea of removal but desired economic development assistance from the United States, and they were worried about being allied with defenders of traditional religion against the United States.[121]

Theda Perdue also has expressed her disagreement with "McLoughlin's interpretation of Cherokee history in terms of anomie and renascence."[122] Perdue contrasted the loss of "cultural moorings" and subsequent cultural transformations by people (especially young men) described by McLoughlin with what she termed a persistence and even strengthening of certain roles (farmers, "socializers of children") for women who were not members of the elite during this time.[123] Finally, Duane Champagne has argued that during this time period, "for most Cherokees these actions did not impair their cultural and social identity," nor did they "fundamentally disturb Cherokee institutions of social and cultural unity."[124]

Nearly ten years later the ball game was still going strong, and Anna Gambold's opinion about it had not changed. On Sunday, April 30, 1820, Gambold wrote that two female "communicants" had passed by "our boys in a ball play with the Negroes."[125] She continued: "After evening devotions, we emphatically *explained* to them this sinful and extremely insolent behavior of theirs, in its greatness and consequences not only to our pain but even more to our dear Savior's pain." The entry for May 1st noted the boys' absence from a love feast because of their actions the previous day, and the following day, May 2, "since we did not yet note any sign of contrition in our boys, Brother Gambold prayed fervently to the dear Savior about this in the morning devotions. And when they gathered soon afterward for school, Sister Gambold had a further very emphatic heart-to-heart talk with them."[126] According to the entry, this approach bore fruit, as the boys broke into tears and asked for forgiveness. I do not doubt that the boys could have been remorseful, and that individuals may in fact have ceased participation in the ball games. Given the other evidence presented from Moravian diaries and letters from the same time period, however, one wonders if there was a cycle of participation, then acceptance of consequences, followed by further participation.

In October 1820 Johann Renatus Schmidt and his wife, Gertraud, came to live at Springplace, where they served until 1827. Anna Gambold died of angina in 1821, and after her death John Gambold moved to the Oothcaloga Mission, where he remarried and served until his death in 1827.[127] While Schmidt's diaries are not available in published form, there are English translations accessible to the researcher at the Moravian Archives in Winston-

Salem, N.C., along with the correspondence of the Gambolds and other missionaries.

On Sunday, August 7, 1825, Schmidt wrote the following in his diary:

> A good number of Indians came for the sermon, which was given about the Gospel for Sunday and translated by D. S. Taucheechy. In the 2nd service we sang a liturgy. Today 13 miles from here, near Coosawatte, there was a large Ball Play, for which about 3000 people had gathered from all areas of the Nation. Different localities played against each other. The betting which was set during this amounted to more than 3500 "Dollars" and consisted of horses, cattle, pigs, guns, copper pots and articles of clothing.[128]

This must have been quite an event. Teams from all over the nation played each other. The crowd size was tremendous, and the aggregate amount of the goods wagered was staggering, quite a sum of money in 1825. In addition, the event was held on a Sunday. The event made such an impression on Schmidt that he was still writing about it a week later, though he revised his estimate to "2000 'Dollars'" worth of items wagered.[129]

In 1923 Edward Schwarze published a history of the Moravian missions in which he cited particular diary entries and freely editorialized about them. About this particular event he opined:

> Times of spiritual revival are usually marked, likewise, by special activity on the part of the powers of darkness. Around Springplace the evils in connection with the frequent ball-playing among the Cherokees were especially marked. The game, innocent enough in itself, was generally attended with much bad behavior, drunkenness and licentiousness. At one such game in 1825, not far from Springplace, Schmidt estimated the crowd in attendance at about 3,000, and he had information, on good authority, that the bets made during the game aggregated $3500.[130]

The original accounts say nothing of the game being "innocent" or not, nor is there any mention of the "authority" of the information. No "powers of darkness" stalk the scene that Schmidt described. These are Schwarze's interpolations that reflect his own particular viewpoint. Interestingly, Schwarze was careful to mention that the game was "innocent enough in itself." As with McLoughlin's comments above, the narrative focus remained on alcohol, gambling, and spectator behavior.

Apparently, at least according to certain scholars, the wagering also was an issue to missionaries in terms of the survival of the missions. Both William McLoughlin and Raymond Fogelson asserted that Schwarze himself was critical of the lack of monetary support from Cherokee people to support the missions. According to McLoughlin, "Schwarze was aware of the argument that the Cherokees were too poor to sustain churches, but he noted sardonically that they always seemed able to raise plenty of money 'in bets at a ball game'—sometimes as much as $3,000 in money, clothing, guns, and produce was bet on a single game."[131] McLoughlin cited the above passage from Schwarze, which upon review does not appear to convey sardonic intent (at least to me); in any case, it is once removed from Schmidt's original account. McLoughlin asserted that while the lack of surplus wealth for some individuals may have been the reason for lack of support, interest in other municipal projects and the failure of the missionaries to allow Cherokee people to be ordained and run the churches themselves also were factors.[132] As with other matters in the community at the time, there were divided opinions on the usefulness of the mission agencies.

Review of this one passage and how it has been interpreted by scholars illustrates the issues involved in utilizing such material. Both Schwarze and McLoughlin were mixing their own interpretations with what they were reading in the accounts, and the combinations produced evidenced this admixture.

A few weeks after his entries about the game in which thousands of dollars of property was gambled, Schmidt discussed a particular student who had participated in the ball game: "August 24th. Our pupil Gardiner Green was taken home for a visit some weeks ago. Today we heard that his father forced him to participate in a Ball Play, where he was hit with the Ball stick by an Indian and trampled so that from noon until sundown he just lay there completely lifeless. However, he finally came to himself again and was taken home on horse by his father."[133] Less than a month later, on September 27th, Schmidt submitted another injury report on Green, who "allowed himself to be talked into going to another Ball Play, where he twisted his leg." Just four days later Schmidt reported on a "big Ball Play two miles from here in our neighborhood." He also noted that "people claimed that a certain sorcerer had forbidden rain, so he was bound and beaten."[134]

"Indeed Veracity is a rare Article among Savages"

There is some amount of debate among historians regarding the general tenor of the relationships between Moravians and Cherokees. In her epilogue to *The Moravian Springplace Mission to the Cherokees*, McClinton concluded that "unlike the Anglo-American world around them, Moravians had profound respect for the Cherokees"; the diaries "suggest that there was an alternative to the racism and dispossession that characterized the interactions of

Cherokees and most Americans of European descent."¹³⁵ She continued, "different worlds, Moravian, Cherokee, and African, did indeed meet at Springplace and again at New Springplace; individuals challenged each other's most deeply held beliefs, but then human beings sat down together at *unser Tisch* (our table), where there was room for all."¹³⁶

However, according to Daniel B. Thorp, the "irony of silence" concept I invoked at the beginning of this chapter was not the only sense in which irony entered into the relations between Cherokee people and the Moravians: "There is a certain irony to all the Moravians' dealings with their neighbors in North Carolina. The Brethren clearly looked with thinly veiled contempt on many of the people around them; in the privacy of their own meetings and records the brothers and sisters frequently described their fellow Carolinians as 'rabble,' as 'the discarded refuse of Ireland and America,' and in other unflattering terms. Yet they seldom showed this contempt openly."¹³⁷ Thorp continued, "although the Europeans did concede that individual Indians might sometimes be admirable men or women, the stereotype among whites on the southern frontier was, in one Moravians' [sic] words, of 'murdering Indians.'"¹³⁸

At the American Philosophical Society Library in Philadelphia, Pennsylvania, I found support for Thorp's contention in the form of letters from John Gambold to Peter S. DuPonceau, who was for many years the secretary of the American Philosophical Society's Historical and Literary Committee.¹³⁹ In this capacity DuPonceau requested information about Cherokee language and customs, and Gambold was quite candid in his responses. In a July 20, 1818, letter to DuPonceau, Gambold explained that because none of the Cherokee students were able to instruct the missionaries, he had no "Satisfactory" information regarding the Cherokee language, or cultural traditions.¹⁴⁰ It is interesting to note that apparently no adult was considered for the task, which would lead one to wonder how much time the missionaries spent in the company of Cherokee adults.

Gambold's next statement in the letter revealed additional reasons for the lack of research on his part: his "ardent desire that old things might pass away and all things become new" coupled with his conviction "that unless the Cherokee Indians adopt our Language, our Laws & our holy Religion, they will at no very distant Period either become extinct, or else degenerate into a kind of gypsies."¹⁴¹ As Francis Paul Prucha has argued, this paternalistic attitude has long been a common feature of relations between First Nations peoples and European colonists and their native-born ancestors.¹⁴²

The attitude in and of itself is not surprising. What is surprising was Gambold's remarkably candid response in a December letter that same year regarding the same issue. Apparently DuPonceau was persistent in his requests, to which Gambold responded: "From many things, which have long passed for true, and at Length have been found to be without Foundation, and more especially from the Observation that generally so many different Tales are produced as there are Informers—and indeed Veracity is a rare Article among Savages—I have contracted a Habit of generally discrediting, and consequently disregarding such Information."[143] Gambold went on to say that he was "prevented by several concurring Circumstances from rousing my Inclination for Researches, which I candidly own is well nigh dormant, into action." The "circumstances" Gambold related were that he and his wife had to do all their chores themselves, and that the Cherokee people were being constantly harangued to remove to other land.[144]

Gambold's comments are revealing and, unfortunately, illustrate Thorp's assessment above. Not to put too fine a point on it, but while the Moravians may well have had "room for all" at *"unser Tisch,"* at times there must have been a number of vacant seats on one side. I have juxtaposed these two historians' perspectives in order to underscore two points that I made in the first section of this chapter: one must recognize the complex relationships hinted at in the diary entries as well as the complicated enterprise of assessing scholarly accounts of them. Perhaps in the end a balance of these two scholarly views is most appropriate.

"This scene of national iniquity": Anetso in ABCFM Journal Reports

While the Moravians had settled in by 1801, in 1816 the American Board of Commissioners for Foreign Missions sought entry into the Cherokee nation. As McLoughlin noted, although "ostensibly interdenominational," "it was essentially a Congregational organization run from Boston."[145] Incorporated in 1812 by Trinitarian Congregationalists, by 1816 the ABCFM included both Presbyterians and Dutch Reformed Calvinists, but they always remained a minority. According to McLoughlin, "Because there were no Congregational ministerial associations in the South, the American Board's missionaries eventually asked to be received as Presbyterians into the Union Presbytery of Eastern Tennessee in order to establish formal ecclesiastical relations in the region."[146]

The American Board established their first mission at Chickamauga Creek in Tennessee in 1817, and a year later the name was changed to the Brainerd Mission. It remained open until just before the Cherokee Removal, closing on August 19, 1838. By 1830 ten mission stations were open, most with schools and churches.[147]

Like their Moravian missionary counterparts at Springplace, the missionaries at the Brainerd Mission corresponded with their headquarters by means of a formal journal from January 1817 to December 1823; this correspondence to their Boston headquarters was edited and published as *The Brainerd Journal*.[148] In these journals, like those of the Moravian missionaries, there were comments and complaints about the Cherokee ball game. And, as in the Moravian journals and letters, there also were reports about boys who participated in the ball game.

For example, the July 5, 1822, entry reported that three boys had skipped school and "were seen on the path where it is said there is a ball play three or four miles from us." The account continued: "From the character of these plays, and the intemperance which generally attends them, they must have a demoralizing effect. We therefore do not allow the children under our direction to attend them."[149]

One of the boys, a student at the school for several years, had asked for and been denied permission to attend the ball game two weeks before. The next day's journal account reported that the three boys were "examined" about this event, and of the three, one was fined, one was pardoned, and the leader, who had asked permission to go, was expelled.[150] The boy who was pardoned had only been at the school for a few weeks and "appeared to be in a great degree ignorant of the evil of going from school without permission—and totally so of the evil of ball plays."[151]

What seemed to be important to the missionaries was that the leader, the veteran student, should have known better. But the boy would have known that the missionaries frowned upon the ball game, so why would he have asked permission in the first place? He must have been torn; it was important for him to go, so much so that he knowingly risked expulsion after investing several years of his life at the school. Yet because he had asked permission, he also wanted to have the missionaries' approval at some level, or at least be allowed to continue in school.

Ultimately, the student made his choice; as students in the Moravian school had done in 1808, as students in the ABCFM school would do again in 1827, he spoke with his actions. The ABCFM missionaries signified the ball plays as "demoralizing" and of an "evil" nature. To the student, it was a part of his culture, an emblem of his identity that he would not deny.

The struggles of the boys exemplify tensions in Cherokee society at that time. In *The Cherokees and Christianity*, McLoughlin commented that by 1825, "the whole Nation was divided into bitterly opposing factions, the Christian and the traditionalist."[152] These divisions ran deep in the Cherokee nation. Like the young student, some people simply refused to relinquish their cultural traditions, including anetso.

As Johann Schmidt had done, an ABCFM missionary and Congregationalist minister Moody Hall wrote about the August 1825 ball game in which thousands of dollars in goods had been wagered. Hall's statements appeared in his August 20, 1825, diary letter to Jeremiah Evarts, in which he noted that on July 11 there was a "great Ball-play within two miles of us."[153] Just a few weeks later, on Sunday August 7th, he reported: "Meeting quite full. It is a trying time for Cherokee professors. There is on this holy day a kind of national Ball-play near the center of the nation. Some of the Judges & principal men, were seen on their way, yesterday to this scene of national iniquity. Those who truly love Christ better than this wicked amusement will not be corrupted to go."[154] Hall returned to the topic when he next made an entry, on Tuesday August 9th. He had been told by another missionary "that many of those who belong to the different [churches] in the nation attended the Ball-play on last sabbath, among the rest was *Elias Boudinott*, of whom better things were hoped!"[155]

Buck Watie, who changed his name to Elias Boudinot, was a mixed-blood Cherokee convert who rose to political prominence in the Cherokee Nation, established the bilingual newspaper the *Cherokee Phoenix*, and was a strong advocate of removal. He was a leader among the group of Cherokee people who signed the fraudulent Treaty of New Echota with the United States government (see below), and was executed in Oklahoma for treason in 1839 along with other relatives who were members of what was known as the Treaty Party.[156] Hall and Daniel S. Butrick, whose signature appeared on the letter, referred to the incident once again in another report to Evarts in December 1825.

Butrick had apparently written a letter to another colleague praising Boudinot's character, which he now regretted. Butrick wrote that "playing ball sometimes" had been the only thing "injurious to the moral character of br. Boudinot," which he "did not think . . . censurable" since apparently "the scholars at Cornwall were allowed to do this, though perhaps in a different form."[157] However, Butrick considered Boudinot's attending "a ball play on the Sabbath" to be "unchristian conduct."[158]

In his history of the Cherokee nation written in 1946, Marion Starkey summarized Hall's comments, writing that there was a "national ball play" in the Cherokee capital of New Echota, which conflicted with both a "council of chiefs" and the Sabbath.[159] Starkey included Hall's memorable description of the event as a "'scene of national iniquity'"; he added that the missionaries believed this to be "backsliding into heathenism on a grand scale."[160] Starkey also had read of some schoolboys' decisions to attend ball games. He commented: "To the missionaries it was an abomination; they exhorted their

Hani! 91

congregations to keep away from the heathenish spectacle and gave a stern refusal to little schoolboys who asked to be excused from class so that they could attend."[161]

Starkey referred to the ball game as a "moral equivalent of war," but he noted that for the missionaries, "these moral considerations were eclipsed by the excesses of the game, its violence, the use of conjure, and the gambling that attended it." The ball game was at the center of what apparently was a large-scale, national expression of an ontological position, a cultural and symbolic event. It certainly seems plausible that the organizers were aware of the scheduling conflict, and indeed purposely created it. According to Starkey, because most of the leaders, "well aware of the attitude of the missionaries," chose to attend rather than stay away, "it looked almost as if National Council had deliberately designed to insult them." The missionaries certainly thought so, and signified it accordingly.

As Hall's letter demonstrated, some missionaries were particularly upset with Elias Boudinot, who was being groomed for a possible leadership position in the mission, but who "attended that ball play and visibly enjoyed it as much as any other heathen."[162] Other missionaries as well were reporting back to their superiors regarding who and what they considered heathen, and anetso typically was on the list. One missionary in particular who was interested in matters of heathenism was the ABCFM missionary Isaac Proctor, from whose letter I quoted at the beginning of the chapter.

"These are purely heathenish sports": Isaac Proctor's Reports

In 1823, at the request of local Cherokee headmen, the American Board sent Isaac Proctor to Etowah, or "Hightower" (a mispronunciation of the Cherokee name) to open a school.[163] A year later Proctor and his "converts" were the subject of complaints. On May 26, 1824, a group of Cherokee headmen had a letter describing their displeasure written for them and sent to Charles Hicks, who at that time was Second Principal Chief of the Cherokee Nation. Among the more serious complaints were that converts were not attending meetings in the townhouse or participating in all-night dances, along with the following: "We, the Chiefs of this place, En,hal,la [Etowah], . . . have for some time beeng [been] [in] Darkness with respect of the indulgence given to the Missionary Teacher [Isaac Proctor] here at this place. . . . As for the [missionary] teachers, they are complained of very much by the young people [who] are under their care for Edducation."[164] Hicks, who as noted above was a convert to the Moravian church, responded to the chiefs in a letter in which he dismissed the claims and sent "apologetic copies of this correspondence to his spiritual advisor among the Moravians," Johan R. Schmidt.[165] Hicks replied in the letter that the new religion of the converts forbade their participation in such activities and dismissed the claims of the students.[166]

Isaac Proctor left the Etowah mission in 1826 and moved on to the mission at Taloney, or Carmel. Daniel S. Butrick, who figures in several accounts discussed in this chapter, replaced him. The school was closed in 1828 because of poor attendance (five students), and Butrick remained at the mission until it was "closed in 1831 by the actions of the State of Georgia."[167]

Proctor complained about Cherokee boys playing ball in a December 11, 1827, letter, and I quoted this passage at the beginning of this chapter. The letter began cheerfully enough, with Proctor reporting that "their conduct in school, however, is good. They are affectionate, harmonious obedient & studious. I have no difficulty in governing them. They are scholars of good minds and are quite promising."[168] However, after another sentence in which he expressed hope for their future development, Proctor wrote the passage quoted above, in which he vented about the boys: "Some of them the other day assembled in plain sight of the Mission house, stripped themselves entirely naked, and for some time played Ball."[169]

William McLoughlin concluded that the students, tired of Proctor "constantly denouncing the sin of ball playing," played ball "in order to show their contempt," and "thus mocked his preaching."[170] The quotation and accompanying explanation were compelling enough that I wanted to consult the original source. Proctor concluded this passage as follows: "But when it is remembered that many youths in civilized Society who have enjoyed the best means of improvement are often seen at almost every place of dissipation it is not so surprising to find those who have lived so many years in ignorance doing such things."[171]

According to Proctor the behavior of the Cherokee boys in class was not a problem, so the situation seems to be a bit more complex than McLoughlin suggested. Though their behavior did not please him, Proctor acknowledged that he observed such behavior in what he considered to be "civilized" boys. Therefore, another interpretation could be that the boys were not as much showing contempt and mocking the preaching against ball playing as they were engaging in an expression of identity and autonomy. Again, to invoke Joel Martin's phrase, they were "in creative contact with history": offensively and proactively expressing themselves. Alternatively, the best conclusion might be that a combination of both intents resulted in the described event.

Later in the same letter Proctor focused his attention again on the ball game, discussing its effect on adults. His commentary was at the same time so vituperative and so evocative that I think it justifies quoting several passages. He began this section as follows: "But I am sorry to add that they still retain their grossest vices. Those that are the most heathenish are their 'Ball Plays,' 'All-night Dances,' & 'Eagle Dances.' These are often held & well attended by both full & mixed Cherokees-especially their Ball plays. These are purely heathenish sports."[172]

The assertion that anetso was one of "their grossest vices" is memorable enough, but Proctor's statement that it was a "purely heathenish sport" is a definitive sound bite that remains even more striking almost two hundred years later. The notion of "pure heathenism" is interesting enough in itself; review of period documents demonstrates that in all forms the scourge of "heathenism" was constantly on the minds of ABCFM missionaries. As John Andrew III has noted: "Behind the missionary efforts of the ABCFM, lay a general missionary theology. That theology, which sprang largely from the religious transmutations of the Second Great Awakening, embodied four essential elements: a belief in the millennium, the concept of disinterested benevolence, a commitment to Christ's last command ('Go ye unto the world'), and a determination that those who remained mired in their indigenous cultures were 'perishing heathen' in need of salvation."[173]

Proctor's comments certainly reflected this final element; moreover his issues with the ball games and accompanying dances clearly seem to be bodily, reflecting what seem to be almost prurient interests: "At their Ball plays the players are literally naked and yet a large proportion of the spectators are females. The All-Night dances are attended by wives without their husbands and husbands without their wives, and as they are held during the night, we may safely infer that all the deeds of darkness are committed."[174]

In addition to this passage ending with yet another memorable line invoking "the deeds of darkness," it is the second time in this particular letter in which Proctor asserts that players were naked. Though many accounts state that players wore breechclouts, I am not aware of any evidence supporting the contention that players played naked. I will discuss the "All-Night dances" in the next chapter, but here I will note that in fact men and women danced separately, and wives and children often camped for the night within view of their male relatives. As for the Eagle Dance, Proctor had this to say: "I possess no information, but have lately been informed that it is more heathenish than either of the others."[175]

This letter also contained a description of a ball game scheduled to coincide with the national council:

> Perhaps it will not be improper to mention here that there was a "National Ball-Play" last summer near New Echota, at a time when there was a called

Council in session & it was considered of so much importance that the Council adjourned for a day to give an opportunity to the members to attend it, and nearly all attended. [p. 10] The first men in council it is said were present—Old Mr. George Sanders with his daughters were also present there. Great sums for Indians are bet at the Plays. At the aforementioned Play one man lost a large yoke of oxen. A woman lost all her best clothing & a good Poney. The Players play in a truly savage manner; entirely disregarding their lives & limbs, so much so that at almost every play more or less [one, are?] crippled.[176]

Here we have quite an informative synopsis of several key features of the complex: the gambling of property as well as money, the style of play, and evidence of its stature as a national pastime.

There were still other activities Proctor had to sort through in compiling his lists of "heathenish" activities. In a letter from July 1827 he complained: "I shudder when I call to mind the abominations that have been committed by the members of this Ch'h. Almost all the crimes mentioned in the 21st Chap. of Rev. have been committed by some of the members of this Church since they united with it."[177]

In this letter, one abomination in particular was at the forefront of his mind. Proctor complained about two Cherokee individuals, Old Zacharias and Charles Moore, who were reputed conjurers. Fellow ABCFM missionary Daniel Butrick had spoken with Old Zacharias about these activities, and Proctor reported that "their conjuring is as purely heathen as almost anything to be met with on the River Ganges—When conjuring, they pray to almost every creature such as white *dogs, butterflies, turtles,* ⟨&c &c⟩."[178] Again, I find this excerpt to be particularly instructive. Though secondhand, Proctor's information about Cherokee conjuring led him to christen it "pure heathenism" and equate it with Indian religious practice ("Hinduism"). Apparently, at least for ABCFM missionaries, this was the gold standard for heathenism at the time.

As it turns out, Proctor did not limit his hyperbolic discourse to descriptions of Cherokee individuals and their customs; Methodists also annoyed him. The Methodists "were first invited into the nation in 1822 by a man of mixed blood named Richard Riley who asked a circuit rider in Alabama to come across the Tennessee River and preach at his home."[179] The circuit rider, Richard Neely, sensing an opportunity, convinced the Tennessee Annual Conference to open a school by the end of the year. The Methodist preacher Andrew Jackson Crawford was tapped to be the teacher, but "like most Methodist missionaries, Crawford preferred preaching to teaching."[180] He began holding camp meetings, which according to McLoughlin, "resembled in tone and excitement the all-night dances of the Cherokee religious tradition." He was so successful that by November 1823 he claimed 108 converts, which convinced the Tennessee Conference "to initiate two regular circuits within the Cherokee Nation" that same month.[181]

By 1828 the Methodists were claiming 700 converts. Proctor was not impressed by their efforts, complaining in a letter to his superior that "'no more than one out of twenty of their members was a real Christian.'" Not only were their calculations off, Proctor continued, but "'their manner of receiving members is directly calculated to lead souls to hell.'"[182] With the circuit riders living alongside Cherokee people, in some cases marrying Cherokee women and becoming citizens of the Cherokee Nation, the Methodist "manner" continued to reap corporeal dividends. By 1830 there were 1,028 Cherokee people in Methodist classes or societies, while the "other three denominations combined had fewer than 300 converts."[183] As McLoughlin noted, the fact that they "were willing to throw in their lot personally with the Cherokees . . . contributed to the feeling that this denomination was truly egalitarian and committed to the nation's welfare."[184]

Unfortunately this was not to remain the case, as most Methodist preachers supported the idea of removal: "By 1834 the denomination had lost over half the converts it had made up to 1830. With the total at only 508, the Tennessee Conference decided to close its missionary effort."[185] The Methodist schools did not keep any records, which may help to explain why I did not locate any references to the ball game from Methodist sources.

The years 1825–27 were particularly tumultuous in the Cherokee Nation, as long simmering differences between different factions in the Cherokee government, (the "traditionalists" and the "progressives") threatened to break into organized conflict. In what became known as "White Path's Rebellion," the Cherokee headman Nunnatsunega, or White Path, called a rival council against the national legislature which drew thousands of people to engage in traditional dances and ceremonies.[186] According to McLoughlin, this was essentially a traditionalist offensive designed to assert control as well as to challenge the new republican form of government and the Christian belief system that it accompanied.[187]

McLoughlin termed it "an assertion of national pride" and "an effort to keep faith with their own heritage and identity as a people." White Path and his followers "were not opposed to all acculturation, but they resented the constant missionary assault upon their 'polluting customs' and 'heathen superstitions.'" Therefore "the goal of the rebellion was to achieve tolerance toward and self-respect for the majority who still adhered to the religion and traditions of their culture." Asserting that they "already had a respectable identity" that "was sufficiently progressive and productive ... it was precisely this necessity for apparently totally transforming their identity which the Cherokee rebels repudiated."[188] Once again Cherokee people were speaking with their actions, and like the national ball game in 1825, this council can be interpreted as a symbolic expression of existence and an expression of an ontological position on a national scale. This crisis that threatened to tear the nation apart was averted for the sake of the only possible common cause, avoiding removal, and an uneasy truce was reached between Principal Chief John Ross and White Path in the summer of 1827.[189]

"[A] faithful testimony against this abominable practice": Evan Jones Weighs In

Throughout the 1820s Cherokee people continued to play in and attend ball games, and missionaries continued to complain about their influence. In 1821, the same year the Sequoyan syllabary was perfected, the Baptist Reverend Evan Jones arrived in Cherokee territory. Arriving two years after the first Baptist mission was founded, he lived in Cherokee communities until 1872. Among his other noteworthy activities, Jones completed a translation of the New Testament into Cherokee using the Sequoyan syllabary and walked the Trail of Tears.[190]

Conjuring vexed Jones as much as it had Proctor. To his credit, because he knew the language, Jones recorded Cherokee terms for these individuals. In one 1828 journal entry he referred to a particular individual who was "a celebrated ... Adonniskee. Priest or conjuror", in another he distinguished between conjurers and doctors, whom he called "Ankanagatee ('Doctors') and Deedanaweskee ('Curers [physicians of the 2nd degree])."'[191] Given the shift in the Cherokee religious system that I will discuss in Chapter 3, it is worthy of note that terms such as "priest" and "conjuror" were used interchangeably.

Evans also mentioned the ball game in several journal entries from 1827 to 1829. As Robert G. Gardner noted in *Cherokees and Baptists in Georgia*, "Two final categories of activities with religious ramifications attracting Jones's opposition were the ball plays and dances, both of which involved elements of magic and—sometimes—extensive drunkenness. Jones wrote of the 'revelry of superstition,' no doubt with these in mind."[192]

In successive journal entries, dated Sunday, June 22, and Monday, June 23, 1828, Jones described the popularity of ball games among Cherokee people and Anglo American spectators and made his own opinion plain.[193] On Sunday evening, stopping in a town (unnamed) for the night, Jones encountered several "white people," who had come from Georgia, "on purpose, to an Indian Dance, to-night, and a Ball-play tomorrow."[194] Jones said he, "considered it my duty to bear a faithful testimony against this abominable practice, though I had no expectation of preventing their going."[195]

The people went ahead to the dance, and Jones passed the evening reading sermons to a small group of Cherokees in the house of his Cherokee host. The next morning, at "family worship," Jones spoke his mind, due to the fact that "several of the white advocates for Indian dances and ball-play" were present. He "endeavoured earnestly to warn them of their dangerous situation," but "afterwards found out that some of their feelings were grated by so much plainness of speech." At noon the same day, Jones went to preach a sermon. A "small company" was present, due to "the Ball play having more attraction to the carnal mind, than the Gospel."[196] Apparently Jones was used to the competition: the July 15, 1827, entry in his journal stated matter of factly, "Friday the Indians had a great Ball-Play just by where I had appointed preaching in the evening and having no interpreter I was obliged to give it up."[197]

Given the landscape features and preparation time necessary for a ball game, it is more likely that Jones chose that site because he knew he was guaranteed a crowd rather than that ball game participants reacted to his decision in order to make a statement. Jones's frustration must have been palpable as he watched so many people arrive, realized they were not there to hear him preach, and was reminded that he could not speak Cherokee. Perhaps this was one of the events that spurred him to learn the Cherokee language so well and ultimately to translate the New Testament.

Yet Jones must have felt he was making some headway. In a February 2, 1829, journal entry, he reported that two men came to him for spiritual advice: "One said he had been much troubled about his ways, and is resolved to leave them. He had already left drinking, dancing, Ball plays and other sinful gatherings. He is afraid to die, and wishes to trust in the Savior. The dying redeemer is constantly in his mind."[198]

Constantly on Jones's mind was the task of conversion, and whether or not this particular individual remained faithful to the church has not been recorded, though like many of his fellows he may have incorporated elements of Christianity or ultimately rejected it. Theda Perdue reported that "relatively few Cherokees" abandoned their faith during this time.[199] In 1830 approximately one in every fifteen of the estimated fifteen thousand people in the Cherokee Nation professed Christianity; one missionary reported in 1828 that half the members of his church had been suspended.[200]

From Jones's comments, we know the ball games continued to be popular tourist events. He classed them with other "sinful gatherings" such as traditional dancing and the nontraditional activity of drinking, and warned Cherokee and non-Cherokee people alike of their "dangerous position" when they observed this "abominable practice." But this cultural battle would soon be dwarfed by a battle for survival that would occupy Jones and everyone else living in Cherokee territory.

The John Howard Payne Papers

There are accounts of anetso and ceremonial complex elements extant that equal or surpass all others in this time period in terms of description and specificity. They are included in the John Howard Payne Papers, part of the A. J. Ayer Collection at the Newberry Library in Chicago, Illinois.[201] Shortly before Principal Chief John Ross left for Washington in 1835 to testify before Congress regarding the proposed removal, the well-known journalist and poet John Howard Payne visited him. Payne had previously written articles against removal, and was intent to collect "historical and ethnologic material relating to the Cherokee" for a proposed book.[202] While visiting Ross, both men were arrested, held for a time without charge, and then released without explanation by the Georgia guard.[203]

Payne continued his sojourns in Cherokee territory, and in 1835 he enlisted the aid of Daniel S. Butrick. Traveling with a letter of support from John Ross, Butrick began collecting material regarding the "original customs and manners" of the Cherokee people.[204] According to McLoughlin, this information was collected between September 1835 and January 1837.[205] As Butrick stated in a letter to Payne about his research, such information was privileged and could not be obtained "from any individuals who are not experimentally convinced of the superior efficacy of the christian religion."[206] Thus his primary sources were several Cherokee converts to Christianity.[207]

Apparently Butrick gave a manuscript to Payne in 1837, and Payne composed a synthesized document based on Butrick's data and his own observations sometime after 1840.[208] It remains unclear how or when the Butrick material entered the Payne collection; the Newberry Library gives the composition date as "circa 1836."[209]

Butrick arrived in Cherokee in 1818 with the first group of Congregationalist missionaries and immediately set to work learning the Cherokee language, living with a Cherokee-speaking family.[210] He stayed with the community until the forced removal, choosing to march along the Trail of Tears with them.[211] Butrick's literary output was limited to one short book, *Antiquities of the Cherokee*, published after his death, as well as various surviving letters.[212] The subject of the book, and apparently of the manuscript given to Payne, seems to be one that consumed him.

Because he was fascinated with a particular Cherokee origin theory, Butrick undertook "intensive research into their customs, sacred myths, and religious rituals."[213] Butrick's thesis was that in the past there had been some sort of "orthodox religion" that had been "'departed from', forgotten or distorted."[214] This religion, he believed, was Judaism; he believed that the Cherokee were among the Lost Tribes of Israel.[215]

Butrick began his first account of the ball game with the following comments: "Akin to war was the ball play, that is, the ball play was called the friend, or companion of the battle. . . . In each town of any note was a respectable man, having been selected to attend the ball plays. The ancient priests had nothing to do in ball plays. They were therefore never considered as being connected with their religious ceremonies . . . Anciently ball players must be men of good character, who would play honorably, without fraud or deception. They were famous,—men of renown."[216]

Even though his consultants were converts to Christianity, and his devotion to his origin theory compromised his judgment, Butrick collected valuable information, much of which is corroborated by other sources. His account was very detailed and made no overt value judgments. He also made several interesting statements.

Based on information from his interviews, Butrick was convinced that the ball game, while an ancient activity, was not connected with religious ceremonies, but was linked to warfare. He did not extend the analysis, however, beyond noting that the "ancient priests" were not involved. Butrick also rejected continuity between traditional practitioners, or conjurers, and the "ancient priests."

He went on to describe the selection of nineteen people, including a conjurer, to perform various functions at a dance begun the night the town accepted the ball play challenge. As the account noted, this dance took place every night for seven nights before the day of the challenge. A list of seven "rules of the play" included abstinence from sexual activity, seclusion from women, scarification for some players, and dietary prohibitions.[217] He also provided detailed descriptions of the going-to-water activity as well as tools and activities of the conjurers, such as divining with beads (all discussed in Chapter 3).[218] Butrick continued with a description of the remainder of the preparations leading up to the ball play, including the chewing and application of a root. All being ready the players marched to the center of the ball ground and faced their "antagonists," each showing what he had to bet personally on the outcome.[219]

Butrick described the game itself in much less detail than he did the other activities, discussing only the basic elements. He also noted that on the fifth and seventh nights after the ball play the victors appointed all-night dances.²²⁰ Like his other observations, his detailed description of the players being taken to water was presented without making a value judgment.

A document written by a certain "J. P. Evans" accompanied the Butrick document. Evans concentrated his attention on the ball play itself, which reminded him, "of the description of the olympic and other oriental games and tilts and tournaments of the crusading periods."²²¹ According to Evans, "to excel in it, is considered a proof of manhood, and adds greatly to a man's respectability and standing in society"; certainly the boys in the Moravian school felt this way about it. Players behaved "as if they expected the performance would procure them unbounded fame and renown."²²²

Evans also provided interesting commentary on the makeup of teams: "In arranging a ball play, it is common for two towns to be engaged, one against the other; but when a great display is wanted, or where considerable wagers are laid, two or three towns are engaged on a side." This comment suggests to me that games continued to be tourist attractions. He spoke of bribes and fraud being concerns on both sides, particularly when large bets were made.²²³ Though thematically both the Butrick and Evans accounts tend toward heroic, somewhat idealized portrayals, here Evans made a less-than-sanguine comment that is certainly plausible, though uncorroborated by any of my research.

In terms of preparatory activities, Evans noted the all-night dance the night before the game, "a peculiar ceremoney [sic] called the Ball Play Dance"; he also noted that "Conjurors are appointed, who profess to ensure victory, by performing certain magical spells, calculated to enfeeble the rival party, or to render their own invincible." The conjurers were so important to the success of their party, Evans wrote, that they would, "invariably predict a favorable issue to their party." Were they to do otherwise, "such is the confidence placed in their sorceries, that it would probably, in many instances, damp the spirit and energies of the party to such a degree, that defeat would be the consequence." Evans also provided a colorful description of ball play action: "The principal respiratory tube is handled in such an uncourteous manner, that the jaws fly open involuntarily, followed by a protrusion of the tongue."²²⁴

As was the case with Major John Norton's 1810 account, the fine detail of both these accounts is impressive, and the similarities between these descriptions, later accounts, and even my own observations are striking. Unlike Butrick, Evans did make several comments that revealed an attitude of superiority and unbelief, particularly with regard to conjurers. Payne, Butrick, and Evans left a valuable if uneven record that gives researchers some sense of what at least one segment of the population felt that they could share with non-Cherokee people about the past in the face of an uncertain future. In the span of two years, that future would reveal itself, at least in the short term, to be very bleak indeed.

"Indications of contemplated hostilities"

At this time outside forces were marshalling for an all-out assault on Cherokee lands. Andrew Jackson was campaigning hard for the presidency of the United States on the platform of "Indian Removal," and he was elected in 1828.[225] One month after his election, the state of Georgia annexed all Cherokee land within its chartered limits.[226] In 1830, the United States Congress passed the Indian Removal Act, authorizing an exchange of Cherokee land for comparable parcels in the West.[227] However, this piece of legislation was consistent with and the culmination of decades of government policy that Thomas Jefferson, among others, had supported.[228]

The missionaries as a rule openly opposed the removal policy until 1832. In that year a legal test case in the United States Supreme Court was concluded between two missionaries and the state of Georgia. The case concerned a law passed in that state requiring all white men in annexed Cherokee territory to sign an oath of allegiance to Georgia.[229]

In 1831 two Congregationalist ABCFM missionaries, Samuel A. Worchester and Dr. Elizur Butler, had defied this order and refused to sign the oath; they promptly had been arrested and jailed. Chief Justice John Marshall and the Supreme Court ruled in favor of the two men, and so in favor of the sovereignty of Cherokee people, their nation, and their right to the disputed territory. Upon hearing of the court's decision, President Jackson is said to have remarked (likely apocryphally), "John Marshall has made his decision, now let him enforce it."[230] Whether or not he actually spoke those words, the message was clear—the Cherokee people would have to go.

According to William McLoughlin, mission agents received regular financial support from the federal government, and the federal government considered missionaries "paid agents and thus bound to support all official policies."[231] The Moravians, attempting to remain neutral, were forced out of Georgia and moved just over the border to Tennessee.[232] From this base they continued itinerant missionary activities until the removal. Some Baptists, including Evan Jones, did an about face and supported the Cherokee cause secretly while continuing publicly to refrain from supporting removal.[233] The Methodists and even the remaining ABCFM Congregationalists seem to have ceased opposition with the conclusion of the court case.[234] As McLoughlin noted, the result of the missionaries ceasing opposition to the removal after 1832 while continuing "to preach salvation without social justice was predictable.... There was not only a tremendous falling off in conversions and mission church membership but a concomitant revival of the traditional religion."[235]

Cherokee people pursued every imaginable avenue in the next few years to stave off the removal, but to no avail. In August 1837, with the spring 1838 deadline to remove less than a year away, the *Raleigh Register and North Carolina Gazette* carried the following item:

> CHEROKEE INDIANS.—We understand that difficulties are apprehended with Cherokee Indians in this State: Those Indians have heretofore been entirely pacific; but the time is now drawing near for their departure to the far West.—They express great dissatisfaction, and declare they will not remove. We are informed that they had several Dances and Ball Plays recently, which the Whites amongst them consider as indications of contemplated hostilities.[236]

It was the ball playing season, and Cherokee people had been playing anetso regularly until that time, according to various accounts. What makes this item particularly interesting, of course, is the final clause. The report, which is at least secondhand ("We are informed"), presents the ball games and dances *themselves* as "indications of contemplated hostilities." Why did the "Whites amongst them" so consider the dances and ball games? Did people overhear the phrase "play ball against" being used in reference to the United States government, as in the two accounts from the eighteenth century that I presented at the end of the previous chapter? Perhaps they were unaware that the "Quallatown Indians" had petitioned federal commissioners to remain in North Carolina; preliminary approval would be granted in September 1837.[237] One wonders if the figure of speech somehow was misconstrued once again.

One thing is for certain: Cherokee people were playing ball regularly the summer before the removal deadline. As discussed earlier in this chapter, there are several historical situations in which Cherokee people appeared to "revive" or increase participation in traditional activities as responses to then-current situations. I will discuss one additional example in Chapter 4, and the affinities between the ball game and warfare in depth in Chapter 5, but here I will say that I am not aware of another example in which ball games were, or were said to be, precursors to armed conflict.

Although an estimated two thousand removal advocates moved before the deadline, the majority of the Cherokee people were removed forcibly from their lands in the East to territory in Oklahoma in the winter of 1838–39. This tragedy does not seem to have a standard name in the Cherokee language among members of the Eastern Band; in English, it is known as the Trail of Tears. Federal troops rousted Cherokee people who had refused to emigrate out of their homes and confiscated many of their possessions, burning houses and crops as they did so.

Approximately sixteen thousand Cherokee people were confined in concentration camps until they began their journey, most by foot. Many thousands of people died either in the camps, in transit to Oklahoma, or soon after their arrival, and the accounts of both Cherokee survivors and the United States soldiers charged with guarding them are a horrific testament to the brutality of this government action. All told, it is estimated that as much as a quarter of the total Cherokee population may have perished during this time.[238] Those people who had managed to avoid removal now began the process of forming what would come to be called the Eastern Band of Cherokee Indians.

Conclusion

Marion Starkey, the ABCFM mission historian who wrote particularly colorful ball game accounts, stated that "the ball play was a noble game, ruled at its best by exacting ethical standards worthy of a more sympathetic study by the missionaries."[239] Raymond Fogelson said the missionaries "were almost unanimous in their disapproval of the game. It was not the game so much as the dancing, drinking and gambling that accompanied it that disturbed them."[240] Theda Perdue said the missionaries were concerned primarily with the attendant drunkenness and near nudity of the players.[241] Yet she also said ball games were traditional rituals that had strong ties to the Cherokee religious system, which would be reason enough for the missionaries' condemnation. Perdue herself interpreted ball games as "essentially ritualized warfare accompanied by many of the same ceremonies as those associated with war."[242]

William McLoughlin stated that for the missionaries, "the practices themselves were sacrilegious."[243] Ball plays, conjuring, and dances all were "polluting customs," and participation in any of these activities was grounds for censure.[244] As discussed above, McLoughlin argued for a model of Cherokee culture based upon anomie and renascence and used evidence of what he said was the secularization of the ball game and ostensibly religious activities to support this contention. McLoughlin believed that Cherokee people who accepted Christianity underwent an important religious transition, transitioning from "a religious system to which all belonged from birth and that was integrally related to all community activities" (including sports), to "voluntary church membership."[245]

Missionaries signified anetso in related terms. The scholars I cited above all agreed that it was not the ball games themselves, but the drinking, near nakedness, and quarreling that were the main factors missionaries opposed. Yet those same scholars also recognized the ritual aspects of the ball game.

This to me seems a bit incongruous. Were the missionaries unaware of the scope of the ceremonial complex? While several of the missionaries did complain about the all-night dance and conjuring, it seems to me that most missionaries were unaware of either the extent or the interrelationship of the ceremonial complex activities, or both. If there were those who knew about them, they did not make the connection between them and anetso as ritual events. Besides, they were worried enough about the public drunkenness and near nudity.

Cherokee people at the time no doubt recognized that the missionaries could not oppose elements about which they were unaware. Thus I suggest the following scenario: Cherokee men and boys on ball teams listened to the missionaries rail against known aspects of the ball game complex and defiantly continued to participate; other Cherokee people defiantly continued to attend. This indeed was "talking back," exemplifying "values [being] given body"; it was the ironic expression of identity and the expression of an ontological position.

But I think there was another part to the story, played out in private. While the game and some of the activities such as dancing continued to be public, Cherokee teams also quietly continued to perform the other necessary ceremonial complex activities privately. This brings me back to Joel Martin's concept of "cultural underground" and the notion of silence derived from Charles Long's work. In this case, the silence might very well have been voluntary. As Martin suggested, activities took place "beyond the gaze" of certain constituencies. Furthermore, as I will illustrate in the next two chapters, this dyadic public/private structure no doubt has contributed to the preservation of the ball game complex through periods of great change.

Anetso was an important part of public life in the period from 1799 to 1838, as it was before and after this time. Time after time anetso was played during political events, in the presence of tourists, and despite the protestations of missionaries. Though it was not an omnipresent symbol, and not the only symbol, it continued to be a vehicle for expression of Cherokee identity, as well as an emblem or symbol of that cultural identity for both Cherokee and non-Cherokee people. This remained the case in the ensuing years as the Cherokee people in North Carolina worked to reconstitute their community identity.

Ahaquo!
(Still there!)

The Anetso Ceremonial Complex

This chapter will situate the anetso ceremonial complex in what I am calling "the Cherokee religious system." First I will discuss a transition in the Cherokee religious system from a hereditary priestly caste to independent individual practitioners. An overview of green corn ceremonialism will follow; these were the most durable elements that survived the transition from what was once a yearly cycle of ceremonies. Then I will provide basic information on those constituent activities of the complex that are key elements of the Cherokee religious system and summarize continuity and change in the performance of these activities since the late nineteenth century. In addition, I will present a thorough report of one of these ritual actions, translated as "going to water," in order to assess persistence and change. Since detailing all of the complied data about every element of the complex would require a separate volume, I will highlight this action for reasons that I will explain below.

Privatization of the Cherokee Religious System

According to both Cherokee oral tradition and prevailing scholarly opinion, at one time there was a hereditary priestly caste in Cherokee society known as the Anikutani.[1] Members of this group officiated during the seasonal ceremonial round of six regular festivals, as well during other festivals held at different intervals.[2] In short, the yearly round included a "'festival of the first new moon of spring . . . about the time the grass began to grow . . . [a] preliminary or new green-corn feast, held when the young corn first became fit to taste . . . [a] mature or ripe green-corn festival . . . forty or fifty days [later] when the corn had become hard and perfect . . . [a] great new-moon feast . . . [on the] the first new moon of autumn . . . [a] propitiation or cementation festival . . . about ten days [after the previous celebration] . . . [and] the festival of the exulting or bounding bush which came somewhat later.'"[3]

Historical accounts of these festivals and Anikutani priests are available from the eighteenth and nineteenth centuries. Alexander Longe, the controversial trader at the center of the Chestowe scandal, remarked in his 1725 account that "there is a certain family that the priesthood belongs to and they always hold that it is the fisick family [sic]."[4] The editor of a published version of this account commented, "the Cherokee society of Long's account is a society of hierarchies of rank and privilege more or less directed by hereditary priests of the 'fisick family' who held their People in fear of the Great Being Above. This picture corresponds strikingly to that set forth in the John Howard Payne Papers by Cherokee informants of a century later."[5]

According to Mooney, Cherokee oral tradition contained accounts of the Anikutani becoming increasingly prideful. While other men were out hunting, the Cherokee priests would enter homes and rape women, believing they were above punishment. One hunter returned from the hunt and found that his wife had been treated in this manner. Community members viewed this indiscretion as the last straw in a series of excesses by this group, and led by this hunter, they slaughtered all Anikutani.[6]

Major John Norton related a similar account in his journal, and as was the case with his accounts of ball games, it is very detailed. He was told about an individual who had entered a Council House "at a very distant period," saying that he had traveled "to the Country above" and returned "with the commands of the Great Spirit whose abode is there."[7] This individual "then appointed several ceremonies, dances, and purifications to be observed"; he "was joined by many others in his office," such that the group grew in numbers and "became sacred in the eyes of the people." They called themselves the "Anikanos" and indulged "their evil passions, without the least regard to the rights of others, or the restraints of modesty and decorum." They "carried their wickedness to such a height, that the indignation of the people was roused . . . [until] they were finally all put to death wherever they were found."[8]

Two articles in the 1980s by Raymond Fogelson remain significant to the scholarly discourse regarding the Anikutani. The first is still the most detailed discussion available of the group; the second contains a brief but crucial amplification of comments he made in the first article regarding their demise.[9] Fogelson noted that a series of vicious smallpox epidemics ravaged Cherokee towns in the late seventeenth and eighteenth centuries, and he cited accounts of priests burning all their implements in frustration at not being able to cure the disease.[10] Other theories incorporated evidence for the group's migration, its being an indigenous population, and its survival as the Anigilohi clan.[11]

In this same article Fogelson included the opinion of Charles R. Hicks, whom he identified as "an important mixed-blood Cherokee and Moravian convert, who was elected Principal Chief in 1827." According to Hicks's account, the priests "might have shifted their profession to that of the Jugglers and Doctors, for it is found in our days that the Jugglers and Doctors possess more knowledge of the Traditions of this nation than any others among the present race."[12]

The second of Fogelson's two articles, written five years after the first, discussed events and "nonevents."[13] Fogelson wrestled with the question of how scholars can "account for the histories of so-called 'people without history,' those who lack accustomed libraries and archives of documents."[14] He argued for an approach "taking seriously native theories of history as embedded in cosmology, in narratives, in rituals and ceremonies, and more generally in native philosophies and worldviews. Implicit here is the assumption that events may be recognized, defined, evaluated, and endowed with meaning differentially in different cultural traditions."[15] What this meant to Fogelson was that scholars needed to consider alternate modes of historical narrative construction rather than "event-centered history."[16] Here he proposed several categories of nonevents, including "the imagined event: one that never happened but could have occurred, or according to the ethnologic involved, should have happened."[17]

Fogelson argued that the demise of the Anikutani was a "subtype" of imagined events he called "the epitomizing event": "Epitomizing events are narratives that condense, encapsulate, and dramatize longer-term historical processes. Such events are inventions but have such compelling qualities and explanatory power that they spread rapidly through the group and soon take on an ethnohistorical reality of their own."[18] In the first article, Fogelson stated that "it is unimportant whether the events recounted in the legend actually occurred"; but in the second article he declared, "such an event probably never occurred."[19]

In terms of assessing the different theories, an important question is when such an event, shift, or culmination of a historical process might have occurred. There are accounts suggesting that there were certainly memories and even some vestiges of this priestly heritage still extant in the early nineteenth century. A Cherokee individual told Major John Norton that when he was a boy, "a venerable person" at a Green Corn Ceremony "preached in a kind of poetic strain, and in a dialect of which only a few words were intelligible to the younger part of the people."[20] The John Howard Payne Papers also contained accounts of these people and their duties.[21] In Chapter 2, I discussed a passage from the Payne Papers which reported that the ancient priests had nothing to do with the ball play, but certain individuals ("respectable men") were selected to attend each contest. This statement suggests that conjurers may have constituted a separate coterie even in the days of the priests.[22]

Missionaries used terms such as "priest" and "conjuror" interchangeably to describe individuals who were their adversaries in the spiritual war or possible influential converts. Furthermore, Fred Gearing's discussion of eighteenth-century Cherokee political and social structures in which a "priest chief" and other priests ("white" officials) were balanced by the "war chief" and "war priest" ("red" officials), lends credence to the notion of a bifurcated system.[23] Whatever the events (or nonevents, according to Fogelson) may have been, a system of autonomous ritual and medicinal specialists was in place by the early nineteenth century.

By the end of the nineteenth century complete ceremonies seem to have ceased or at least to have been significantly truncated, but certain constituent activities proved to be more durable, particularly those activities connected to the growth and harvest of corn. So the Anikutani seem to have disappeared, but religious and medicinal specialists, selected ritual activities, including constituent pieces of the yearly ceremonial round, as well as memories of previous ceremonial cycles and functionaries all survived without interruption throughout the twentieth century. In the early twentieth century designated community leaders oversaw the community events until they abated, and often these were the autonomous ritual and medicinal specialists. As this book was going to press, individual practitioners continued to work on the Qualla Boundary.

Green Corn Ceremonialism

Activities surrounding the harvest of corn have taken several different but associated forms among the Cherokee. There were at one time two distinct festivals related to the harvest of green corn: an initial celebration when the corn was first eaten, and a second festival forty to fifty days later when the corn had ripened.[24] These were part of the seasonal round of festivals listed above. Of these activities, only the Green Corn Dance and certain actions performed before eating the first green corn of the harvest survived into the early twentieth century. The Green Corn Dance has been cited repeatedly by scholars as being a religious ceremony of great importance and historical durability.[25]

Cherokee people traditionally had two corn ceremonies, yet worked two crops of corn a year. Witthoft said a "major harvest festival" was what he called the "New Corn Festival, held in August when the green corn first became fit to eat. It marked the beginning of the winter half of the year."²⁶ Accounts of the community celebration were furnished to Witthoft by Will West Long, who relied on conversations with his mother and older brother "to supply some information about this extinct ceremonial complex."²⁷ Everyone present would drink an emetic, go to water, and then take the corn medicine. Social dancing would then follow all night. In the morning, the conjurer would take all present to water, where he would divine to see if each would live until the next Green Corn Festival.²⁸

The two Cherokee festivals eventually were replaced by two activities: a curing ceremonial feast with no connection to the calendar; and a medicine, or drink, that families consumed before partaking of the first green corn of the season.²⁹ In a 1946 article, Witthoft quoted Mooney (from a somewhat obscure publication), who said the last "tribal" Green Corn Dance had been held in 1887.³⁰ Mooney said that he had witnessed two private family celebrations "as late as 1914" that involved "the blessing upon the new corn and on those about to partake of it for the first time."³¹

Older accounts discussed additional activities. An 1818 account in the *Raleigh (N.C.) Register* by the Cherokee chief Charles Hicks told of a festival that lasted four days, with a "conjuror" feeding a fire with grains of seven ears of corn and everyone drinking "a tea of wild horehound."³² Hicks remarked that "it is said that a person was formerly chosen to speak to the people on each day in a language that is partly lost—at least there is very little of it known now."³³

Ruth Wetmore, in an article that combined the findings of several scholars, suggested there was a six-day festival, with the activities described above, and termed it the "Preliminary Green Corn Feast."³⁴ According to her, the "Ripe Green Corn Feast" was held "in middle or late September when the corn had become hard and perfect."³⁵ This seems to have lasted four days.

The Cherokee national council met at this time as well. In addition, since its inception the Cherokee Indian Fair has been held roughly at this time of year, either the first or second week in October. Mooney supplied information from perhaps an even earlier period than that of Hicks's account, in which just before the Green Corn Dance, "every fire in the settlement was extinguished and all the people came and got new fire from the townhouse. This was called *atsi'la gălûñkw'ti'yu*, 'the honored or sacred fire.'"³⁶

Referencing Witthoft's work, Speck and Broom commented that by the time of their fieldwork in the first four decades of the twentieth century the full details of the community activities described above had not survived and agreed with his conclusions, presuming that the corn medicine was administered in August.³⁷ The Green Corn Dance ("akɔhādĭ"), literally, "big foreheads in motion"), remained a key part of the Green Corn Ceremony at this time.[38]

The Green Corn Dance lasted all day and the following night, and had four periods, or stages.[39] Speck and Broom provided detailed descriptions of the movements of each stage, complete with diagrams and photographs. In the first and third stages, men and women began by dancing at the same time, but separately, eventually joining together. The second stage was a "feasting interval," and the fourth stage, an all-night series of dances the night following the feast.[40] The dance ended "just before dawn with the Round or Running Dance, which is preceded by the Corn Dance, an intrinsic part of the harvest ceremony" (and a separate dance).[41]

Will West Long said the predawn performance of the Corn Dance represented "'early spring planting' through the analogy of morning and the springtime of the year." It also was "believed to have been a necessary preparation for planting," linked to the conjurer's prayer for speedy growth of the corn, as well as preventing "the illness believed to result from eating green corn." Of note in the context of my discussion of the Thunders in Chapter 1 is the fact that in the first stage, the men danced counterclockwise in a circle with guns, which they fired one after the other at intervals, symbolizing thunder. The symbolism of the entire dance was unclear to the authors, but they surmised an implication of "a fertilization of vital elements, specifically the grains."[42]

In my research, several written sources and consultants reported the drinking of a medicine before they were allowed to eat the first green corn of the season.[43] Two other practices are worthy of note. People did not blow on the roasted corn to cool it, and the cobs were left in the house for four days.

According to Molly Sequoyah, as told to John Witthoft, "One must not blow on a roasted ear of green corn in order to cool it, as this would cause a thunderstorm."[44] The Thunders being sons and husband of Selu, the Corn Mother, they "would resent such disrespectful treatment of her."[45] In addition, the cobs were kept in the house for four days because Selu's body lay outdoors on the ground for that amount of time after her son killed her. So the Thunders are referenced in the dance, as well as the practices associated with green corn ceremonialism.

In the mid-1980s a group in Big Cove revived the Green Corn Ceremony. In the late 1990s I was shown a dance arbor, including a wood structure with sections where different clans would sit, circling a small mound in a clearing. It appeared much like a portion of the dance ground replica in the Oconaluftee Village. In addition I was told that sweat baths (sing. osi) were constructed for both men and women. Green corn dances were held for several years at the turn of the twenty-first century, but I have no information as to whether or not they have continued. At that time opinions about the dancing were mixed, with some community members supporting this activity, and others citing non-Cherokee participation and the lack of proper authority to conduct the dances and other activities.[46]

Key Elements of the Cherokee Anetso Ceremonial Complex

Mooney observed of Cherokee religion that one can "admire the consistency of the theory, the particularity of the ceremonial and the beauty of the expression"; in short, the "wonderful completeness about the whole system which is not surpassed even by the ceremonial religions of the East."[47] Though many valuable scholarly works have discussed Cherokee religious activities, there is no scholarly treatment of Cherokee religious system elements that is systematic and comprehensive. Production of such a work would be a massive undertaking and would require one or more large volumes.

In what follows I will summarize the rudiments of several key Cherokee religious system elements that are incorporated in the anetso ceremonial complex. My characterizations and classifications of cultural actions into a system and complex are justified primarily in their usefulness as heuristic devices rather than as an inviolable historical record. Where possible I have provided Cherokee terms.[48]

When discussing elements of the ceremonial complex, it is important to distinguish between match games and exhibition games. A match game is a formal contest between two townships or teams of other configurations (multiple towns or settlements, nation versus nation). Historically, community members gambled with rival settlement members on the outcome, and conjurers were employed. These were major social events.[49]

If enough players were in favor of a game, they appointed a manager ("di.tsu.hi.sti.ski"), a team was gathered, and one or more (up to four) conjurers, would be hired.[50] According to a published source from the early 1970s, match games were held on Saturdays at noon, with two o'clock becoming the preferred starting time in later years.[51] Weeknight summertime games also were reported.[52]

Historically, activities that were part of the anetso ceremonial complex occurred in the weeks leading up to the contest, intensified the evening before, and continued immediately after, concluding a week later. In the past, some elements of the complex, such as dances, were public affairs, while others were done in private. While at one time all ball games were match games, in the last sixty or seventy years these mostly have given way to exhibition matches, or scrimmages, between squads of the same team during the

Cherokee Indian Fair. I will discuss possible reasons for this shift in context in Chapter 4.

1. "ana-dóni-ha" ("they conjure [now]");[53] **conjuring:** Both the Cherokee stems "*doni*" and "*lhsdelhdo*" can be translated "conjure."[54] This is the ability of individuals to enlist the aid of other-than-human persons in a variety of human endeavors, as well as to effect transformations or desired effects on other humans, human events, or other aspects of existence by means of specific ritual procedures. There are numerous individual procedures, some of which include the preparation and use of vegetable and animal materials. Such procedures typically include the use of *idigawesdi*, often translated as "formulas" (described below), and a number of other actions discussed below, as well as the propitiation of other-than-human persons.

Since at least the early nineteenth century, these autonomous ritual and medicinal practitioners with various specialties and abilities have been active, and their titles reflect this diversity. Historically the two spheres of activity have been linked in Cherokee culture, and many observers have noted the relationship. James Mooney noted, "Every doctor is a priest, and every application is a religious act accompanied by prayer."[55] Jack Frederick Kilpatrick and Anna Gritts Kilpatrick explained the office as follows in 1965: "The correct term for a Cherokee shaman who, like the Jewish rabbi, is both physician and priest, is *dida:hnvwi:sg(i)* ('curer of them, he')."[56] Alan Kilpatrick, following his parents, also has employed this latter term (although he translated it as "knowledgeable shaman").[57]

In the summer of 1945 the linguist Ernest Bender transcribed an interview with Molly Sequoyah, a Cherokee resident of the Big Cove community on the Qualla Boundary, in which he rendered the terms she used as "adonisgi" and "adáwisgi," both translated as "'conjure-man'"; and "gosʌsgi náwohdi ('he-made medicine')."[58] An additional term listed but not used in the interviews was "a-lhsdélhdo-di," "conjure-man."[59] Raymond Fogelson cited the first two of these terms as well in 1962, though he rendered them differently.[60] Over the course of several articles, Fogelson focused attention on what he variously referred to as "medico-magical beliefs" as well as "sorcery and witchcraft."[61]

In the 1990s, Lee Irwin culled terms from several works and standardized their spelling, including, "*ada'nunwisgi*," "'healers'" or "'curers'"; "*amayi didadzun:stisgi*," "the one who 'takes them to water,'" interpreted as "'priest'"; and his rendering of the term given above, "*dida'nunwiski*" (sing.), "well-known and mature healer."[62] In conversation, members of the Eastern Band of Cherokee often have referred to someone who "doctors," or people being "doctored," and have used the English terms "conjurer," "conjure-men," or "conjure-women."[63]

Certain individuals were and are adept at a variety of tasks, and there also are other designations for the rare individuals who are extraordinarily adept, such as *"adawehi,"* "'master shaman'"; or malevolent, such as *"tsikili,"* "horned owl."[64] The Kilpatricks noted that the "antitype" of the *didanvwisgi*, "the individual who unauthorizedly uses knowledge for evil ends, is a *dida:hnese:sg(i)* ('putter-in and drawer-out of them, he')—a sorcerer, a 'witch.' Any *dida:hnvwi:sg(i)* knows everything a *dida:hnese:sg(i)* knows, and even more; but he uses his knowledge in a selfless and socially sanctioned way to counter and to crush evil."[65]

These statements imply that it would be incorrect to characterize the Cherokee religious system as dominated by or obsessed with the malevolent side of conjuring. While there is no doubt that such activity takes place, it is best understood in a balanced relationship with the benevolent individuals and actions, as the Kilpatricks present. To focus on such elements of a negative or destructive nature is to risk misunderstanding the system as a whole. As an analogue (if I may be permitted a generalized statement to make the point), this is akin to characterizing Christianity as being preoccupied with Satan and demons.

It is clear from my experience that for many non-Cherokee people, whether or not they are scholars, the term "conjurer" can *conjure* various images. These include tuxedo-clad Houdinis pulling rabbits out of a hat and making people disappear and reappear at will, or wily wizards in pointed hats casting spells to turn princes into frogs or to keep princesses locked in towers. Certainly there are Cherokee people who do not adhere to the "traditional" religious system in any way and are in fact opposed to its continuation to the extent that mention of any aspect of the system also would provoke a negative or dismissive reaction. Yet for many Cherokee people there is no negative connotation associated with the term "conjurer"; so much so that now when I employ the term in conversation I usually do not give it a second thought.

Historically, conjuring often has been glossed as a part of a superstitious system to be rejected in favor of Christianity by a certain portion of the population. Yet for other people it was and in some cases continues to be part of a religious system that encompasses the totality of experience, both positive and negative. It is my sense that many people's views lie somewhere in between. For a number of individuals, elements of the religious systems are considered complementary rather than conflicting. This includes some individuals who are conjurers, including a consultant of mine.

In the context of anetso, each ball team traditionally hired at least one conjurer.[66] The conjurer's duties have included dictating the performance of the various activities, endeavoring to learn the outcome and strategy of the opponents, striving to manipulate events and players' actions and abilities, and protecting his team from his opposite number. Traditionally, ritual and medicinal specialists have performed these activities individually, as well as in the context of the ball game complex. In Mooney's opinion, the outcome of the ball game rested with the conjurers, or as he called them, "shamans": "Thus the ball play becomes as well a contest between rival shamans. Among primitive peoples the shaman is in truth all-powerful, and even so simple a matter as the ball game is not left to the free enjoyment of the people, but is so interwoven with priestly rites and influence that the shaman becomes the most important actor in the play."[67]

This excerpt of Mooney's also is illustrative, in my opinion, of the dissonance between conceptual categories different cultures utilize. He interpreted the ball game according to preconceived categories of "ritual" and "game" that were mutually exclusive, even though he clearly recognized the ritual aspects of the activity. Yet rather than identify the ball game with other activities, Cherokee or otherwise, that were similarly "interwoven with priestly rites and influence," instead he assigned it to a separate category and made a value judgment based upon categorical rather than descriptive criteria.

In my own field research I have had the opportunity to discuss aspects of anetso with current and former managers of different teams, current and former players, a ball stick maker, and several conjurers. One of the things I learned was that any information related to conjuring activities continues to be guarded. It is powerful. Each individual interviewed did not and would not talk about certain aspects of the anetso complex, and would only go so far in discussion of others. Each stated that in regard to certain matters he was not qualified to speak, and for other matters that the power of the activities or formulas would be compromised if revealed or even discussed with me.[68]

2. "*i:gawé:sdi*" ("to say, one"); "formula, song":[69] The plural form is "*idi:gawé:sdi*" ("to be said, they").[70] These can be described as standardized speech acts, or ritual combinatory utterances; with the advent of the syllabary many were collected in texts known as "*nv:wo:dhi digo:hwé:li*, or medicine books."[71] These books were in a number of forms, including chapbooks, ledger books, and writing tablets. Above all other material objects these texts have been most coveted by ethnographers; a number of idigawesdi have been acquired and published by scholars, and a number of these collections currently reside in the archives of major museums and libraries in the United States.

As the Kilpatricks noted, "most Cherokee magical rituals consist of something that one says (or merely thinks) or sings, called the *i:gawé:sdi* ('to say, one'), and some recommended physical procedures, called the *igv́:n(e)dhi* ('to do, one'), although some have no *igv́:n(e)dhi* at all."[72] Their opinion was that published information on such Cherokee activities did "not recognize a fundamental truth: in any magical ritual all generative power resides in thought, and the *i:gawé:sdi*, which focuses and directs that thought, alone is inviolate."[73] Solomon Bird (b. 1902) of the Snowbird community was asked in a 1986 oral history interview what the conjurer said to the players when he "took them to water" (described below) before a ball game. He replied, "I don't know, and nobody else knew either. In fact, they didn't speak out. They did it in their minds."[74] The *igawesdi* is typically a prayer or entreaty to one or more other-than-human persons to aid in the action desired,

On the other hand, according to the Kilpatricks, "the *igv́:n(e)dhi*, which merely augments the authority of thought, or serves more effectively to apply or disseminate it," could be altered in any number of ways by the individual practitioner, or even deleted.[75] The *igvnedi* contains instructions for further ritual action, in some cases including preparation of and treatment with *nvwoti*, or "medicine" (see below).[76] Depending upon their abilities, other-than-human persons are either beseeched or commanded to aid or identify themselves with the party in question.[77] Though I will discuss this in context, suffice to say that extremely powerful other-than-human persons are beseeched for assistance, while lesser beings are commanded to act. Included in the igvnedi section is such information as a notation of ingredients, directions for preparation, and information concerning the number of times it should be administered.

Mooney reported that the "formulas generally consist of four paragraphs, corresponding to four steps in the medical ceremony."[78] As he explained in another work,

> The two sacred numbers of the Cherokee are four and seven, the latter being the actual number of the tribal clans, the formulistic number of upper worlds or heavens, and the ceremonial number of paragraphs or repetitions in the principal formulas. Thus in the prayers for long life the priest raises his client by successive stages to the first, second, third, fourth, and finally to the seventh heaven before the end is accomplished. The sacred four has direct relation to the four cardinal points, while seven, besides these, includes also 'above,' 'below,' and 'here in the center.' In many tribal rituals color and sometimes sex are assigned to each point of direction. In the sacred Cherokee formulas the spirits of the East, South, West, and North are, respectively, Red, White, Black, and Blue, and each

color has also its own symbolic meaning of Power (War), Peace, Death, and Defeat."[79]

As for the term "formula," the Kilpatricks stated that "'sacred formulas,' the term confected by James Mooney," while "in many respects . . . fitting . . . possesses connotations of rigidity" and fails to convey an "ineradicable inherent plasticity in the practice of Cherokee magic"; in addition, "many of the 'formulas' are far from 'sacred.'"[80] Based on just the formulas that have been collected by researchers, one can see the wide variety of circumstances in which formulas might be employed. To give a few examples, there are formulas for the following: ease of pregnancy, rain, a good harvest, to cure specific sicknesses, to make someone fall in love with you, and to find something lost. Although not discussed openly, malevolent formulas for harming and even killing others do exist.[81]

There are a number of idigawesdi specific to the anetso complex. A variety of formulas might be employed during preparation for and during a ball game. Formulas exist for taking the players to water, improving performance, producing victory for the team, causing defeat for the opposing team, preparing ball sticks, and a number of other purposes, many of which will be described below. Conjurers recite idigawesdi that call upon specific beings for assistance. In addition, "strong" or particularly talented players are often singled out as subjects (or targets) of the formulas.

Interestingly, there are relatively few published anetso formulas, and Mooney included only one in his *Sacred Formulas of the Cherokees*, titled "This Concerns the Ball Play—To Take Them to Water With It."[82] Olbrechts included one formula in the *Swimmer Manuscript* (#31) for scratching with a snake tooth in preparation for, among other things, the ball game, but there are no specific formulas for anetso included in that collection of ninety-six formulas.[83] It is my opinion that only two such formulas were published because they were hard to come by for both men. It may have been the case that such formulas were still in great use and would not have been parted with easily, no matter what the enticement.

One of the excellent features of Fogelson's study is the inclusion of several ball game formulas, comprising the largest available collection of such information. He said he built a collection of eighteen ball game formulas, and several of these were included, plus a key nonspecific formula from another of his collections and two formulas from Oklahoma.[84] Most, but not all, are from Lloyd Sequoyah of Big Cove, a respected and knowledgeable individual and the son of Molly Sequoyah, who was a consultant for John Witthoft and Ernst Bender and was herself respected for her traditional knowledge.[85]

There are many formulas that appeal to the Thunders or otherwise mention them, and the anetso formulas in Fogelson's collection contain many references to them. Fogelson included formulas for a variety of activities related to anetso. These included several formulas for taking players to water, formulas to select players and "doctor" ball sticks, formulas for use during the march to the ball field as well as the march to the center ground, a few for use during the match, and even one for simultaneously harming a rival and protecting oneself from conjuring.[86]

There are conjurers who are still active, and formulas are available for those who seek them. The Museum of the Cherokee Indian received two donated chapbooks (small ledger books) in 1999, which I have studied briefly, and there is at least one ball game formula in one of them, but to my knowledge it has not yet been translated.[87] Several people have told me they possessed such books, but this is never an issue that I raise in conversation. This is a sensitive subject, due to the thoroughgoing obsession many earlier researchers had with acquiring formulas. Yet several consultants have raised the subject themselves in conversation, and I have discussed such formula books with people.

The books are still in demand within the general community as well. One consultant told me she had such a book, which several friends asked to borrow. It went from one to the other and when the owner got it back there were a few pages missing. None of the people who borrowed it knew anything about the missing pages.[88]

Writing in the 1970s, Charles Hudson noted that the use of formulas for Cherokee people was not limited to special occasions.[89] Day-to-day usage was and is equally prevalent, and my research suggests there are some types of formulas that are common knowledge. Over time, according to consultants, fewer and fewer people have cultivated this knowledge; but it seems to me that there is a resurgence of interest in plants and their uses.[90] It stands to reason that beyond the recognized experts in the community, even people with minimal plant knowledge also would have some knowledge of relevant basic formulas.

3. "*amó:hi atsv́:sdi*";[91] "going to water": Commonly translated as "going to water," the phrase *amohi atsvsdi* literally means "water-place, to go and return, one."[92] This is the Cherokee practice of ceremonially bathing, washing, or laving portions of the body (and sometimes objects) in a running body of water, such as a river, stream, or branch.

There are two forms of this activity: certain occasions or situations call for a religious specialist to accompany the individual(s) going to water, while on other occasions individuals go alone. I refer to these two forms of the activity as "being taken" and "going" to water. About this distinction Frans Olbrechts, working in the early 1930s, observed after discussion of a "typical example of a formula 'for taking them to the water with,'" that "a similar but less elaborate ceremonial may be performed for the less important of the purposes . . . by a layman, without the intervention of the medicine man."[93] Many consultants also have remarked upon this point.[94] Though Mooney did not specifically address this distinction, he did note a separate distinction between "plunging into the water" and "dipping up the water"; as we shall see below, both methods are employed in the ball game complex.[95]

The earliest written description yet located of going to water appears in Alexander Longe's 1725 publication "A Small Postscript . . ."; he described the practice as part of what he called the "Feast of First Fruits" and the ritual when men return from war.[96] References to the activity occurred throughout the nineteenth century, and most scholars who have written about elements of the Cherokee religious system have discussed the significance of this practice.

At the turn of the twentieth century, Mooney wrote, "This ceremony of going to water is the most sacred and impressive in the whole Cherokee ritual"; in another work he noted that it was part of "every important ritual performance."[97] Historically amohi atsvsdi has been a standard component of ritual events such as the Green Corn Ceremony, and families or other groups might be taken to water in conjunction with births, marriages, and deaths. It has been a key component of treatment for various illnesses, and also has been employed as a preparatory or concluding activity for other activities, such as hunting, warfare, the Cherokee ball game, and the formal transmission of cultural narratives. In the context of this activity ritual specialists might diagnose conditions, administer medicinal treatments, beseech other-than-human persons for assistance, or offer prayers for the general well-being of the company.

At one time, people regularly underwent "sweat baths" beforehand in osi, multipurpose structures. Additionally, as noted above, the solitary individual can go to water; this can be done on a daily basis to ensure long life and good health. Mooney reported that the most propitious time to go to water was in "the latter part of autumn," when all the leaves falling into the streams and rivers "are supposed to impart their medicinal virtues to the water."[98] Mooney was told that people were to go to water even if they had to break ice on the surface of the water to do so, and that "to the neglect of this rite the older people attribute many of the evils that have come upon the tribe in later days."[99] Several consultants have discussed going to water both on a daily basis and in the presence of a conjurer, and I have observed bright autumn leaves of trees overhanging the Oconaluftee River falling in as if they were just pouring off into the water.[100] Presently, among people who are members of the Eastern Band of Cherokee, going to water often can be a relatively simple matter, for such is the landscape of western North Carolina that streams or branches are never far away, even right in some peoples' back or front yards.

During the anetso ceremonial complex, players go to water both pre- and postcontest in the company of the team conjurer. For reasons I will discuss in context, at different times in the schedule of the complex the activity is performed privately and publicly.

4. "analhsgi" ("they dance now");[101] **dancing:** Dancing was at one time a major ritual activity in the Cherokee system, and was included in almost every Cherokee ceremonial occasion, including the Green Corn Ceremony. Dances of particular significance include the Green Corn Dance, Eagle Dance, and Booger Dance. Even after public ceremonials had ceased to be performed, in the late nineteenth and early twentieth century, dancing was a regularly scheduled event, and this remained so in to the 1930s. Presently dancing is publicly performed at events such as the Cherokee Indian Fair by the Big Cove Dancers. Another dance group, the Warriors of AniKituhwa, recreates dances of the eighteenth century; they have performed at events in the United States as well as abroad.[102]

Solomon Bird stated in a 1986 Fading Voices interview that people "danced but not all the time. It was for a reason when they did dance—sometimes to be renewed . . . They didn't dance for the fun of it." He further commented that "there were different types of dances for each occasion. They danced first, and they would all sit down to discuss whatever they had to take care of. These were principal members of the medicine men—the wise and powerful in mind men." He concluded by saying that "dance was the important event in the past. It prevented troubles and war among the people."[103] Consultants have stated that both "social" and "religious" dances would be performed in the course of an event.[104]

The most comprehensive study of Cherokee dance is *Cherokee Dance and Drama* (1951), by Frank G. Speck and Leonard Broom, in collaboration with Will West Long. Will West Long was a resident of the Big Cove community who throughout his life was involved with the preservation of Cherokee culture as both participant and observer. Sources have attributed the cessation of the Green Corn Dance to Will West Long's death in 1947.[105] Fogelson cited their book as "an essential outline of the traditional Cherokee ceremonial cycle."[106] It contains collected versions of cultural narratives, an igawesdi (formula), and individual Cherokee dance choreography.

Over half a century later it remains the most detailed discussion of Cherokee dance yet published. Speck and Broom remarked that they wished to "detail the surviving forms of dance and ritual" particularly among residents of Big Cove for the twenty years previous to the publication of the book. While the record was "made too late . . . to achieve a full and rounded account of Cherokee ceremonial life," based on "the speed with which the aboriginal culture is fading," even in that span of two decades much had changed.[107]

According to the authors, "from the beginning of missionary contact early in the nineteenth century until the present, both native and white religious workers among the Cherokee have regarded the dances as competitive systems and treated them as curious practices of ignorant savages to be derided, as symptoms of idolatrous behavior to be challenged, or as a system of decadent revelry and a focus of infection for the forces of sin equated with the forces of intemperance." They argued that "in the combined dance and drama, obscured religious motives are undoubtedly present, but they are no more important than artistic conventions. Surely they are less important in the direct consciousness of the participants and spectators than are the aesthetic and the dramatic elements." In discussing the "heavy dependence on one informant," Will West Long, Speck and Broom stated superciliously that "the people, at least in this late stage of acculturation, are the laity, not unlike the mannikins of a performance who play their parts under the manipulations of the master."[108]

They continued:

> Cherokee ritual dance performance includes some of the aims of a dramatic exhibition. It is only from the leaders—the self-appointed cult of the learned—that deeper meanings and spiritual motives may be discovered, as Dr. Olbrechts found in his study of medicine song formulas and medicine men. The wise men of the dance songs and the dance singers and leaders appear to be also the medicine men, for those chiefly responsible for Cherokee survivals are not narrow specialists in aboriginal lore. West Long himself was an example of this bilateral profession.

One summary statement they offered was that "in general, the dances reveal an equilibrium between the Cherokee and their environment, both animate and inanimate."[109]

The only exception to this was "tsu`nigădu'lĭ," "many persons faces covered over," or what in English is conventionally termed the "Booger Dance." About this dance they noted, "In the Booger Dance the equilibrium is precarious. We make bold to interpret its function in this way: by relating the invasion of the white man to the spiritual forces of nature with which the Cherokee aboriginally learned to cope, the potency of the threat is somehow lessened."[110] This particular dance has been the subject of quite a bit of scholarship.[111]

Not surprisingly, the most detailed account of ball game dancing is in *Cherokee Dance and Drama* as well; the book included schematic diagrams of dances in addition to detailed descriptions. An all-night ball dance, preliminary dances, and a Victory dance were all once part of the anetso complex. The ball game dances were opportunities for other members of the towns to actively participate in the complex and to support their team.

The "Ballplayers' Dance" the night before the game was known by two Cherokee names: "dä`tselä`nūni:", 'things transformed'" and "dane`ksi: natani:", 'they are going to put the things on their buttocks.'"[112] The second name referred to what Speck and Broom said was a former custom of attaching a tail pendant made of feathers (occasionally a deer tail was used) to the back of a belt. These "ornaments were symbolic of speed and strength."[113] The first name was not translated, and though Arnold van Gennep and Victor Turner would no doubt have a field day with this translation, I have not located an explanation for it.

Fogelson considered the all-night ball dance to be the "climax of the pre-game preparations" in many ways and felt that the outcome of the next day's game was thought to "depend heavily on the effectiveness with which these proceedings are carried out."[114] Speck, Broom, and Long provided an extremely detailed account, upon which I cannot improve. I will note that during the dance there are sections in which players line up and advance toward the "enemy," complete with call-and-response led by the *Talala* (see below). At one point in the dance they also "go through motions of catching and throwing the ball."[115]

5. "náwohdi," "nah wa ti," or "nv wo ti"; "medicine":[116] Cherokee people historically have made use of a staggering number of indigenous plants to make "medicine." A 1975 publication coauthored by Mary Chiltoskey, a longtime resident and schoolteacher on the Qualla Boundary, compiled a list from historical source material and thirty years of interviews; the index listed over one thousand plants.[117] One particularly knowledgeable individual who aided the authors was Hester Lambert Reagan, who died in 1986 at the age of 102.[118] The Cherokee Indian Fair regularly held contests in which people would display plants and provide names and explanations for their uses, and the archives of the Museum of the Cherokee Indian has an undated typed list of one year's results. Reagan won first place that year with a total of 216 plants, five more than the second-place finisher, Ethel McCoy.[119]

In his 1891 publication *Sacred Formulas of the Cherokees*, James Mooney

FIGURE 3.1. "Ceremony, Pre–Ball Game Dance 1888." From a series of photographs in which players and other community members presumably staged a ball game dance for James Mooney to photograph. Note how several players are looking toward the camera with their arms crossed, suggesting this is between official "takes." (National Anthropological Archives, Smithsonian Institution, Negative #1044-a [formerly called Negative #1039a], Inventory #06217900; photograph by James Mooney.

FIGURE 3.2. "Pre–Ball Game Dance, 1946." Players and Carl Standingdeer demonstrate the ballplayers' pregame dance for the camera. This unpublished photograph is from the same series shot by Loomis Dean for the 1946 *Life* magazine photo essay. The composition of the photograph recalls the 1888 photographs taken by Mooney of a similarly staged demonstration (see previous figure). Note the "chiefing" regalia worn by Standingdeer; he was an early practitioner of this interaction with tourists. (© Christopher Dean / Photo: Loomis Dean.)

took a sampling of twenty-five plants and their uses and compared it to the United States Dispensatory.[120] He determined that seven, or about one-third, were found to be "actually possessing medical virtues, while the remaining two-thirds are inert, if not positively injurious."[121] He dismissed a number of unnamed herbs because they were not listed in the dispensatory and remarked that it was "absurd to suppose that the savage, a child in intellect, has reached a higher development in any branch of science than has been attained by the civilized man."[122]

Mooney concluded that "Cherokee medicine is an empiric development of the fetich [sic] idea," with an operative principle of "the doctrine of signatures"; his contemporary Sir James George Frazer classed it as "homeopathic magic," operating on the principle of the "Law of Similarity."[123] Frazer remarked in *The Golden Bough* (1922) that Cherokee people were "adepts in practical botany of the homeopathic sort," citing Mooney's discussion of how "Cherokee ballplayers wash themselves" with a decoction of catgut "to toughen their muscles."[124]

Players who wanted an extra edge might bathe themselves in "decoctions" made from a variety of substances to improve performance.[125] The small rush known as catgut, the wild crabapple, and the ironwood tree were three such substances. The rush was said to resist trampling, always standing erect; bathing with it made players' "muscles tough like the root of the plant." The crabapple tree was said to always keep its trunk off the ground "even when thrown down" by its spreading top.

Players rubbed decoctions into their limbs to achieve advantageous properties; they made themselves slippery by using chewed slippery elm, sassafras bark, or eel skin. Likewise players might rub each limb with the fore and hind legs of a turtle to gain the stout legs of that animal. In order to "make themselves more supple," players also might whip themselves with a particular grass (star grass) or a switch made from the bark of a hickory sapling grown bent because of a fallen log. After being scratched for the first time a player might eat a bit of a rattlesnake prepared by a conjurer with the aim of rendering "himself an object of terror to his opponents."[126] Finally, during games players were allowed to drink a "sour preparation made from green grapes and wild crabapples."[127]

As noted above in the section on conjuring, there are terms that designate a conjurer's particular knowledge of medicine separate from or in conjunction with other abilities; two terms designating specific abilities are "gosʌsgi náwohdi ('he-made medicine')" and didanvwisgi. Such individuals prepare medicinal substances that patients ingest or apply to the exterior of the body, often in conjunction with amohi atsvsdi (going to water), recitation of *idi:gawé:sdi,* or scratching. Ball players historically have chewed substances such as particular roots and applied these to the ceremonial scratches (described below).

Whatever one might believe about the efficacy of these plants, either physically, psychologically, or otherwise, there were Cherokee people who used such plants throughout the twentieth century, and certain individuals continue to do so at present, along with using pharmaceutically manufactured and approved substances.

6. *sunikta diktati* or *adela diktati* ("examining with the beads");[128] **divination:** Divination can be performed in a number of different ways; there are techniques that are general knowledge and others that are only known to conjurers. Divination is utilized to predict future events and to locate lost persons or objects. It can be part of a ceremony for future good health, and certain conjurers have the ability to ascertain the course of future events. There are accounts of divinatory techniques utilizing water, fire, and certain crystals, or "ulûñsû´tï" ("it is transparent") stones.[129] The most prevalent method in ball game divination is sunikta diktati or adela diktati, "examining with the beads." The strongest players are chosen for the game in this way, and the outcome of the game is divined, in some cases down to the play-by-play action.[130] Several consultants over the years have discussed divination with me in some detail, but I have never seen the actual procedure performed.

7. "*de´tsinuga´skû*"; "scratching"[131] **(or scarification):** Mooney reported that James Adair in 1775 had made note of the practice. Utilized as an aid in curing maladies of various sorts, it can be done with several different implements including "a rattlesnake's tooth, a brier, a flint, or a piece of glass . . . in accordance with the mythologic theory." At one time many small children were scratched at certain times for various reasons, as were people with certain illnesses.[132] Various mental, physical, and spiritual benefits have been attributed to this practice.

Fogelson said that Cherokee people believe "periodic blood-letting to be a healthy practice, since it removes 'bad blood' from the system."[133] He noted its various uses in the Southeast, including as punishment, to treat rheumatism, and to increase stamina and avoid fatigue when running. He termed it a "highly elaborated rite" among the Cherokee, involving "a specialist to perform the operation and to recite ceremonial prayers, a special scratching device, and the use of herbal medicines to bathe the wounds."[134]

Scratching also was associated with green corn ceremonialism, as Anna Gambold's July 26, 1808, entry in the Moravian mission diary explained. Two Cherokee guests would eat potatoes, but they did not want to eat corn because they had not been *scratched*. Each year before they begin eating the new corn, this operation is carried out by the headman for the old and young who belong to his family. Using a sharp fish bone, he makes scratches over the chest and back crosswise, on the arms and legs, however, in long stripes, so that they become completely bloody. After this is done, a family dance follows, and then they begin to eat the new corn happily. This is also what happens when they eat the first fresh beans in the year. Indeed, in this case, a good medicine and a day of fasting are supposed to do the same thing with respect to their health.[135]

Though other items can be used, the most prevalent tool for scratching ball players is the *kanuga*, an instrument (often with seven points) made of wood and bone splinters, usually turkey.[136] Bamboo briers, rattlesnake fangs, bear's teeth or claws, turkey quills, and deer and fox bones also have been reported.[137] Fogelson linked the use of the turkey bone scratcher to the version of the "Ball Game between the Animals and Birds" that Lloyd Sequoyah dictated to him. In this version Turtle, Wild Turkey, and a few other animals boasted about how humans would use their body parts to succeed in future ball games. Turkey said that if they used his bones to scratch, it would "make the fastest runner you've ever seen. I don't give up when I go running up the mountain."[138]

According to Mooney, the "regular method" of scratching for ball players was as follows: "to draw the scratcher four times down the upper part of each arm, thus making twenty-eight scratches each about 6 inches in length, repeating the operation on each arm below the elbow and on each leg above and below the knee. Finally, the instrument is drawn across the breast from the two shoulders so as to form a cross; another curving stroke is made to connect the two upper ends of the cross and the same pattern is repeated on the back, so that the body is thus gashed in nearly three hundred places. Although very painful for a while, as may well be supposed, the scratches do not penetrate deep enough to result [in serious injury]."[139]

Several consultants discussed scratching, providing corroborative comments about the practice energizing players for the game, players not being allowed to play if they stepped off the rock during the operation (in Big Cove), and the fact that players were not always scratched in preparation for a particular contest but rather were scratched as needed during practices and immediately before a game.[140] According to Fogelson, Big Cove players had to stand on a naturally bleached rock by a stream and face east, the direction associated with the color red and success.[141]

FIGURE 3.3.
"Ball Game n.d." In this photograph illustrating the practice of scarification, Standing Water, an "assistant," scratches Wolftown player Jim Johnson. Johnson is wearing the old-style breechclout, and marks from the kanuga are visible. Close inspection of the photo reveals that some scratches are bleeding. (National Anthropological Archives, Smithsonian Institution Negative #1042, Inventory #06217900; photograph by James Mooney.)

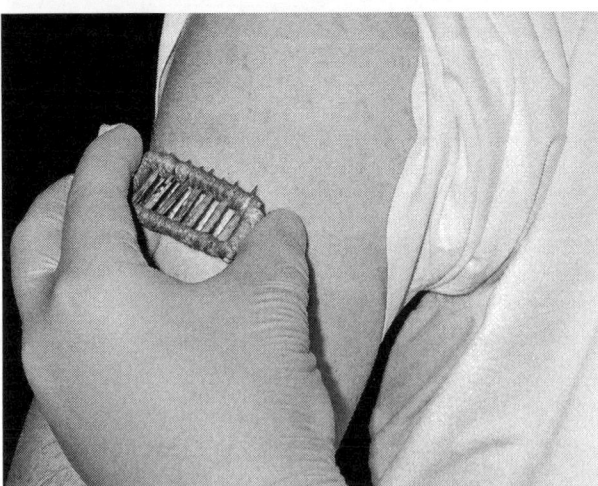

FIGURE 3.4.
Scarifier. The author holds a kanuga up to his arm to illustrate how the instrument is used. The sides of the kanuga are being squeezed, and its seven points are protruding out. (Catalogue no. E130488, Department of Anthropology, Smithsonian Institution; photograph by author.)

Presently this practice is not always evident, yet the possibility of it being used is ever present. During the 2000 Cherokee Indian Fair, Big Cove and Wolftown were scheduled to play their first exhibition scrimmage in many years. Though these were not match games in the fullest sense of the term, on the day of the game several of the players from Wolftown appeared at the edges of the field with one row of four scratches on their upper left chests. Some, but not all, players appeared to have another comb rake on their right upper back. Instead of the scheduled match, they played a scrimmage amongst themselves. In 2001, in preparation for match games that once again did not occur, some Wolftown players were scratched once again; one vertical scratch was visible on the breast of some players.

8. "gaktûñ'ta" ("prohibition" or "injunction")[142]**; dietary and physical contact prohibitions:** Prohibitions typically have been observed during convalescence, and certain prohibitions have been associated with warfare as well as the anetso ceremonial complex. Most important, players were forbidden to have physical contact with women before the match, beginning as early as twenty-eight days before and continuing seven days after the match.[143] If a woman touched a ball stick on the eve of a game it was "rendered unfit for use"; Mooney noted that in the past "vengeance" and "punishment" had been the penalties for such infractions. A player with a pregnant wife was not allowed to participate, as he had lost strength that had gone to the child, and as a result was "heavy and sluggish in his movements." Infants also were not to be touched, and young birds or animals were not allowed to be eaten, for fear that contact with their characteristic brittle bones would result in an early injury. Likewise frog meat was avoided.[144]

The meat of a rabbit was not eaten because of that animal's tendency to become "easily alarmed and liable to lose its wits when pursued by a hunter."[145] The fish called the hogsucker was not to be consumed, on account of its sluggishness; nor were specific greens including *"atûnka,"* or lamb's-quarter, whose stalks are easily broken. Salt and hot foods were not allowed; Mooney said this was in line with "medical gaktûnta."[146] In another article unrelated to the ball game he explained that these two things were usually prohibited when treating illness.[147]

In addition to discussing the *gaktvda* regarding food and drink, Fogelson provided information on spittle disposal. Traditionally, saliva was considered as essential a fluid as blood, and if captured by the opposition the conjurer could "perform ceremonies over it to render the player helpless during the game."[148] Discarded cigarette butts, tobacco spittle, or a recently bitten plug of tobacco were all fertile sources for saliva, so players were forbidden to smoke, chew tobacco, or dip snuff and literally were warned to watch where they spit.

Perhaps most extensive were the prohibitions concerning contact with women, particularly sexual intercourse, which Fogelson termed the "most important taboo of all." Players were to abstain "at least seven days before . . . and . . . four or seven days after the game, depending on the date of the victory celebration." Fogelson included an account of a player active in the early 1960s who disregarded the female avoidance prohibition and was weak and ineffective in the contest. He agreed with Mooney that men whose wives were pregnant or menstruating were considered unavoidably weakened and were "usually not permitted to play or take part in the regular ceremonies." However, contrary to what Mooney reported, Fogelson's sources told him an expectant father could play if he underwent special ceremonial preparation, but he was not expected to last long in the game. Under no circumstances were women to touch the ball sticks, for if they did "their power would be dissipated and new sticks would have to be obtained."[149]

According to Fogelson, who referenced the cultural narrative of *Nvyanvwi*, or Stone Coat, in his explanation, "Menstrual blood is considered a very dangerous and debilitating substance by Cherokee men."[150] In this narrative, a monstrous being male warriors cannot subdue is weakened by seven menstruating women and then captured and burned to death.[151] Recent works have examined Cherokee notions of menstruation in some depth; suffice to say here that while Fogelson's viewpoint is widely accepted, more recently some scholars have highlighted the positive, powerful, and creative aspects of the blood.[152] By some accounts, as Stone Coat died he taught the Cherokee their medicinal formulas and sang hunting songs. In his ashes people found red *wodi* paint that once applied gave them what they prayed for, and an *ulvsvti*, or divining stone.[153]

Alcohol was strictly prohibited during training. Players who were caught drinking were disqualified; Fogelson said that in 1958 two potential players suffered this fate.[154] Players would typically fast from the evening preceding the all-night ball play dance until the morning, when they were fed cold unseasoned corn bread and "tepid parched corn soup."[155] It bears mentioning in advance of my discussion in Chapter 5 that according to Fogelson, "parched corn meal was the standard ration of the Cherokee war party during the 18th century."[156]

Fogelson himself felt the attention to detail in observing these gaktvda was lacking during his observations. Players made token attempts, but in his opinion did not believe in the underlying principles as anything more than superstition:

> The ball game ritualism seems more intact than some other areas of native magic, but subtle signs seem to indicate that erosive forces of disbelief are already far advanced. The system of ball player taboos is still given lip service, but the general trend seems to be one of gradual relaxation of restrictions . . . at least outwardly, the players manifest a reverent attitude toward the rituals. However, one gets the feeling that the performing of these rituals has lost much of its compulsive rigidity and grounding in a viable belief structure. More often than not the rituals seem to be performed as matters of empty form rather than as acts of faith.[157]

Yet Fogelson did interview at least one person who recalled past violations of the sexual taboo, for instance, and believed the results to have proven out the indiscretion.[158]

Fogelson described "the erosive forces of disbelief" at work among players, and there certainly is evidence to support his view. Yet I have found the opposite to be true among at least some players. Some players I encountered abstained from alcohol in preparation for the games and during the days of the Fall Festival, but it is impossible to say with certainty how all players behaved.

In 1999 I observed an interesting correlation between this restriction and current efforts to educate people about drug and alcohol abuse. A poster on the wall in the exhibition building at the Cherokee Ceremonial Grounds featured the Wolftown ball team. The poster read "RESPECT TRADITION—PLAY YOUR GAME SUBSTANCE FREE" and had pictures of the boys playing, surrounding a team picture of the men.[159] Tradition and prohibition thus were linked symbolically in support of substance abuse education.

Regarding avoidance of women, I observed the behavior of a consultant and then asked for an interpretation on two occasions. The first happened in 1998 when I introduced him to a female Cherokee friend. He very politely greeted her without shaking her hand, which she had momentarily outstretched. When I remarked on this avoidance later to him, he confirmed that one did not know what the woman might bring that could affect his play the next day.

In October 2000 I advised my wife as we went to see this person that he might not want to shake her hand, and I explained why. But, to my surprise, he extended his hand and shook hers. When I asked about this later he said out of respect for me, and for her, he had shaken her hand.

He also mentioned, however, that since she was not Native American the issue of her being "contagious" was a moot point. I understood him to mean that she did not have the belief system to support such activity. In any case, he was a driver the next day and did not play; though he certainly came into contact with other players.[160] I cannot say how other players acted, but I think it is fair to assume at least a small percentage of the players maintain such a restriction.

One elderly consultant told me about a certain well-known woman of one community who would spread a concoction along the trail the opposition would take to the contest. She was a conjurer and apparently would perform this action when menstruating. This same individual told of a teammate who was unable to ward off an illness because he did not heed the conjurer's direction to go to water in the week after the contest.[161]

All players participate as a team in some of the activities of the ceremonial complex. The activities discussed above are related to how a player conducts himself when he is not at practice. As I will discuss below, all team members go to water after attending practice; as I noted above, scratching sometimes is performed if the occasion warrants.

9. Fasting: At one time, people would fast in preparation for the Green Corn Ceremony. Players traditionally fast from after dinner the night before a game until after its completion. Women who participated in the all-night dance also traditionally fasted.

10. Marching: The movements of the teams to the field and then to the center ground are ritualized. Each team has a man specially chosen, called the Talala (red-headed woodpecker), who cries out, and his team answers with "whoops," a type of affirmative call.[162] Both teams do this while advancing in a four-part movement to the center of the field.

Now You Don't See it, Now You Do: Amohi atsvsdi, "going to water"

This ritual has been remarkably durable through periods of great cultural change, and at present it is the only one to my knowledge that Cherokee people perform in public on a regular basis, yearly during the fair. Furthermore, as I noted above, amohi atsvsdi illustrates a noteworthy public/private dichotomy in Cherokee ritual practice that is relevant to contemporary scholarly discourse about both secrecy and ethnographic method, particularly with regard to issues of propriety. Thus, I argue that the example of going to water illuminates an important distinction between cultural privacy and secrecy that can inform broader disciplinary discussions. For the purpose of tracing continuity and change since the late nineteenth century, in what follows I will present a three-period comparative description of going to water, juxtaposing James Mooney's late nineteenth-century and Raymond Fogelson's mid-twentieth-century accounts with my own from the turn of the twenty-first century.

Throughout the night of the ball game dance and intermittently in the weeks preceding the ball play, immediately before, and following its conclusion, the conjurer would take the team to a nearby river or stream. The conjurer would line the players up on the bank and begin to recite a formula while "examining the beads." Often red and black beads were employed, representing the team and their opponents, respectively.

The day of the contest involved going to water multiple times. At sunrise the players began their march to the ball ground and halted four times. At each stop, every player went to water individually with the conjurer. As Mooney noted, this took quite a bit of time.

The games were held midway between competing settlements, so often the trip was several miles. Thus the games usually did not start until the early afternoon.[163] Mooney reported a past custom no longer in force at that time that forbade players to sit down on anything but the ground during these trips, or even to lean on anything but a fellow player.[164]

Reaching the ball ground, the players moved to a sheltered area by the river to strip down and be scratched. After each player had been scratched, he plunged in the water and washed off the blood.[165] They then dressed for the game and were ready to go to water for the final time before the match.

Mooney published an example of a formula used to take players to water the last time before they play and included a contextual explanation. This example is a good one because it includes the elements of conjuring and divination. He noted that the conjurer, in selecting an appropriate spot, chose "a bend of the river where he can look toward the east while facing upstream." All the players lined up together on the bank, "side by side looking down upon the water, with their ball sticks clasped upon their breasts."[166]

The conjurer stood behind them, and an assistant laid out a red cloth and a black cloth, with a corresponding number of "sacred beads" of like colors on each cloth. The conjurer picked up one red bead, to represent one player on his team, and one black bead, to represent his opposite number on the opposing team. He then recited a formula in which the Long Man ("Yûwĭ Gûnahi′ta . . . the sacred name for the river") is the first of several beings—the Red Bat, Red Deer, Red Hawk, and Red Rattlesnake are the others—to whom the "shaman prays on behalf of his client" or who are beseeched to aid the player. He asked them to bestow victory as well as particular characteristics upon that individual player, who was identified by name and clan.[167]

Next the conjurer symbolically raised his clients individually to Galvladi ("above," "on high," "the world above"), frequently translated in English as the "seventh heaven"; referenced in my discussion of Cherokee cultural narratives, it is conceptualized as a place of honor, holiness, and safety.[168] The conjurer then asked for the individual's "most dreaded rival" and subsequently beseeched beings such as the Black Fog, Black Spider, and Black Rattlesnake to conspire to remove the soul of the man to the Darkening Land in the west, "never to reappear." As the conjurer finished reciting the formula, he often simultaneously stomped a black bead representing a particularly feared opposing player into the ground. At this moment "each man dips his ball sticks into the water and bringing them up, touches his lips; then stooping again he dips up the water in his hand and laves his head and breast."[169]

In addition, after the game, "the winning players immediately go to water again with their shamans and perform another ceremony for the purpose of turning aside the revengeful incantations of their defeated rivals."[170] Mooney did not mention a victory dance or a related postmatch going-to-water proscription.

FOGELSON

Fogelson noted that the practice of going to water appeared throughout the anetso cycle. The players were taken to water in advance of issuing or accepting a challenge, and "twice daily, in the morning and the evening, for a week or for four days prior to a game."[171] They went to water during the all-night ball dance, during the march to the ball field, at the "stripping off place" (as with Mooney's account, a sheltered place by the river), immediately after the game, and at the victory dance a week later.[172]

The players would go to water with the conjurer in the morning before breakfast. According to Fogelson they would drink an emetic, which removed phlegm, built up a player's wind, and combated conjured spittle. In addition, "notions of purification through the removal of dangerous 'germs' [da.tsu or tsga.yi] are associated with the vomiting exercise."[173]

Fogelson also described the going-to-water activity performed during intermissions of the all-night ball dance, described below. In this case the players would go in groups of seven, with the strongest seven going as the first group. Weaker ball players would go more frequently, and the formula was repeated four times each time they went. During these night trips players dipped their ball sticks, laved their faces and breasts, and drank some of the water.[174]

FIGURE 3.5. "Players Going to Water." Players and conjurer demonstrate "going to water" for *Life* magazine photo essay by Loomis Dean, 1946. As with the previous Dean photograph (fig. 3.2), this is being staged for the camera. The players are employing the laving technique rather than immersion. The caption for the photograph read: "Invocation to gods is made before the game. The players dip their stickball rackets in the waters of the Oconaluftee River, ask victory for their team." ("Cherokee Stickball," *Life*, November 11, 1946, 92; © Christopher Dean / Photo: Loomis Dean.)

ZOGRY

Again, presently to my knowledge, the postgame amohi atsvsdi at the Cherokee Indian Fair is one of the few Cherokee ritual activities done in public. I am aided in my effort to parse the complicated nature of these elements by the work of a number of theorists, but here I must point to Milton Singer's seminal characterization of "cultural performance" as an activity in which people "thought of their culture as encapsulated in these discrete performances which they could exhibit to visitors and to themselves."[175]

Ahaquo! 135

While the ball game itself is presented to tourist audiences and routinely interpreted and reported as an isolated and complete activity, additional components of the ceremonial complex are performed in private, including other instances of going to water. In the three to four weeks preceding the scheduled contests, ball teams go to water as a group after practices; after the games, and a week later, at a team event they go as well. Throughout this time they may also go individually if so instructed.

I have attended several practices, and tagged along with the players as they went to water after games. In 1998, I asked and received permission to film one team going to water after the last game of the fair. In both types of situations, at practices and after the games, they clearly did not go to water for the benefit of tourists. At the practices I attended I was one of the only people there who was not a member of the local community. There were some people staying at the campground who stopped and watched the action for awhile, but most were relatives and friends of team members. When practice was finished the players, led by the team manager, went to a stream in the woods at one edge of the field. Respecting their privacy I did not follow, and the stream is not visible from the field; but simply observing their drenched bodies when they emerged from the woods about ten minutes later told me they had gone to water.

At the fair, most of the tourists who had just watched the teams play had no idea that the players made their way across the street and down a small incline to the Oconaluftee River. However, as the players made their way across the street backed up with traffic it was no secret where they were going either. The river is clearly visible from the road, and indelibly etched in my mind are the looks of puzzlement from car passengers as they slowly made their way down the street and caught a glance of the team performing the ritual. Because the river is not hidden, anyone who might happen to be around could see them.

Though I observed some players splashing and joking, all players observed seemed to dunk themselves four times before they engaged in horseplay or left the water. Some rubbed water on the backs and arms of their teammates as well. A line of backed-up traffic on this busy weekend made for a captive audience, and fishermen down the river a bit no doubt wondered what was happening. Many observers, if they happened to recognize them as ball players, probably thought they just were washing off from the game.

Herein lies the important distinction between the occasions I observed. The numerous times the players go to water before the contest they do so in private. According to my consultants, this last time the players go to water, in public, is unlike all the other occasions, as the action washes away all the medicine and conjuring that were part of the anetso complex.[176] This explains both why I was allowed to film it and why it can be done in a public location.

A profoundly meaningful activity, going to water might be mistaken for an everyday swim by uninformed observers; yet several otherwise careful scholars have characterized it as a "magical" or "mystical" practice in addition to noting its ritual nature. In his 1994 book *American Indian Lacrosse: Little Brother of War*, former senior ethnomusicologist at the Smithsonian Institution Thomas Vennum Jr. was on less-than-solid ground when he presented the view that in order to "penetrate the Indian game, one must enter a world of spiritual belief and magic."[177] He continued in dramatic fashion, "the magic is still there in the Indian game, but it is just under the surface, easily overlooked by the unsuspecting."[178] Vennum did not explain what he meant by "magic," but as the comment above illustrates, magic was equated with "spiritual belief" in some kind of hazy amalgam that titillated the reader's imagination with thoughts of the "other" and his or her mysterious ways.

James Mooney also resorted to similarly evocative language when describing the practice to his readers. He noted that during the all-night dance that preceded match games, the conjurer and an assistant would take players "to a retired spot at the river's bank, where they perform the mystic rite known as 'going to water.'"[179]

In thinking about these portrayals of their subject matter, I was reminded of a comment Tomoko Masuzawa made in her essay entitled "Culture" for the book *Critical Terms for Religious Studies*.[180] Masuzawa asserted that scholars who studied other cultures yearned for a particular reward from their inquiries: "Thus, over and above the chastely scientific purpose of research, there is room for the student of culture to hope that any given culture, however alien and idiosyncratic some of its constitutive elements might appear, could in the end be saying something, imparting a secret message, a forgotten promise, perhaps even a hidden anecdote of destiny."[181]

Disjunctions and tensions exist between what people *want to know* and what other people *want to tell them*, as well as between what people *want to hear* and *what they are told* by other people. Such issues create an interface between my own work and the contemporary scholarship regarding the concepts of secrecy and privacy by such scholars as Paul Johnson, Michael F. Brown, Hugh Urban, D. Michael Lindsay, and Michael Barkun, as well as key earlier works by Vine Deloria Jr., Murray L. Wax, Luther H. Martin, Hans G. Kippenberg, and Guy G. Stroumsa.[182] In a 1991 article, Vine Deloria Jr. noted: "In the old traditional ways of most tribes, knowledge of the ceremonies, dreams, and messages received in vision quests were a private affair.... Religious knowledge was a strictly private affair. An individual had knowledge because higher powers intended that he or she have this knowledge; it was not for distribution to the masses simply because it was a nice message because this knowledge imposed duties and responsibilities on the individual who was so chosen."[183]

Here Deloria made plain the key distinction between privacy and secrecy. The knowledge was not to be distributed because it "imposed duties and responsibilities on the individual." Conversely, in Deloria's explanation there was no admonition to "keep it secret"; Deloria did not even mention that concept. The strategy Deloria explains accords agency to those indigenous peoples who are and have been for centuries actively working to maintain and transmit information within communities irrespective of extrasocietal fluctuations.

Now I do not assert that Deloria was or should be the arbiter of what are "the old traditional ways of most tribes" and what characteristics that statement implies. I readily admit that this concept is debatable and at least somewhat problematic. But in my opinion these generalizations, which Deloria employed to make his point, do not divest his statements of their significance with regard to current academic discussions. I contend, following Deloria, that the notion of "secrecy" is dependent upon an a priori cultural assumption: religious knowledge (substitute "experience of the sacred" if desired), if it is genuine, is something to be shared.

Thus an important distinction between privacy and secrecy is articulated. In this regard, in my opinion the category "cultural privacy" suggested by Michael F. Brown is applicable not only to discussion of the Cherokee religious system, but to more global discourse in the discipline of religious studies.[184] Brown commented that "cultural privacy is defined as the right of possession of a culture—especially possessors of a native culture—to shield themselves from unwanted scrutiny. A right to cultural privacy is presented as self-evident and morally unassailable, even if its scope remains unspecified."[185]

This is a particularly relevant issue both historically and at present for First Nations communities, as for hundreds of years they have confronted an odd combination of a United States governmental program of quasi-legal cultural suppression and what today is known as "ethnotourism." While such overt governmental suppression is no longer an issue, religious freedom continues to be an ongoing process for First Nations in the United States. Furthermore, with regard to ethnotourism and its academic and religious counterparts, the ceaseless migration pattern of a gaggle of gawkers, hawkers, and talkers (I include myself in this group) has continued unabated.

This view echoes that by Murray L. Wax, who argued that there are "no statutory provisions for protecting ritual secrets," though there are "provisions to protect commercial secrets as well as limited protection of the communications between some professionals (lawyers, physicians, priests) and their clients."[186] As a result, in the United States (and many European countries) while there are legal protections for conversations with one's lawyer, doctor, or religious leader, and the exact formulas or recipes for such products consumed by millions daily as Coca-Cola Classic and Kentucky Fried Chicken remain safely locked in vaults, there are no legal protections for "ritual secrets" or cultural privacy.

As I stated at the beginning of this section, amohi atsvsdi illustrates a noteworthy public/private dichotomy in Cherokee ritual practice. In terms of the Cherokee religious system, I argue that this traditional public/private structure has contributed to the continuation of amohi atsvsdi through periods of great cultural change, though this notion remains to be explored more fully. The title of this section references the artificial mystification of this activity by certain scholars and the relationship between this type of interpretation, a priori assumptions, and cultural propriety. It is in this regard that going to water might prove to be a useful example in broader disciplinary discussions of secrecy as well as ethnographic method.

Features of the Contemporary Religious Landscape of the Eastern Band of Cherokee Indians

Many if not most members of the Qualla Boundary community are active Christians and avid churchgoers, and for this segment of the population identity in many ways revolves around the house of worship. The scholarship attesting to the acculturation and Christianization of the Eastern Band is extensive.[187] Cherokee hymns and preaching in Cherokee are elements in some congregations; though in the majority they are not.

In 1966 Harriet Kupferer listed twenty-one churches on the Qualla Boundary: "15 Baptist churches . . . 3 Methodist, 1 Pentecostal Holiness, 1 Catholic, and 1 Episcopal."[188] Laurence French estimated that there were "a dozen or so Baptist churches and one Methodist church serving the Eastern Band prior to World War II" and listed twenty-seven in 1978, including Church of the Latter-day Saints and Church of God congregations and six additional Baptist churches.[189] Twenty-one churches (eleven of them Baptist) are listed on a fact sheet about the town of Cherokee included in educational materials distributed by the Museum of the Cherokee Indian.[190] Absent from the list is the Latter-day Saints church located on the edge of the Qualla Boundary, which counts as members Cherokee individuals as well as local non-Cherokee businessman and educators.

With regard to the religious affiliations of conjurers, Raymond Fogelson has said in reference to the Eastern Cherokee that "as far as can be ascertained, all of today's conjurers consider themselves to be good Christians and feel that their work is completely consistent with Christian doctrine. The importance of faith and the power of prayer are fully recognized by the conjurer."[191] I respectfully disagree with this opinion.

In my experience, while Fogelson's view holds true to a large extent, there do exist individuals who strongly reject any assumption of Christianity on their part, and do not attend Christian worship services other than out of respect for family events. These individuals continue to refer to the "Creator" instead of "God."[192] Granted, these people make up a minority of the total population, but conjurers are already a small minority in the Cherokee population.

Such individuals display similar approaches to that of Will West Long, who in addition to working with Frank Speck and Leonard Broom was a Cherokee consultant for Mooney, Frans Olbrechts, and John Witthoft, among others. Witthoft reported that "Will had never been a church member, and I understood him to say that he had never been christened, despite the fact that his father was a Baptist lay preacher. He was, of course, raised by his mother. He once told me of how many of the older men had very unwillingly become Christians because of the constant pressuring from their daughters. He said he would never give in to the churches."[193]

That being said, I have met a conjurer who believes God and Christ act through him or her. In this case, the individual engages in many of the same activities as non-Christian individuals, but the theology involved is Christian. However, I would not rule out the fact that this individual may have wanted to put his or her activity in a context he or she thought might be more palatable for me, whether or not that was actually the case.[194] In addition, there seems to be a common strategy of merging the two systems, and most conjurers are not averse to attending church and being married and buried there as well.

Of the conjurers I have met, both living and now deceased, I would say the following: I have met at least one who rejected Christianity outright. There have been three or four who combined the activities of conjuring with Christian practice to some degree, from mostly Christian to mostly not. One has openly advocated Christianity; and two or three have an unknown affiliation.

Today there are certainly more conjurers who live on or near the Qualla Boundary than those I have referenced, and I have heard many stories of them in peoples' lives. Based on my experience, it is likely that I have come in to contact with several more conjurers and not realized it. As I discuss in Chapter 4, the most traditional people go to great lengths not to advertise themselves, so I do not hesitate to speculate that there are others who reject Christianity outright.

In addition, as I also discuss in Chapter 4, there are those who fashion themselves as conjurers, either within the community, or more regularly, to non-Cherokee clientele. I have witnessed individuals being privately derided and ridiculed by other members of the community, though not while in their presence. Although in these instances of self-promotion derision is straightforward, in other cases such ridicule can be a backhanded compliment. A competitive spirit does exist among practitioners, and several times I have been told a certain individual was a dabbler or only concerned with harming others, only to hear the same charges being leveled at the bearer of that information.

It is important to reiterate the point from earlier in this chapter that Cherokee conjurers do not associate in societies, as is the case with ritual or medicinal specialists in other cultures. Theirs is an individual craft. Two conjurers may share knowledge if one or both deem it worthwhile, but such people definitely do not (and do not have to) advertise. In fact, many will do the opposite and reveal abilities only in situations when they feel comfortable doing so.

Conjurers reflect attitudes and beliefs of community members. In my estimation, the religious landscape of the Eastern Band of the Cherokee can, for the purposes of explanation, be imagined as a continuum or spectrum, with Christianity at one end and the Cherokee religious system on the other. There are people all along the spectrum, and based on my experience there are fewer people at the Cherokee religious system end. But there are many more individuals than one might think located all along, and such "location" is difficult to plot conclusively, for different stances might be taken based on the individual situation.

For example, there are some individuals who attend church regularly and say they reject traditional medicinal practices, yet turn to these if standard medical techniques fail. As another example, several years ago a consultant made an interesting observation. He said that several of the local non-Cherokee preachers had at one time or another become interested in conjuring. He named three preachers, at least one of whom was still active in 2000.[195]

Furthermore, several other factors must be taken into consideration. For a variety of reasons people might not want to make public, especially to a non-Cherokee researcher, adherence to traditional religious practices. In my experience such information is parted with very carefully, and often in bits and pieces. That such strategies are still in use again reflects the strength of tradition.

In terms of the Cherokee religious landscape, there are still people who have beliefs consistent with, or participate in elements of, a Cherokee religious system, yet who do so completely outside of a Christian context. A larger group of people blend many of these beliefs and behaviors with a devout Christian faith. These people, too, attest to the perseverance of Cherokee traditions in their practice, as continued consultations with medicine people and recourse to traditional remedies are intermingled with regular attendance at twice weekly church services and prayer meetings. Now the degree or percentage of one to the other, of course, varies with the individual. There also are many people who reject any perceived non-Christian beliefs or behaviors. Of course such an assignment of people to "types" ultimately is a generalization, but it can be helpful in terms of assessing trends and providing a broad outline or contour of the landscape.

In the end, it is reasonable as a general statement to say that many Cherokee people have been, and continue to be, able to harmonize the religious and social ideals of two or more cultures.[196]

Although there is no question that many Cherokee cultural activities are not practiced as frequently as they once were, presently some activities actually are undergoing a revival. If one peers just a little below the self-consciously constructed, "made-for-tourist-America" surface, one will find certain medicinal, religious, social, and artistic traditions thriving. Funeral customs still include the sit-up, or "sitting up," a practice common in other local communities. And the Cherokee Boys Club has taken over an activity once performed exclusively by community aid societies, providing coffins for individuals who request them. Such community groups also continue to dig graves in some instances.

Recourse to herbal medicine is an element few will bring up but many will discuss if asked. Even though some see it and its practitioners as not consonant with Christian beliefs, others incorporate both into their way of life. Some on the Qualla Boundary, led by an elder from one township, have revived the traditional dancing; a regular schedule of social dancing is punctuated by other events such as the Green Corn Ceremony. As noted above, participants have revived components of this ceremony, including the *osi*, or sweat bath, and reconstructed a dance ground complete with separate arbors for different clans. Some people from other townships dislike these events; they are criticized as breaches of tradition due to the presence of non–Native Americans, and in some instances, their participation.

Conjuring is an activity that has continued and has very real and serious consequences in the lives of some people. As I noted above, it also seems to have consumed many studies of the Cherokee people, both east and west. Conjuring is rejected by many Cherokee people as part of a superstitious system cast off in favor of Christianity; yet for others who do not identify themselves as Christians it continues to be part of a religious system that encompasses the totality of experience, both positive and negative. As I also noted above, most people's views lie somewhere in between.

One final type of source material offers another perspective on how at least certain Cherokee people think about the ball game and religion. Going back through some of my older files, I found two calendars published in 1997 and 1998 by the North Carolina Cooperative Extension Service. Community members staffed the local agency, and the calendars were distributed to local businesses and community members. Thus they were produced expressly for the local community. The cover of the 1997 calendar read, "Bridging Our Past With The Present, Looking Ahead . . . Looking Back," while the 1998 calendar cover read, "Continuing the Tradition. Looking Ahead . . . Looking Back."[197]

Each month's page had the names of the months and days in both Cherokee and English, and facing pages featured collages with black-and-white as well as color photographs. Every month had a thematic caption, such as, for January, the importance of elders; for February, the importance of young people gaining skills for the future; and for October, the Fall Festival as a time of homecoming and friendship. The September captions were similar as well: "Indian Stickball has been a part of our culture for generations. . . . Our youth continue the tradition at the Cherokee fall festival," and "We preserve our culture and tradition through archery, stickball, crafts, blow-gun contest, and native dance."[198] These first-person statements in calendars produced for members of the local community clearly link anetso to Cherokee identity.

The 1998 calendar had one color picture of what looked to be a recent boy's game at the fair along with black-and-white and color pictures of people demonstrating other activities. All of the pictures on the 1997 facing page featured the ball game. Included were two undated black-and-white team photographs of ball teams, one of men and one of boys, and a more recent color photograph of a young man wearing a Cherokee ribbon shirt demonstrating stick technique to three young boys.[199] The only mention of religion in either calendar was the December 1998 caption: "Religion and spirituality is an important part of the Cherokee people's lives. We are proud of the many different churches on the reservation."[200] Clearly this viewpoint highlighted the cultural significance of anetso, but just as clearly separated the ball game from "religion and spirituality."

Conclusion

In addition to my suggestions about the public/private dichotomy in the Cherokee religious system, I think two conclusions can be drawn from the data presented. First, as I discussed above, there have been changes in the complex; yet to repeat Fogelson's relevant statement from above, the "basic outline of the ceremonial cycle surrounding the game remained intact."[201] Secondly, both Mooney and I did primary research in the township of Wolftown, while Fogelson worked mostly with Big Cove residents. There are distinct differences in the two communities.

Over time, in other words, based on the comparison of the three descriptive samples of Mooney, Fogelson, and myself, the complex has maintained a relative amount of stability as a distinct and enduring cultural element. While the ball dance is apparently no longer performed, one cannot be sure it is not conducted in private, especially considering the security at such events as Mooney described. The Victory Dance apparently is no longer performed, though another type of team celebration seems to have taken its place in the cycle.

Prohibitions, related activities such as going to water and scratching, a postgame event, "doctoring," and a preparatory period of practice all were part of the complex in the first decade of the twenty-first century, much as they have been for at least the last hundred years. Generally speaking, I have seen an increase in the number of players across the Qualla Boundary in the years I have attended. In fact, in the future Wolftown may split into two teams to accommodate the number of players who have joined the team. In addition, a recent phenomenon has been the emergence of women's teams. I have not followed these teams as I have the men's. Be this a revival or the emergence of new ritual, this controversial development will be discussed in Chapter 4.

Both Wolftown and Big Cove have longstanding ball game traditions, but several differences can be observed. Based on my research, it seems that Big Cove residents and participants have been much more open with researchers about anetso ceremonialism and symbolism.[202] In examining these sources, one finds many references to the Thunder family. Wolftown residents and participants, at least the people I have met, are generally more reticent about discussing such matters. In some cases, as I described in Chapter 1, this extends to not referring to or discussing members of the Thunder family or uttering their collective name.

Based on written sources, in the past Big Cove consultants reported conjuring against the other team, as well as conjuring or doctoring for one's own side. Contemporary Wolftown consultants reported that conjuring is only employed for their team, and not against the opponent. I have not broached the subject with Big Cove consultants. The tradition of women playing anetso seems to be centered in Big Cove, though Wolftown women played ball in 2000 and 2001. This suggests that a difference of opinion exists in Wolftown; several consultants I asked about this issue said that female participation was not part of their received tradition.[203]

Cherokee men, and in more recent times Cherokee women as well, gather together on ball game practice fields and forge a commitment to the community; or perhaps as a symbol of that unity they field a ball team. The ethic of participation, the way the players carry themselves and acquit themselves on the field, the honor of performing to the best of their ability in a contest that their ancestors once played on the same land, these remain meaningful reasons to participate for Cherokee adults and teenagers.

I conclude that facets of participation in anetso are still indicative of a world view that is consistent with the Cherokee cultural narrative tradition and other traditional beliefs, and continue to be to the extent that the participants believe in the efficacy of their actions. Some participants believe strongly, and some do not. The tradition of anetso participation gets passed on in some families; in others it does not; and in still others it is picked back up after being put down for a generation or two—but it continues. Whether or not this will continue to be the case is, of course, unknown.

My experience suggests conjurers are still in the community; they are still called upon for service if the circumstances dictate; and players respect this activity when they participate in anetso. It is presumptuous to assume that players do not really "believe" in the efficacy of these actions anymore. Some do and some do not, but as in any religious community, there is no lock-step adherence to belief.[204]

Tseduga!
(Pass it to me!)

Performing the Cherokee Ball Game
in the Twentieth Century

In 1900, James Mooney concluded his "Historical Sketch" of the Cherokee with the following line: "The older people still cling to their ancient rites and sacred traditions, but the dance and the ballplay wither and the Indian day is nearly spent."[1] In 2009, despite Mooney's dire prognosis, it is clear that the sun has not set on the Eastern Band of Cherokee Nation. As I discussed in Chapter 3, while the majority of Cherokee people identify themselves as Christians, there are Cherokee individuals of various ages who adhere to selected elements of an identifiable Cherokee religious system.

As for the Cherokee ball game, or as Mooney referred to it, the ballplay, a season of regular match games between townships was the norm, concurrent with exhibition games at least until the early 1930s or 1940s (the exact time frame is a matter I will address). Presently people play it regularly two or three times a year during the annual Cherokee Fall Festival, and occasionally elsewhere. If Mooney was correct and it is in fact withering, then it is taking its own sweet time in doing so. Whether it will continue is not for me to speculate, for I hold no crystal ball. However, as I will argue in this chapter, the concept of withering, or degeneration, particularly when part of an organic metaphor, is a problematic assumption both in general and specifically with regard to anetso and the ceremonial complex.

I contend that Mooney was one in a long line of observers, both before and after him, who believed the activities and beliefs that they were encountering were on the wane. They genuinely felt that they were visiting Cherokee people in North Carolina at a critical time, and were recording information that would not be available to later researchers. Time and time again in my research I came upon observers' statements to the effect that the ball game at that time was not as it once was. These statements appeared not only in the primary literature, but in the secondary literature as well, often couched in language suggesting the sad inevitability of the situation.

I can say this with confidence not only because there is ample evidence of such attitudes in the scholarship, but because I count myself among such observers. I felt this way when I first began poking around the Qualla Boundary in 1993, and in 1997 when I began the video documentary project Enduring Voices. It slowly began to dawn on me that this was not the case. Today, sixteen years since I first began visiting the Qualla Boundary, I am more circumspect. Not surprisingly, the situation is more complex than I first imagined.

Still, such interpretations bothered me, beyond the obvious cultural determinism. Of course diachronic change is a given, but based on my research it seems to me that the prevailing opinion *at almost any given time* was that the anetso ceremonial complex was a shell of what it once was, thus evidencing degeneration and decline. In other words, if one steps back and looks at the accounts and interpretations, the ball game seems to be eternally declining. The only exceptions were when "revivals" were reported, but even in these situations the result always seemed to be on the negative side of the ledger.

As I conducted my research it became clear why observers repeatedly said that the anetso complex was in decline. They based their assessments on two generally acknowledged facts and one widely held impression: the cessation of a regular season of intertownship games, the contraction of the complex or cycle of activities, and the lack of belief in the principles underlying the complex activities. While I do not disagree with the first two points, I do wish to problematize the overall interpretation of the three assertions.

Also implicit in these assessments is a recognition that the ball game complex provided public display of selected Cherokee cultural beliefs and customs, including "religious" activity, and a determination that these beliefs and activities in general were on the wane. Observers argued that this process of degeneration is evidenced by a decrease in the actions or activities reported historically (through time) as accompanying the event; a sloughing off of elements and even, seemingly, whole structures of "meaning" and "belief." Thus the game itself was really a cultural artifact, a husk of an evolved societal behavior. In simple terms, it now was devoid of any "real" or binding significance that it once possessed.

Because the notion of degeneration is endemic in the study of First Nations cultural practices, it is important to understand what preconceptions inform it. My understanding of degeneration in the context of this discussion begins with the following assumption on the part of the observer: that he or she is able to discern possible latent meanings encoded in the form or literal meaning of a cultural activity or event. Usually there is one prevalent latent meaning observers describe that presupposes a single purpose of an event, from which the present form of the event has degenerated. Therefore acceptance of a theory of degeneration necessitates identification of an "original" purpose of the ball game.

Implicit in such formulations is the conception of some sort of ur-complex centered on an ur-game, as well as an epoch in which people "believed" more uniformly. In this regard I side with Dell Hymes's comment about performance that "there is no more an '*Ur*-performance' than there is an '*Ur*-text.'"[2] Hymes stated that it is difficult to assess when performance is, in his words, "authentic or authoritative"; in the examples he presented he said this "occurs only at a certain point or in a certain respect." This is the case "especially in an oral tradition, [where] performance is a mode of existence and realization that is partly *constitutive* of what the tradition is."[3]

I understand Hymes to mean that variation is a crucial, vital element in performance.[4] In my view there is no "original meaning" of the Cherokee ball game that is being deviated from or adhered to strictly. Hymes's theory of performance offers an alternative to prevalent historical notions about anetso that posit degeneration as the primary explanation for difference in the event and the general lessening of activities associated with it.

In many books and classrooms, religions such as Christianity, Judaism, and Islam are presented as entities that change but endure. Few if any scholars would think, for example, of characterizing the Protestant Reformation, or the Reform movement in Judaism, as degeneration, even though both resulted in a radical redefinition of ritual activity for many. On the other hand, religious traditions of First Nations peoples often continue to be portrayed as archaic, quaint, and vanishing.

Change in any culture is inevitable, and for historians change is a particularly key notion and is always assumed. In my opinion, many studies of First Nations religious systems have overly stressed degeneration and loss. James Merrell, discussing the Catawba Nation, argued that Catawba history had "something of a rollercoaster rhythm" rather "than the tragically plummeting trajectory so commonly charted."[5] I find this notion of a roller coaster rhythm useful, and I agree with Merrell that it more accurately describes the process of cultural change and continuity.

Several Cherokee consultants discussed this issue with me, and offered their own theories. Comments by some community members expressed the belief that "all the old people are gone," or all of the really powerful individuals have passed.[6] This reinforces the idea introduced above that it appears to most every generation of ethnographers as if they are arriving at the last possible moment to record information. As I said above, at times in the past

I certainly was not immune to such a conclusion, reinforced by comments like these; but there were other theories consultants discussed as well.

Another set of comments were similar but put an interesting spin on the above concept. Several consultants told me elderly people had said to them that the traditional ways would eventually fade away. This was explained as inevitable and foretold. Therefore, significantly, several consultants did not consider this development in tragic terms.[7]

One consultant's elders, however, had relayed a different message entirely. In this scenario, the metaphor of a soda bottle was used. The fat bottom of the bottle represented a time when traditions were in full bloom. As time passed, traditions would lessen bit by bit, until a time when very few would be practiced. The neck of the bottle represented this point in time, which the consultant said was the current state of affairs when we had the conversation. After a further period of time, the traditions would reemerge more strongly, practically rushing out of the bottle, so to speak.[8]

In addition to the obvious benefit to my project of having Cherokee people assessing their own culture, I find these Cherokee theories of cultural change and continuity to be compelling in other ways as well. They strip away the romantic stereotype of "the Native Americans" as anachronistic museum pieces stolidly awaiting their inevitable cultural assimilation, or in other cases helplessly bemoaning their loss of tradition. Even in this sampling of what consultants discussed with me, the diversity of opinion in the community was expressed clearly.

Taking such opinions seriously challenges scholars to undertake critical reexamination of paradigms and tropes employed in historical "narrativization" of First Nations histories. As Winnifred Sullivan has argued, drawing in part from Johannes Fabian, "History has been the way to study 'us'; anthropology or history of religions the way to study 'them.' Thus, American religion has been studied by historians, while other religions have been studied as reified ahistorical systems."[9] I too think there is a difference in how scholars portray such cultural processes.

Of course people and communities modify, combine, or even reject religious beliefs. I am not questioning that there have been serious and difficult circumstances in which particular elements of indigenous nations' religious systems have abated, lessened, or disappeared either due to forcible suppression, coercion, or pragmatism. In some cases particular elements have resurfaced or reappeared independently or in combination with elements from other religious systems.

I submit that the concepts "revitalization" and "perseverance," though both certainly accurate to some degree, nevertheless ring somewhat hollow, even romantic and patronizing, in the context of the standard frameworks or narratives of U.S. religious history. Unlike the term "perseverance," I choose to employ the term "persistence," because it "may be used in a favorable or unfavorable sense" and "implies a steadfast, unremitting continuance in spite of opposition or protest."[10] The example given in my dictionary for the unfavorable sense is as follows: "an annoying persistence in a belief."[11] "Persistence" thus is a more fluid term: indigenous North American peoples and their cultural traditions did not just persevere—they have *persisted*—like it or not, independent of any relationship with broader U.S. cultural trends, and with no necessary referent to a broader U.S. historical narrative.

The fact remains that certain Cherokee traditions or elements of the religious system are guarded very carefully. This strategy has resulted in many observers being unaware of their existence to the point of declaring Cherokee traditions to be in a state of decline. In turn, scholars who rely on these sources have accepted this conclusion as well. What I argue is that there is continuity to many indigenous traditions that in particular synchronic instances can be described in the current coin as subaltern, subterranean, or evidence of what Joel Martin called a "cultural underground." Not visible to the outside observer, no matter how dedicated or well meaning the individual might be, this strategy affects how a particular ritual, cultural narrative, or other religious element is portrayed in a diachronic framework.

Cherokee people in North Carolina have long been familiar with the tourist trade. According to historical documentation Cherokee people have been presenting or performing the ball game for nearly 150 years, and they likely have been doing so for longer. The numerous accounts I will cite throughout this chapter attest to the fact that for hundreds of years Cherokee people have presented anetso to tourists of all sorts, including visiting dignitaries, government officials, missionaries, and anthropologists. From the Duke of Orleans asking for a game to be held in the late eighteenth century to Fogelson asking for a game to be presented in the early 1960s, and many times in between and subsequently, the game has been played by request in addition to the regular games during the annual Cherokee Indian Fairs.

An interesting consideration about these games at the fair is that beyond the presentation of the game to others, Cherokee people, at least in the twentieth century, seem to have presented the game to themselves in exhibition form. I say this because during my trips to the fair I would estimate that the vast majority of the people who gather to watch the games live nearby. Of course there are many tourists, but the games always draw a local crowd.

There are sporadic accounts of teams traveling to present exhibitions of anetso at the beginning of the twentieth century. The accounts increase through the teens and twenties to an apparent peak in the 1930s, when this practice ceased at some point during that decade, and then begin again at a more irregular rate. Most often Cherokee players divided into two teams and played; but occasionally a team from the Qualla Boundary played other teams, as I will discuss below. These performances were in addition to the "match" or "real" games that were regular events until sometime in the 1930s and that have occurred periodically since then, as I noted in the previous chapter.

When and why match games ceased remains a matter of debate, as I will discuss below. Though I have not found any information about a formal ban, I have located a document that is suggestive of formal action taken by an agency superintendent, which I will discuss below. Possible factors for the cessation of traveling exhibitions include the change of superintendents and the burgeoning tourist industry in the local region. Cherokee people may have stopped traveling as much to perform exhibitions, but still played anetso regularly during the fair.

Another interesting consideration is whether or not the significance of the game actually has increased during the last century. One can make the argument that because regular match games are no longer played, the significance of the game has changed. I say this because year after year, with changes in fair administration, at least one game, if not several, has been a constant at the fairs. Newspaper articles from the 1920s until the present routinely have featured the activity. Significantly, the fair programs regularly feature pictures of anetso, even in years when one could argue that its relevance has diminished.

However, if an activity that once was a regular event within a community becomes an activity that people only engage in during an event such as a fair, and as an exhibition no less, what does that mean? Does the activity necessarily lose significance, for both participants and spectators? I do not think that this is uniformly the case, but a number of observers in the past have disagreed, as I will explain later in the chapter.

Signification and Self-Presentation

I would like to return to Charles H. Long's discourse regarding signification and correlate it with Leah Dilworth's discussion of the First Nations tourist trade in the twentieth century. Both sources conceptually support my argument that anetso historically has been an important clearinghouse for notions of "Cherokee identity" as apprehended by both Cherokee and non-Cherokee individuals. Of course within these two constituencies there is a great diversity of opinions.

Reflecting on his own childhood experiences, Long noted, "my community was a community that knew that one of the important meanings about it was the fact that it was a community signified by another community. This signification constituted a subordinate relationship of power expressed through custom and legal structures. While aware of this fact, the community undercut this legitimated signification with a signification upon this legitimated signifying."[12]

I take this to mean that an appearance-level deception of acquiescence can obscure a different mode of identity unbounded by social circumstances. Once again I reference Joel Martin's notion of a "cultural underground" to describe Cherokee people who have retained a certain conscious ulterior identity recognizable to fellow community members. I believe this creative strategy of interaction describes the stance of a certain portion of the Qualla Boundary population in the twentieth century as well as the nineteenth.[13]

Leah Dilworth has provided additional support for this interpretation, focusing her attention on representations of First Nations peoples in the southwestern United States. She noted that "part of my task has been to find a way to reveal Native American 'subalterns' in these representations as having a 'constitutive rather than a reflective role in colonial and domestic imperial discourse and subjectivity.'"[14] Dilworth employed several metaphors in her important study, including "collecting" and "spectacle," which she applied "in the Debordian sense of a social relationship among people mediated by commodified images." She noted further that this "spectacle—in which what did not appear was as significant as what did—was a discourse in which meaning and power relationships were continually constructed and negotiated."[15]

Significantly, Dilworth, like Long, highlighted the factor of silence, for in many of these narratives, "the silence of the Indians . . . parallels their 'blindness'; they do not possess the power to see tourists, nor can they speak."[16] Thus this "touristic encounter becomes an event through which one establishes one's subjectivity in relation to an other."[17] Dilworth returned to this theme later in the book, citing "Susan Stewart's statement that, 'Narrative is seen . . . as a structure of desire, a structure that both invents and distances its object and thereby inscribes again and again the gap between signifier and signified that is the place of generation for the symbolic.'"[18]

Dilworth astutely characterized the "tourist narrative" as "a story of a quest for contact with authenticity" that "gains its authority from the journey into and return from the realm of the other." According to her, many in the modernist art movement expressed a "primitivist understanding of Indians . . . emptied of any sense of historical context and agency." Dilworth deemed this process a type of commodity fetishism: "In the case of Native Americans, what is elided is history, and Indians emerge as free-floating signifiers available for all kinds of signification."[19] At both the beginning and end of her book, Dilworth used the now-familiar metaphors of "contact zone" (from Mary Louise Pratt) and "borderland" (from Michael J. Riley) to describe various situations of social interaction.[20] The resonance of these observations with Long's statements about silence and signification is clear.

I suggest that there are at least three additional modes of this interaction, all illustrated by examples from First Nations communities. An easily recognizable contemporary Cherokee example of the first strategic mode is "chiefing." This is when Cherokee men dress up in "Plains-style" headdresses and buckskin and stand next to teepees on the side of the road. Tourists stop and pay a fee to take a picture of or with a "real Indian," and this can be a lucrative seasonal job for people. Of course the "chiefs" know that Cherokee people never wore headdresses or lived in teepees, but at least one Eastern Band member researched the market and found that wearing traditional Cherokee garb was bad for business.[21]

By means of this strategy, Cherokee people have turned the non-Cherokee signification, "what Cherokee/Indian people should do," to their advantage, but it also has another benefit: it obfuscates the dialogue concerning "what Cherokee people do." Though many people who "chief" may not engage in traditional activities, some consultants who do so have stated that their behavior is advantageous in terms of maintaining privacy about traditional behaviors and beliefs.[22] It serves a general purpose, effectively using stereotype as a blind alley. Again, this is exactly the conclusion Martin reached in his discussion of a "cultural underground."

Another layer of this interaction complicates matters. Though change is afoot, for many years nonresidents owned most of the tourist shops on the Qualla Boundary and stocked them with kitschy "Indian" objects made in China. Kermit Hunter, a non-Cherokee, nonresident playwright wrote the script for an outdoor drama, *Unto These Hills*, which debuted in 1950. For over fifty years millions of tourists saw a play that featured European American actors in all the major roles, replete with brown face and body makeup, the equivalent of black face. Recently the drama was rewritten, and Cherokee people now direct it and have assumed most lead roles.[23]

This idea of "giving the people what they want" also extends to activities that are considered traditional in many cultures. In such cases traditional activities have continued to be performed, but only on specified occasions due to religious or social pressures. Good examples of this second mode of interaction are the Roman Catholic feast-day dances of several New Mexico and Arizona communities ("Pueblo" groups), which are traditional festivals performed as Christian events, sometimes merged or overlaid with Christian symbolism. While ostensibly they are then "celebrating" the saints and the tradition they represent, in many cases they continue to represent older community beliefs for participants.[24] In these cases many communities allow tourists to attend and usually forbid photography, video and audio recording, or other means of documenting the events.

The third mode is related to the second and encompasses the performance of traditional activities with tourists present, but without overlay. Hopi ceremonial dances are examples of this mode. Tourists who inquire at hotels and other locations are told whether villages are open and if they are allowed to attend.[25]

The question is, where does the anetso ceremonial complex fit? Not explicitly connected to any "religious ritual," yet incorporating "ritual activities" during the public presentation, it defies easy characterization yet again. Non-Cherokee people have been attending ball games for several hundred years and recording their experiences for others to read. As I will illustrate below, what is remarkable to consider is that in addition to regular games, Cherokee people have been exhibiting anetso by request for that long as well.

"To the no-small amusement of an European spectator": Performances of the Ball Game in the Latter Eighteenth Century

In 1762, the British lieutenant Henry Timberlake, attached to the command of Captain John Stuart, noted the ball game both in his memoirs and in his mapmaking. He commented on the "great dexterity" displayed in the "ball plays" and noted that women played their own games.[26] He also noted that the women "pulled one another about" when they played, "to the no-small amusement of an European spectator."[27]

On his map of the Cherokee territory, Timberlake identified a small body of water between the towns of "Toqua" and "Tommotley" as "Ball play creek."[28] This may have been where he witnessed the ball games he mentioned; as he depicted the creek on the map, it ran through the middle of a large, level plain. A later source reported that "Ball Play Creek, a tributary of Tellico River, afforded a natural amphitheater for hundreds of spectators."[29] Thus it would have provided a good field and access to a running body of water, both necessities for the ball game. Further, it would have provided ample space for spectators and access to the creek from two sides.

This account indicated that the ball game was a regular, well-attended event that was popular enough to have a landscape feature named after it. It also was a something of a tourist event at that time, though Timberlake did

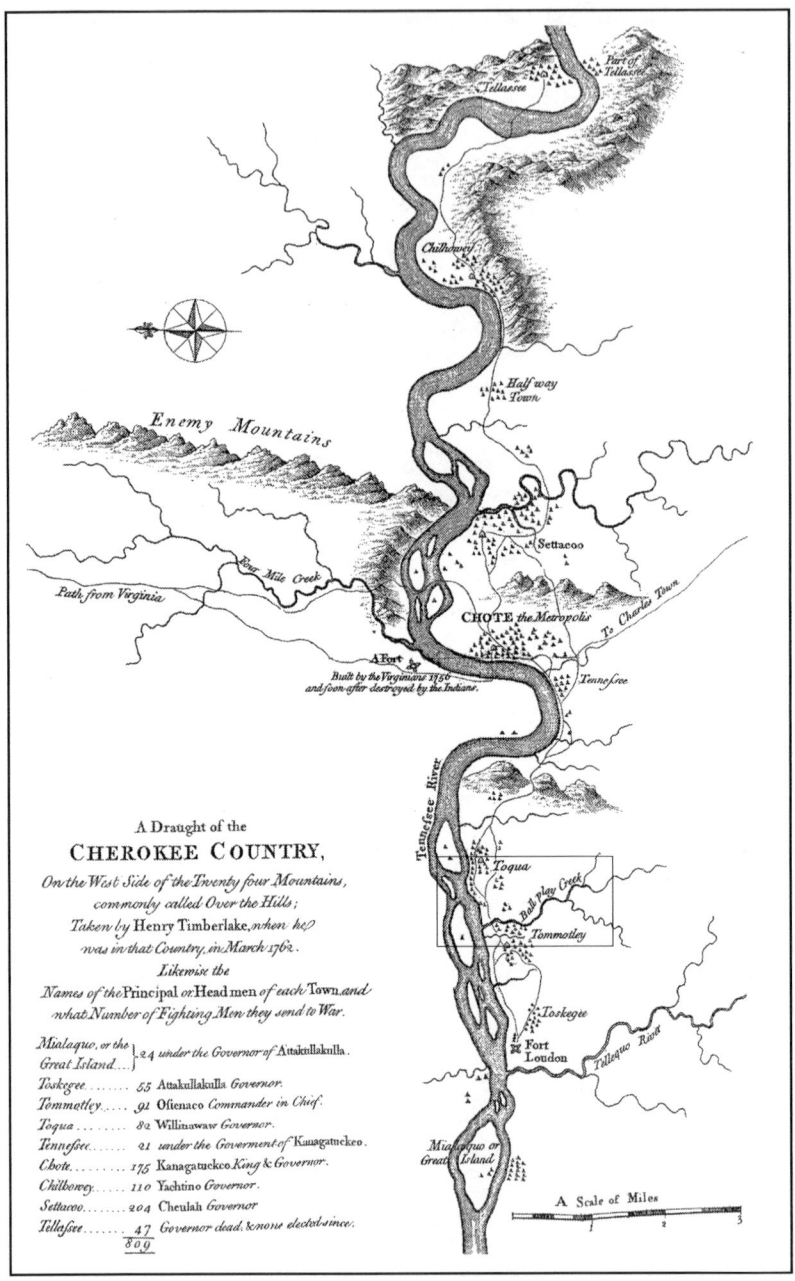

FIGURE 4.1. "A Draught of the Cherokee Country, On the West Side of the Twenty four Mountains, commonly called Over the Hills; taken by Henry Timberlake, when he was in that Country, in March 1762. Likewise the Names of the Principal or Head men of each Town and what Number of Fighting Men they send to War." Timberlake located "Ball Play Creek" between the towns of Toqua and Tommotley on his map, a testament to the popularity and frequency of the activity during this time.

not say whether or not he was the amused European spectator in his account. Moreover, at least in that area at that time, women as well as men played anetso.

On April 12, 1774, Alexander Cameron, the resident agent for the British crown in Cherokee territory, wrote a letter to Captain Stuart, who was elsewhere at the time. Though his letter dealt with other matters, Cameron began with the following paragraph:

> Sir:
> Since I had the pleasure of writing to you last all is well in this quarter.— great ball Plays are weekly exhibitings, Betting their all; and Whole Towns returning home in their Buffs. Sugar Town has carried off every Prize, which is judged by all to be owing to the great gift of Big Sawney's conjuration: [Thikafsse?] of Seneca whom I cloathed from Top to Toe, before he went to the Creeks, Returned home last night Stark Naked; lost his horse & most of his wife's Apparel.[30]

This paragraph is wonderfully descriptive and informative. Ball games at this time were weekly events, and apparently Sugar Town was on a winning streak. Big Sawney, he of the "great gift" of "conjuration," was no doubt the conjurer for Sugar Town, and was said "by all" to have made the difference in the contest. Cameron's account suggested that the activity of conjuring was common knowledge to at least some British personnel.

In addition, Cameron reported the conjuring and the information about gambling without making any overt value judgments, as was the case with other military officers' accounts. Quite obviously, many spectators gambled, and some lost whatever they were willing to wager. Cameron apparently sold or gave clothing to a man who wagered and lost it, his wife's clothing, and even his horse. The custom of betting clothing was common through the nineteenth century, and probably continued until the 1930s. While people did indeed "bet the clothes off their back," in all the accounts I have ever heard or read people who did so wore several layers, betting the outer one or two layers. Horses, cows, wagons, and other smaller items also were fair game, as several missionaries pointed out in letters and journal entries.

In 1775, the year after Big Sawney's triumph, the Cherokee people suffered the most egregious treaty land cessions to that time, culminating in the Henderson purchase: "By these treaties the Cherokee were shorn of practically all their ancient territorial claims north of the present Tennessee line and east of the Blue ridge and the Savannah, including much of their best hunting range; their home settlements were . . . left still in their possession."[31] More land cessions soon followed. On July 2, 1791, as Tennessee governor William Blount presided, "forty-one principal men of the tribe" signed a treaty making further such concessions.[32]

Beginning on May 20, 1792, Governor Blount conducted a "parlay and annuity distribution," stipulated by the 1791 treaty.[33] As discussed in an earlier chapter, William McLoughlin portrayed the treaty of 1791 as a watershed event, arguing that it was the harbinger of the massive cultural upheaval experienced by Cherokee people during the decades before and after the beginning of the nineteenth century. According to a report, two ball games occurred during this summit, which began with a day of "getting acquainted through informal conversation."[34] A summary of events written in 1938 noted that Eskaqua, an "important Cherokee Chief," requested that the second day of the meeting be spent in "eating, 'seasonable drinking of whiskey', in holding private talks with the chiefs, and in a ballplay."[35] This account stated that he apparently wagered heavily on the outcome of the contest and lost.

Eskaqua convinced the governor to postpone the meeting one more day and recovered his losses at the ball game the next day, a Tuesday. According to the account, he and others "staked their clothes on the second game, reserving only their flaps." This account sounds more plausible than people walking around naked. In a successful effort to weaken players on the opposing team, Eskaqua, who did not play, allegedly got drunk on Monday night with those players, while his players did not drink heavily.[36]

The final mention of the ball game in the eighteenth century that I have found also discussed alcohol consumption by players.[37] In this instance, Cherokee people seemingly were pressured to perform for distinguished guests. The account comes from the journal of the touring Duke of Orleans, later to become King Louis-Philippe of France.

Louis-Philippe certainly reflected the time in which he lived. He had the following to say about Cherokee religion: "None of these Indians profess any formal religious creed. Nonetheless, they believe that there is The Great Man Above who made everything here below, but they are too lazy to pursue that idea further and too refractory to be strict about ceremonies or religious duties. (Certainly they observe a few practices or rituals unfamiliar to us. They are reluctant to describe such activities, or even to identify them, but they do observe rites that each of us may interpret for himself.)"[38] His ridiculous comments about people being "too lazy" and "too refractory" notwithstanding, Louis-Philippe would have been a successful ethnographer had royal duty not called. Comments such as, "they observe a few practices or rituals unfamiliar to us," and, "they do observe rites that each of us may interpret for himself," revealed a keen eye for such matters.[39]

According to the duke, a ball game was arranged for his edification in 1797 near the village of Tokono. As I mentioned above in the discussion of Henry Timberlake's 1762 map, this area was noted for its ball games. An editorial comment from another edition of the duke's journal supported this point: "The annual ball-game of the Cherokees gave to that region of the country on the west side of the Tellico River, where it emptied into the Little Tennessee, the name of Ball Play."[40]

Louis-Philippe was anxious to see a ball game, and the commandant asked the "chiefs" if they would comply. They apparently were not excited about the idea, "having played several games in recent days for the entertainment of the boundary commissioners. But six gallons of spirits that we promised the winners decided the matter."[41] The next day, May 2, 1797, at two o'clock, the Duke and his entourage arrived and "bore the two hogsheads (of whiskey) in triumph onto the battlefield where all was being readied for the ball game."[42]

Once again the future king proved to be a careful observer. Louis-Philippe said the Cherokee game was called "*Hannatsôké*, with a long *o* and a very distinct last syllable." This transliteration is obviously a variant of "anetso." He was told about a series of four yells the players normally made: the challenge, and then a war cry, a scalping cry, and a death cry; but he was disappointed to find that due to the many recent games, the tired players dispensed with such preliminaries. Though as I have described, the players, led by the talala, do call out a certain number of times, I am aware of no corroborating evidence for the names he gave them. He also noted that "for an inspired and exciting game, they have to wager among themselves, and unfortunately that is just what did not happen."[43]

The duke provided details of players' uniforms and rackets and gave a good overview of other rules and method of play. He wrote that though the players "buffet one another mercilessly and produce horrible spills," what is "most admirable is that neither during the game nor afterward is there ever the least argument." After the game, Louis-Philippe immediately returned to Tellico, and he reported that much carousing ensued on "the far bank" as the whiskey began to flow; late that night representatives of one of the chiefs attempted to procure more, but they were told that the trading post was closed.[44]

This account contained the first written mention of the march to the center ground. This is the earliest definitive evidence that Cherokee ball games were played for the benefit of visitors, as tourist events, rather than visitors simply being allowed to attend regular games or games being integrated into gatherings such as treaty meetings. Significantly, the players did not march

Tseduga! 159

to meet at the center of the field, nor did anyone gamble. Furthermore, the Duke noted they had played several exhibition games recently.

As I discussed in Chapter 2, William McLoughlin argued that this period produced great cultural decline. He cited consumption of alcohol by players, non-Cherokee spectators, and gambling as evidence of this cultural decline from better days when "the Ball Plays were hallowed by sacred prayers, dances, and rituals," players observed gaktvda, and players were of "high integrity and honor."[45] Again, this is a conclusion that I dispute.

First of all, evidence of individual players' behavior, then as now, is not necessarily a sign of cultural decline across the board. Second, exhibition contests, such as the one in the 1797 account, are not the same as regular ball games, and players may not be subject to the same restrictions. Based on my research, I suggest that alcohol as payment for playing, and the consumption of alcohol by players at the games, are linked to the performance of ball games as tourist events. As the previous examples suggested, this appears to have been the case when the games were scheduled as part of annuity distributions or performed by request for or in the presence of non-Cherokee visitors.

I conclude that by 1797, and likely much earlier, Cherokee people were adept at negotiating the presentation of their culture. The practice of playing the ball game before dignitaries and other tourists was firmly established, and the march to the center ground, wagering, and other ceremonial complex activities were regular features in future decades and centuries. I contend that anetso continued as a tourist attraction, among other functions, from this time period until the present. At times there have been separate ball games for community members and visitors; and at times ball games have fulfilled both functions simultaneously.

After the monumental upheaval of the forced removal to lands in Oklahoma, Cherokee people who remained in North Carolina and those who made it to Oklahoma continued to participate in many traditional activities in its aftermath, including anetso. As John Finger has noted, this behavior concerned some neighbors. In 1840, a man named Andrew Barnard complained that Cherokee people near the Valley River in North Carolina were "forming Settlements, building town houses, and Show every disposition to keep up their former manners and customs of councils, dances, ballplays, and other practices, which is disgusting to civilized Society and calculated to corrupt our youth, and produce distress and confusion among all good thinking people."[46]

In the face of such opinions, Cherokee people continued to uphold their traditions. Visitors continued to comment, but some were more circumspect. John Mullay, who visited in 1845, praised the Cherokee people he observed, noting they were "'advancing encouragingly,'" in spite of continuing to participate in their "'wild and grotesque dances.'"[47]

The journalist Charles Lanman visited Cherokee people in North Carolina in 1848 and described ball games and ceremonial complex activities in some detail. He commented that "the manly game of ball-playing is still practised after the ancient manner with one or two restrictions."[48] Lanman reported that no gambling was allowed other than handkerchiefs or belts, and players were prohibited "from choking each other, and breaking their heads and legs, when excited, as was their habit in former times."[49]

In 1851, the Methodist missionary Elizur Butler noted that many in his church "'believed they should go to heaven because they did not attend all-night dances and go to ball plays.'"[50] While I did not locate any Methodist accounts of ball games during the time period discussed in Chapter 2, this statement is similar to one the Baptist missionary Evan Jones recorded in an 1829 journal entry that I did cite. Clearly other Cherokee people had reached the same conclusion years earlier.

But Cherokee people continued to participate in and attend ball games, and as an account published in 1855 illustrated, curious onlookers continued to inject themselves into the proceedings. In this account, the Rev. George White presented a letter from an unnamed "gentleman" who attended an August game between the towns of "'Chattooga and Chicamauga.'"[51] The account described the rules of play, teams of fifty players with faces painted "'in a fantastical manner,'" wagering, and the march to the center ground in some detail, but the most interesting section had to do with the observer's description of, and interaction with, the "'conjurers.'"[52] The narrator approached the men, and "when I spoke to one of them he did not deign even to raise his head; the second time I spoke he gave me a terrible look, and at the same time one of the Indian women came and said, 'Conagatee unaka,' 'Go away, white man.'"[53] Attendance at the ball games, then as now, was not the issue: the problem was that a non-Cherokee visitor had failed to respect certain boundaries.

Given the exigencies of these turbulent times, many Cherokee people still no doubt found it ironic that for several decades of the nineteenth century their political fate rested largely with an Anglo-American man. Though he was not Cherokee by birth, William Holland Thomas was an important political leader who had a great deal of influence in affairs of state.[54] In this capacity he represented the Cherokee people of North Carolina in Washington, D.C., and elsewhere and also "presented" Cherokee culture to visitors in a certain sense, hosting politicians and other observers, including Charles

Lanman for a portion of his stay.[55] From 1838 to the beginning of the Civil War he was a state senator.[56] One of the most influential political leaders of the Eastern Band up to and following the Removal, Thomas held title to most North Carolina Cherokee people's lands until 1866.[57]

Thomas encouraged the ball games, and according to at least one source he periodically participated in them; but "more often he staged a ballplay as entertainment for some visiting dignitary."[58] According to John Finger, Thomas was quick to use the games to further his own political gains: "for many years he scheduled the ballplay in conjunction with political speeches and rallies, guaranteeing large crowds for his own electioneering."[59] Tracking down citations from two sources, I examined two documents located in Duke University manuscript collections that further display both Thomas's support of ball games and their continued appeal to tourists.

The first item is a daybook entry from Thomas's store dated August 23, 1860, in which he wrote "paid Indian ball players (cash)—$15.00."[60] One wonders if this was payment to one team (and a conjurer, perhaps?), say at a dollar apiece, or if it was somehow divided by two teams. The second item is a July 24, 1860, letter from Thomas Lenoir, a local non-Cherokee resident, to his brother. In this letter, Lenoir wrote, "I have not time to write much now, that wonderful Indian ball play comes off day after tomorrow—the whole neighborhood will be flooded with visitors—I expect to have a good deal more company than will be agreeable." He went on to say that some recent guests would be returning for the ball game, including relatives from South Carolina as well as visitors from both Russia and France.[61]

These documents make it clear that at least some of the ball games at this time were large tourist events, with paid players. Nevertheless, the games remained serious and dangerous. While many ball game accounts I present throughout this study note the possibility of players sustaining serious bodily injury, an entry from an 1860 census roll documented the fact that the game could be deadly. The roll listed "Tsaki, Jake," twenty-five years old, as having been "killed at Qualla at a ballgame."[62]

Of course many young men would lose their lives in the years to come in a different pursuit. During the Civil War, Thomas led Cherokee men in the Confederate Sixty-ninth North Carolina Infantry, known as the Thomas Legion.[63] According to one source, camped Cherokee soldiers played ball occasionally, and sometimes did so at the request of Thomas, as they had before the war.[64] James Mooney reported that at Strawberry Plains in eastern Tennessee in the summer of 1863, where the Cherokee men were guarding a railroad bridge over the Holston River, a game was suggested to alleviate boredom, and the "preliminary ceremonies were dispensed with for once."

The game was interrupted when, "in the middle of it an advanced detachment of the 'Yankees' slipped in, burned the bridge, and were moving forward, when the Cherokee, losing all interest in the game, broke for cover and left the Federals in possession of the ground."[65] Mooney doubly signified the Cherokee soldiers in this anecdote, portraying them as childlike (bored with guard duty, in need of something to do) and militarily naive (engrossed in the game and surprised by the enemy).

After the war, Thomas experienced financial and mental difficulties and by 1866 was no longer considered the official representative of the Cherokee people.[66] However, he must have retained some measure of influence, for on May 27, 1867, Thomas issued a notice calling for a ball game from the settlement of Stekoa, in which he called upon the "Chiefs. of cherokees" to have a meeting "at the Big meeting House on friday 12 o clock instead of Saturday." He continued, "In the evening a ball play for a deer (with sticks) also 4 lbs tobacco to be given to the players, by me. At night—dance old dancing ground 2 bushels meat to feed the hungry." He concluded the note by saying that whiskey was not allowed at the dancing ground.[67] The reason for the meeting is not known, but it may be as discussed above that Thomas had a political motive and wanted to guarantee a large crowd.

Based on my archival research, I conclude that beginning in the late nineteenth century anetso became one of a handful of the most visible "traditional" Cherokee cultural activities. It also was an activity that Cherokee people presented to non-Cherokee people. To "present" can mean many things, of course.

In 1888 and 1889, the *Raleigh News and Observer*, the state capital's news paper, reported on two separate exhibitions of Cherokee culture. The first was what they called a "Cherokee's Gala-Day," held in "Murphy, the 'capital' of Cherokee," on the occasion of the completion of a section of railroad line. The account continued, "The celebration took place yesterday. A feature of the day was an 'Indian War Dance,' engaged in by about thirty native Cherokee Indians. There was also a game of base ball played by native Indians."[68] Though the account says they played baseball instead of the ball game, it is interesting to note that the game was played among Cherokee people as part of the exhibition.

The second account was more detailed and reported on a group of Cherokee people who would be coming to the North Carolina State Fair: "An Indian chief will be one of the number, and the whole party will be costumed in native Indian regalia. They will play their native game of lacrosse, which is a regular rough and tumble game. The presence of the Indians will be a great draw at the fair."[69] An account in the newspaper after one exhibition reported that "the Indians played with spirit and created as much excitement and enthusiasm as an intercollegiate football game ever did."[70]

At the beginning of the twentieth century, anetso was part of a strategy to effect political change. In 1900, Democratic registrars in North Carolina refused to register members of the Eastern Band on the grounds that they were noncitizen wards of the United States. Henry Spray, the federal agent in charge of the Cherokee agency, reported that this action led to a "revival" of certain traditional Cherokee practices. In his annual Department of the Interior report for 1900, Spray reported that a "revival of ball play, with its accompanying dances and the superstitious rites of the 'medicine man,' is having a bad influence."[71]

Spray endeavored to find out the reason for this resurgence of activity and quoted a representative explanation: "If we are not citizens, we are Indians; then let us act as Indians." Based on these comments, Spray concluded in the report that once their right to vote was restored, such activity would cease. He concluded that the revival was "a step backward, which should be retrieved by an early settlement, beyond cavil, of the political status of the Eastern Cherokee."[72]

This did not prove to be the case, however, and there is no support for the argument that they intended to desist. The explanation given to Spray in conversation suggests a strategy of using participation in the ball game as a kind of bargaining chip. Whether or not the intention of the participants was to curtail this activity once voting rights had been restored, members of the community were making a strong statement to the agent by drawing his attention to it.

My conclusion is that what Spray termed a revival was in fact an element of a strategic package of response to the local disfranchisement. James Mooney had detailed the activities associated with the anetso complex a decade earlier, and though Mooney suggested the tradition as a whole was waning, there is evidence of its continuation. Spray began his tenure at the Cherokee Agency in 1898. Perhaps the practices he described had been in abeyance for the two years he had been there; but evidence presented in previous chapters weighs against this view.

I interpret this "revival" as an identity-affirming Cherokee response to the local political situation, in the context of wider policies of reform promulgated by the Bureau of Indian Affairs and Congress that reflected the spirit of the Progressive Era. As with several incidents I presented in Chapter 2, this revival showed Cherokee people in "creative contact with history," expressing their identity by playing the ball game. In an unusual twist, the federal agent reported a Cherokee perspective explaining the rationale of the action.

Cherokee people were used to certain duties as citizens, including exercising their right to vote. Court cases that muddied the legal status of the Cherokee and unscrupulous partisan politicians are blamed for the resulting loss of this right in 1900.[73]

When told their right to vote had been taken away from them, legal challenges, lobbying, and displays of identity such as participation in traditional practices were all part of a strategy of response. It was not until 1930 that Cherokee people in North Carolina regained that undisputed right. However, only a formal protest by World War Two veterans finally forced the issue and resulted in Cherokee people being physically registered and actually voting.[74]

At the beginning of the twentieth century, after Mooney's early visits, people still were playing the ball game. As this incident displayed, some people were using it to protest the loss of Cherokee voting rights. Henry Spray was replaced in 1904, and subsequent government agents had different responses to the ball game. Some even promoted it, and over the next several decades it was a large part of the image Cherokee people presented to the world.

The Public Face of Anetso in the First Half of the Twentieth Century

It is clear that as a cultural symbol, anetso has had wide currency both within and outside the Qualla Boundary community. Particularly in the context of the preceding discussion of degeneration, an assessment of the ball game as part of the tourist trade is in order. Anetso also has been a featured activity at the annual Cherokee Indian Fair, or Fall Festival, since it began in 1914. John Finger summarized its significance at this time: "By the early twentieth century the ballplay was a common feature of Cherokee efforts to attract white attention and money. It was always a major feature of the annual tribal fair, and nearby white communities often invited teams to compete before enthusiastic crowds on special occasions like the Fourth of July."[75]

As we have seen, as early as 1889, and probably earlier, Cherokee teams were invited by local communities to play ball against each other on special occasions in addition to the fair. Over and above written accounts, there are a number of photographs that document exhibition games in the early twentieth century. For example, a Cherokee consultant has shared with me a team photograph from such an event that took place in Asheville, North Carolina, in 1911.[76] The agency superintendent at the time, Frank Kyselka, appeared in the photograph with the teams (including the father of my consultant). Finger stated that "Frank Kyselka believed the ballplay was a model of decorum. In 1910, when fatalities among collegiate athletes had become

Tseduga! 165

FIGURE 4.2. "The players before taking places on grounds for playing game of 'La Crosse.'" Players lining up before an exhibition game, probably Asheville, N.C., circa 1921–23. (Courtesy Museum of the Cherokee Indian Archives, Shepherd Photo Collection, MSS 99-04; photograph by George Masa.)

a national scandal, he expressed the belief football's rule makers could learn 'valuable points from a study of the Indian game.'"[77] Other photographs of ball game action in Asheville are in the collection of the Museum of the Cherokee Indian archives.[78]

Cherokee Indian Agency records from 1910–34 add valuable detail to discussion of this issue. In this quarter century of reports, the ball game frequently was mentioned. Statements ranged from classifying it as harmless to references about steps being taken to stop it, at least during certain times of the year. In every report the language was quite similar, particularly when the superintendent was the same and had been on the job for more than a year. In fact, many sections were copied almost virtually word for word from year to year; in other instances they varied only slightly.

In most cases, the only Cherokee cultural activity that was mentioned in the entire narrative report was the ball game, or the ball dance, or both. The green corn dance was mentioned once, and conjurers were noted several times, but every single report except that from 1913 made specific mention of either the ball game, the ball dance, or both. This was quite surprising, and, to me, it speaks to the persistence of these activities.

In what I would term a reassuring or borderline dismissive tone, the superintendent almost every year made some statement to the effect that the dance and game were benign, and that the dance had lost much of its previous significance. Perhaps wary of their superiors' wrath for allowing such a custom to persist, the superintendents highlighted the factors of gambling and drunkenness. In the earlier years these features were problems they said they were addressing. In the later years the ball game and ball dance seemed unobjectionable because they posed no threat to "law and order." Repeatedly they assured their readers that the game and dance were either soon to fade away or were so benign as to not be a concern.

A few examples in particular will suffice to make my point. The first is from the 1915 report. The superintendent, whose name is not given, stated that "The dance is giving [sic] the night preceding the playing of la-crosse and is a religious ceremony connected with the game. There is less harm done at the dance than at the games. There is perhaps more disorder at these games than at any time during the year. . . . These dances and games are given no official recognition by me and a healthy sentiment is being worked up against the evil tendences [sic] connected with the game."[79] The next year's report, also without a name, stated in reference to the dance that "It was originally a pagan ceremony connected with the game but it has lost much of this element and is very much a matter of form rather than that of a religious ceremony." The author also noted that "when school is in session the pupils are not allowed to attend."[80]

James Henderson was the author of the 1917 report, which contained the evidence I spoke of regarding action taken by the agency superintendent against the ball game. Henderson stated: "I do not consider the dance as harmful to the Indians as the ball game which is played the following day which is usually attended by a tendency toward disorder and gambling. Only a few of these games were played during the year and steps have been taken to entirely prevent any being played during the present summer."[81] The next year's report said of the dance that in addition to its pagan nature "the medicine man figures largely"; while "formerly they were drunken orgies . . . since whiskey has been eliminated from the reservation little harm is done by them." The report also included a fine picture of two ball teams that to my knowledge has never been published.[82]

By 1920 Henderson felt comfortable enough to report of the dance that it "has lost much of its ancient significance. The purely orthadox [sic] Indians

FIGURE 4.3. "The 'Indian Ball' Teams." Two Cherokee anetso teams, Cherokee, N.C., 1918. The man standing in the middle between the two teams was designated to oversee the contest. (Superintendents' Annual Narrative and Statistical Reports from Field Jurisdictions of the Bureau of Indian Affairs, 1907–1938. Annual Report 1918, Cherokee Indian School, Cherokee, N.C. National Archives Microfilm Publication M1011, Roll 12. National Archives and Records Administration, Washington, D.C.)

will not attend them and it is only a question of a short while until they will have gone the way of the other dances and customs of this people."[83] Three years later he reported that the dances "have ceased to be a problem to the community."[84]

Perhaps because of his belief that the dances had degenerated, in 1921 Henderson corresponded with the Greensboro, North Carolina, Chamber of Commerce secretary about a "Scalp Dance and Harvest Carnival." The chamber was "anxious to have some real Indians with us at our Scalp Dance and Harvest Feast," and asked if "they could come prepared to dress up in real Indian regalia and give us some War Hoops and Indian Dancing."[85] Henderson responded in the affirmative, but explained that "the old fellows will not take part in a public performance such as you want.... In this connection let me say that the Cherokees do not wear primitive dress any more and that the young men who do go will have to provide costumes for themselves."[86] After receiving this letter, it seems that the chamber's anxiousness waned; they responded that it had been "decided that it will probably be best not to bring any of the Indians from Cherokee. We thank you very much for the offer."[87]

If they could not have the Cherokee people do what they wanted them to do while looking like they wanted them to, then apparently they were not interested.

In 1923, Henderson permitted a ball team to travel to a Shriner's convention in Washington, D.C.[88] Evidently Henderson had changed his view from his earlier belief that the games encouraged "idleness" and violence. One consultant, when asked about the event, remembered his father leaving for the game.[89] According to John Finger, circa 1920 agency superintendents understood the ball play of the day as a "pallid reflection of the earlier game." To Finger, by the 1920s participation in any of the accompanying activities of the anetso complex was "more a cursory bow to tradition" than "part of any deeply ingrained belief." At that time, "perhaps the best example of cultural continuity on the reservation was the daily use of the Cherokee language in most households, though increasing numbers of Indians could also speak English."[90]

Throughout this period several newspaper articles featured anetso. A 1927 article in the *Asheville (N.C.) Sunday Citizen* by Anne D. Bryson began, "When this part of Western North Carolina is spoken of or written about, mention is usually made of the Cherokee Indian reservation, the home of the eastern band of the Cherokee tribe. Tourists who come here ask to be routed to it as it is known all over the United States."[91] Bryson stated that "six thousand visited the school during the summer of 1926," and that "last October 10,000 people attended this Fair during the four days. More are expected this years [sic] as the main highways are completed."

Bryson reported in some detail about conjuring, the fair, and the ball game, distinguishing between exhibition matches and "real games." She recalled, "The only real game I ever saw was played at Birdtown several years ago and the winner broke the collar bone of his opponent. The man continued playing for at least ten minutes after it was broken, before he would accept defeat."[92]

A year later, in 1928, the Sunday edition of the *Charlotte (N.C.) Observer* devoted the entire second page and part of a third to a feature article about the Cherokee people living on the Qualla Boundary. In the fashion of the time, successive headlines prefaced the text of the article. One of them read, "Ancient Indian Games Will Be Played for Edification of Whites."[93] Majel Ivey, the author of the feature stated, "The Cherokees will be one of the greatest attractions to tourists visiting the Smoky mountains national park. Though the government has instituted here a comprehensive system of education and modern methods of living, the ancient ceremonies and sports are still preserved as racial customs."

Ivey also provided a good deal of description of conjuring and the ball game, reporting that "the old superstitions hold sway at these ceremonies preceding their games, for this ball game religion is an obsession with the Cherokees. At the Indian ball game a squaw will almost bet the clothes off her back on her brave who is on the team." Photographs of a ball team and ball game action were included. Ivey wrote that the ball game was "mainly a test of strength and endurance and on account of the savagery of the game, it has been modified considerably at the instance of the government."[94]

This piece dealt with a variety of topics, such as education, legal status of the reservation, historical background, Cherokee medicinal practices, and a description of the fair. The article also had a separate section on the ball game, and it was surprisingly detailed on a number of subjects, including the ball dance, going to water, scratching, divination, and selection of players. In addition it included details of formulas, as well as several ball game terms.[95]

A 1934 *Asheville (N.C.) Citizen-Times* article on the Southeastern Fair in Atlanta, Georgia, touted the "cross-section of Indian life under the approval of John Collier, United States commissioner of Indian affairs," that would be on display. The article began with comments about an "extremely peaceful invasion" by some Cherokee people, who "used to hunt at will where Atlanta, Ga., now stands." It also noted that the ball game was "a general mixture of rugby and soccer football and lacrosse, involving the roughest elements of each."[96]

Though the article itself was short, both of the photographs included were of Cherokee ball players. One picture was of the team, and the other was of a "star player," Ben Powell, and his daughter. Powell was pictured wearing a Plains-style headdress and holding a bow. The team was pictured in short pants, with a few of the players giving mock presentation of the legal two-handed stick blow to the head.[97]

As the article noted, Powell had played on the famous Carlisle Indian School football teams of 1910 and 1911, led by Jim Thorpe and coached by the legendary Glenn "Pop" Warner.[98] Again, as seen above, the ball game was presented as a defining image of the Cherokee people to the general American public. Furthermore, this image was linked both to a misconceived image of Cherokee people as part of the Plains cultural area, as well as to the more familiar image of American football. The photographs were attributed to the Associated Press, suggesting that they were reprinted across the country.

Sarah H. Hill's *Weaving New Worlds: Southeastern Cherokee Women and Their Basketry* provided excerpts from an *Atlanta Journal* article that proclaimed the Cherokee ball game as "'more entertaining than any other activity'" at the exposition, as well as being "'probably the roughest game in America.'"[99]

Hill went on to say that despite, "reporters' assurances that fairgoers would see them in realistic settings, Cherokees stayed in 'six large wigwams' that were 'nearly exact copies of their former dwellings' of the eighteenth century. . . . Moreover, the men wore feathered headdresses, carried tomahawks for newspaper photographs, and participated in archery and blowgun contests, wrestling matches, and ball games."[100] Though the dwellings and costumes were inaccurate, the contests were all part of the annual Cherokee Fairs. Hill noted that the Cherokee Tribal Council had voted to change the date of that year's fair to allow about fifty Cherokee people to attend the Southeastern Fair and participate in the Indian Exposition, as per the suggestion of John Collier.[101]

In addition to newspaper articles, my archival research has produced correspondence related to several exhibitions of anetso during the 1930s and 1940s. I will focus on one in particular, the 1935 Dogwood Festival in Chapel Hill, N.C. The Dogwood Festival committee had been interested in having "Indian Ball" teams participate since the festival began in 1933 and had written then-superintendent R. L. Spalsbury to inquire about teams giving an exhibition. Spalsbury directed them to contact Chief Jarrett Blythe, which they did; and he responded in the affirmative.[102] However, there is no archived correspondence after this letter until the secretary of the Dogwood Festival committee, Felix A. Grisette, wrote to Superintendent Harold W. Foght in 1935 to ask again (it is unclear why he bypassed Blythe). Grisette estimated that there would be "1500 boy scouts plus their families and friends" at the festival.[103]

Foght replied to the request by saying he thought teams could be raised, even though "the only difficulty is that the Indians are rather out of training at this time of year."[104] After the details had been worked out, Foght responded to confirm the arrangement: "The statement of condition [sic] as set forth in your letter meets in every respect with our approval. I will do my best to bring you two teams that will really put up a fight."[105]

Further correspondence focused on proper publicity, with the fair official asking for a description of the game that could be used in the advertising campaign, as well as pictures "of the teams in action preferably, but good group pictures if you have no action photographs."[106] In response, Foght apologized that a description had not been sent, explaining that he had asked Carl Standingdeer to come to the agency office and provide a statement, but that Standingdeer had not done so. Foght was able to include photographs, about which he said, "The boys will this year be tattooed up somewhat and be made to look quite a bit more like Indians than in this group."[107]

Two letters from Foght to Standingdeer also were archived. The second, sent on April 19, was more formal than the first, and expressed some amount of irritation. It began, "It is high time now for us to have the details of the ball game completed," and concluded with, "I find at the last moment, it will be impossible for me to make the trip with the team, which I regret very much. . . . But I do want to see you on Monday."[108] He also discussed the players' appearance: "I feel that we should dress up the players a little better than ordinary this time. For example, each team should have its own color and each one should have his hair dressed properly with the required feathers. I believe, too, that we ought to do what the Navajos and others do, paint up the naked part of the body in fantastic colors. I believe it would add to the spectacle."[109]

This statement is revealing, but not only because of the comment about body paint. By asking for each player to "have his hair dressed properly with the required feathers," Foght demonstrated that he knew that Cherokee players do this in match games. In other words, he was trying to make the performance "more realistic" in one way while simultaneously attempting to introduce other inauthentic elements that he thought would appeal to the audience. A description of the ball game, along with a handwritten diagram of the players' positions, eventually was sent.[110]

In addition to this correspondence, an event program and financial statement were among the Dogwood Festival records, providing a level of specificity about a public event that was out of the ordinary. The event program stated that a "Cherokee Indian Ball Game" would be played April 27, 1935, on Emerson Field in Chapel Hill. An asterisk next to this item directed the reader to an emendation at the bottom of the page that read: "Two teams, of ten players each, from the Cherokee Indian Reservation in North Carolina will play in the ball game. It is one of the oldest games of Indian origin and will be played in its primitive form. When played on the reservation the game follows a series of tribal ceremonies based upon ancient customs of the race."[111] The festival organizers were well aware of at least some elements of the ceremonial complex, and the inclusion of buzz words such as "oldest," "primitive," "tribal ceremonies," and "ancient customs" was calculated to pique the interest of people and make the upcoming event more appealing.

Apparently the advertising worked, because a lot of people came to see the game, and it made money. It was the central event of the festival, held at 3:00 P.M. on a Saturday. The admission was fifty cents, making it quite an expensive event in 1935; in fact it was the most expensive event of the festival. According to the financial statement, the gate receipts amounted to $293.02 (the .02 was unexplained), which means there were 586 paying spectators. Assuming the Boy Scouts were given free admission, one could conservatively estimate another several hundred spectators. The ball game exhibition also was the highest netting event of the festival, making almost $85, again, a good bit of money at the height of the Depression.[112]

The ball game was not the only cultural activity that was exhibited that year. Just a month earlier a group of dancers from Big Cove led by Will West Long applied for permission to attend the National Folk Festival in Chattanooga, Tennessee. Long noted in his letter that the group had not been able to attend the Southeastern Fair the previous year in Atlanta; he also reiterated their qualifications: "as you know we are oldest group and really Cherokee dance and song [sic]."[113] A program from the festival lists the Cherokee group as performing "Tribal Rites and Dances."[114]

The next year the dance group was headed to the National Folk Festival in Dallas, Texas, and Foght wrote to Long to ask him to come down to the agency office "in order that we may take a good picture of you. Be sure to bring the head band and feather so as to make it as truly Indian as possible."[115] Another letter to Long followed a week later in which Foght reminded him "to bring along your headband and feather. I will find you a costume at school to use in the photograph." Apparently there had been some discussion of a ball team going to the 1936 festival as well, but Foght had decided against it because "it is better to do one thing well then to do two things poorly."[116]

During this time, the Qualla Boundary also was receiving national attention for its yearly fair. A 1936 *New York Times* feature reported, "Probably the most picturesque event scheduled for this Fall is the annual Cherokee Indian Fair. . . . An ancient Indian ball game, the forerunner of the present game of lacrosse, will be revived as a featured event of the fair. Played with 'ball sticks' like miniature tennis racquets, the games will be contests between the Cherokee warriors from Bird Town, Paint Town, Big Cove, Yellow Hill and Qualla."[117]

Archival research also yielded additional correspondence from other events that Cherokee performers attended, such as the 1936 Asheville, North Carolina, Rhododendron Festival, in which the chairman of the "Indian Committee," Holmes Bryson Jr., complained about the Cherokee men's attire. He also asked, "if we couldn't have a few Indian yells from the boys as they march down the avenue. The whole thing is only a make-believe show and we want to make it as exciting and spectacular as possible. It would be fine if the ball players would consent to having their bodies *painted* in a savage manner. Your experience with the Western Indians has undoubtedly proved to you that such little things go over big with a crowd of pale faces."[118]

I find it quite interesting that in this case, as above, the event organizers knew perfectly well that they were creating a "make-believe" show; however it is doubtful that the crowds knew this. As with the Dogwood Festival organizers, Bryson was keen to have information about the history and rules of the ball game and other activities that could be used in the publicity campaign; he noted that "if the writer of the ball game article could make it sound as brutal as the sport really is, the results would be most successful."[119]

Sarah H. Hill discussed this correspondence, and her summation of the events was as follows: "The efforts to preserve native customs in order to educate white audiences thus slid hopelessly and inevitably into an endeavor to entertain."[120] She went on to say:

> The end of the thirties brought a different superintendent and another performance policy. Incoming Superintendent C. M. Blair informed festival promoters that "in the future our policy should be to confine this type of program to the environs of Cherokee." The superintendent claimed that the decision to circumscribe native performance was in part "sentimental," but it also "would result in the increased financial returns to the Indians." In 1939, the tourism generated by the Great Smoky Mountains National Park held great promise for economic relief.[121]

However, a 1938 letter from Bryson to Blair discussed the Rhododendron Festival for that year, so clearly Blair's opinion had changed, perhaps due to the national park opening.[122]

In the years that followed, Cherokee Chief Jarrett Blythe once again became involved in the process. In the spring of 1941 divisions of two major motion picture companies, Grantland Rice's Sportlight (Paramount Pictures) and MGM News of the Day, both asked to film ball games. Blythe noted in one letter that "defense work and the draft have broken into the regular routine of games, and I am quite sure that there will be no games staged this spring or summer"; he suggested that the best time for such filming would be during the Cherokee Indian Fair.[123] C. M. Blair received a letter from an Indian Affairs official relating that the producers "would like very much to have this ball game staged for their special benefit with crowds present if possible."[124]

Further correspondence between Blythe and Jack Eaton, a *Sportlight* producer, reveals the latter's disappointment that no games would be scheduled; Eaton asked if players could be gathered so they could "stage the game just for the cameras."[125] Blythe responded, "after reading your letter and noting that you only want a demonstration and not a regular match game among the Indians I feel that it would not be so difficult to arrange for that."[126] I have not been able to determine if in fact either *Sportlight* or *News of the Day* did film a ball game.

Two additional letters from 1948 are interesting as well. In the first, Joe Jennings, then the superintendent of the Cherokee Agency, responded as follows to a request for an exhibition of the ball game: "From time to time efforts have been made for various organizations in cities to secure Cherokee Indian teams for the purpose of staging Indian Ball games. Practically all of these efforts have been unsuccessful. Most of the boys who play this game are employed and would naturally hesitate to interrupt their employment."[127]

Jennings went on to say that he would pass on the request, and if enough people were interested they themselves could arrange the event.[128] I do not know if this event came to pass. In the second letter, Blythe responded to a July 1948 request for ball teams to play in Asheville by saying that he had "checked with leaders of the various teams, and they advise that they are unable to get their respective teams together at this time of the year."[129]

These comments by Blythe are quite significant because they are evidence that match games were in fact still being played in 1941, and possibly even in 1948, years after most sources say the last "real" match game was played. John Gulick expressed the generally held opinion that "in 1934 was played the last stickball game in the old tradition.... It is questionable whether the strong sense of community rivalry (and therefore identity) which had been associated with the game has subsequently found any comparable outlet. It is therefore doubtful that that sense of identity was felt by more than a handful of enthusiasts in 1934."[130] In another article that same year (1958) he wrote that in the 1930s, "Stickball was still played in earnest, but it was to be discontinued (except for exhibition purposes) before 1940.... Although there was extensive knowledge of the old dances in Big Cove in the 1930's, few of them were still performed." In the same article he stated that the ball games "were effectively suppressed by Indian Agency personnel before 1940."[131]

In yet another article Gulick asserted that "as regular township organizations, the stickball teams were abolished at the instance [sic] of the Agency for apparently two reasons: first, injuries to the players due to its roughness which had apparently become disproportionate in terms of a game rather than a battle; second, the frequently unruly behavior among the spectators which led to drunken brawls, knifings, and so on. (The second reason has also been mentioned by various informants as having been operative in the cessation of the few remaining aboriginal dances)."[132] This also was supposed to be the last time an all-night ball dance was held, and that gambling was permitted.

Though there is no textual evidence to support this conclusion, the superintendents' reports discussed above suggest it would be plausible. According to Mary Chiltoskey, a longtime Qualla Boundary resident and educator, "betting on the game and finally the game itself was outlawed for several decades in this century by white authorities."[133] Lloyd Sequoyah told Fogelson that "the Cherokee gave up the match games of their own volition."[134] Fogelson further stated that the last match game "of which the writer has record took place in 1938 at a flat bottom near the present-day National Park Ranger Station with Big Cove defeating Yellow Hill by a score of 12 to 5. This game marked the last time that the all night ball game dance was performed in Big Cove."[135] According to my consultants, Wolftown and Big Cove last played a match game in the early 1980s, possibly in 1982 or 1983.[136] What these comments reveal is that a regular series of games continued past the 1930s, and this practice was stopped not by the agency's request, but by the exigencies of war.

Throughout the 1940s it seems that anetso continued to be a part of Cherokee culture that Cherokee people presented to the rest of the world. In 1946 an employee of the Travel Information Division of the North Carolina Department of Conservation and Development took a series of photographs at the Cherokee Indian Fair and elsewhere on the Qualla Boundary. Many featured ball game action, and there were even some pictures of pregame activities. These appear to have been staged, including one photograph in particular of players presumably going to water before the contest. However those depicting ball game action, including a few of injured players, clearly were not staged.[137] In another photograph a portion of a bus is visible, and on the side one can see the partial phrases "America's Oldest Ball" and "Cherokee Indian Ball," suggesting that this was a travel bus used for performance tours such as those discussed above.[138] Though it is unclear if these photographs were used in an advertising campaign to promote tourism, below I will discuss a 1951 film produced by the Travel Information Division that did use footage of Cherokee people in this way.

The ball game received attention from the national press as well in this time period. Fogelson quoted passages from features in three magazines, including *Life* (1946), *True Magazine* (1948), and *Literary Digest* (1928).[139] As he noted, *Life* described the game as "the world's roughest ball game," and the article in *True* was entitled "Homicide: a sport."[140]

The *Life* magazine piece was a three-page photographic essay featuring the work of renowned photographer Loomis Dean. According to the short

FIGURE 4.4. "Wolftown 1939 Ball Team." The 1939 Wolftown team before "going to water" in the Oconaluftee River. Left to right: Jeff Toineeta, Albert Crowe (driver), Noah Powell, Jeff Thompson, John A. Crowe, Jesse Washington (conjurer), Noah Smith (kneeling), Noah Arch (driver), Jonah Washington, Homer Powell, Bill Stamper, Russell Hornbuckle (not pictured, Enoch Sampson). The drivers pointed out the ball to the players and monitored the game action. (Courtesy Museum of the Cherokee Indian Archives, Ph. 482.)

paragraph of text, the game pictures were of the "Wolftown Bears" versus the "Wolftown Wolves."[141] In one photograph, Noah Powell, who would serve as Principal Chief of the Eastern Band of Cherokee Indians from 1971 to 1973, was shown running with the ball in his mouth while an unidentified player grabbed at his throat.[142] Another featured a group of players kneeling before a river and dipping their ball sticks in the water, while a man stood behind them, apparently looking at beads in his hands.[143] (See fig. 3.5) Players with feathers in their hair appear in two of the pictures, and in one photograph of game action one of the players is wearing shorts with cross or "X" markings.[144]

Though I am not a print media historian, considering the almost legendary reputation of *Life*, I think it is fair to assume that a great number of people saw these pictures. I venture to guess that a comparable number of people learned about the Cherokee ball game from these three magazine pieces, indeed perhaps from the *Life* magazine essay itself, as did people from all of the other publications I discuss in this study combined. From the comments Fogelson quoted and my own review of one of the articles, it is fairly clear that the articles highlighted what for the average reader would be the physicality and relatively "exotic" nature of the activity.

Tseduga! 177

The Public Face of Anetso in the Second Half of the Twentieth Century

The Eastern Cherokee are not necessarily more guilty of propagating noble savage ideas than other groups. However, with their sophisticated cultural entertainments, Unto These Hills and Oconaluftee Village, and their proximity to the population centers of the East Coast, they were probably more influential than other tribes in establishing certain ideas about Indians during the 1950s and 1960s.
—Michael Harkin, "Postmodern Tourism and Aboriginal People," 2003

In the first half of the twentieth century, in addition to various newspapers and magazines featuring anetso, Cherokee Agency superintendents had promoted it, and the Travel Information Division of the North Carolina Department of Conservation and Development had collected a series of photographs of the game and surrounding events. Therefore it is not surprising that a 1951 full-color film to promote tourism produced for this agency contained footage of a ball game during a fair.[145] The brief segment began with Cherokee people engaged in various activities such as basket weaving and carving. It then switched to footage of a bow-and-arrow shooting contest and a ball game from the Fall Festival, and the segment ended with action shots of the game, while a Ferris wheel revolved in the background.

As the camera panned the crowd and then focused on the game action, the narrator intoned, "With a hickory nut for a ball and a no-holds-barred rule, these original Americans have played this game for hundreds of years." After a pause in narration while players wrestled and struggled for the ball to the strains of an overdubbed organ, the narrator remarked, "Don't ask us who's winning—we can't figure the game out either."[146] Like the articles above, these brief images highlighted the exotic physicality of the subjects to the potential tourist; the message in this case seemed to be that "Cherokee people are strange and wonderful, and even the 'tour guides' don't understand, but that doesn't matter—come visit anyway." As technology advanced, movie cameras focused on anetso, like still cameras, drawings, and written accounts had before; and as it was part of the Fall Festival, it continued to be a part of their culture that Cherokee people presented to the rest of the world.

In addition to the fair, important tourist draws during this era were the outdoor drama *Unto these Hills* and the re-created 1750s-era Oconaluftee Village, in which Cherokee community members exhibited various arts and crafts. Gulick noted that these were controversial because "the revivals of aboriginal culture for tourist exhibition purposes were originally planned and designed, and are maintained, on the initiative of White people, with some non-conservative Indians in consultation, by means of an organization called the Cherokee Historical Association [CHA]. The Association does employ a large number of Indians, among them quite a few conservatives."[147] John Finger concurred: "The CHA was clearly a white-dominated organization."[148]

With regard to the ball game, in the late 1950s John Gulick reported, based on information from Fogelson, that "the meaningfulness of the game in terms of aboriginal cultural patterns would not seem to have been entirely lost.... There is evidence, also, that at least some of the present-day teams undergo a token of the elaborate pre-game rituals." He noted that the scratching of players was still being done and continued, "It is not known whether they also observed the various abstinences which were once obligatory, but at least the ritual at the stream was observed directly. It took place, furthermore, in a secluded spot, so that there was no question of its being done purely for the benefit of tourists and outsiders."[149] Gulick further reported that in 1959 a regular series of games had taken place, which "led to its being played in earnest, with the result that a number of serious injuries were inflicted; and on some occasions, the spectators became belligerent."[150]

All of these tourist attractions gained much national attention, as illustrated by this 1960 *New York Times* feature, entitled, "The Cherokees: A Proud Race Tells Its Story," and headlined, "Museums and a Reconstructed Village Recall Tribal Life of Centuries Ago." After some detail about the drama, including "an age-old tribal dance" being featured, the article concluded, "Tourist events in this Cherokee region reach a climax with the annual Cherokee Indian Fair on Oct. 4–8. Apart from the exhibits, there will be Indian ball games, singing, a baby show and other events."[151] Echoing earlier observations to some degree, Fogelson remarked in 1962:

> The fact that the ball game is a salable tourist amusement should assure its continuance for some time. The public portion of the ritual such as the whooping, stylized march to the center ground, and ritual at the water after the game probably will survive as part of the tourist presentation. The future persistence of the non-public ritualism is less assured. This non-public ritualism must remain covert in order not to incur the wrath of the church and other agencies of moral "uplift." However, as long as the game lives up to its title as the "world's roughest sport" a certain amount of danger and uncertainty will always be present and, if ones takes a Malinowskian position, probably aid in the survival of a considerable amount of the complex ritual.[152]

There are several activities that one could place in such a category of cultural presentation that also are important for identity maintenance, and one of the most important is the Cherokee language. John Gulick argued in the late 1950s that the language "is the only major aspect of the aboriginal culture which survives to any important degree in directly observable form. . . . Our hypothesis is that the Cherokee language survives primarily because its use is a symbolic expression of resistance to the continued socio-cultural pressures of the Whites." He continued, "Unable to account satisfactorily on any other basis for the persistence of the language, we are led to conclude that speaking Cherokee by preference is a symbolic, and to some extent instrumental, act of resistance. This conclusion is further strengthened when we consider that until 1933, the attempt to eradicate the language through the school system was an open and painful issue for all."[153]

More recently Margaret Bender has argued that the syllabary itself, "through its broader semiotic functioning," has "an extremely meaningful role in contemporary Cherokee life." Because it "has been such a potent and polyvalent symbol since its invention" and "has been taken to represent both adoption and rejection of the dominant society's values and practices . . . it plays an important part in Eastern Cherokee self-representation through tourism and in other contexts." Thus "the syllabary is an important representation of Cherokee culture and identity."[154]

I agree with analysis; however, to my knowledge there are no exhibitions of people sitting around speaking the language. I realize that such a concept sounds ridiculous, but I mention it because of something that happened to me when I was working on the Enduring Voices Project. My base of operations for the project was the archive of the Museum of the Cherokee Indian. As there was no staff archivist at the time, sometimes I fielded questions from the public. Occasionally I pitched in when the staff was short-handed at the admissions counter or in the gift shop, which is where the following interaction occurred.

One day I was manning the shop's audiovisual counter and a woman asked for Cherokee language materials. I showed her what we had in stock, including books and compact discs, but she did not seem interested in any of those choices. She then asked, "Could you get a couple of Cherokee staff members to come out here and talk so we can hear what Cherokee sounds like?" At first I did not know what to say, but I recovered and answered politely that as she could see we were quite busy right then. She persisted. "I'll bet there aren't two people who work here who can speak in Cherokee," she challenged.

"Actually, ma'am," I replied curtly, "there are several people here who do speak Cherokee fluently, but they are not zoo animals whom you simply can command to perform for you." Her eyes widened; then she turned on her heels and huffed, "Well I never!" as she stormed away. "That's right," I thought to myself, "and now that you have, maybe you'll think twice before you say something like that again." Staff members told me they get that all the time, but one of the managers explained that if they all responded as I had whenever something like that happened then they would lose a significant number of sales. Clearly I learned something about retail customer service that day. My point in narrating this encounter is not to mock the customer involved, but to illustrate this expectation of cultural performance sometimes expressed by members of the non-Cherokee public to members of the Eastern Band.[155]

Every year the Cherokee Indian Fair has both an exhibition of artwork and a judged contest. Cultural performances do abound, linked closely to the tourist industry. Baskets, carvings, and a host of other arts and crafts items including ball sticks are on sale year-round at several locations on the Qualla Boundary. These include the Qualla Boundary Cooperative and the Museum of the Cherokee Indian, across the street from one another in the center of town. A feature for the last several years has been the Cherokee Voices event sponsored by the museum, in which Cherokee artisans, storytellers, and other individuals participate. Anetso continues to be a regular event at the fair; in 2009 games were scheduled for three of the four days. However, the official tourism sites for the Eastern Band did not mention the ball game on the information page for the 2010 fair; nor was it mentioned in the 2008 and 2009 press releases about the fair linked to that page. Oddly, the "History and Culture" index page of the website features a picture of a ball stick, even though the game is not explained on any of the linked pages.[156] To reiterate my point from earlier in the chapter, I think one can make a strong case that in this context, at this point in time, as exhibitions the games are performances Cherokee people present to themselves as much as to tourists. Large local crowds continue to attend the games.

Other cultural performances are presented by Cherokee people who travel to engage in storytelling and dancing, and the North Carolina Arts Council has recognized several Cherokee artists and storytellers for their cultural presentation work. As I noted in Chapter 2, the Warriors of Anikituhwa dance troupe presents selected Cherokee dances, including two based on Timberlake's eighteenth-century descriptions, dressed and painted as history suggests their eighteenth-century forefathers were. The outdoor drama *Unto These Hills* was rewritten three times between 2006 and 2008 and still continues to draw crowds, though not in the numbers it did in its 1950s heyday.[157]

In 2007 there was only one ball game scheduled, when in other years two or three have been the norm, including a young boy's game. That year, upon purchasing a ticket for the fair, fairgoers received a brochure containing a schedule of events. The colorful cover of the brochure featured three black-and-white pictures: one of a dance group performing at the fair, one of ball game action, and one of the team line-up before the game.[158]

It is reasonable to assume that in choosing images for the brochure, fair officials strived to invoke tradition, and thus picked "classic" pictures from previous fairs. I may be wrong, but in my opinion the only picture that the average tourist would immediately recognize would be that of the dancers. They could interpret the picture of the ball game action as some sort of contest, but unless they had studied the game they would not know what the lineup photo was. Therefore I think the pictures were as much for the local community as they were for tourists.

Further review of schedule brochures, commemorative books, and t-shirts from the past several years, reveals that ball game imagery is regularly part of the designs. Every year as a fund-raiser, Cherokee High School sells t-shirts at the Cherokee Indian Fair with an original student design. The shirt for the year 2000 depicted a ball player, along with the Cherokee syllabary symbols *Tsa la gi*. A Cherokee student in a summer school class gave me another shirt from several years before that also featured the ball game. The cover design of the 2001 fair program featured a black-and-white drawing combining several images, among them a pair of ball sticks. The 1997 fair ticket displayed a similar design.

Cherokee nonparticipants also make use of the notion of anetso in the process of self-definition. Consultants often brought up the subject before I did, as was the case with several of the Enduring Voices documentary project participants (see cited interview material in Chapters 1 and 3). Many individuals had vivid memories of particular games, players, and conjurers, of family members who participated, and of the all-night dancing, the food after the game, and the wagering.[159]

My research indicates that many practices and beliefs associated with the complex have not ceased; it may be the case that anetso is in fact undergoing something of a revival. I also noted in Chapter 3 that more communities have been participating in the men's ball games at the fair in recent years. In addition, the appearance of women's teams is an interesting phenomenon, whether or not it is the revival of an old custom or the beginning of a new one.

Women Playing Ball: Evidence Past and Present

When I arrived in Cherokee in October of 2000 I was surprised to learn that women's teams would be competing in the Fall Festival. None of my consultants could remember women's teams, or any such competition in their lifetimes. Yet women from Wolftown, traditionally one of the townships with strong ball teams, were among the leaders in organizing the games. High school athletic events are hotly contested and well attended across western North Carolina, as is the case elsewhere in the United States, and on and around the Qualla Boundary it is no different. In 1993, for example, the Cherokee High School girls' basketball team won a state championship.

In 2001, there was a controversy over women playing anetso. Women's teams had competed as part of the fair the year before, in colorful team t-shirts and shorts, before enthusiastic crowds. Action was rough; an ambulance had come out on to the field during one game to transport an injured player. At a meeting held at the fairgrounds, the fair committee heard both sides of the issue. After a close vote, women were allowed to play.[160]

Again in 2004 a minor controversy arose because the fair committee did not approve a game between women's teams, but the women took the field and played after the scheduled men's game concluded. The announcer for the game was using the public address system that had been supplied for the men's game, and the Cherokee Tribal Police came and ordered him to turn it off. This incident illustrates the current community debate regarding the women's game. To my knowledge, as this book was going to press women have continued to play at the fair.

The issue of women playing ball is interesting. Some people say there was a time when both men and women played. I even have been told that women originated the activity, and the men took it from them. One woman told me she remembered girls playing with a rag doll instead of a ball during one fair.[161] Other consultants maintain the various prohibitions against contact with women before and during a match preclude their participation.

As noted above, in 1762, Lieutenant Henry Timberlake, a British colonial officer, witnessed women playing ball, noting that the women "pulled one another about" when they played, "to the no-small amusement of an European spectator."[162] This is the earliest reference to women playing that I have located, and Fogelson concurred. Fogelson stated that often immediately after the male contest the "women of the defeated settlement challenged the women of the victorious settlement in an effort to salvage some measure of town pride."[163] Though none of Fogelson's "informants" remembered women's ball games, he cited several additional accounts of women's games, which he said "confirms its former existence."[164] He concluded that, "before the removal in 1838 . . . women's games seem to have been frequent, either as an encore to the main game or in mixed forms as a social recreation within a town."[165]

According to Fogelson, at one time there were two kinds of games, a

Tseduga!

female ball game and a mixed game, in which the men played the women or mixed teams competed.[166] These games apparently were for recreation only; Fogelson did not mention, and I am not aware of, any accounts that mention other ceremonial complex activities.[167] I have not interviewed any female players, and do not know what activities accompany the contest. The further study of the women's games past and present would be a fruitful area of future research.

Conclusion

Anetso is one of the hardiest Cherokee "traditional" activities, one that was ubiquitous in Cherokee life for many years and continues to this day. It is not done for power or prestige, for gain or glamour. Yet, people just keep doing it. Many tourists who see Cherokee people doing it are completely unaware of what they are watching. Cherokee young people are run through the same movements and ceremony as their older counterparts, who use the same motions that are embedded in Cherokee identity and history.

What I think is significant is that anetso, though not always played for the same reason, has been played in basically the same way. The ceremonial complex has changed, but it has not disappeared. Some Cherokee people have found and continue to find religious significance in certain activities of the ceremonial complex even in the context of the fair; thus the question of inherent "religiosity" is situational. In addition, variation in activity, belief, and reasoning for participation are all natural parts of any religious system.

On an individual level there is deliberate identity maintenance that persists, through family and community interaction. This activity is neither unilateral nor of one voice. Furthermore, identity maintenance does not express itself in rigid adherence to doctrine and practice that produces anachronistic human museum pieces. It is a fluid and multiplex process. In the words of Gerald M. Sider, discussing the Lumbee people of North Carolina, it is a process of continuing "to try to bind new and different futures to ongoing pasts."[168]

Many people are privately ensuring continuation of Cherokee cultural traditions on a day-by-day basis simply by living their lives. Focused inward, into the community, this most crucial identity cultivation often remains the least discussed, and rightly so. But some individuals will express their sentiments if asked, and others offer opinions; some people also consent to have their comments recorded or repeated elsewhere. Others really do not have to say anything; one only has to observe the traditional activities they maintain, such as anetso. In these situations, identity cultivation and maintenance speak loudly.

5

Woye!
(Foul!)

Theory and the Meaning of Anetso

In these text-mediated disciplines and factions, theory is in discourse with theory, texts with texts. Living persons, living collectivities get uneasy, sidelong glances, for they are out of sync with abstract ideological programmatics.
—Don Handelman, "Critiques of Anthropology," 1994

When the manager of the Wolftown anetso team and the players walk across the street to the bank of the Oconaluftee River and stand single file facing the water, he talks to them before they engage in amohi atsvsdi, the "going to water" activity. In October 2005, a cultural consultant told me that the manager speaks to them about why they continue to play anetso and participate in associated activities. At that time he also tells them why and for whom they are playing:

    1. For mothers and grandmothers, because they are where the blood comes from, they determine your clan

    2. For the community—old, young, sick, weak, because they need to be protected, and this is part of the warrior code

    3. For themselves, with honor and respect, as the old ones taught.[1]

I had never heard this information, nor mention of the Cherokee warrior code before. I had consulted with the individual who imparted this to me since I first came to Cherokee in 1993. According to other Cherokee consultants and based on my observations, this individual is quite knowledgeable regarding the activity. However, this meeting was different from previous interactions with this consultant and other people, in which it was understood that when we talked I was not to bring a notebook, tape recorder, or laptop. This meant that I wrote down information later that day or the next.

In this case the individual dictated the statement, sitting and watching as I typed the statement into my laptop, and then read it when I was done.

Furthermore, this conversation took place at a table at the Cherokee Indian Fair, with other people going about their business all around us—eating, talking, laughing, and visiting. Yet this person still insists on anonymity. I do not wish to make a fetish of this statement; it is one person's opinion at one point in time. However, because it is one person's opinion at one point in time, it is important. In a work in which I, as author, pick and choose ideas, events, impressions, and reminiscences to represent this Cherokee cultural activity, such a statement provides an important counterpoint. The fact that it was transmitted to me in this way also is reason for its inclusion.

The statement is quite straightforward. People play anetso to express their identity: as Cherokee, as members of particular clans, as community protectors, and as caretakers of a tradition. There is no mention of other-than-human persons. There is no stated purpose of honoring, propitiating, beseeching, or thanking. No explicit link is made to any other event, although there is the suggestion that anetso is linked to warfare, or at least to training in order to protect those who cannot protect themselves.

Case closed: anetso is not a ritual. Activities of the ceremonial complex focused on it? Rituals? Connection between them? No mention. Case closed? Not so fast. As I have argued in previous chapters, just because such information related to the religious system is not discussed publicly does not mean it does not exist. Perhaps my consultant did not feel it was appropriate to share such information with a non-Cherokee person; other information consultants provided in other contexts suggests the issue is not so easily resolved.

The Relationship between the Ball Game and Warfare

The Cherokee term *anetso* (rendered variously) occurs most frequently in the written record as the name of the Cherokee ball game, but the term translated "little war" also appears. Several consultants noted it as well.[2] Raymond Fogelson provided a nice summary of the most common explanation given for the ball game that included this term: "The game was, and still is, regarded as a war surrogate, a fact borne out by: the translation of one of its Cherokee names, da.na.wah́ u'sdi', as 'little war'; the frequent use of the phrase, 'play ball against them,' as a figurative expression to denote a contest or battle (Mooney 1900: 312–3; 384; 433); and the general similarity of the ball game ceremonialism with the earlier war ritual."[3]

Elsewhere in his 1962 study Fogelson added to this comparison. He noted that warfare, "as traditionally practiced, can be conceptualized as but a further extension of blood revenge, whereby family and clan are replaced by tribal groups as units of cooperation. Warfare took the form of continued episodic raids and counter-reprisals."[4] Fogelson also stated that in "the 18th century, inter-tribal games between the Creek, Choctaw and Cherokee often served as alternatives to war in the settlement of boundary disputes," though he did not provide a footnote.[5]

Citing the John Howard Payne Papers, William H. Gilbert agreed when he summarized that "war can be said to have been a ritualized recurrent event of immense importance in Cherokee society."[6] Fred Gearing lent further support to this conclusion when he stated that, "Periodically, during the summer when warfare was rare, the young men joined together for ballplays with other villages. They assumed then a set of relations with one another, and with the village at large, which was analogous to the structure of the village for war."[7] My consultant's statement above is consistent with all of these interpretations.

According to Fogelson's interpretation, the ball game, as "a surrogate of war," followed the same socio-structural pattern as war; this mode Fogelson termed "equilibrated aggression."[8] He explained the concept in terms of the interactions between two parties, in which the "action and reaction sequences are temporarily stabilized, but no final resolution of conflict is implied . . . and the pattern is likely to start all over again." This notion "implies a set of rules or value premises shared by the contending parties" in a society's attempt to control aggressive action: "In short, unstructured, uncontrolled displays of aggression, particularly among the Cherokee, can have dangerous consequences."[9]

Fogelson suggested an important Cherokee ideal, the "harmony ethic," is just such a set of rules or premises in Cherokee society. Operative in the ball game and the cultural narrative about the contest between the birds and the animals, it is an "ideal behavior pattern that can be approached, but never fully attained."[10] The originator of the concept was Robert K. Thomas, a member of the Oklahoma Cherokee Nation who conducted fieldwork as part of a research team led by the anthropologist John Gulick in the late 1950s. Thomas sought to describe "the covert cultural patterns of conservative Cherokee life" as a "philosophical system—world view."[11] He continued, "the Cherokee tries to maintain harmonious interpersonal relationships with his fellow Cherokee by avoiding giving offense, on the negative side, and by giving of himself to his fellow Cherokee in regard to his time and material goods, on the positive side."[12]

Though a fairly general statement, this notion of the harmony ethic is to Cherokee religious studies scholarship what Max Weber's notion of the

"Protestant ethic" was at one time to some scholars of American religion: a kind of touchstone. Thomas's views were based on his conversations with Eastern Cherokee people, and he was concerned primarily with elucidating behaviors and the worldview held by those Cherokee people he described as "conservative."[13] Thomas's concept is regularly quoted by scholars, and to my knowledge the formulation never has been critiqued in print.[14]

Though I recognize the usefulness of Thomas's list of characteristic traits as well as his insightful observations, I question the broad application of it to Cherokee society by other scholars. The ideas discussed in the paper that explained this idea are intriguing, and are useful in assessing interpersonal relationships. Thomas's desire to present Cherokee beliefs as similar to the beliefs of evangelical Christian doctrine may have affected his discussion. Nevertheless, almost every Cherokee scholar who has discussed such matters has accepted the viability and explanatory capacity of the notion of the "harmony ethic."[15]

Fogelson believed a function of the ball game was communal reinforcement of this ideal of the harmony ethic. In his study, Fogelson examined two versions of the cultural narrative about the game between the birds and the animals — Mooney's collected version and the version Lloyd Sequoyah related to Fogelson. As we have seen, Fogelson adopted Kenelm Burridge's understanding of a "myth-dream", ("A community day-dream as it were"), employing the notion as a "unifying device serving to make intelligible certain symbolic content of the Cherokee ball game."[16] In this way he interpreted the ball game as a "ritual drama" that enacted "premises implicit in the myth-dream"; chiefly the "the management and control of . . . the process of equilibrated aggression."[17] This was a task the harmony ethic also served to fulfill.

Fogelson, as stated above, believed both warfare and the ball game followed a pattern of equilibrated aggression. As he noted, "After the first game is played, the process of equilibrated aggression is set in motion, since ball games are usually serial events with the losing team generally challenging the winners to a re-match." Like warfare, so this interpretation goes, the serial event is itself an extension of clan or blood revenge, and all three were mechanisms, according to Fogelson, designed to control aggressive behavior and promote social unity and consensus.[18] I will expand briefly on his theory here, and again below in the following section.

This custom of clan revenge was a hardy tradition not formally abolished in Cherokee communities until the beginning of the nineteenth century. My interpretation of Fogelson's theory is that with clan revenge abolished, and with warfare having come to an end decades earlier, the ball game remained as a key social institution for maintenance of the harmony ethic.

The harmony ethic remained an active rationale for other surviving social institutions as well, such as the *gadugi*, or free-labor groups.[19] Again, Fogelson's interpretation argued for the ball game as a surrogate for war in which competing townships, villages, or clans manage aggression.

Later in the study Fogelson compared this optimistic paradigm, which he supported with then-current anthropological theory (the "Gluckman-Turner position"), with a more pessimistic view that also had its adherents at that time (the "Siegel-Beals position").[20] He theorized that the ball game was an expression of the lack of cohesion and solidarity within and between communities, and that ethics were transgressed as hatred and cycles of revenge spilled out past the ball field and into everyday life: "The intensity of the ritualism and actual events reveal the fact that the ball players sometimes entered the game with deliberate intentions to maim, or even kill, members of the opposing team. Besides perpetuating chains of intentional ball game violence, these grudges, many of which were originally engendered in game situations, sometimes extended beyond the playing field and resulted in sorcery, fights and even homicide."[21]

What Fogelson concluded was that the Gluckman-Turner eufunctional explanation was more appropriate during the "aboriginal and early historic periods." During these times, the ball game provided a secondary outlet to warfare, gambling on the matches "served as a device to facilitate the circulation of commodities throughout the tribe," and the occasions when it was played, including treaty negotiations, became more festive as a result. He stated that the Siegal-Beals dysfunctional explanation was more appropriate from the end of the eighteenth century onward, when, "with the disappearance of the war path . . . the game may have taken on more of the attributes of real warfare." According to Fogelson, this second pattern "seems to have continued among the Eastern Cherokee through recent times and may help explain the survival of the game." He reported that interest in the game intensified in the years following World War Two, owing to the participation of veterans.[22] In a later work he summarized, "While the game is unquestionably aboriginal, and while several accounts of ballgames survive from the colonial period, it seems probable that ballgames assumed greater importance and, perhaps, greater ritual elaboration in post-Revolutionary times as a symbolic surrogate for actual warfare."[23]

Without relying on the social theory Fogelson invoked, Alan Kilpatrick, citing the work of William H. Gilbert, argued for a balanced assessment. He noted, "The interplay between social solidarity and opposition most often finds ritual expression in the heated rivalry between villages at stickball games."[24] Gilbert noted that "conflicts between villages were symbolized and to some extent given vent to by means of the ball games, which resembled regular battles in their ferocity."²⁵ Gilbert said that during his research visits in 1932 the ball game held "special importance in Cherokee culture as a basic form of organization of town units in opposition to each other."²⁶ Town was pitted against town, conjurer against conjurer, and clan brother against clan brother.²⁷

As I noted above, Fred Gearing also had something to say on this subject. He argued that the Cherokee "ethos" (the aforementioned harmony ethic) resulted in "periods of required deference" that in turn "created aggressive energies but blocked their expression"; therefore, "periods of relief," which warfare provided, were "probably necessary psychologically." Since warfare was by and large a winter activity, in the summer months there was the "ball play, seen as a harmless release from deference (and closed also by ritual purification)."²⁸

My own experience suggests that this notion of the interplay of social solidarity and opposition could be favorably applied to recent times, if it is not couched in the social and psychological determinism favored by Fogelson and Gearing and limited to this one function. I also agree with Gilbert's assessment, though he could have made a distinction between exhibitions and match games in this remark. While these notions are part of the story, they do not exhaust anetso's reservoir of meaning.

Similarities between Ball Game and War Ceremonialism

Gilbert divided the war complex into three phases: "preparation, the actual campaign, and the return."²⁹ Each description was very similar to the corresponding phases of the ball game complex. It is clear that warriors prepared themselves for battle much as ballplayers did for matches.

James Mooney included one war formula with ball game references in his work *Sacred Formulas of the Cherokees* that will help to demonstrate the affinities between the two activities. The formula "What Those Who Have Been to War Did to Help Themselves" is for men about to go to war.³⁰ As Mooney noted, this formula could be recited for up to eight men at once. To quote Mooney, who described the Confederate Cherokee Legion's preparations in the Civil War, "Almost every man of the three hundred East Cherokees who served in the rebellion had this or a similar ceremony performed before setting out—many of them also consulting the oracular (ulû^n-sû'ti) stone at the same time—and it is but fair to state that not more than two or three of the entire number were wounded in actual battle."³¹

The formula begins with the phrase, "Hayĭ'! Yû! Listen! Now instantly we have lifted up the red war club," and also includes the phrase, "You . . .

have shielded yourselves . . . with the red war club."³² These war clubs, as ball sticks might do, are "continually buffeting the doomed souls under the earth"; as the formula states, "the black war clubs shall be moving about like ball sticks in the game, there his soul shall be, never to reappear."³³ The formula also mentioned a "war whoop," which was "believed to have a positive magic power for the protection of the warrior, as well as for terrifying the foe."³⁴ This whoop is similar to that of the Talala in the call-and-response performed by this individual and the ball players.

This formula was recited for four consecutive nights before setting out. Then, on the fourth night, the conjurer gave each player a "small charmed root that has the power to confer invulnerability." The players went to water in the presence of the conjurer, and then, having chewed a bit of the root, spit the juice on their bodies "in order that the bullets of the enemy may pass him by or slide off from his skin like drops of water."³⁵ Ball players traditionally have included this action when going to water the final time before the contest in order to elude the grasp of their opponents.

Gilbert reported more details of the warriors' preparations. The "season" for "offensive and voluntary war was in the spring or fall"; after assembling, warriors fasted, prayed, and stood vigils for a day and a night. The first day after assembling "some bathed in the river and underwent purification." They performed a war dance throughout the night, and "before dawn all went to the river and plunged in seven times."³⁶

Beginning at daybreak the appointed "red war priest" performed divinations, first by casting a deer's tongue in the "sacred fire," next using beads, then with a crystal. These events and pre–ball game preparations share many similarities. Warriors, like ball players, observed gaktvda (prohibitions) that included avoidance behavior: "No intercourse with women was allowed throughout the course of the war." On the war march all were required to go to water and plunge seven times morning and night, along with a host of other rules.³⁷

At one time both players and warriors wore bird feathers, which were collected, dyed, and ritually treated by members of the Bird Clan.³⁸ Fogelson observed feathers attached to players' hair and ball sticks and noted that "birds appear to have played an important role in traditional war symbolism." For the ball game, the particular feathers were chosen on the basis of the individual's abilities or position. For example, the center fighter, usually the best player on the team, wore an eagle feather, symbolic of the captain of the bird team in the cultural narrative of the game between the four-legged animals and the birds.³⁹

In preparation for both anetso and warfare, ritual specialists would apply red paint to the faces and bodies of Cherokee men. As Thomas Vennum has noted, also from review of the John Howard Payne Papers, "in case of a small war expedition, or of a ball play, [the feathers] were painted at the request of the leader."[40] For a larger or "general" war, the war counselors asked these "sacred painters" to ready the feathers, and "different prayers were recited during the body painting."[41]

Fire, snakes, and lightning are additional elements that appeared in the context of both activities. Early accounts of Cherokee warfare reported that a war fire was sometimes carried into battle in a pot, and Fogelson noted that some conjurers have been known to carry portions of the ball dance fire to matches in pipes or lanterns concealed in gunny sacks.[42] When both players and warriors marked their bodies "with charred pieces of lightning-struck wood before confronting their enemies," the power of snakes, along with their symbolic analogue, lightning, was invoked.[43]

In Chapter 1, I cited Fogelson's comments that the "powerful Sons of Thunder, the Little Red Men, are frequently associated with snakes in Cherokee myths and ritual formulae, particularly those dealing with war and the ball-game."[44] This connection between anetso and the Sons of Thunder will be explored later in this chapter. One other similarity between warfare and the ball game was the use of items referencing rattlesnakes: masks with carved coiled rattlesnakes were used in dances to recruit warriors; while in the ball dance rattlesnake rattles were often affixed to the dance leader's gourd rattle and players' hair.[45] I will discuss the presence of rattlesnake symbolism in more detail below.

Cherokee warriors and ball players were similar in another way, as Vennum has summarized: "Cherokee warriors and ball players alike were considered to be in a 'red condition' for the entire cycle of their activities—susceptible to danger, injury, and even death—and while they continued their rituals after the principal event (battle/game) until they were 'released' ceremonially by a conjurer through ritual purification. It also explains their fear and avoidance of menstruating women, who were also considered 'unclean' and therefore dangerous because of their bleeding."[46] He noted, quoting the trader Alexander Longe, that "the warriors were said to be u-ta-la'-wa-shu-hi', meaning in a 'red' or bloody condition."[47] Fogelson agreed, at one point commenting that "the ball play, as a 'moral equivalent of war' . . . was definitely classified as a red activity."[48]

This notion also supported Fred Gearing's theory of red and white "structural poses" in Cherokee society. Gearing linked the ball game and warfare, and drew from the Payne Papers as well: "Teams had [war] priests to conjure for them and after games had to pass through purifying rites analogous to the rites on return from war (Payne MS, IVb: 61–64).... It is probably no accident, as a Buttrick informant reported (Payne MS, IVb: 16–64), that 'ancient priests [meaning the village priests who led ceremonies and councils] had nothing to do in ballplays,' and that the players were ritually impure after the game."[49]

Gilbert reported periods of "purification" and avoidance lasting from four to twenty-four days after returning from battle.[50] Purification activities included drinking emetics for four days while sitting by the "war fire," and going to water and passing arms through a fire on the fourth night.[51] As we have seen, it remains essential for some players to go to water not only after the final game, but also seven days later, usually at a team gathering. However, I am not aware that this activity or the Victory Dance done in the past included emetics or the ordeal of placing arms through a fire.

Vennum concluded that the final element of the anetso complex, the Victory Dance, was "unquestionably a vestige of the Scalp Dance of former times."[52] While I do not share his certainty, his comparison of Lieutenant Henry Timberlake's 1762 observations of a returning Cherokee war party with the Speck and Broom and Fogelson accounts of the anetso Victory Dance is convincing: there is an unmistakable similarity between the Scalp Dance and the Victory Dance.[53] Drawing once again on the Payne Papers, Gilbert said that the custom of giving war heroes goods on both occasions "has some resemblance to the allotment of the winnings in the ball game as stakes of victory."[54] During the time of his research, in 1932, Gilbert commented that the "chief function of the Eagle Dance at the present time is the celebration of victory in the Ball Game."[55] Regarding the postwar events, Fogelson felt that the "nature of these transformation mechanisms corresponds closely to those of the ball game."[56]

Gilbert linked war, the ball game, and hunting together when he stated that in "war, as in hunting and the ball game, the expectation of success or failure was determined by the use of various forms of divination."[57] There was "constant invocation of protective powers over, and the dissolution of uncleannesses from," both the warrior and ball player. He noted that both hunting and warfare required purification before and after the event, as is the case with the ball game.[58] The possible relationship between anetso and hunting also will briefly be considered later in this chapter.

Whether one considers specific similarities between the war and ball game complexes, or considers the activities more broadly in terms of social meaning and impact, there is much to compare. In the two historical accounts I presented in Chapter 1, the Cherokee figure of speech "to play ball against," as discussed in the "Kanati and Selu" narrative, was employed in both by their non-Cherokee authors.

Little Men and God's Great Guns: Witthoft's Theory of Anetso as Ritual

To my knowledge several tape-recorded comments that John Witthoft made have never been transcribed and published. In these comments he unequivocally stated that anetso itself was a religious ritual, and he explicitly linked the "twin gods" to it. I believe these twin gods to be the sons of Kanati and Selu, *Anisgaya Tsvsdi*, the "Little Men."[59] To quote Witthoft, the ball game was "a major religious ceremony" that "had to do with rainmaking and with the worship of the twin gods."[60] Located in the archives of the Museum of the Cherokee Indian, these audiocassettes were produced for the staff of the Oconaluftee Indian Village to aid in the design and construction of the first facility.[61]

Because these never have been published, I will quote several lengthy sections. Witthoft's initial comment regarding games was as follows: "The first and most important of them all was the Indian ball game, or Cherokee lacrosse which was not only a game of men and the national game, but it was also a major religious ceremony, that had to do with rainmaking and with the worship of the twin gods. Boys played at this game, in learning expert skills at it, in order to play in the big games, the real rituals, of men. Most lacrosse games, most Indian ball games, were played in the spring."[62]

In a later section of these taped remarks he noted, "All of these games had sacred meanings, and there are references to them in the myths, and this is probably the reason why the times when they were played were in the late evening and the early night before a major ritual."[63]

Even in his description of the Green Corn Ceremony, the ball game was mentioned: "At sunset, the night before the Green Corn Ceremony started, the old year ended. At this time all of the hunting for the Green Corn to provide meat for the feast had been completed, and all of the arrangements for the ceremony were done. At that sunset, when the old year ended, the last lacrosse game of the year had been played. And this was in many ways the most important lacrosse game of the year."[64]

Witthoft's comments, again, to my knowledge never published, offer an important and unique interpretation of the ball game. There is one other reference in Witthoft's work regarding this connection between the Little Men and the ball game. In a piece entitled "Cherokee Beliefs Concerning Death," originally not intended for publication but published in the *Journal of*

Cherokee Studies after Witthoft's death, he made some extremely interesting comments regarding conjuring: "I am sure there were two kinds of conjuring in ancient times. One was practiced in part at the town-house fire, the ball-dance fire, and the war-camp fire, and 'red' functions, and involved the male twin gods. The other was practiced in part at the square-ground fire and domestic fires, had 'white' functions, and involved some female deities. They meet in the magical conflict of funeral."[65]

These comments are provocative and suggest an explanation that may link disparate sources together. Both Gearing's theory of "red" and "white" structural poses in Cherokee society and the passage in the John Howard Payne Papers in which the commentator reported that the ancient priests were said to have nothing to do with the ball play express the same idea. I have interpreted this passage from the Payne Papers as suggesting the existence of two groups of religious specialists and functionaries, with anetso the provenance of conjurers. Witthoft's statement supports that conclusion.

To fully understand the implications of Witthoft's statements, however, it is necessary to understand the significance of the Little Men and their various connections to anetso, which is why I provided a basic introduction to them in Chapter 1. My conclusion is that though this is not an interpretation widely discussed, it is consistent with some information given in cultural narratives and displayed in ritual activity. Consultants today do not suggest this interpretation, and though I am not sure how widespread the belief was, I conclude that it at one time was extensive and may still be an aspect of Cherokee religious observances connected to veneration or propitiation of the Thunder Beings. There is no question that the Thunder Beings have held a significant position in the Cherokee religious system.

Furthermore, players accessed the power of the Thunders in a variety of ways. They have been ever-present in the anetso complex, though Cherokee people seldom if ever discuss them publicly. Mooney reported that charcoal was procured from the dance fire, and "whenever possible is procured by burning the wood of a tree that has been struck by lightning, such wood being regarded as peculiarly sacred and endowed with mysterious properties." The tree must have been struck but not killed by the lightning, and the wood should be burned along with wood of a honey-locust tree. The pulverized charcoal of this mixture was used to make a cross over the heart and a spot on each shoulder, and was dispensed from an empty cocoon that held a red and black bead. According to Mooney, this marking made "the player swift like the lightning and invulnerable as the tree that defies the thunderbolt, and renders his flesh as hard and firm to the touch as the wood of the honey-locust."[66]

Fogelson said such lightning-struck charcoal was "regarded as a most powerful substance, since it represents non-lethal contact with the thunder spirits." He also reported ball sticks that were engraved, painted, or burned with designs, frequently "jagged lines representing lightning, diamond cross-hatching to resemble a rattlesnake, and scallopped [sic] edges on the lip of the cup." He observed many sticks that were painted red or had red string entwined in the netting of the cup; small wrapped pieces of bat wing, peewee, chimney sweep, or hummingbird feathers were often affixed to the base of the cup. He also learned that some sticks were "burnished in the fire to improve their magical potency."[67]

I have been given ball sticks as gifts that exhibit certain of these design elements, and in the course of my archival research, I have located material evidence that is instructive in this regard as well. In both the Smithsonian National Museum of the American Indian and National Museum of Natural History collections, I came upon examples of almost all of the objects mentioned above.

The two most prominent design elements of these objects were the color red and reference to the rattlesnake, either by design, such as the cross-hatching design of rattlesnake markings, or attached body parts of the snake. The third most common motif was the cross, or "x." One item of particular interest was a "white duck feather with crossed rattlesnake fangs and red thread attached, symbolizing red lightning," according to the card catalog identification card.[68] Frank G. Speck deposited it in the collection in 1931, and the card stated that it was "used as a scarifier by ball players to give speed and fierceness."[69] Though the fangs were missing from the feather, this object combined three design motifs: red color, the rattlesnake, and the cross or "x."

Ball sticks themselves exhibited a few specific design motifs, including the cross-hatching design noted above. One common marking is an "x" or cross mark incised and burnished into the sticks just below the point where the bent piece of hickory wood comes together to form the cup of the racket. One pair of sticks had a kind of "reverse stripe" burnished design to produce black diamonds that seem clearly to mimic the rattlesnake's skin pattern. Another design, a spiral wrapping around the stick like a barbershop pole design, is less clear. It may be depicting the design on the rattlesnake's skin right above the rattle, or perhaps a snake coiled around the stick. A third variation had dots strategically placed along with the spiral design, again to mimic the rattlesnake's pattern.[70]

The color red was evident on sticks as well, such as a piece of red cloth attached to the metal webbing of the cup of a ball stick, and ball sticks with

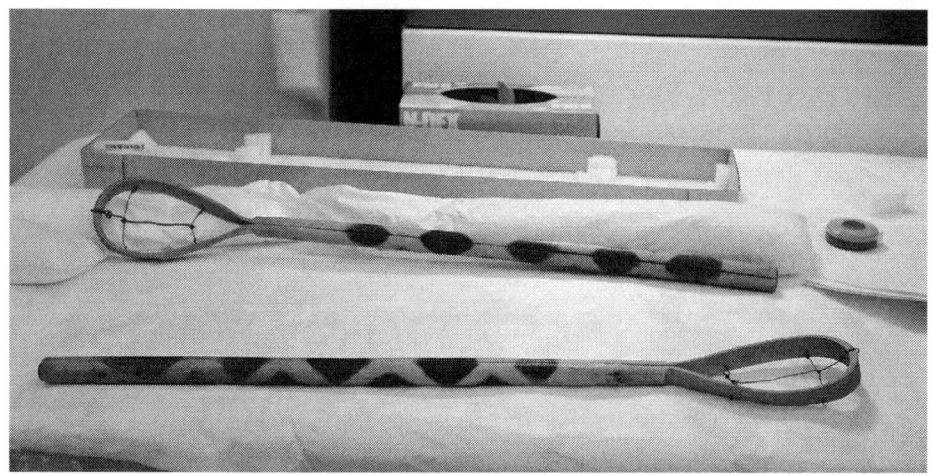

FIGURE 5.1. Pair of ball sticks. This pair of ball sticks has a burnished design of "reverse stripes" to produce black diamonds, a stylized rendering of a rattlesnake's markings. Collected by Mark R. Harrington, 1908. (Courtesy National Museum of the American Indian, Smithsonian Institution, Catalog no. 018993.000; photograph by author.)

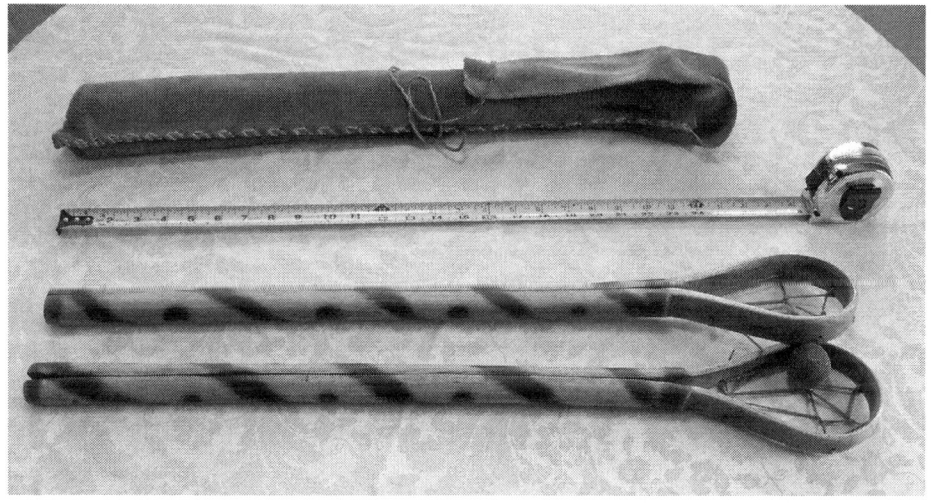

FIGURE 5.2. Ball sticks, ball, and case. This pair of sticks, ball, and carrying case were presented to the author as a gift in 2007. The stylized design of a spiral and dots seems to be a combination of the two common motifs on sticks, the spiral and the diamond or reverse cross or "x" marking, both of which reference a rattlesnake's markings. (Photograph by author.)

faint traces of red paint as part of their designs.[71] On most stick cups, cross-hatched incisions were located on the top edges of the cups, or as Fogelson said, the scalloped edges. On some sticks this edging went the entire length of the cup, but the two pairs of sticks given to me had three sets with seven points each.[72]

Fogelson said bathing suits or blue-jean shorts were the normal ball playing attire; he also noted that the short trunks Mooney described ("a.su.ló") were "decorated with symbolic stripes, crosses, and other designs."[73] The shorts I observed, some of which appear in photographs taken by Mooney, have red cloth appliqué and piping with these designs.[74]

One additional item worthy of note is a "War Dance Mask." According to the collection card, it was a human face, "with a rattle snake [sic] carved on top, red and black painted decoration, used in the ancient war dance. He who joined the dance, taking the mask and putting it on, signified his intention of joining the raiding party."[75]

The Thunders clearly are involved in the anetso ceremonial complex, but beyond this physical evidence, the commentary about its significance, and Witthoft's comments, no other information has surfaced to suggest that anetso was or is explicitly a religious ritual about the Thunders, or an attempt to gain their favor. It is fair to assess Witthoft in light of the academic work of his time. This interpretation exists nowhere else in the written record, and, as mentioned, current consultants reject it. In addition, several factors militate against forming such a conclusion.

Witthoft's best-known book, entitled *Green Corn Ceremonialism in the Eastern Woodlands*, was published in 1949 and discussed affinities among various groups in both the northeast and southeast cultural areas. He also contributed to a later Bureau of American Ethnology publication that was a symposium on Cherokee and Iroquois cultures.[76] Such works assessed Haudenausaunee (Iroquois)–Cherokee affinities (among other groups) in terms of cultural characteristics. Witthoft may have been overly influenced by data concerning the Haudenausaunee that clearly links a lacrosse-type activity with supernatural personages known as Thunder Beings.

In my opinion, it is possible that a scholar might interpret a visible element of one religious tradition with known explanations (according to that scholar) as similar to an element of another religious tradition without the attendant explanatory scholarship.[77] As an area scholar, it is likely Witthoft knew of the scholarship discussing the ball game as a religious ritual propitiating or pleasing to the Thunder Beings. In the absence of information for this hardy Cherokee activity, he may have borrowed from another culture to

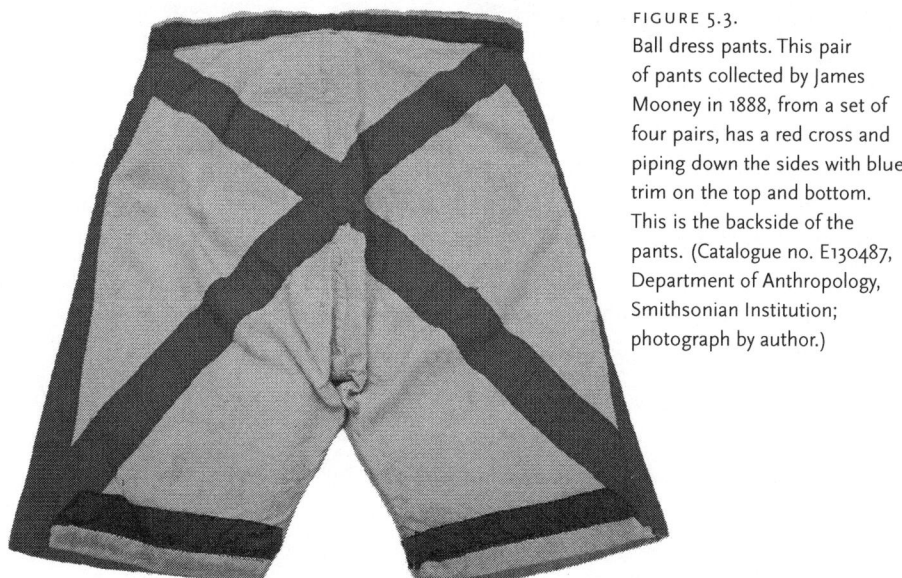

FIGURE 5.3. Ball dress pants. This pair of pants collected by James Mooney in 1888, from a set of four pairs, has a red cross and piping down the sides with blue trim on the top and bottom. This is the backside of the pants. (Catalogue no. E130487, Department of Anthropology, Smithsonian Institution; photograph by author.)

FIGURE 5.4. War dance mask representing human and rattlesnake. This dance mask has the figure of the rattlesnake on top of the human face. The crosshatching and striping on the rattlesnake portion of the mask are similar to certain design elements on the ball sticks. Collected by Frank Speck, 1933. (Courtesy National Museum of the American Indian, Smithsonian Institution, Catalog no. 185764.000; photograph by author.)

characterize what he thought to be a similar component of a similarly constructed system.

What one can say is that his statements do corroborate other evidence discussed above about the close relationship the Thunders have with anetso, even if they do not conclusively mark anetso as a ritual. A more global consideration is whether or not presently there is evidence of games that are rituals, or evidence that there have been such ritual games in the past. That broad question is the subject of the next section. I will begin by investigating the question in terms of First Nations cultures, and then offer selected observations about other possible examples.

Theories of the Relationships between Game and Ritual

It follows that a correct understanding of the origin and final significance of our Indian games can be obtained only through a more or less perfect knowledge of the rituals and symbolism of the various tribes.
—Stewart Culin, "American Indian Games," 1903

Unpacking the various aspects of the anetso ceremonial complex calls for reference to a range of scholarly perspectives on the subjects of play, ritual, game, spectacle, and performance. Because several works of some vintage still inform contemporary scholarship on the Cherokee religious system, anetso, and First Nations games, it also has been necessary to exhume somewhat dated, primarily anthropological academic literature. As I explained in the book's introduction, the scholarship of Mooney and Fogelson remains significant. Other anthropologists working from the 1930s through the 1960s also provided valuable accounts of these three subject areas that scholars working today continue to cite. Thus as I noted in the introduction, this book will serve as an up-to-date and much-needed reappraisal of scholarly discourse on these subjects.

In terms of theoretical perspectives, the situation is much the same. Statements about the nature of rituals and games by the anthropologists Stewart Culin and Claude Lévi-Strauss, made in 1907 and 1966 respectively, seem to have dominated the discourse since the dates of their composition. Paradoxically, as I will discuss below, Culin's conclusions have been dismissed roundly in spite of a preponderance of evidence, while Lévi-Strauss's formulation remains touted in spite of its rather flimsy supporting evidence.

Most, though not all, contemporary scholars have dismissed Culin's conclusions about the relationship between game and ritual as overly generalized, benevolently racist, and humanistic attempts to justify the actions of First Nations peoples. However, I think the interpretive pendulum has swung too far away from his position, and I hope to nudge it back toward the center. Conversely, Lévi-Strauss's distinction between the "frames" of ritual and game continues to inform contemporary scholarship. This is in spite of the fact that, as I will detail below, Lévi-Strauss based his conclusion on but two examples: one from an Eastern Highlands society in New Guinea that conventional academic discourse terms the "Gahuku-Gama," and one from the "Fox," now the Sac and Fox Nation.

My specific contribution to the ongoing discussion, though modest, will be to modify Culin's main conclusion and in the process, employing anetso as my primary example, seek to problematize if not refute Lévi-Strauss's distinction between game and ritual. Culin argued that every game devolved from or originated in a ritual practice. I agree emphatically with the generally held opinion that this is *not* the case. On the other hand, I do agree with Culin that according to received categories, there have been and are "rituals" that are "games." By this I do not contend that all games are rituals. I mean that, contrary to Lévi-Strauss, I argue that whatever we may venture by way of a defining distinction between ritual and game, his criterion that in "ritual" the outcome is predetermined, either by repeated games until both sides have won an equal number of times, or by prearranged determination of the victors, is problematic. While I share the prevailing viewpoint that collapsing structures into broader generalities is counterproductive to the task of definition building, inaccurately rendered assertions of difference and distinction are equally unproductive.

Certainly First Nations or Native American activities have received their share of attention with regard to these issues. Scholars such as Joseph Oxendine and Michael Salter have argued for the religious meaning of selected lacrosse-type games with data from cultures in what are now the northeastern and southeastern United States, respectively; other scholars have made similar assertions in other contexts.[78] In many instances, theories supporting religious meanings of games, either presently or in the past, have been allied with the concept of degeneration, where "game" devolves from a "loss of religiosity," although this does not apply to the theories of Oxendine and Salter.

Pursuant to this line of thinking, in a 1933 study of the Pawnee Nation Alexander Lesser considered an activity that had functioned at different times as both a "game" and as a "ritual"; in this context he suggested a modified theory of change that incorporated the notion of degeneration. Leonard Broom posited a useful explanation in 1937 for persistence of the Cherokee ball game and attendant complex activities against a broader landscape of cultural degeneration, as Fogelson would do a quarter century later. Broom collaborated with Frank G. Speck and Will West Long on the important 1951 study *Cherokee Dance and Drama*. After reviewing Culin's and then Lévi-Strauss's arguments, I will survey these and other selected viewpoints.

....

Stewart Culin published his signature work, "Games of the North American Indians," in 1907 as the accompanying paper of the *Twenty-Fourth Annual Report of the Bureau of American Ethnology*.[79] This massive volume, over eight hundred pages in length, is basically an edited reader. Along with introductory material and commentary, it included many reproduced articles from a variety of sources, either in whole or in part. While contemporary scholars are quick to point out its interpretive flaws, generally speaking, scholars regard it a relevant scholarly work due to the large amount of linguistic and ethnographic data Culin collected.[80]

Scholars looking to Culin for theoretical justification to support a thesis of degeneration did not need to read very far. In the introduction to this work, Culin asserted that the games were "the direct and natural outgrowth of aboriginal institutions in America," and that they showed "no modifications due to white influence other than the decay which characterizes all Indian institutions under existing conditions."[81] His matter-of-fact assertion of degeneration is not surprising for the time period; but as I will discuss below, additional comments in the work suggest that his view is more nuanced than this statement suggests.

Beginning with his "comparative study of the stick-dice game," Culin argued for a general correlation between "gaming implements and many ceremonial appliances," leading him to conclude "that behind both ceremonies and games there existed some widespread myth from which both derived their impulse." Drawing from Frank Hamilton Cushing's "Outlines of Zuñi Creation Myths" (*Thirteenth Annual Report of the Bureau of American Ethnology*), as well as other sources, Culin concluded that many origin narratives among First Nations peoples presented a main character or characters engaging in a game with an opponent bent on destroying humanity. In many cases these individuals were "those curious children, the divine Twins, the miraculous offspring of the Sun, who are the principal personages in many Indian mythologies." These "primal gamblers" succeeded by "superior cunning, skill, or magic," and now control seasons and the earth's daily routine; "always contending, they are the original patrons of play, and their games are the games now played by men."[82] While such a broad conclusion about origin narratives is difficult to substantiate, obviously there are affinities between this description and other cultural narratives, including the Cherokee narrative featuring Kanati, Selu, and their sons, the Little Men.

Culin concluded that, "in general, games appear to be played ceremonially, as pleasing to the gods, with the object of securing fertility, causing rain, giving and prolonging life, expelling demons, or curing sickness."[83] He ended the text of the introduction by saying that the Zuni "sholiwe" game "is ceremonially played to-day to secure rain."[84] Importantly, he employed the *present* tense, not the past tense, in both of these quotations. His opinion was that certain games continued to be "played ceremonially." In spite of his certainty about degeneration of First Nations cultural activities, he was clear, as he would reiterate in the conclusion, that such a characteristic was not universal, or at the very least not to the same degree across First Nations groups.

It is at the end of the work where Culin provided his succinct "summary of conclusions," which I reproduce in its entirety:

(1) That the games of the North American Indians may be classified in a small number of related groups.

(2) That morphologically they are practically identical and universal among all the tribes.

(3) That as they now exist they are either instruments of rites or have descended from ceremonial observances of a religious character.

(4) That their identity and unity are shared by the myth or myths with which they are associated.

(5) That while their common and secular object appears to be purely a manifestation of the desire for amusement or gain, they are performed also as religious ceremonies, as rites pleasing to the gods to secure their favor, or as processes of sympathetic magic, to drive away sickness, avert other evil, or produce rain and the fertilization and reproduction of plants and animals, or other beneficial results.

(6) That in part they agree in general and in particular with certain widespread ceremonial observances found on other continents, which observances, in what appear to be their oldest and most primitive manifestations, are almost exclusively divinatory.[85]

A century later, readers can find much to disagree with in this passage, but it is not all chaff. Certainly the definitively universalistic nature of his first, second, and fourth conclusions are theoretically problematic, impractically unlikely, and difficult to prove. However, there certainly are games and, as he noted, cultural narratives about them that are common to more than one community or nation. How one might classify games in relationship to one another (i.e., ball games, stick-and-ball games, etc.), while useful in some contexts, has no bearing on the issues at hand in this context.

More importantly, as Culin's comments should make clear, despite applying an evolutionary framework to his data, he did not argue for degeneration across the board. In the third conclusion he clearly stated his opinion about games: "That as they now exist they are either instruments of rites or have descended from ceremonial observances of a religious character." Additionally, conclusion five, despite its initial overly general clause, remains useful. It stated that the games "*are* performed as religious ceremonies" (my emphasis) and neatly summarized many *different* possible utilitarian motives or reasons why people engage in these activities. The final conclusion also is overstated, as he argued for some sort of "primitive" divinatory function, but again, the indication that games shared characteristics with "ceremonial observances" is provocative.[86]

I maintain that many scholars have simplified Culin's argument, and I think I know why. There are several examples in print of scholars who characterized his views based on the following oft-quoted statement that appeared in a general entry entitled "Games" in the 1907 Bureau of American Ethnology publication "Handbook of American Indians North of Mexico": "Back of each game is found a ceremony in which the game was a significant part. The ceremony has commonly disappeared; the game survives as an amusement, but often with traditions and observances which serve to connect it with its original purpose. The ceremonies appear to have been to cure sickness, to cause fertilization and reproduction of plants and animals, and in the arid region, to produce rain."[87] Here he used the past tense for the most part, though the second sentence did leave open the possibility that there were exceptions to the rule. Obviously this statement is different than the sum of his conclusions presented in "Games."

Interestingly, the first two sentences in the "Handbook" quotation already had appeared in his 1903 *American Anthropologist* article "American Indian Games," almost word for word. However, the next few sentences were quite different, focusing not on the past but on the present. The article passage continued with the sentence that serves as the epigraph to this section of the present chapter: "It follows that a correct understanding of the origin and final significance of our Indian games can be obtained only through a more or less perfect knowledge of the rituals and symbolism of the various tribes. Fortunately there remain certain tribes in which games occupy their original place in the religious life of the people, or a middle stage in which they are practised [sic] both as a rite and as an amusement. This is true both in Zuñi and in the Hopi towns of Arizona."[88]

To me this is a huge difference in emphasis. Though he maintains his view regarding degeneration, he acknowledges the full range of the relationship between game and ritual, including instances past and present when they were performed both as ceremonies and as games.[89]

Whether or not the emphasis in the "Handbook" was the result of an editorial change or a change in Culin's theory I cannot say, but it is important to recognize that he did say basically the same thing in both the 1903 article and "Games." At the time he was working on these two projects, at least, in his opinion there were games that were rituals. While the later passage may in fact be a refinement of his conclusion, the point of this exegetical exercise is that his viewpoint is different in the article and the major work than it is in what essentially is an encyclopedia entry.

In addition, what he said later in the same 1903 article was quite revealing: "The ball games have yielded least fruitful results to my comparative study."[90] In the end, Culin speculated based on Mooney's work that "the game of ball with rackets may be a dramatization of war. Mr. Mooney has pointed out that the ball game receives the name of war among the Cherokee."[91] Unlike the other activities, which he clearly could link to a particular goal or function, he was unable to do the same with anetso. Culin all but acknowledged that the ball games did not quite fit the rest of the data: anetso was not and is not played for any of the reasons Culin listed, and thus defied description in these ways. This is one of the most important points about anetso; indeterminacy remains about anetso's *meaning*, not about the presence or absence of ritual elements. Ultimately, this aspect is what confounds scholarly analysis; if it had a clear "function," the argument simply would be about categories or frames.

Claude Lévi-Strauss made the classic distinction between realms of ritual and game in *The Savage Mind* (1966 [1962]). For Lévi-Strauss, games are "defined by a set of rules which in practice allow the playing of any number of matches." He distinguished games and ritual by commenting that ritual, "which is also 'played', is . . . like a favoured instance of a game, remembered from among the possible ones because it is the only one which results in a particular type of equilibrium between the two sides." Thus for Lévi-Strauss, in instances when games are played repeatedly to allow both sides to "reach the same score," then this "is treating a game as a ritual."[92]

Because contemporary scholars continue to invoke this distinction, it is instructive to examine the source material that led him to this conclusion. Lévi-Strauss presented two examples to support his contention. Both were from fieldwork reports of other anthropologists. The first was "the case of the Gahuku-Gama of New Guinea who have learnt football but who will play, several days running, as many matches as are necessary for both sides to reach the same score."[93] His source for the information was a 1959 *American Anthropologist* article by K. E. Read.

Read stated that the aim of the contest was for a team to "equal the goals scored by the other and no team should win, that is establish its outright superiority." According to Read, the "guiding principle" of "equivalence" explained this behavior, as well as the "traditional feuding" that football had replaced, and warfare. Likewise, he reported, "the major cycle of festivals is governed by rules which are expressly designed to permit parity."[94] However, it is important to note that Read did not identify the football games as part of the festivals, or as rituals.

Lévi-Strauss's second example was a ball game that "accompanied" a Meskwaki (Fox; today part of the Sac and Fox Nation) adoption ritual, the purpose of which "was to replace a dead relative by a living one and so to allow the final departure of the soul of the deceased."[95] Here he relied on Truman Michelson's "Notes on Fox Mortuary Customs and Beliefs," in the *40th Annual Report, Bureau of American Ethnology* (1918–19) (1925).[96] Lévi-Strauss relied much more heavily on the Meskwaki example, devoting a page and a half to it in comparison to two sentences about the Gahuku-Gama example. Additionally, the Meskwaki game in question is an indigenous form of lacrosse. For both of these reasons I will devote more attention to it than to the first example.

According to Lévi-Strauss, "the main aim" of the rituals was "to get rid of the dead and to prevent them from avenging on the living their bitterness and regret."[97] He further reported that "the adoption rites necessary to make the soul of the deceased finally decide to go where it will take on the role of a protecting spirit are normally accompanied by competitive sports that pit the two moieties against one another."[98] All of the accompanying papers in the Bureau of American Ethnology (BAE) volume dealt with Meskwaki culture and bore Michelson's name as author. However, large segments of the volume consisted of accounts written down in the standard Meskwaki (Fox) syllabary and rendered in English by several individuals, including Michelson.

Lévi-Strauss drew from an account by a man named Sam Peters when he related that the outcome of the ball game differed; whichever team won was that of the moiety, "Kīckō" or "Tō'kān," adopting the individual for whom the adoption feast was being held. He presented a portion of the following passage to illustrate this point:

> And when an adoption-feast is given for these men, they would play cards. Sometimes they play the moccasin game (according to the games) the

men were in the habit of playing. And they would play ball. They used lacrosse sticks. It is as if they were playing with him for the last time, so it is said. This is how it is when they play ball. When the man for whom the adoption-feast is held is a Tō'kānna', the Tō'kānagki' win the game. The Kī'ckō'agki' can not win. And if it is a Kī'ckō'a' woman for whom the adoption-feast is given the Kī'ckō'agki' win, as in turn the Tō'kānagki' do not win. And that is the way it is.[99]

Lévi-Strauss interpreted this fixed outcome as follows: In the "great biological and social game" which the living and dead constantly play, "it is only the living who win." He commented that, "as all the North American mythology confirms, to win a game is symbolically to 'kill' one's opponent; this is depicted as really happening in innumerable myths." Thus, "by ruling that they should always win, the dead are given the illusion that it is they who are really alive, and that their opponents, having been 'killed' by them, are dead." As a result of this interpretation, the "formal structure of what might at first sight be taken for a competitive game is in fact identical" with such Algonquin rituals as the "Mitawit or Midewinin . . . in which the initiates get symbolically killed," feigning death "in order to obtain a further lease on life."[100]

Lévi-Strauss concluded that games have a disjunctive effect, while rituals have a conjunctive effect. According to Lévi-Strauss, games begin with symmetry—the same rules for both sides—and end with asymmetry—winners and losers. Ritual, on the other hand, begins with asymmetry, "profane and sacred . . . dead and living . . . initiated and uninitiated"; it ends with symmetry—"the 'game' consists in making all the participants pass to the winning side by means of events," presumably the "playing out" or successful completion of the ritual. As he ended this particular chapter, Lévi-Strauss further commented that "the game produces events by means of a structure," while "rites and myths, on the other hand, like 'bricolage' . . . take to pieces and reconstruct sets of events . . . and use them as so many indestructible pieces for structural patterns in which they serve alternatively as ends or means."[101]

While this is an interesting, if not entirely persuasive, exposition derived from the initial quotation, as it happens there is another account of the adoption feast lacrosse game in Michelson's work. It was written by Alfred Kiyana, whose contribution seems to have been roughly equivalent to that of Sam Peters in this as well as several other papers bearing Michelson's name that appeared in the same BAE volume. Kiyana's manuscript output was considerable, and his work has been the subject of recent scholarship.[102] The Kiyana account is quite detailed, yet no mention was made of the fixed outcome.

At the beginning of his account, Kiyana wrote that those giving the adoption feast "are playing with each other for the last time. They are stopping to play with their relatives for the last time. They play only the kinds of games (their relatives) enjoyed (playing) while alive."[103] He also provided two detailed passages about the games:

> Ball players play ball there. Those who first hurl this ball, hurl it toward the west. When the Kī'ckōs first touch they hurl it in that direction. And when the Tō'kāns touch it first they hurl it in that direction. The ball players (always) use lacrosse sticks: that is what they call them. When the Tō'kāns win, they are supposed to eat. Tō'kān-bowls: that is what they are called. And when the Kī'ckōs win, they are called Kī'ckō-bowls. [Those holding the adoption-feast] desire that all the people dine sumptuously. That is how the people hold adoption-feasts. No one is supposed not to eat. Every one of those there, as many as went to play with the one for whom the adoption-feast is held, are expected to eat. They desire that no one go away from there hungry: they desire that all of the people eat, even children, no matter what they eat.[104]

In this account Kiyana stressed the element of the postgame meal. As written, the passage described what the bowls are to be called when one or the other side won, but there was no mention of a predetermined outcome. There also was no mention of the adopted individual's moiety.

The second quotation described the women's game in some detail, but there was no mention of a predetermined outcome. To be sure, the fact that Kiyana did not mention this aspect in either of these passages is not conclusive—perhaps he felt this information should not be shared, or for some reason was not important—but it does give one pause.[105] Even though the texts differed on the point that I have highlighted, Michelson stated "that the Indian texts presented all supplement and confirm, rather than contradict each other," and "that the data correspond very closely to that obtained from other informants."[106] My aim is not to make the specious assertion that Kiyana was a more "true Meskwaki" source than Peters, but only to illustrate the fact that another source who wrote very thorough accounts did not include this particular detail. Perhaps there were variations in how the ritual was performed; again, perhaps Kiyana either did not want to write about it or did not know about it, but the discrepancy is curious.

An earlier account of a Meskwaki adoption feast by the anthropologist William Jones provided additional detail that potentially problematizes Lévi-Strauss's conclusion in this way as well as in another way.[107] In the game described in this article there were two boys being adopted and the Kīckō side prevailed three to one. A feast had been prepared by the family adopting the boys, and in winning the Kīckō victors "had the right to claim the food as theirs"; as hosts they then invited the other side to join the feast. As they did so, the victors "twitted [the losing side] of the ease with which they disposed of them in the game." This is a most significant point. Jones further observed that only a few Tōʻkān men accepted, "placidly submitting themselves to the fun poked at them during the feast."[108]

Yet again, there was no mention of the outcome being predetermined, or of the family's moiety. In many ways this account agreed with that of Kiyana, and in fact they reinforce each other in suggesting that the outcome may not have been predetermined.

Lévi-Strauss's interpretation focused on equilibrium between the living and the dead. In the Jones account, the victors invited the losing team to the feast, only a few team members accepted, and subsequently they were teased during the event. This raises two questions. First, if the outcome of the Meskwaki game was predetermined, i.e., if this was a "ritual," then why didn't everyone on the losing team attend the feast? Secondly, what was the point of the winners teasing the losers about how easy their victory was?

This begs an additional question: Is the issue of equilibrium between the moieties of the living not relevant? If it is, perhaps the implication is that these contests occurred over a period of time as both moieties adopted individuals, eventually resulting in a long-term equilibrium. In that context, perhaps one could offer a psychological theory about both moieties getting the chance to lord their victories over the others and tease them, thus providing a safe outlet for aggression. Though this is not a theory that I would put forward, the proposed function is what Read suggested above for the Gahuku-Gama football game, and is in fact what Fogelson suggested at one point about the Cherokee ball game, as discussed above.

To my mind, the two factors of the majority of the losing team not attending the feast and those who did being subjected to teasing clearly illustrate one thing: that at least among living humans, equilibrium did *not* result. What does one make of this distinction? If equilibrium of living people in this context is not relevant, then is it then an issue of "games" between living humans versus "rituals" that feature either dead versus living humans or the involvement of other-than-human persons? Even if Lévi-Strauss was correct in the end and picked the one account that included this important detail, the complexity of the relationship between the activities remains unclear.

In a section on "lacrosse" later in the text, the editor of the text, Margaret Welpley Fisher, related a cultural narrative in which "the manitou came among them and gave them the knowledge and skill of playing lacrosse"; he also told them that though others would learn the game from them, "the game would belong to them."¹⁰⁹ Fisher repeated the same Michelson citation as above in a footnote, and added valuable detail: "The game is called bagahatuwitni, the stick, otchi, and the ball pekwaki." She also noted that the rackets and ball Jones collected were illustrated in Culin's *Games of the North American Indians*.¹¹⁰

In a third section of Jones's text, entitled "Feasts of Thanksgiving," he described gatherings at the time of new corn (when it is first ripe enough to eat) when each moiety invites the other to a feast. At a certain point in the festivities the moieties sit on the ground facing each other in the middle of the bark house where the event is held. At this point the invited were all to eat before the hosts did. The passage continued, "The feasting is often a rivalry between the To'kans and Kickos, who endeavor to outdo each other in rapidity, completeness, and skill in putting away what is placed before them to eat. These services are purely religious and no one ought to come unless invited."¹¹¹

This description is of a ritual contest without a predetermined outcome. In the introduction to the translation of a text written by Alfred Kiyana, Michelson remarked, "The text starts out with a general description of how a gens festival is conducted; and it will be noticed that my contention that the tribal dual division into Kī'ckō'agki' and Tō'kānagki' is ceremonial as well for purely athletic purposes is sustained."¹¹² Fisher supported Michelson's contention about the nature of the game by citing an account by Paul Radin of a "Winnebago fast-eating contest, which good form demands that the host's phratry be allowed to win."¹¹³

What I have presented above does not invalidate Lévi-Strauss's theory, and he did provide the Gahuku-Gama example, but since the Meskwaki example is so central it does have some bearing in terms of assessing Lévi-Strauss's conclusions. Additionally, as I have discussed, there are Cherokee narratives featuring ball games that pitted various beings, including humans and other-than-human persons, against one another. Both Lévi-Strauss's and Culin's general assertions about First Nations narratives, while overstated, do point to the fact that other nations (not all) have certain narratives with similar components. Is there a necessary link, then, between narrative and practice? It seems to me that Lévi-Strauss's conclusions leave this issue unresolved as well.

Can there be ritual games that display elements of both parts of his dichotomy? In the case of the Meskwaki lacrosse game, there is a clear "meaning" that one can isolate and therefore identify the game, as well as the women's double ball game, as games that are rituals, or "ritual games." But if the outcome is proven *not* to be predetermined, then does that immediately exclude an action from the category of ritual? There is no way to catalogue every single activity in the world to determine structurally if they comply with this distinction, so what is the utility of this theory?

Anetso complicates the discussion one level further, because the "religious activities" are focused on anetso, not the other way around. If one cannot assign a "religious" meaning or function to anetso, because of its autotelic nature, does this disqualify it as well? My conclusion is that game, more particularly its subset, sport, and ritual *cannot* be separated so cleanly as Lévi-Strauss argued; not in the Meskwaki example and not in several others, including anetso. But both his and Culin's formulation continue to inform influential scholars, whose work I will discuss below.

....

Having sketched out the positions of Lévi-Strauss and Culin, I turn now to selected examples of scholarship informed by their work. After all of my research, Alexander Lesser's 1933 book, *The Pawnee Ghost Dance Hand Game: Ghost Dance Revival and Ethnic Identity*, and Leonard Bloom's 1937 Ph.D. dissertation, "The Acculturation of the Eastern Cherokee," remain key sources. In her introduction to the 1996 edition of Lesser's book, the anthropologist Alice Beck Kehoe felt the need to offer an apologetic, stating that the book was not "Trivial Pursuit esoteric," but rather was "a history of the Pawnee nation over the century of its greatest tribulations, and a detailed I-was-there description of a sociable ritual embedding central tenets of Pawnee worldview."[114] Kehoe's comments suggested perceived scholarly suspicion regarding such topics, which in my opinion was warranted, then as now, though perhaps not to the same degree.

As Kendall Blanchard has neatly summarized, Lesser took issue with Culin, arguing that "although some Native American games may have evolved from ritual, such is not necessarily the case."[115] Lesser himself wrote that the "general character of the transformation of the Pawnee hand game can be summarized by the statement that a gambling game was transformed into a Ghost Dance hand game ceremony." According to Lesser, the details of the change were most significant, and "the three aspects of change" to be considered were "persistence," "loss," and "addition" of traits.[116] He summarized again: "What persisted was the game itself, with its forms of play and of arranging for play; what were eliminated were the gambling aspects, and the associated war party simulations; what was added to make the new form was the generic type of ceremonialism and ritualism of the Pawnee, and the concepts and suggestions of the Ghost Dance religion and the Ghost Dance ceremonial forms."[117]

Lesser then considered what he called the "history of the game rituals," and stated that the "games, as the Ghost Dances themselves, were cultural instruments for revivals."[118] He estimated that the hand game became part of the Ghost Dance complex about 1892 and was linked to the Ghost Dance of 1890, associated with the Numu (Paiute) prophet Wovoka.[119] Lesser noted that before 1890, the game was associated with "war party patterns," but that like the Ghost Dance elements, these could have attached to the game core, and thus were not irrefutable evidence "of ultimate origins in rite or ceremony." He concluded that "as the doctrine which called these rituals into being weakens, the rituals tend to relapse once more into mere games," thus "games may become rites, as well as rites games."[120]

Lesser argued that the play of the game was "the nucleus or core of meaning"; understanding the process of change entailed "dealing with types of association and dissociation of extrinsically related themes to and from a certain analytic core or constant."[121] Because the doctrine of the Ghost Dance included Christian concepts, concomitant rituals were incorporated into the games and replaced Pawnee traditions; for example a Baptist blessing took the place of a smoke offering.[122] Lesser also stated that "the elements of gambling of the earlier game were eliminated," because "the Ghost Dance hand game was a ceremony." Between 1902 and 1919, the games "disintegrated" from four-day into one-day events, and some became church games; by 1930–31, when Lesser visited, ceremonial games were "less and less played," and "those games which are demonstrated are attended by many primarily as a form of social amusement."[123] Thus the cycle of change went "from gambling game to ritual to church game to social game," with the result that "a gambling game has finally become a cultural institution for social gatherings."[124]

Lesser began his book's conclusion by quoting several of Stewart Culin's conclusions (numbers 3, 5, and 6 above), and stating his opinion that Culin abandoned his view that the games were originally divinatory rites.[125] Ultimately, Lesser said, all such "contentions are at best hypothetical" and did not affect his argument. Reiterating earlier comments, Lesser summarized his general conclusion as follows: "We have considered a game, and the particular additions to it were of a ritual or ceremonial nature, hence we may say a game became a ceremony, or, as the process is tending to reverse itself, a ceremony is becoming a game."[126]

As for the Ghost Dance hand game specifically, he argued it was, "composed of at least two 'systems,'" or "separable complexes," the game play and Pawnee ceremonialism, and importantly, that the game existed before it was associated with ceremonial actions. Lesser argued that the hand game became a ritual because it was a well-known traditional activity, perhaps the most accessible of any such activity to the widest group of Pawnee people. Both its stature as an indigenous cultural form as well as its ubiquity transformed it from a "leisure" activity to a ceremonial activity in times when many forms of ceremonialism either were suppressed or discarded (it later changed back to a leisure activity again). Lesser understood the Pawnee hand game play itself as having constituent "persistences" that were the "nucleus" around which other "associations," or "meanings," accrued (Pawnee ritual elements, Ghost Dance ideology, Christian ritual elements) or were sloughed off (gambling, war party simulations) from around the core of the game, itself not a constant entity.[127]

He did however argue for broader application of his own findings. In particular, he noted the relevance of plotting a "cultural institution or complex," asserting that a "persistent core constitutes an analytic unit or constant against which the changes can be visualized," and "that the total institution at any one time, viz., the core plus its analytically revealed associations, is a manifold which is not a unit system."[128] I find Lesser's characterization useful, because anetso, like the Pawnee hand game, is a "manifold," composed of a nuclear core (the ball game itself) plus a "separable complex" that I can at least provisionally term "Cherokee ceremonialism." The notion that as a nucleus the hand game had the ability to support various meanings at different times provides an example of what I am asserting is the case for anetso. I also agree that the accessibility of the activity was significant.

Though there are similarities in Lesser's project and my own, there are several crucial differences. One difference between Lesser's interpretation and mine is that I suggest that collateral meanings are transported as a function; they do not attach or fall away but are held in trust as constitutive of the ball game's multivalent nature. My interpretation of diachronic change is based on interpretation of discrete primary meanings of the ball game that have emerged in particular historical moments.

Another way my interpretation differs from Lesser's is that he understood the hand game to have no connection to the realm of religion in the time prior to the period he treats. I argue that for Cherokee people, realms or frames of the received categories religion and game have interfaced continually for at least several hundred years; longer according to Cherokee cultural narratives. In addition, Lesser's opinion that the hand game fulfilled "intellectual and social needs . . . in the midst of cultural barrenness . . . produced by uncontrolled assimilation" is extreme in hindsight, and his functionalist approach is antiquated, as are the psychological approaches over against which he privileged his own theories.[129] However, his basic insights remain rock solid.

In his 1937 Ph.D. dissertation, Leonard Broom, who went by the last name of Bloom at that time, reported on anetso. He was of the opinion that it had "a secure place in the customs of the modern community," and that its significance lay in "the fact that its survival has had a part in preserving a whole gestalt of ritualistic and ceremonial appurtenances."[130] In a lengthy quote he provided a survey of anetso ceremonial complex activities at that time:

> One of the best preserved of dance forms is the ball game dance. Only in the pre-game ritual is scarification carried out in an extreme fashion. Scratching once may have been an actual ordeal; today it is ceremonial. Although they are all practiced in a much diluted manner, we still find associated with preparation for the ball play, scratching, conjuring, going to water, fasting, continence, and the post-game dance of celebration. No doubt the game will outlast all its attendant customs, but it has been a potent factor in lending artificial respiration to a whole body of lore. The axiom seems to present itself that *gestalten of lore will survive longer when they have as a core some salient institution of marked vigour.*[131]

This is a statement of great utility for my project. Bloom's statement resonated with certain of Lesser's comments in that the ball game is a nucleus around which other activities aggregate, including those of a "religious" nature, and that as a cultural form the ball game proved to be unusually persistent. He reported seven of the ceremonial complex activities still being performed, albeit "in a much diluted manner." However, I have serious reservations about Bloom's assessment that the ball game provided "artificial respiration" for the continuation of elements of the religious system. In part my disagreement lies with the inherent aspect of degeneration in his theory. But also, as I have discussed, several of the activities, particularly going to water and conjuring, are stand-alone activities. I also find it noteworthy that he used "ceremonial" to mean "not actual."

In *Cherokee Dance and Drama*, Broom and his coauthor Frank Speck made a related statement about the ball game dance, but broadened their scope:

> The Ball Game or Ballplayers' Dance is but a small part of a long, involved, and esoteric ritual preparation for the team, to add spiritual strength to its efforts and to weaken those of its opponents. Its analogies are martial and

the entire performance corresponds with ancient rites of the war party. The gaming feature need not be regarded as a step toward profanation, for it is associated with rites throughout eastern North America in the Iroquois Bowl Game, Lacrosse, and the Tug of War, as well as the widespread Moccasin Game.[132]

This statement speaks to several of the issues treated earlier in this chapter, including the perception of a close relationship between anetso and war. Also noteworthy is the statement, with supporting examples, that the "gaming feature need not be regarded as a step toward profanation." Clearly the authors were responding to an unspoken notion that such features were evidence of "degeneration." This narrative posture has been adopted by a number of contemporary scholars, some of whom relied upon Culin's work.[133]

Joseph Oxendine has provided further perspective on the discussion, noting that "Culin emphasized, perhaps unduly, the connection between ritual and sport," and citing Blanchard's characterization of Culin's attitude as "benevolent racism."[134] He then clearly stated his position with two key passages: "The abundance of evidence from as long ago as 1636 and continuing through the 19th century overwhelmingly identifies sport with ceremony and spirituality. That so many observers, reporting independently, would concur in support of a positive Indian image seems unlikely. Some of those reporting a strong cultural connection, in fact, predated Culin's work by more than two centuries."[135]

Oxendine further reported that, "Oren Lyons, traditional Faithkeeper of the Iroquois and also a former All-American lacrosse player at Syracuse University, informed me in July of 1986 that the connection between games and healing continues today. According to him, it is not unusual for friends to arrange a lacrosse game for a sick person's benefit. The individual is taken in his or her sick bed to the sidelines of the field, and the game is played in that person's honor."[136] In addition, Oxendine said that Blanchard's critique of the "ritual-to-sport evolution" did not "refute the notion of a strong interrelationship between traditional sport and ritual."[137]

John MacAloon discussed Culin's work along with that of British classicists such as Jane E. Harrison, who postulated that games, as well as theater, dance, music, and poetry, had "separated from an original religious ritual matrix in the primitive and ancient worlds." According to this argument, religious or magical elements in games such as Shrovetide football contests among peasants in "early modern France and England," and sumo in Japan, were seen as "backward 'survivals' of an archaic past in 'fossil' social structures still partially attuned in cult to cosmological and agricultural rhythms."[138]

MacAloon surmised that such conclusions were based on an evolutionary theory of society that scholars such as Max Weber believed explained the transition from "'traditional' to 'modern' societies under the impact of the industrial revolution and modern science." MacAloon also noted that such views have been criticized as Eurocentric and imperialist, and further, "that in the West itself religion has not regularly and inevitably declined and that the cultural history of forms like games has not followed any simple unilinear pattern." MacAloon dismissed as "humanistic speculations" the theories of ethnologists such as Stewart Culin, citing as evidence the concluding passage from Culin's introduction to "Games" discussed above. MacAloon argued that Culin's work was influenced by and contributed to "evolutionist trends of European thought variously styled 'rationalization,' 'modernization,' and 'secularization.'"[139] However, like other scholars mentioned in this survey, MacAloon simplified Culin's argument and ultimately undervalued its significance in the study of First Nations games.

. . . .

Why have so many observers struggled with the concept of "game" for so long and so inconclusively? Why have observers located it on opposite ends of a spectrum, either, à la Huizinga, overshooting its universal significance, or not taking it seriously, deeming it not fit for scholarly investigation? One reason is because games are arenas for people to try out, to act out, to have their efforts "count"—but not really.

What separates game from ritual in this general formulation are the voluntary quality and the aspect of fun. These characteristics translate to an absence of expectation to participate that can produce personal or social conflict. Both contribute to its interpretation as "not serious." As Victor Turner noted, one willingly pays to go to the Super Bowl, yet feels "moral pressure" to attend worship services.[140] Both rituals and games have spectators, but rituals do not have fans, at least not in the generally recognized sense.[141]

A common example is the following: a priest leads a team in prayer before a college basketball game in the United States, and a victorious player thanks God afterward in a postgame interview. The specific focus of the prayer beforehand is the game. The indication is that God has an interest, if not in the outcome, then in the fair play and safety of the players. The specific focus of the action after the game, which is literally thanksgiving, remains the game.

It is fair to say that in such a situation, no one involved—priest, coaches, players, spectators, reporters—considered the game itself to be a ritual, though religious beliefs and actions were involved. Conventional scholarly opinion would be the same. On the other hand, the action of the priest leading the team in prayer before a game, I argue, just as readily *would be* considered a ritual as not, especially by scholars. The praying is isolatable as a ritual from the game, but not the other way around. Why? Because presumably the prayer is directed toward an other-than-human person or persons, and such belief is part of a recognizable religious system. The game, while also part of a larger cultural system, is not accorded the same distinction because there is no perceived direct link to a recognizable religious system.

In her later work *Ritual: Perspectives and Dimensions*, Catherine Bell discussed sport, play, and war in the same section. She noted: "Much interest and conjecture attend the question of how sports may have originally emerged from religious ritual or been closely linked to it, as in the Mayan-Aztec ballcourt game or the Greek Olympic games. Whether or not such lineage is relevant to understanding modern sports, some observers are fascinated by the way in which sports attracts various taboos, pollution beliefs, and 'magical' practices."[142]

The comparisons to the Mesoamerican ball games and the Greek Olympics are provocative, and this issue deserves consideration of its own. Citing "patently nonutilitarian gestures" employed by athletes, Bell said that "such miniature rituals, defined as proscribed behavior that is scrupulously observed in order to affect an outcome, may not be part of the game in itself but on close examination seem nearly inseparable from real participation in sports." Other scholars have focused on the idea that "the ritualism of sports derives from the importance of the more encompassing sets of rules . . . [that] constrain the contenders and force them to follow very controlled patterns of interaction." The result is that, "in the tension between the brute human energy being expended and the highly coded means of engagement, the sports event seems to evoke in highly symbolic ways a fundamental conflict or experience at the core of social life."[143]

Such an interpretation is not unlike that of Fogelson, who strove in his dissertation to interpret the ball game with the prevailing theory of the day. Bell went on to say that,

> Similar considerations are behind the tendency to describe some forms of play as ritual. While the chess match is more like a sports contest than not and thus shares in some of the ways in which sports can appear ritual-like, most characterizations of play as ritual-like focus on examples that are communal, repetitive, and culturally patterned. These characteriza-

tions see in play a social license to manipulate, invert, or ridicule cultural symbols and patterns, even though such manipulations can effectively reinforce deeply embedded social assumptions about the way things are and should be.[144]

She also made a statement about war: "War is another social analog to the rule-governed expressive activities of sports and play that also appears ritualistic in many circumstances. Naturally, as with the previous examples, war usually involves many explicit rites and ceremonies, but observations concerning the ritual-like nature of war itself point to the role of rules in channeling, constraining, and simultaneously legitimating the violent interaction of opposed groups."[145] Obviously the interesting relationship Bell outlined between ritual, sport, play, and war is relevant to my discussion of anetso. The "role of rules" in regulating violence has particular application.

Of course, issues of violence are significant in the history of religious systems, though unlike scholars such as René Girard, I do not accord violence a central role in the formation of such systems.[146] In several cultural contexts, enduring physical hardship or violence in a cultural presentation seems inextricably linked with identity and the perpetuation of culture. To engage in such activity within the bounded space and time of the ball game, with retaliation after the contest frowned upon, is an interesting variation on the theme. In a fairly well-known article (Bell cited it in *Ritual*, for example) regarding the relationship of violence, rules, ritual, and game, Mary and Max Gluckman argued that,

> Again, it has been said that some North American Indian games were ritual; but this does not emerge from the following account taken from Culin's book, or elsewhere there. The contestants may use magic to seek success, and the presiding elders ask for a peaceable game, with none hurt and fair play observed, but there is no suggestion that unfair play or assault or attempts to damage an opponent bring occult retribution, or that the course of the game or its outcome influence in occult manner the course of outside events.[147]

They continued by citing accounts of Chippewa lacrosse games, stating that "'the rules of the game' apparently provided an ethos which kept the games within bounds."[148] The authors then contrasted these examples with the description of rough play in Mooney's 1890 article, noting that "these fracas occurred despite an address by an old man." "This breaking out of violence, despite the ethos of the game and the initial supplication, as well as the fact that the players can make choices and the outcome is uncertain, also distinguish most games from ritual. Except when prescribed and limited license, within bounds, is allowed, violence at a ritual may destroy its efficacy."[149]

The Gluckmans' point is that "it is also inappropriate, but not blasphemous, for competition and struggle to break the rules of games," but that people do so anyway; yet this "is not destructive of efficacy of the rules."[150] The authors' reliance on Lévi-Strauss's distinction between game and ritual is clear, as are the normative assumptions regarding what rituals are (need for exterior referent, controlled violence, threat of both "occult retribution" and inefficacy for improper conduct), and are not (the "uncertain outcome," individual choice, uncontrolled violence). Plainly the notion of rituals being autotelic is antithetical to the Gluckmans' interpretation; patently anetso does not conform to their model (nor to their characterization, for that matter).

Allen Guttman's delineation of seven distinguishing characteristics of modern sports from "primitive, ancient, and medieval" sports in *From Ritual to Record: The Nature of Modern Sports* (1978) has continued to influence the discourse among certain scholars.[151] Guttman concluded that, "whether or not one considers the passions, the rituals, and the myths of modern sports as a secular religion, the fundamental contrast with primitive and ancient sports remains. The bond between the secular and the sacred has been broken, the attachment to the realm of the transcendent has been severed."[152]

He also offered this concise statement: "We do not run in order that the earth be more fertile. We till the earth, or work in our factories and our offices, so that we can have time to play."[153] Guttman's primary illustration for this argument was Morris Opler's 1944 article, "The Jicarilla Apache Ceremonial Relay Race."[154] For his part, Opler stated that there was "probably less concern over which side will win the race than there is that the ceremony takes place at frequent intervals."[155]

In his book on First Nations running traditions, Peter Nabakov dubbed Opler's work the "most detailed study of any Indian running ceremony."[156] Nabakov himself asserted that beyond the functions of communicating, fighting, and hunting, First Nations peoples "also ran to enact their myths and to create a bridge between themselves and the forces of nature." Though the book concerned running, Nabakov invoked the Cherokee ball game. He noted that "ballplayers sought animal and plant powers before each game," and thus, "they made themselves composites of their flora and fauna," an evocative, if not entirely accurate statement.[157]

Guttman also referenced "the ritual ball game of the Cherokee Indians," comparing the conjurer's role to that of a contemporary "witch doctor" working with Zulu soccer teams in Durban, South Africa.[158] In a later work Guttman argued that, modern sports are not ordinarily perceived by athletes and spectators as religious ceremonies in the obvious ways that a Roman Catholic mass or an African Methodist Episcopal Zionist funeral are. No matter how important they seem to their players and spectators, modern sports do not provide encounters with what theologians refer to as "the numinous." The games played by adult members of the Indian tribes, however, were normally occasions for interaction with the mysterious realm of the sacred. . . . Such games, "played ceremonially," were part and parcel of fertility ritual, the exorcism of demons, and . . . sometimes functioned as vehicles for divination.[159]

Guttman chose two activities to typify such "ceremonial games" (my phrase), and he had used them both before: the Jicarilla Apache "relay race" and the "stickball" games of the "Southeastern Indian" tribes. He argued that "the lockerroom prayers of the local priest at a high school football game and the elaborate rites of the shaman on the eve of the stickball game are formally comparable." For him, the differences between "ourselves and our hunter-and-gatherer ancestors" outweigh similarities: "Lockerroom priests are expected to ask the Lord's blessings and to remind their psyched-up auditors to leaven the mayhem with a modicum of Christian charity; the shaman, on the other hand, performed a number of symbolic actions associated with human fertility. Without the priest, the football game is unimpaired (some might say enhanced); without the shaman, there *was* no stickball game."[160]

But of course who is the "we" that he is invoking; and what of the people who play the game today and would be most displeased if they were referred to as anyone's hunter-gatherer ancestor? Cherokee conjurers, like priests in locker rooms, make use of relationships with various beings to try and gain assistance or advantage (and thwart the efforts of their opposite number).

I suggest that there is a fundamental similarity between this sort of ball game propitiation and that of "modern" football players (among others) who, with the help of team spiritual leaders or advisers, make use of relationships with, to use a Christian example, God and/or Jesus Christ for propitiation purposes toward a corporate goal. In other words, they ask for assistance in securing victory. Payment in this case is giving the "credit" or "glory" or "thanks" to God or Jesus Christ.

Of course this comparison has its flaws. For example, the conjuring activities are considered to be integral to the anetso complex, while such activities related to football can most properly be termed peripheral, if not approaching incidental. But one of the points I am trying to make is that these activities are not considered "mystical" or "mysterious" or "magical" when directed toward a culturally familiar superhuman being. When a Christian minister prays to God with members of the team, this is not "mysterious" to a non-Cherokee observer may who understand the Cherokee activity in such a way.

As I have endeavored to show, in Guttman's terms the "shamans" are asking for "blessings," not doing human fertility pantomime or magic. Football, like anetso, provides a cultural locus for a range of activities, some that can be termed "ritual" and some "religious." Preliminary and postgame activities, propitiatory activities, community involvement, even gambling serve to weave the experience of this game into the social lives of players and spectators. Though Guttman often simplified matters, his recognition of what the philosopher Ludwig Wittgenstein has termed "family resemblances" helps the discussion.[161]

Another helpful viewpoint is that of Victor Turner, whose application of Arnold van Gennep's notion of liminal phenomena in a ritual process is well known.[162] In a 1974 article Turner discussed the Cherokee ball game in the context of postulating the category "liminoid," which he distinguished from his well-known category "liminal."[163] Turner made a distinction between "ergic-ludic ritual liminality and anergic-ludic liminoid genres of action and literature." Basically, he argued that in tribal societies liminal phenomena tend to be ultimately eufunctional, while in industrial societies liminoid phenomena expressed in genres of literature, drama, and sport are not; in some cases they are social critiques and sometimes are revolutionary. In "complex modern societies" both types are present, with the liminal being located in churches, initiation rites of fraternities, and Masonic orders, and the liminoid categories above being commodified. To repeat Turner's idea from above, one willingly pays to go to the Super Bowl, yet feels "moral pressure" to attend worship services—"One *works at* the liminal, one *plays with* the liminoid."[164]

Turner argued that the distinction between work and leisure, "which includes but exceeds play *sui generis*," was "an artifact of the Industrial Revolution."[165] He listed the ball game among a group of activities he thought exemplified "'ludic' aspects of tribal and agrarian ritual and myth." Grouping the "ancient Maya and modern Cherokee" ball games together as "sacred games," Turner argued that these activities, along with other types of activities such as "joking relationships . . . riddles, mock ordeals, holy fooling and clowning" as well as Trickster tales, were in fact, "as Durkheim says, 'de la vie sérieuse.'"[166]

Turner believed such activities were "intrinsically connected with the 'work' of the collectivity in performing symbolic actions and manipulating symbolic objects."¹⁶⁷ Like MacAloon I do not agree with his evolutionary social model or his general conclusions. However his comments about the symbolism and "sacred" nature of the ball game are thoughtful; clearly Turner recognized some aspect of both Mayan and Cherokee ball games that illustrated an element of his argument.

Clifford Geertz's "Deep Play: Notes on the Balinese Cockfight" certainly is one of the best-known scholarly articles on the subjects of play and games. In his exposition of "deep play" he stressed that the cockfight was "fundamentally a dramatization of status concerns."¹⁶⁸ Geertz suggested that the cockfight was set aside from ordinary life as "only a game" and "reconnected to it as 'more than a game.'"¹⁶⁹

Ultimately, according to Geertz, the cockfight is "interpretive," a "metasocial commentary: a story they tell themselves about themselves." For Geertz, the cockfight provided a window to explore the entire culture: "As much of America surfaces in a ball park, on a golf links, at a race track, or around a poker table, much of Bali surfaces in a cock ring. For it is only apparently cocks that are fighting there. Actually, it is men."¹⁷⁰ Several other scholars have made similar comments regarding the display of American culture through baseball (Jacques Barzun) and football (William Arens); Raymond Fogelson said as much about anetso in his dissertation.¹⁷¹

The difference between the positions of Geertz and Fogelson is that while both expressed the same basic opinion, Geertz developed the idea in terms of the activity itself more than in the personality characterizations it might have revealed. According to a critique by Margaret Wiener, Geertz's conclusions about cockfighting complicated rather than explained the cultural implications of the activity. She asserted that Geertz's conclusion "obscures Balinese intentions" and "does not take indigenous discourses seriously into account," thus "recapitulating many of the claims made by Dutch colonial officials."¹⁷² Oddly, Geertz did not fully consider the overtly religious aspects of the cockfights, which, ironically, raised further questions about his explanation.

The concepts of game or sport as deep play, and the cockfight as religious ritual and metasocial commentary, are quite useful in terms of my theoretical approach to the Cherokee ball game, though I strive to provide an alternative to metaphors of text. One scholar who is at the forefront in the theorization of a range of related issues is John MacAloon, whose work I will engage next. At present, MacAloon stands alone in terms of the interdisciplinary scope and theoretical sophistication of his work on performance, ritual, and game. Though I do not share his views of religion and ritual, and he did not directly address the ball game, his assessment of the general theoretical scholarship is the most studied, and thus essential to my project.

In an important 2006 essay, MacAloon reflected on his research program focused on the Olympic Games, including two essential essays published in a volume he edited in 1984, *Rite, Drama, Festival, Spectacle*. In key sections of the essays and the accompanying endnotes, as he tracked his own intellectual journey MacAloon provided a quick survey of major theorists of play, performance, and game. I will return once more to consider his work below, but first I want to highlight his continued allegiance to Lévi-Strauss's theory.

MacAloon recalled that in the first 1984 essay, he highlighted "a model of complex types of cultural performance, what I call 'nested and ramified performance forms,' exemplified by the Olympic Games (MacAloon 1984b)." In the second 1984 essay, he "intended a double intervention with respect to the field of cultural performance theory, as it had come to be known due largely to a senior Chicago colleague, Milton Singer (MacAloon 1984a)."[173] MacAloon's aims here were first to distinguish between the "master performative genres of game, ritual, and festival" and then to assert "that spectacle had to be treated carefully as a performative genre in its own right" in order to fully interpret the Olympic Games.[174]

Drawing from the work of Boorstin, Debord, and Baudrillard, he characterized their work on spectacle as "imperialist 'critical theories' claiming that it is all just a big show." According to MacAloon, his goal was "retaining the critical edge without lapsing into the hyperboles that in the end reveal the critiques of Boorstin, Baudrillard, and Debord (and many derivative others) to be themselves compromised participants in the logic of the spectacle." For MacAloon, "breaking out of this pseudo-critical prison made inquiry into the actual cultural meanings and social functions of concrete spectacles in relation to other performance genres the imperative task at hand."[175]

At this point in the essay MacAloon rehearsed the intellectual journey that, in his words, "led me to abandon my teacher Victor Turner's insistence that a single paradigm of the ritual process could serve to interpret very diverse performative genres (Turner 1969)."[176] According to MacAloon, despite the fact that the Olympics are the "hyperbolic epitome" of the "classic *rite de passage* paradigm," "the sports contests did not easily fit within it, for they are anything but ritual games in the technical sense of ludic contests whose outcomes are known in advance."[177] With this sentence he clearly expressed his allegiance to Lévi-Strauss's formulation, and the next sentence reiterated his position: "But as total social facts in Mauss's sense, games simply are not rituals."[178]

MacAloon related that he next attempted "to derive both games and rites from then an underlying order of play, à la *Homo Ludens* and the existential phenomenologists, but this ended me up in the famous Huizingan dead end, where the concept of the ludic becomes so abstracted as to be nearly indistinguishable from the concept of culture itself, and the most interesting genre differences (particularly ones most vexed or politicized in the multicultural contexts of the Olympics) were pushed completely out of focus."[179]

It was at this point in the article that MacAloon invoked Lévi-Strauss:

> Lévi-Strauss had famously articulated the oppositional complementarity of the logics of games and rites at a structural level (Lévi-Strauss 1966, 30–33). By collapsing the two genres into one another, one could scarcely hope to understand their mutual attractions and interactions—Olympic contests and Olympic victory ceremonies, for example—or the curious failure of other sports events—the football World Cup, most notably—to bring any novel or evocative ritual forms into being. Finally "getting it" about the conceptual autonomy of ritual and game made it easier for me to pay attention to my own empirical studies and to recognize other genres composing the nested Olympic system.[180]

I agree with MacAloon that collapsing the two together as interpretive genres is counterproductive, but again, marking difference because it makes the task easier only works if the distinction is accurate. I argued above that it is not. Yet again, MacAloon's note to this last quoted statement proved as instructive as the text itself. About his notion of the "conceptual autonomy of ritual and game" he further stated: "World Cup researcher-partisans tend toward a negative kneejerk reaction to this observation, until you ask them to honestly evaluate the World Cup opening and closing and victory ceremonies. Inevitably they then agree that these are silly, derivative, insignificant performances in contrast to the Olympic ritual system, and these days much more a matter of spectacle than ritual anyway."[181]

MacAloon would no doubt agree that what is "silly, derivative," and "insignificant" and what is not, just like what is "ritual" and what is not, are subjective notions. As a counterexample to his example, consider the case of the Swedish Olympic Greco-Roman wrestler Ara Abrahamian who was disqualified from the 2008 Beijing Olympic Games and stripped of his bronze medal. According to the news account, Abrahamian argued with the referee and judges after his loss to the eventual gold medal winner. During the medal presentation, after receiving his medal, Abrahamian took it off his neck, placed it in the center of the competition mat, and walked off.

The International Olympic Committee (IOC) determined that he was in violation of "two rules of the Olympic charter, one that bans any sort of demonstrations and another that demands respect for all Olympic athletes."

The article quoted the IOC's statement as follows: "'the awards ceremony is a highly symbolic ritual, acknowledged as such by all athletes and other participants. Any disruption by any athlete, in particular a medalist, is in itself an insult to the other athletes and to the Olympic Movement. It is also contrary to the spirit of fair play.'" The article also noted that in an apparent addition of insult to injury, "Abrahamian never expressed regret or offered an apology."[182] I reiterate my point that in terms of "highly symbolic rituals," silly and serious are matters of opinion.

After dismissing World Cup ceremonies, MacAloon next turned his attention to those "authorities" who,

> will proceed then to assert that the football matches themselves are ritual forms, with these writers ending up in the same conceptual confusion I am describing. Instead, they should devote their expertise, in my opinion, to answering this very interesting question of difference that from my point of view is correlated with the presence or absence of developed ideology. Whatever one may think of "Olympism," "footballism" and much less "World Cupism" are hardly equivalent if they can be said to exist at all as self-conscious ideological projects.[183]

Now Jonathan Z. Smith certainly would agree with his suggested focus of attention; the "very interesting question of difference" being close to Smith's theoretical heart. I too think it is important, as is the stipulation that the difference is based on the "presence or absence of developed ideology." However, MacAloon did not include for consideration cultural forms such as the "ancient Maya and modern Cherokee" ball games, as Turner among other scholars had noted. Whether they are examples of a cultural form that weakens his theory or even if they are simply the exception that proves the rule, they bear mention. While I do not expect MacAloon to have surveyed every single activity in the world, based on his *Encyclopedia of Religion* article he was aware of Stewart Culin's work. I repeat my assertion that he simplified Culin's argument and did not properly address Culin's collected evidence.

Again, to reiterate my conclusion from above, game, including the subset sport, *cannot* be distinguished from ritual as easily as Lévi-Strauss and MacAloon suggested. The different-frames argument makes conceptual sense, and does (as noted above) stress difference over similarity, but it does not necessarily describe the forms and their relationship most accurately. The stipulation that ritual features undeniable assertions, and that these are concepts play suggests and games present is interesting, but difficult to illustrate. If one grants that one can "discover" in play a means to express beliefs, emotions, or even tenets, games would display only the variability. In other words, the best or hardest-working team does not always win, sometimes cheating goes unnoticed, and so forth.

I think one result of MacAloon's formulation is a functionalist assumption that any ritual presentation must transmit or convey one message. Based on his other scholarship I do not think this is what he means at all, but one byproduct of dividing performance types into nested or otherwise differentiated categories is that one runs the risk, in my mind, of reifying the "purpose" or "meaning" of each of those performance types. In the case of ane-tso, as I assert throughout this book, there is no single identifiable external "reason" or "function"; interpreting it as autotelic remains the most viable option.

CONCLUSION

Taladu ogisquodiga
(12, we finished)

The cultural cachet of anetso is notable for members of the Eastern Band of Cherokee Nation. At least three generations of Cherokee players and spectators live on or near the Qualla Boundary. Played regularly only one week of the year at the Cherokee Indian Fair, the Cherokee ball game nevertheless remains important to many Cherokee people for what it is, what it represents, and what it recalls. There is no question that for a number of Cherokee people anetso has little or no significance, nor is there any question that the complex as a whole has contracted. Yet the information required to expand it again remains known, and the anetso ceremonial complex still has utility both as a repertoire or repository of cultural information and as a vehicle for the transmission of this information from one generation to the next. Anetso itself also continues to be a symbol of Cherokee identity, and it helps to sustain the other activities surrounding it in the complex.

In an era of indigenous cultural resurgence, anetso certainly is not as celebrated as Cherokee language programs, arts and crafts, dancing, or storytelling. But it is a hardy example of an indigenous Cherokee practice, with both a discernible oral history and a traceable documentary history, which continues to link Cherokee people with indigenous cultural narratives and traditions that are centuries old. Religious, political, economic, and social values all have at one time or another passed through the complex and are encoded in its structure.

As I conclude this book I would like to recount one final vignette from my cultural consultation or "fieldwork" experience. I juxtapose it with the 1855 account of the Reverend George White, who, when he approached a conjurer during a ball game and attempted to speak with him, was first ignored and then scowled at and scolded with the phrase "'Conagatee unaka,' 'Go away, white man.'"[1] Over a century and a half later, Cherokee people continue to deal with visitors who are invited (tourists), those who are not (researchers), and people attempting to document or reconnect with their supposed Cherokee heritage.

In 1998, when I was working on the Enduring Voices Project in conjunction with the Museum of the Cherokee Indian, a document made the rounds of Cherokee tribal offices and the museum. Portions of it also appeared in the *Cherokee One Feather*, the newspaper of the Qualla Boundary. It was entitled "Tracing Your Hysterical Roots," and the listed author was the mysterious "Dr. I. M. Uneg." "Uneg," or *unega*, meaning "white," is the common Cherokee term for a white or European American person.

The document was produced anonymously within the Qualla Boundary community, primarily for the amusement of community members.[2] According to several Cherokee consultants the document gave voice to opinions regarding the endless stream of "wannabees" who would appropriate Cherokee identity. It also skewered those scholars who would interject themselves into the community, proceed to classify and describe Cherokee people and their culture, and then market themselves as experts.

One additional point of interest about the document is how exactly a copy of it came into my possession. One day, a Cherokee staff member at the museum handed me a copy of the document, teasingly inquiring as she did so if in fact I was the good Doctor. By her delivery I gathered the double meaning of her question: was I the author of the document (she knew I was not); and was I a "Dr. Uneg" in the flesh?[3]

The document consisted of three parts: a "Brief Forward," a survey of twenty-eight questions to determine "hallmark signs" of Cherokee ancestry, and an "Official Cherokee Indian Native American Tribal Enrollment Form."[4] The foreword shared some biographical information about Dr. Uneg and explained the research that led to the survey. He had the obligatory "BS" degree from college and had "recently discovered his Cherokee roots" during a visit to Cherokee.[5]

Dr. Uneg came to realize that before Removal there was a system of monarchy among the Cherokee; this "was plainly obvious because so many of the people who said they were Cherokee stated that their great great grandmothers were 'full blood Cherokee princesses.'" Realizing that Cherokee princes and princesses did in fact exist, Uneg then calculated based on what people told him that there must have been at least one hundred Cherokee princesses for every prince. Because of this imbalance, he concluded, "the women were forced into the arms of Europeans."[6]

Uneg prefaced the survey proper by noting that, in fact, "9 out of 10 people are descendants of the Cherokee Tribe." He instructed the reader to fill out the paperwork at the end if they discover they have Cherokee roots. Here I will mention but a choice few of the survey questions. In the immortal words of Dr. Uneg, "Join me now as we delve into the mystery, the myth, the magic behind discovering your very own Cherokee roots."[7] (Feel free to play along.)

1) First and foremost, let us begin with the largest common denominator—skin color. We know the Great Creator has made people of many flavors—some chocolate, some lemon, some vanilla, and so on. We also have been told that to "walk in beauty" we must never judge a book by its cover. However, in this case, we must be forced to look at skin color. Are you pasty and extremely white? For instance, when you wear shorts are other people compelled to put on sunglasses? If you answered "yes" to this question then you may be Cherokee.

2) If at any point you answer "no" to any question, you may stop because you most likely aren't Cherokee. Thus, having said that, if you answered "yes" to question one then by all means proceed to this next question. Do you lay in a tanning bed until you are golden brown (like a big, fat, juicy Thanksgiving turkey) because you are "stuck indoors all winter" and are trying to retain your skin's "natural" tan? . . .

13) Do you want to own a wolf really bad, and if you did, would you name him Two Socks? If you answered "yes" then you are well on your way to Dancing with Wolves!

14) If you had a choice between a pair of Levi's, a Nike T-shirt, and a pair of sneakers OR a loin cloth, breastplate, choker, and a pair of knee-high moccasins which would you choose? If you chose the "Indian" outfit then you are on the right path towards inner beauty. . . .

17) If you killed a deer would you cut out its heart and take a bite so that the deer's spirit might pass on to you? If so, then you are an Indian hunter.

18) Do you often tell people that when you were a child and you played "Cowboys and Indians" you were always the Indian? This is a BIG clue that you are Indian! . . .

20) Do you complain about how much baskets and beadwork cost at the local craft shops? Every true Cherokee knows that these things are quite easy to make and is insulted at the people that try to take advantage of them at the stores. If you complain about the price of crafts then you must be a local!

21) Do sales people *never* follow you around the store to see if you are trying to shoplift? Then you must be Cherokee because nobody ever treats them badly when they go shopping. . . .

27) Last but not least, do you have absolutely no proof whatsoever that

anybody in your inbred family tree was ever even remotely near an Indian at any time in the past let alone romantically involved with a Cherokee Princess? If you answered "yes" then you have only one question left to answer!

28) Are you convinced that you can prove your Cherokee ancestry through a blood test? If you answered "yes" then you are a full-blood![8]

The enrollment form on the last page has a space for your "current" name, as well as spaces for your "Indian name" and an alternate choice in case that name is already being used. A note reminds one to "remember to make it as Sioux as possible!" The applicant also is asked to pick a tribe they think they are descended from (one that has some money), and to provide an address and phone number ("remember, if you are claiming to be Cherokee you must not live within three states of North Carolina!"). Finally, directions are given to send the form, along with $10 (non-refundable), "and we will be contacting you about where and when your ceremony will be held when we will induct you into the Tribe. Please remember to bring your best regalia to the ceremony as we will be dancing around a fire like a bunch of heathens."[9]

Reverend White, Dr. Uneg. The more things change, the more they stay the same, goes the old chestnut. More incisively than I could ever express, this document gives voice to opinions and emotions concerning Cherokee identity. It is a document produced within the community, primarily for the community, though its pointed comments are certainly directed at others. It combines a number of different types of questions to lay plain, in reverse, some of the defining characteristics of the Eastern Band, as seen by members of that community.

Though only a few questions were included, it should be obvious that certain questions mask serious issues that only have meaning for locals or for people who have spent time in that community. For example, several people, including the woman who shared the document with me, have told me stories about how on occasion they had been followed around in stores in nearby communities on suspicion of shoplifting.[10] Other questions, such as the first and last, dealing with skin color and "blood," address various aspects of the obvious "wannabe" issue that plagues the community.

Both the Reverend White and Dr. Uneg vignettes, separated by a century and a half, offer effective illustrations of selected dynamics of people interested in Cherokee culture, the way they often approach learning about them, and reactions these interchanges can provoke. In fact, researchers, academic and otherwise, can provoke some of the strongest reactions. As Linda Tuhiwai Smith has noted,

> The word itself, 'research', is probably one of the dirtiest words in the indigenous world's vocabulary. . . . The power of research was not in the visits made by researchers to our communities, nor in their fieldwork and the rude questions they often asked. In fact, may individual non-indigenous researchers remain highly respected and well liked by the communities with whom they have lived. At a common sense level research was talked about both in terms of its absolute worthlessness to us, the indigenous world, and its absolute usefulness to those who wielded it as an instrument. It told us things already known, suggested things that would not work, and made careers for people who already had jobs.[11]

Even after spending time over the course of sixteen years visiting people on and around the Qualla Boundary, including working, teaching, and living there for a short time, when I visit I always feel trepidation and a sense of awkwardness upon arrival. I have realized that that is how it should be; it is an awkward business. There also is a serious undertone of wariness that is palpable, a reminder to respect privacy and propriety, even in the midst of joking.

In my experience, Cherokee people deal regularly with sojourners searching for something, and it seems that they have done so for hundreds of years. These people are different than the run-of-the-mill tourists who are an important part of the economy, who visit attractions and stores, and more recently the casino, constructed to woo them to town. Some of these sojourners seek heritage; others, spiritual self-affirmation. Some seek a First Nations group on which to hang their academic, social work, or other career upon, while others simply are looking to make a living. In every case, what people, including me, ultimately learn depends heavily upon what consultants want us to know.

Ann T. Jordan has spoken eloquently about her interchange with David Lewis Jr., her primary consultant and coauthor of her book on Muskogee religion. At one point Lewis "was explaining why I was not getting it right and, by extension, why anthropologists so often do not get it right." As Jordan goes on to reflect,

> Our "informants" are in control of the knowledge we gain. They can choose to share, or choose to leave us with misunderstandings or no understandings. No amount of participant observation would have prevented my misunderstanding as I would never have been able to witness the sacred event he described. No matter how much time we spend with them, we anthropologists who are outsiders do not live in

the worlds of the people we "study." Without those lived experiences, we do not know the right questions to ask.[12]

These interactions are handled by different people in different ways; with grace and humor, aggravation and resentment, and even bemused resignation, which can mask a fierce commitment to safeguarding certain cultural elements. What this means to my present study can be summed up by what a longtime consultant reiterated to me in October 2007, which I rendered in shorthand in my notes: "Identity bound up with the activity; cease activity or give it away, cease to have individual identity."[13] Cherokee identity is bound up with anetso and the anetso complex. If Cherokee people cease participation in their indigenous activities or give them away, i.e., reveal all the details of all of the activities to those who ask, then they will cease to have identity as a distinct community.[14]

As my consultant stated at the beginning of Chapter 5, to play the game as one's ancestors did, in the same place they once played, remains compelling for people today. The anetso complex provides continuity, perhaps, in the way only communal activities such as a ceremony or a contest can, because so many are involved through time. Indeed people's bodies become inscribed by the activities performed; physically, by scarification and other pregame rituals, during the ball game itself, and, alongside it, by the motions of the dances and ceremonies.

In this study I also presented several accounts from the last two hundred years that reported the imminent demise of the ball game. At the end of the nineteenth century, a quarter of a century later at the beginning of the twentieth century, and then again shortly after midcentury, anetso was characterized as a shadow of its former self. More recent accounts also mentioned this trend. The ceremonial complex has endured great change, and despite a general minimization of constituent activities of the complex, as my research has shown, Cherokee people continue to play anetso. In fact, it actually may be undergoing resurgence, as increased community participation and the formation of female teams suggest.

I have assessed the prevalent explanations for anetso in this study and argued that the complex has transported multiple meanings through time. The activity itself can be considered a reservoir of cultural gesture, symbol, and metaphor, for it has continued to support different meanings beyond the literal for both Cherokee and non-Cherokee people. Historically, Cherokee people have recognized the cross-cultural, or international, currency of anetso and have used this to their advantage. It has been a marker of identity deployed in both religious and secular contexts.

Anetso figures in all manner of Cherokee cultural narratives, from "Kanati and Selu" to "The Ball Game between the Birds and the Animals." Scholarly interpretations suggest a host of themes: coming of age, test of manhood, liminal transformation, agon, the necessity of struggle to overcome hardship, and the ethic of participation in the face of possible negative consequences. These themes suggest that at one time anetso was a natural analogue to warfare, although this reading by no means exhausts its possible meaning as an activity for men. Players can tap into this well of narrative for inspiration, but the anetso complex itself teaches these lessons. Granted, every participant does not draw such inferences, but they are available.

Though certain agents later promoted it, anetso drew the ire of many missionaries and Bureau of Indian Affairs agents. Missionaries attacked the ball game not so much for what it was as for what it engendered. At times it attracted unseemly behavior to its sidelines (promiscuity, drunkenness, gambling, and brawling) that made government and religious officials wary.

Played in response to missionaries who forbade it, and used as part of a strategy of reenfranchisement in negotiations with government agents, anetso was an expression of identity, a definitive statement of existence. These events also can be interpreted as examples of ironic silence, for such observer-reported games speak to the researcher, even though written history has included little Cherokee commentary about such events.

In the eyes of some ball games were physical manifestations or bodily metaphors for behaviors thought to be strange, violent, possibly antisocial, and even to some, evil. Other observers have described ball games more with a sense of wonder than anything else. To them it was a bodily metaphor for "Indian," "primitive," "authenticity of culture," "manliness," and other constructions.

Anetso is different from other Cherokee activities such as storytelling and craft making. It is different because it cannot be commodified in the same way; it cannot be packaged up and taken home. In a way, it is more accessible than many other traditional activities, because anyone who is willing to endure the practice schedule can join the team. Like traditional dancing or speaking Cherokee, the practice can be learned or copied, but it needs to be in context to have any sort of meaningful impact on those involved.

By the same token, it differs from those expressions of tradition as well. Two people can speak Cherokee together, and just a handful of people can perform a dance. Both activities can be done inside, in private, though they do not need to be. The ball game, on the other hand, requires more people and open space. A group of people is needed, and they cannot play a game of ball in someone's living room.

Enjoying a good ball game can be as much about being Cherokee as participating in it can be if there is a background of tradition that drives one to take interest. No longer the focus of community attention as it once was in the past, there still are groups dedicated to the continuation of anetso because members believe that participation is an indication of being what a person should be in Cherokee society. In other words, it is a public display of a dedication, or adherence, to the preservation of a certain mode of living, or stance toward life.

Today games are only played at the very public Cherokee Indian Fair, where other traditional activities also are on display for community members and tourists alike. The ball field is a "contact zone" that lies in the center of expanding concentric circles, within the larger zones of the Ceremonial Grounds, where the fair is held, and the tourist-friendly town of Cherokee. People can videotape the games, and ball sticks are for sale, like baskets, beadwork, pottery, and a myriad of items with Cherokee words on them. When players go to water after the games, it is unavoidably public, as I described in context. But much of the ball game complex remains private.

The ball game itself is the public surfacing and communal rendering of traditional practices and beliefs that are private and individual. This mode is consistent with many other Cherokee practices, and in particular, religious traditions. As I discussed in Chapter 3, the early nineteenth-century shift from a priestly hierarchy to individual practitioners altered the religious system. Perhaps it was the influence of Christianity in combination with this shift that "privatized" the system.

Though once there were public communal rituals, such as dancing, that have been revived recently, I think there has been an individualistic, private focus in Cherokee religious behavior for quite some time. Conjurers, both conjure-men and conjure-women, "doctor" alone for the most part. Dances and ball games are times when the traditions surface for the outsider; when patterns and behaviors become public because of the nature of the contest or activity.

In my opinion, anetso is clearly a form of routinized behavior of long duration, the performance of which accommodates but does not demand interaction with other-than-human persons, or agents. If my historical survey supports the conclusion that the categories of ritual and not-ritual are skewed, or have the wrong holes for Cherokee pegs, I have succeeded in making my point. But I recognize that any individual delineation of ritual still hinges on the lines drawn around it; it too is an interpretive tool. The evidence presented in this study confirms that anetso itself satisfies the conditions of commonly held definitions of "ritual." Though it contains many ritual elements, the complex is not wedded to a religious observance or goal.

Unlike many religious actions, the ball game is self-referential, or autotelic. Instead of being an activity to secure a result such as a good harvest, to cure a disease, or to give thanks, anetso is its own goal; it is not consciously performed for any extraneous reasons or in service to another Cherokee activity. At the same time, the ball game's outcome depends on the proper performance of many elements of a Cherokee religious system: inherited, formalized symbolic activities that are understood to be distinctly Cherokee, either by Cherokee or non-Cherokee people or both, and that Cherokee commentators and area scholars alike have termed rituals in other contexts.

Studies of such "borderline" activities should increase, to help understand more clearly how scholars ourselves create and manipulate the boundaries in which we place the "objects" of our studies. In this way my study is as much about how the scholar approaches the problem as it is a resolution of a problem. My critique of Lévi-Strauss's distinction between "game" and "ritual" and my divergence from the position on the matter taken by other contemporary scholars might seem to muddy the waters. Of course I am not doing so in order to assert that ritual and game are identical, but rather to allow for rethinking the categories in a manner that hopefully is more accurate, a task that challenges us to reflexively question the historically and culturally specific bases of our analysis. Inaccurately rendered distinctions and differences are just as counterproductive as generalized umbrella categories.

My desire to present a carefully detailed study of the anetso ceremonial complex (with attendant space considerations) and to contextualize it in the Cherokee religious system has necessitated the exclusion of sustained discussion of certain realms of concern. These include issues of violence, gender, and economics. Further study in all of these areas with regard to the ball game would be fruitful, and I may take them up in future work.

There are a number of First Nations or Native American lacrosse-type activities that bear interesting comparison with anetso, some with clearly stated external foci and goals. I briefly mentioned Haudenosaunee (Iroquois) and Meskwaki activities in context, but there are others as well, including the Choctaw ball game, about which Kendall Blanchard has written.[15] Mesoamerican ball games are the next logical comparative group, though they are not ball-and-stick games, and there is an increasing amount of scholarship available.[16]

There are several other First Nations "games" or "sports" that beg for careful, sustained, contextualized contemporary interpretation. As I briefly noted in Chapter 5, footracing, including Hopi, Tewa, and Jicarilla Apache versions, is another example of an activity that potentially bridges the "game/ritual divide." My approach also has precluded a more global consideration of activities that straddle this divide as well. Other examples of activities that skirt the boundaries of game and ritual abound: the Greek Olympics, historical and contemporary *matsuri* and *sumo* in Japan, Shrovetide football in Europe, contemporary football ("soccer") in a number of countries in Europe and Africa, and the modern Olympics. A check of any academic database suggests that scholarship on these activities is limited, but is increasing of late.

In the end, the contribution of this book is not to come to a conclusion about what anetso "really means." Nor is it an explanation of what anetso means to Cherokee people. That is up to the Cherokee people who play and watch it. The book does seek to convey a clear sense of the import of a longstanding and vital element in Cherokee culture, and to consider the manifold ways in which Cherokee people have represented it to themselves and to outside observers, some of whom in turn have represented and signified it.

An allied goal of the book has been to interrogate received categories with anetso as an example, with particular attention to its relationship with elements of a putative Cherokee religious system or repertoire. For the most part, other than brief introductory treatment, I have engaged with such data only to the extent that it is linked to anetso.

There is much work to be done in the study of those Cherokee cultural elements that might be termed "religious." The challenge remains to engage in this endeavor with the respect and commitment that the community deserves. And to listen the next time someone tells you that you might be standing a little too close to the action.

Notes

Introduction

1. Personal communication, October 2000. In the body of the study I offer additional discussion of this term and alternate terms. Consultants repeatedly have rejected the term "stickball" as erroneous; one consultant remarked that stickball is what little kids play with a broom handle and any available type of ball. That being said, there are Cherokee people who do refer to the activity as stickball. After conversations with several consultants and review of the scholarship, I have chosen the transliteration "anetso." This I think is a clear way to render the three discrete syllables "a/ne/tso," with no diacritical marks.

Cherokee orthography is not uniform in scholarly literature; syllable representations and diacritical marks vary. In this book, I use a very simplified form of transliteration. As I am not a linguist, this seems the best way to present Cherokee terms for ease of reading in English and to minimize errors on my part. I render the syllables as they appear in standard Cherokee syllabary charts, as continuous words with no linguistic marks of division, emphasis, or accent. Cherokee vowels are a, e, i, o, u, and v. The v is a nasalized "uh," as in "under."

When quoting other scholars I have tried to reproduce their transliterations as closely as possible. At first mention, such words are enclosed in quotation marks and put in italic or roman type per the original. When I introduce a term or employ a different form than previously presented, I italicize it and subsequently render it in roman type. For Meskwaki terms, I follow the works that I cite.

2. For example, see Molly Sequoyah, in Ernest Bender, "Cherokee II." Sequoyah, a member of the Eastern Band, used the term "a-nahnezóʌsgi" in conversations transcribed by linguist Ernest Bender, who translated it as "ball-team," as well as "they-played-ball." Ibid., 2.2 Free Translation, 225. The accompanying morpheme list included "a," a third person marker; "na," the "pluralizer of third person"; the "hnezo stem" meaning "play"; and "sgi," denoting "that." Ibid., 2.4 Morpheme List, 226. Bender stated, "The crude data was obtained from two informants. Molly Sequoia dictated the texts and translations in the summer of 1945." Ibid., 223.

3. Personal communications, 1993–2007.

4. Tambiah, *Buddhism and the Spirit Cults*, 1, 3. Also see ibid., 337–40. Several scholars have employed something akin to the "ceremonial complex" term. Raymond Fogelson used the term "ritual complex." Fogelson, "The Cherokee Ball Game," 156. Lee Irwin used the phrase "ceremonial cycles," to describe the entire seasonal round. Irwin, "Cherokee Healing," 254n18. This term should not be confused with the concept of a "Southeastern Ceremonial Complex," or "Southern Cult," which was popular in the field of archaeology for many years but more recently has been critiqued on several different levels and its explanatory capacity greatly reduced. As originally conceived, the theory was that based on archaeological evidence from "late prehistoric sites," the societies in a large geographical area in what is now the southeastern United States shared many similar material characteristics, suggesting broader religious and political affinities, during the Mississippian and early historic periods. Muller, "The Southern Cult," 11, 19.

5. My emphasis. *The Oxford American Desk Dictionary and Thesaurus*, 122, 723.

6. Lévi-Strauss, *The Savage Mind*, 30–31.

7. Eastern Band of Cherokee Indians website, ⟨http://www.nc-cherokee.com/⟩ (accessed August 2008). The last word on the official seal was changed from "Indians" to "Nation" in 1997, but both names remain in use. A total population figure for "Eastern Cherokee, NC" of 8,092 was given in "No. 36. Population Living on Selected Reservations and Trust Lands: 2000," in *American Indian, Alaska Native Tables from the Statistical Abstract of the United States: 2004–2005*, ⟨http://www.census.gov/statab/www/sa04aian.pdf⟩ (accessed 5/29/09); a total population figure of 10,210 was given in "Table 1. American Indian and Alaska Native Alone and Alone or in Combination Population by Tribe for the United States: 2000," in "Census 2000 PHC-T-18, American Indian and Alaska Native Tribes in North Carolina: 2000," ⟨http://www.census.gov/population/www/cen2000/briefs/phc-t18/tables/tab001.pdf⟩ (accessed May 2009).

8. Personal communications, 1993–2007. For a cogent summary of information concerning the Eastern Band of the Cherokee, see King, "Cherokee," 105–8. Also useful is "Cherokee, N.C. Fact Sheet."

9. ⟨http://www.nps.gov/grsm/⟩ (accessed May 2009).

10. National Park Service Public Use Statistics Office, National Park Service, U.S. Department of the Interior, "Ranking Report for Recreation Visits in: 2008," ⟨http://www.nature.nps.gov/stats/viewReport.cfm⟩ (accessed May 2009). Figures were 16,309,307 and 9,044,010, respectively. There is some dispute about these figures because of the complicated way in which the number of visitors is counted, including apparently anyone riding on the Blue Ridge Parkway or through the park. The Golden Gate National Recreation Area ranked second with 14,554,750 visitors.

11. Associated Press, "Agreement permits Cherokee to double size of casino," *Raleigh (N.C.) News and Observer*, November 16, 2000. The article stated that the casino had drawn 3.2 million visitors in 1999. Also see Joseph Martin, "Luxury Casino Hotel Construction Starts," *Cherokee (N.C.) One Feather*, October 4, 2000.

12. Jon Ostendorff, "Harrah's expansion continues in lean times," *Asheville (N.C.) Citizen-Times*, July 7, 2008, ⟨www.citizen-times.com⟩ (accessed August 2008).

13. Jon Ostendorff, "Harrah's Cherokee to cut jobs," *Asheville (N.C.) Citizen-Times*, January 13, 2009, ⟨http://www.wbir.com/news/local/story.aspx?storyid=74522&provider=rss⟩ (accessed May 2009).

14. James Mooney, "The Cherokee Ball Play," 108.

15. Ibid.

16. Anonymous, review of "Cherokee Ball Play."

17. Ibid.

18. I would like to thank Jonathan Z. Smith for first suggesting this source to me in a conversation about anetso many years ago.

19. The project was funded by the North Carolina Arts Council and administered through the Museum of the Cherokee Indian; it ran from September 1997 to September 1999. There is not a consensus regarding the official name change noted above. The museum's name was not changed, and the Tribal Council and the U.S. government both continue to employ "Eastern Band of Cherokee Indians." I will alternate between the terms. The resulting individual videos total approximately twenty-four hours and are a valuable resource. I conceived the project as a continuation of the late 1980s audiotape project entitled Fading Voices. For an overview of this project, see Joan Greene Orr and Lois Calonehuskie, "Fading Voices Project Introduction," 5.

The museum has continued interview projects since then, under the title Cherokee Voices.

The interview materials are now housed both in the Museum of the Cherokee Indian Archives and in the Southern Folklife Collection at the University of North Carolina at Chapel Hill. Enduring Voices Collection, MSS 99-11, Interviews, 1997–1998 (Museum of the Cherokee Indian Archives, Cherokee, N.C., videocassettes and transcriptions); Michael J. Zogry Collection (#20339), Interviews, 1997–1998, Southern Folklife Collection (Wilson Library, University of North Carolina at Chapel Hill, Chapel Hill, N.C., videocassettes and transcriptions). The materials are the same in both collections.

20. All of these sources as well as those in the next three paragraphs will be discussed in context, and proper citations provided.

21. Michael J. Zogry, field notes, October 11, 1998.

22. Gill, "Dancing Ritual, Ritual Dancing," 45.

23. Ibid.

24. Ibid., 46.

25. Gill, "Embodied Theology," 81–92.

26. Ibid., 82; also see 81–83, 91–92; Gill, "Dancing Ritual, Ritual Dancing," 47.

27. Sam Gill, email to the author, June 30, 2005.

28. Catherine Bell, *Ritual Theory, Ritual Practice*, 80.

29. Bourdieu, *Outline of a Theory*, 72. Emphasis in the original. It bears mentioning that Marcel Mauss used the term *habitus* in an article that discussed "techniques of the body"; yet he remains "a largely unacknowledged source of this aspect of contemporary thought concerned with the body." Mauss, "The Notion of Body Techniques," 97, 101. The quotation is from Lechte, "Marcel Mauss," in *Fifty Key Contemporary Thinkers*, 24. For a good discussion of Mauss's article, see Asad, "Toward a Genealogy of the Concept of Ritual," in *Genealogies of Religion*, 75–77. Asad commented that Bourdieu "was later to popularize the word *habitus*, but it is strange that he gave Mauss no credit for having originated the concept." Ibid., 75.

30. Bourdieu, "Sociology of Sport," 162.

31. Ibid., 166.

32. Ibid., 163.

33. Ibid.

34. Ibid.

35. Catherine Bell, *Ritual*, 164.

36. Ibid., 164.

37. Smith, "Religion, Religions, Religious," 269.

38. Ibid.

39. Campany, "Very Idea of Religions," 316, 318. See, in particular, 291–96, 312–19. I agree with Campany's critique that new metaphors are needed and that those in current use, such as organic metaphors, are ill-advised, but I am not convinced of the utility of "repertoires." As Campany noted, terms such as "Christianities" or "Judaisms" work fairly well in the interim; since neither "Cherokeanity" nor "Cherokeism" are words as of yet, however, pluralizing is not really a viable option in this case. Therefore, until a better metaphor comes along, I am sticking with "religious system." See ibid., 291–92.

40. Mindful of Campany's critique and the bad form of including a derivative of a word in the word's definition, I explicitly avoided the term "systematized."

41. Geertz, "Religion as a Cultural System," in *The Interpretation of Cultures*, 90; discussion of phrase, 90–94.

42. See Campany, "Very Idea of Religions," 293–94; 318. He juxtaposed Geertz's formulation with Émile Durkheim's "'conceptual systems'" and Robin Hortin's "'theoretical schemes.'" Ibid., 318.

43. Kapferer, "Ritual Dynamics and Virtual Practice," 35.

44. Ibid., 36.

45. Ibid.

46. Ibid., 39.

47. Ibid., 38. For example, he commented that "Bell's recent surveys (1992, 1997) on approaches toward ritual blend many of these together, for this commentator, in a less than successful manner." Ibid., 36.

48. Staal, "The Meaninglessness of Ritual," 8.

49. Ibid.

50. Ibid., 9.

51. Ibid.

52. In his response to this article Penner wrote: "This essay is not a review of Staal's article. The article is neither profound as scholarship, nor specific in its description of either theory or the present status of ritual analysis." Penner, "Language, Ritual and Meaning," 1.

53. Don Handelman, introduction, in Handelman and Lindquist, *Ritual in Its Own Right*, 3. He cited his own work as "Handelman 1998, n.d.a."

54. Ibid., 28n1.

55. Ibid., 4.

56. Ibid., 10.

57. Ibid., 11.

58. Ibid., 11, 14.

59. Turner, "Liminal to Liminoid," 161. The paper of which Turner spoke eventually became a chapter in Mihaly Csikszentmihalyi's *Beyond Boredom and Anxiety* (MacAloon and Cziksentmihalyi, "Deep Play," 361–84). Cowritten by John MacAloon, "Deep Play and the Flow Experience in Rock Climbing" introduced its project by invoking the notion of "deep play" as developed by the eighteenth-century British philosopher Jeremy Bentham. Quoting Clifford Geertz's article on Balinese cockfighting, Cziksentmihalyi and MacAloon wondered, "Why are people attracted to an activity that offers no 'rational' rewards?" Ibid., 362. They said that the Dutch scholar Johan Huizinga "first elaborated the paradox that play forms are 'good for nothing' in terms of existing economic, biological, or psychological needs, but are 'good for everything' because they serve as experiments for new ways of living." Ibid., 377. Accepting Geertz's theory of the cockfight as a metasocial commentary, they then wondered, how "can an autotelic activity like rock climbing provide a base from which one can perceive culture more clearly? And are the interpretations of society thus obtained protostructural as well as antistructural?" Ibid. Cziksentmihalyi and MacAloon concluded that Geertz represents the cockfight as ultimately eufunctional, to quote Turner from above. Yet, "for the rock climbers, on the contrary, the alternative vision induced by climbing is intensely critical of the normative order." Ibid., 379. Thus, it is, as Turner would say, liminoid. For some, but certainly not all, of the climbers, adjectives such as "*transcendent, religious, visionary*, or *ecstatic* are traditionally employed" in their descriptions of their experiences. Ibid., 373.

60. Kapferer, "Ritual Dynamics and Virtual Practice," 39.

61. Grimes, "Defining Nascent Ritual," 541.

62. Grimes, "Ritual and the Media," 163n32.

63. Ibid.
64. Ibid.
65. Ibid.
66. Grimes, "Putting Space in Its Place," in *Rite Out of Place*, 101–13.
67. Ibid., 101. Notable exceptions include the discussion of Jonathan Z. Smith's paper, "The Domestication of Sacrifice," in Hamerton-Kelly, *Violent Origins*, 206–35; Gill, "No Place to Stand"; Kimura, "Bearing the 'Bare Facts'"; Ray, "The Koyukon Bear Party"; McCutcheon, Review: "Relating Smith." McCutcheon makes the same point about Smith's scholarship and lists the examples above save for the first, as well as a few additional examples. Grimes's book apparently had not been published yet, for it was not listed either. Ibid., 295–96n30. As this book was going to press another example was published: Roberts, "All Work and No Play." This article included a critique of several of Sam Gill's related works as well.
68. Grimes, "Putting Space in Its Place," 102.
69. Ibid.
70. Jonathan Z. Smith, in discussion of Jonathan Z. Smith paper, "The Domestication of Sacrifice," in Hamerton-Kelly, *Violent Origins*, 206.
71. Catherine Bell, *Ritual Theory, Ritual Practice*, 74.
72. Ibid., 80–81.
73. Ibid., 83.
74. Ibid., 85.
75. Ibid.
76. Ibid., 91.
77. Ibid., 219.
78. Ibid.
79. Ibid.
80. Ibid. Emphasis in the original.
81. Huizinga, *Homo Ludens*.
82. Ibid., 20.
83. Ibid.
84. Ibid., 19.
85. Ibid., 13.
86. Ibid., 203.
87. Ibid., 20.
88. Ibid., 197–98.
89. MacAloon, "Games," 3265.
90. Ibid.
91. Staal, *Rules Without Meaning*, 427.
92. Callois, *Man, Play, and Games*; Callois, "Structure and Classification of Games," 44–55.
93. MacAloon, "Games," 3267. Also see Blanchard, *The Anthropology of Sport*, 51.
94. MacAloon, "Games," 3267.
95. Ibid., 3267–68.
96. A good general survey is Alf Hiltebeitel, "Gambling," in *The Encyclopedia of Religion*, 2nd ed., 3259–64. Originally published in the first edition of the *Encyclopedia* (1987), this entry has a revised bibliography for the second edition.
97. Of course here I expressly do not refer to the casino operations of the last several decades.

98. Jonathan Z. Smith, Conversation with University of California Santa Barbara graduate students, 1997.

99. Board of Commissioners of Indian Trade of South Carolina, Minutes, May 4, 1714, 53.

100. Isaac Proctor to Jeremiah Evarts, December 11, 1827, Papers of the American Board of Commissioners for Foreign Missions, [No. 189] p. 9 / microfilm #502.

101. I will discuss several examples of this disapproval in Chapter 2.

102. Spray, "Report of Superintendent," 307.

103. Gulick, *Cherokees at the Crossroads*, 114. Though Gulick stated that the Cherokee Indian Agency had banned the activity, he had no footnotes to support this claim. Though there may in fact have been a ban, I have not yet found evidence of it.

104. Mooney, *Myths of the Cherokee* (hereafter *Myths*), 181.

105. Finger, *Cherokee Americans*, 58. A team was sent to Washington, D.C., in 1923 to perform at a Shriners' convention. I discuss this and related events in Chapter 4.

106. I will discuss several such accounts in Chapter 4.

107. Alan Kilpatrick, *Night has a Naked Soul*.

108. Enduring Voices Collection, MSS 99-11, Interviews, 1997–1998 (Museum of the Cherokee Indian Archives, Cherokee, N.C., videocassettes and transcriptions); Michael J. Zogry Collection (#20339), Interviews, 1997–1998, Southern Folklife Collection (Wilson Library, University of North Carolina at Chapel Hill, Chapel Hill, N.C., videocassettes and transcriptions), same materials as the Enduring Voices Collection.

109. Field notes, 8/1/98.

110. Deloria, *Custer Died for Your Sins*, 86.

Chapter 1

1. Throughout the book I will use the term "cultural narrative" to mean what is commonly referred to as "myth." In my opinion, the latter term is burdened with a sense of being "not true," and I want to stress the idea that no truth judgment is implied when I discuss the narratives.

2. For the concept of "other-than-human persons," see Hallowell, "Ojibwa Ontology," 145.

3. Genesis 32:24–32, *New Oxford Annotated Bible*, 56.

4. Ibid., verse 28 and note to verse 28.

5. Mooney, *Myths*, 433. This work and another publication, Mooney, *Sacred Formulas of the Cherokees*, 301–97, were reprinted together as *Myths of the Cherokee and Sacred Formulas of the Cherokees* (Nashville, Tenn.: Charles and Randy Elder, 1982). As these are two separate works, they will be cited hereafter separately as *Myths* and *Sacred Formulas*, and in all cases page citations are to the reprint edition. Other important sources contain various versions of cultural narratives and some analysis, and in this group I include works by John Witthoft, Frank Speck and Leonard Broom with Will West Long, William H. Gilbert, Raymond Fogelson, Frans Olbrechts, and Jack F. and Anna G. Kilpatrick. Most of these sources will be cited in context in this or upcoming chapters. In addition, my fieldwork on the Qualla Boundary, including work for the video documentary project Enduring Voices, resulted in the documentation of several narratives, some of which were taped. Other collections of narratives for popular readership continue to be published.

6. Mooney, *Myths*, 229.

7. Ibid.; and "Contents," in ibid., 5–7. His two divisional frames do not match; as I

discuss below there are sacred myths mixed in with other traditions and narratives, and other category mixtures.

8. Basso, *Wisdom Sits in Places*, 48–50.

9. See Raymond J. DeMaille and Elaine A. Jahner, "Further Comparative Materials for the Study of Sioux Religion," and "Part 1: James R. Walker: His Life and Work," in Walker, *Lakota Belief and Ritual*, xxxix, 42. Also see Walker, *Lakota Myth*. Walker was a physician assigned to the Pine Ridge Reservation in 1896 and undertook research on elements of traditional Lakota culture at the request of Clark Wissler of the American Museum of Natural History in New York. Walker left Pine Ridge in 1914 but continued working with the material he had gathered until 1925; he died in 1926. Ibid., "Walker: His Life and Work," 6, 13–14, 33–34, 43.

10. Gilbert, "The Eastern Cherokees," 169–413, 301.

11. Ibid., 302. He only published one narrative, "The Story of the Creation of Man," in Gilbert, "The Cherokees of North Carolina," 549–50. He remarked that he intended to publish them at a later time, "as part of a formal study of Cherokee ethnology," though he apparently never did. Gilbert, "Eastern Cherokees," 302n36.

12. Mooney, *Myths*, 235–36.

13. Ibid., 229.

14. Ibid., 232.

15. Ibid., 234. He gave as examples the characters Flint and Rabbit. Ibid. In addition, Cherokee historical traditions, in Mooney's opinion, were "strangely wanting." Even though the Cherokee had been involved in war and treaty making for three centuries with several European and Native American nations by that time, Mooney found "little evidence" of such encounters. This he attributed to "the temper of the Cherokee mind," which he said was "accustomed to look forward to new things rather than to dwell upon the past." He concluded that whatever the reason "may have been, their national legend is now lost forever." Ibid; Mooney, *Myths*, 231.

16. William H. Gilbert agreed with Mooney that "extremely fragmentary remnants" were all that survived of a complete account of the origins of the Cherokee people. Gilbert, "Cherokees of North Carolina," 548. John Witthoft suggested there might be two migration traditions, according to different sources. Witthoft, "Cherokee Migration Story," 304. I also have heard the story about Sequoyah dying somewhere in South America looking for a long-lost band of Cherokees. Personal communications, 1993–2007. But my cultural consultation experience also suggests another option: the Cherokee have always inhabited that land. This point was stressed in several conversations. Though there are fragments of migration traditions that survive, there are some people who reject this idea completely and say the old people always told them that the Cherokee had always inhabited that area of land. Personal communications, 1993–2007. In sum, there are an interesting and suggestive number of "fragments" that have become woven into the Cherokee narrative tradition. It should be clear that any attempt to favor one migration tradition over another is purely speculative.

17. Mooney, *Myths*, 229.

18. Ibid., 231.

19. Ibid.

20. Gilbert, "Eastern Cherokee Social Organization," 334.

21. Gilbert, "Cherokees of North Carolina," 548.

22. According to Mooney, the animals in these narratives "were larger and of more per-

fect type" than the animals now on earth, in the same way that "the traditional hero-gods" were. Mooney, *Myths*, 231. The animals "had chiefs, councils, and townhouses, mingled with human kind upon terms of perfect equality and spoke the same language." Ibid. They even had the same hereafter, in the "Darkening land of Usûñhi′yĭ." Ibid., 261. Mooney noted that the present-day animals were not descendants of those mythic animals, "but only weak imitations," except the one or two "present creatures" descended from monsters. These mythic animals, for unexplained reasons, each moved to "Gâlûñ′lătĭ, the world above, where they still exist." Ibid., 231.

23. Ibid., 229.

24. Mooney, "Myths of the Cherokees," 98. In this quote he did not add diacritical marks; in the title and the text of the narrative he did so. Mooney, *Myths*, 506. I will continue to render quotations of his transliterations as he did, but also to present this word, as well as other Cherokee words, in their widely accepted forms.

25. Mooney, *Myths*, 230. Mooney rendered the term "âsĭ". Ibid

26. Ibid., 232.

27. Ibid., 230. "Going to water" will be discussed in a later chapter.

28. Ibid. John Ax told Mooney that as a boy he was sometimes admitted to the osi to tend the fire, and thus was able to learn about some stories and rites. Mooney noted this was a "special privilege," although Ax did not claim to be an "adept" as a result of this. Ibid.

29. The Green Corn Dance and related observances comprise perhaps the most important and certainly the hardiest of the Cherokee festivals that once revolved around a lunar cycle. I will discuss these topics in more depth in Chapter 3.

30. Mooney, *Myths*, 462. Frans M. Olbrechts, in Mooney and Olbrechts, *Swimmer Manuscript*, 99.

31. Mooney and Olbrechts, *Swimmer Manuscript*, 99.

32. Irwin, "Different Voices Together," 13. Beginning in the eighteenth century, there are reports of menstrual huts and birthing huts for women, but I have not located a record of women gathering together on winter nights as the men did. As Theda Perdue has noted, "In Cherokee society, home and hearth were part of a woman's domain. Whatever time she could spare from the fields was spent at the homestead with other women. . . . While men did make appearances at the households of their wives and of their own lineages, they could be found most frequently at a communal site in the company of other men." Perdue, *Cherokee Women*, 46. For discussion of such structures, see ibid., 29, 32; Mooney and Olbrechts, *Swimmer Manuscript*, 34, 99–101. There is some uncertainty as to whether the winter sleeping houses, which at one time were apparently connected to every house, were the same as the structures in which narratives were transmitted. See Lewis and Kneberg, "The Cherokee 'Hothouse,'" 224–27; Schneider, "Brother Martin Schneider's Report," 260–61; Faulkner, "Cherokee Winter House."

33. All, personal communications, 1993–2007. Visitors also sometimes included conjurers for a period of a few days to tend to a sick family member.

34. Mooney, *Myths*, 232. This point further supports my argument that the latter story belongs in the "sacred myths" category.

35. Ibid., 242.

36. Ibid., 319. The presence of this linguistic device aids in categorization of narratives, as I note below.

37. Personal communications, 1993–2007.

38. Obviously the issue of "race" or "blood" is contested and complicated. I only present

this information because it informs the topic at hand, and I make no assertions about particular individuals.

39. Personal communications, 1993–2007.

40. Ibid.

41. My phrase; for speech acts, see Searle, *Speech Acts*.

42. There were some participants in the Enduring Voices oral history project who told complete narratives.

43. I also was told several versions of other narratives, such as that of Nun′yunu′wi, or Stonecoat, and Utlun′ta, or Spearfinger.

44. Mooney, *Myths*, 5.

45. Ibid., 239–40.

46. Ibid.

47. Ibid., 240. Mooney gives the full name for this location as "Gûlkwâ′gine Di′gâlûñ′lătiyûn." Ibid., 240. This term and the simpler construction Galvladi seem to refer to the same location, suggesting no distinction is made between the area immediately below the sky vault and above it. The latter term is most often invoked when the world above is referenced in narratives.

48. Ibid., 231.

49. Ibid., 240.

50. Ibid.

51. Ibid., 240–42.

52. Ibid. This is a type of small bowl. Ibid., 540.

53. For several Cherokee narratives there are a number of variant texts extant, and I will provide more detailed information about these variants for selected narratives in which anetso figures prominently. Different individuals related portions of this narrative to me at different times, but no one presented an entire account. The primary source text for the narrative as I present it here is Mooney, "Kana′tĭ and Selu: Origin of corn and game," in *Myths*, 242–48. Additional versions not discussed or cited below include Mooney, "Myths of the Cherokees," 97–108; and Baillou, "A Contribution to the Mythology," 93–102. Two versions of the narrative are contained in the John Howard Payne Papers (hereafter JHP). I will discuss this source in great detail in Chapter 2 and include the full reference information there. The first is in "Section the Second. Legends connected with the departures from the religious system considered as the orthodox one among the Cherokee," JHP TS 1:32–38 (MS 43–52). A footnote to the title attributes the narrative to "*Sick, a, towah*, through two Interpreters, to the author." Ibid., 32. For a discussion of this individual see Irwin, "Different Voices Together." A second version of this narrative is in JHP TS (NL) 2:51–62, attributed to "Sickatower," followed by a very short version of the same narrative given by "Dr. Butler, a missionary residing in the Nation." Ibid., 62. This was Elizur Butler, the well-known missionary of the American Board of Commissioners for Foreign Missions.

54. Mooney, *Myths*, 524, 531. Consultants I have spoken with say the meaning is "successful," or "good," not "lucky." Personal communications, 1993–2007.

55. Ibid., 242.

56. Ibid.

57. Ibid.

58. Ibid., 243–45.

59. Ibid., 246–48.

60. Ibid., 431. Here Mooney used geographic distinctions to differentiate the North Carolina and Oklahoma communities. He collected these versions in 1887–90, from Swim-

mer and John Ax (Eastern Band) and James D. Wafford (Cherokee Nation). Ibid. Swimmer, or "A'yûñ´inĭ," was Mooney's main "informant." Ibid., 512, 236. Mooney said Ax was known as "Ităgû´năhĭ," and Wafford was known as "Tsuskwănûñ´năawa´tă," or "Worn-out-blanket." Ibid., 237, 238. According to Mooney, Wahnenauhi was the "anonymous writer" of a manuscript in the archives of the Bureau of American Ethnology, "Historical Sketches of the Cherokees, together with some of their Customs, Traditions, and Superstitions, by Wahnenauhi, a Cherokee Indian." Ibid., 214, 431. This manuscript was edited and published by Jack F. Kilpatrick. See Jack F. Kilpatrick, "The Wahnenauhi Manuscript," 175–214.

61. Ibid.
62. Mooney, "Myths of the Cherokees," 98.
63. Mooney, *Myths*, 230.
64. Ibid., 243.
65. Ibid., 244. In this version it is not immediately apparent to the reader why this method of production, while perhaps unorthodox, was so distasteful as to require her execution. The second sentence seems to insinuate something, but it is not specified. However, a version of the narrative told by Mollie Sequoyah to John Witthoft in 1946 provided key detail that makes their decision at least somewhat more intelligible. In this version at this point there is only one son, for the second son will be born from the blood of Selu's neck after she is killed. The son watched through a crack in the storehouse wall and "saw her shake herself and beat her body with her hands, and corn and beans came spilling out onto the floor from beneath her dress." He thought to himself, "'Why that stuff is only excrement, and she makes us believe it's food.'" It was then that he resolved to kill her. Mollie Sequoyah, "Mollie Sequoyah's Version," in Witthoft, "The Cherokee Green Corn Medicine," 217. Also see "Moses Owl's Version," in ibid., 218.
66. Mooney, *Myths*, 244–45.
67. Ibid., 245.
68. Ibid., 433.
69. James Mooney, "Origin of Game and Vegetables, 2d Version," no. 1905, Bureau of American Ethnology Catalogue of Manuscripts, 38, National Anthropological Archives, Washington, D.C. (hereafter JM MSS). These are handwritten shorthand drafts, with some transliterated data, that are among the many manuscripts, notes, and other materials of Mooney's located in this collection. The catalogue card states the following under "Remarks": "Original mss. of Cherokee stories pub. In 19th Annual Report of the B.A.E." Mooney's written notes at the beginning and end of the versions direct the reader to the following variants also contained in that manuscript collection: "The Thunder Family-Origin of Game and Vegetables," 29–30; and "Origin of Game and Vegetables 5," 44. These two differ in length and amount of detail. As with the published works, I have endeavored to duplicate most of Mooney's diacritical marks on the Cherokee terms as closely as possible.
70. Mooney, *Myths*, 247.
71. Ibid., 247–48.
72. Ibid., 248.
73. Mollie Sequoyah's version in Witthoft ended with a one-sentence summary about the sons traveling west together with their father "to take up their station as the Thunders." Sequoyah in Witthoft, "The Cherokee Green Corn Medicine," 218. "Moses Owl's Version" did not contain this final detail. Ibid., 218. Neither mentioned the ball game, nor did the "Wahnenauhi Version" in *Myths*, which also concluded with Selu's directive to the boys regarding what to do with her dead body. This version also incorporated elements and

language which more closely approximate notions of Christian sacrifice. This aspect may reflect either beliefs of the narrators or a desire to present the story in a particular way that might resonate with the non-Cherokee audience. See Mooney, *Myths*, 248–49. For a similar example of a version of a Cherokee narrative that might also integrate a notion of Christian sacrifice, compare the version of Stonecoat, or Nun´yunu´wi collected by Mooney with Will West Long's. See Mooney, *Myths*, 319–20, and Will West Long, "Legend of Stone Coat: His Sacrifice and the Bequest of Medicine Dances and Song Formulas to the Cherokee," in Speck and Broom, *Cherokee Dance and Drama*, 13–16. All subsequent citations are to this edition.

74. Mooney, *Myths*, 250–52.

75. This concept is expressed in the cultural narratives as well as in formulas, yet it does not manifest itself as some sort of idyllic, romanticized "love all nature" attitude. It has an ethical component. One example of this is the deer hunter asking the pardon of slain deer, lest he be followed home and stricken with rheumatism by their chief, Little Deer. Thus the punishment for insensitivity to and disrespect of other beings is disease. Mooney, *Myths*, 250–51, 263–64. The cultural narrative that expresses this ideal to its fullest is this narrative of the origin of disease and medicine.

76. Ibid., 261. Lee Irwin has argued that there was no Edenic harmony and that Cherokee people have always been in conflict with animals. See Irwin, "Cherokee Healing," 240–41.

77. Mooney, *Myths*, 252.

78. Personal communications, 1993–2007.

79. Mooney, 252–54.

80. "Contents" in ibid., 252–54. He omitted the subtitle in the body of the text.

81. Ibid., 252.

82. Ibid., 436.

83. Ibid., 253.

84. Ibid., 253–54.

85. Consultants have related entire accounts, and different individuals have related portions of this narrative to me at different times, including Enduring Voices participants. Zogry, personal communications, 1993, 1998, 1999, 2000; Enduring Voices November 1997, December 1997, June 1998. The primary source text for the narrative as I present it here is Mooney, "The ball game of the birds and animals," in *Myths*, 286–87. Additional versions not discussed or cited below include: Mooney, "The Ball Play between the Birds and Animals," no. 1905, JM MSS, 12; Mooney, "The Ballplay Between the Birds and Animals—How the Flying Squirrel and Bat Got to Fly," no. 1905, JM MSS, 21; Mooney, "Cherokee Ball Play," 108–9; and Lloyd Sequoyah, "Ball Game between the Animals and Birds," in Fogelson, "Cherokee Ball Game," 10–14.

86. Personal communications, 1993–2007.

87. Mooney, *Myths*, 286–87.

88. Additionally, Lloyd Sequoyah's version includes portions not recorded by Mooney, which Fogelson described as "conscious formulation of a great deal of the latent meaning of the myth. Fogelson, "Cherokee Ball Game," 8. Much of the additional material is explanatory detail and commentary, in addition to the epilogue. Fogelson noted that Sequoyah had been drinking prior to the session and said the alcohol "facilitated" the inclusion of this additional material. Ibid., 8, 7. He also said the narration was "marred by occasional repetition, discursiveness, and occasional incoherence." Ibid. While I did not experience factors of repetition and incoherence, I did observe discursiveness when being

told narratives by some members of the Eastern Band. But in my experience the aspect of discursiveness Fogelson described is stylistic and is not the result of imbibing alcohol; it perhaps is better termed "parenthetically explanatory." In this sense only I agree with Fogelson when he notes that the version given by Sequoyah "more closely approximates the typical Cherokee style of storytelling than do the smooth, closely edited texts published by Mooney." Ibid., 7. However, as noted above, Mooney did preserve some shorter discursive elements, most notably the explanation of the metaphorical meaning of the ball game. Finally, as Fogelson noted the fact that Sequoyah had been drinking, one wonders why the men did not reschedule.

89. Ibid., 14.

90. In addition to the variant versions noted above, other versions have appeared, and in a variety of formats, including newspapers, children's books, and other publications. Some examples are Kathi Smith Littlejohn, "The Birds and Animals Stickball Game," in Duncan, *Living Stories of the Cherokee*, 66–67; Owl, "The Big Ball Game." David Owl's book *Stories From a Wise Old Owl* also contains a section on the ball game. Ibid., 57–63. It was reprinted as "Cherokee Indian Ball," *Cherokee (N.C.) One Feather*, October 5, 1988, 6–7. Also see Arneach, *The Animals' Ballgame*. This is a book for children, with text at the end of the book and a tape recording of it to accompany the book of illustrations. Arneach noted that he learned the narratives from his uncles George and David Owl. Ibid., publication data page. Other newspaper articles include Bird Partridge in John Parris, "Lore: Animals, Birds Played a Ball Game," *Asheville (N.C.) Citizen-Times*, September 22, 1988, 1A, 2A. Though the narrative was attributed to Partridge, a well-known traditionalist, the narrative was told by Parris and was not a transcription of Partridge's words; Parris said the conversation had taken place "almost forty years ago." Ibid., 1A. This narrative is a slightly edited version of another entry in Parris's Roaming the Mountains column that appeared eleven years earlier. See John Parris, "About the Bat and the Flying Squirrel," *Asheville (N.C.) Citizen-Times*, September 4, 1977, 1A, 5A. Both columns contained a few comments from Partridge and Hayes Lossiah, who was seventy-three at the time and was another well-known traditionalist on the Qualla Boundary. While these accounts were edited and their overall tone rendered somewhat romantic, quotations from Cherokee individuals make these articles useful, though to what extent their words were edited is unclear. Many years earlier Parris also published a book with similar features, *The Cherokee Story* (1950).

91. Personal communication, October 1998. This detail has, to my knowledge, never been published.

92. Ibid. Consultants transliterated the Bat's name in this way.

93. No consultants related this narrative to me. The source text for the narrative as I present it here is Mooney, "The Moon and the Thunders," in *Myths*, 256–57.

94. Ibid., 257. This information has not been corroborated by any consultant or published source.

95. Mooney said in the notes to this narrative that "the myth connecting the moon with the ballplay is from Haywood (Natural and Aboriginal History of Tennessee, p. 285), apparently on the authority of Charles Hicks, a mixed-blood chief." Ibid., 441. Again, this information has not been corroborated and may be a garbled account.

96. I did not hear any part of this narrative. The primary source texts for the narrative as I present it here are Mooney, "The End of Untsaiyi'," no. 1905, JM MSS, 27–28; and Mooney, "Ûñtsaiyĭ´, the Gambler," in *Myths*, 311–15.

97. Actually Thunder lived "a little to the south of west, near the place where the sun goes down behind the water." Mooney, *Myths*, 311.

98. For details on Vtsayi see ibid., 464. This is the game played with the gaming wheel mentioned in the version of Kanati and Selu discussed above.

99. Ibid., 312.

100. Ibid.

101. Ibid., 313.

102. Ibid. Though he gambled his life away, the narrative reported that "Brass never died, and can not die until the end of the world," so he lies imprisoned in water until that time. Ibid., 314.

103. Ibid., 464. As I will discuss in more detail in Chapter 5, other consultants and sources have suggested this was the case.

104. Mooney, "The End of Untsayi'," no. 1905, JM MSS, 28.

105. My title; it should not be confused with the similar narratives that are listed as variant texts immediately below. Unlike the variant texts listed with the other narratives these differ more substantially, yet are similar enough to note. I did not hear any part of this story. The primary source text for the narrative as I present it here is Moses Owl, in Witthoft and Hadlock, "Cherokee-Iroquois Little People," 419. Additional versions not discussed or cited below include: Mooney, "The Man who Married the Thunder's Sister," no. 1905, JM MSS, 21–22; and Mooney, "The man who married the Thunder's sister," in *Myths*, 345–47.

106. Owl, in Witthoft and Hadlock, "Cherokee Iroquois Little People," 419.

107. Ibid.

108. See Mooney, "The Man Who Married the Thunder's Sister," in *Myths*, 345–47, in which the ball game is not mentioned, there is only one brother, and the man returns to his people but dies soon after. He is offered bracelets of snakes, as in the story of "Brass" or Vtsayi (above) and he is offered a mount of a giant snake, in this case an Uktena, as is the case in Owl's narrative.

109. Richard King, *Orientalism and Religion*, 35. Cicero's quote, from *De Natura Deorum*, is in ibid.

110. Fogelson, "Cherokee Ball Game," 10.

111. See Burridge, *Mambu*.

112. Fogelson, "Cherokee Little People Reconsidered," 95.

113. I discuss Western Cherokee beliefs below, but briefly. My work has been solely on the Qualla Boundary reservation, and my arguments and discussions should be understood only in that context.

114. Personal communications, 1993–2007.

115. Alan Kilpatrick, "Note on Cherokee Theological Concepts," 394. I have retained the citations in order to display his use of his parents' research to support his assertion.

116. Ibid., 401n4. He went on to say that his parents would sometimes "lapse" into use of this term even though they were firm about their translation.

117. Mooney and Olbrechts, *Swimmer Manuscript*, 20. Olbrechts gave the first Cherokee word as a version of *une:hlanv'hi* and the second as *ge:yagv:gu* (my approximation); his orthography is virtually impossible to reproduce.

118. Ibid.

119. Ibid.

120. See, for example, "Catechism of the Ten Commandments." The foreword stated that the catechism was "based on a work by A. N. Chamberlin . . . found in *Cherokee Pictorial Book* printed at Talaquah, Indian Territory, in 1888." Ibid.

121. Mooney and Olbrechts, *Swimmer Manuscript*, 20.

122. Mooney, "Cherokee Ball Play," 130.

123. Gilbert, "The Cherokees of North Carolina," 549.

124. Ibid., 548.

125. Payne-Butrick Manuscript, 25 (mss. 33–34). As I noted above, I will discuss and provide full citation information for this source in Chapter 2.

126. Ibid., 25 (mss. 34).

127. Longe, "A Small Postscript," 8, 9. Corkran placed his edited version and the original version on facing pages. The first quotation is from the edited version and the second quotation is from the original, because Corkran wrote "ouga Olaster the vola" and I have not ascertained which is the typo.

128. Ibid. The quotations are from Corkran's version. The four beings are described as corresponding in color to "us Indians," "black like the negro," "white as you English are," and "the color of the Spaniards." In Longe's "very fair and plain account" the priest says that the white being of the south is the most favored, as are the white men. The "black god" of the north is "very cross," the "white" god of the south is "a very good one," and the fourth (brown?) god is "pretty good and assistant to the messenger of the south." The god of the east is propitiated so he "should not send strong east winds and over set all our corn when a tasselling or in the ear." He is "something better" than the black god, but according to the account Longe relates, it is the gods of the south and west who "are good and has compassion on the people of the earth." Ibid., 12, 14.

129. Starr, *Early History of the Cherokees*, 16–17. For information on Starr, see Strickland, "Emmet Starr," 609–610. About Starr, Strickland commented, "Sequoyah, it is said, gave his people 'talking leaves.' Starr gave his people a recorded history." Ibid., 610. Starr's most well-known work is *History of the Cherokee Indians and their legends and folk lore* (1922). The book contains a wealth of information regarding all aspects of Cherokee culture and history, including rare photographs. One famous photograph is of the 1916 Council of the Nighthawk Keetoowah, considered conservators of cultural traditions in Oklahoma. There are seven men in the picture, and all are either wearing or holding "the ancient Cherokee wampum belts, never previously exhibited." Strickland, "Emmet Starr," 610. In front of them on the ground are several items, including a drum, a gourd rattle, and two pairs of crossed ball sticks. Starr, *History of the Cherokee Indians*, 487. This item arrangement clearly displays the cultural significance of the ball game, and the fact that it was a marker of Cherokee identity eighty years after the Trail of Tears. Ibid.

130. Personal communications, 1993–2007.

131. See the comments of "L.S." in Fogelson, "A Study of the Conjuror," 79; Witthoft, *The Cherokee Green Corn Medicine*, 213–19; Enduring Voices interview, November 1997. This individual told a story about his mother speaking to "uncle" and the subsequent parting of the thunderclouds as a storm approached. Ibid.

132. Longe, "A Small Postscript," 38.

133. JHP TS 1:27 (MS pp. 36–37). This information is attributed to "Sick,a,htow,ah," or Sickahtowah. There is an error, "vice-gerents," in the typescript. In this source the Red Man, confusingly, seems to "signify," yet not be identified as, the sun. Ibid.

134. Ibid., 30 (MS p. 40). The information before and after the section in which this included is attributed to "Sick,a,htow,ah," but it is unclear if he was the source of this particular item.

135. Mooney, *Myths*, 435.

136. Ibid., 257. See also his statement in which he terms "The Thunderers" or "They who make the Thunder" as "Aní-Hyûñ′tikwălá′skĭ" and distinguishes them as the "great

Thunderers" from the "inferior thunder spirits" that inhabit cliffs, mountains and waterfalls such as Tallulah. Ibid., 441.

137. Mooney, "The Thunder Family-Origin of Game and Vegetables," no. 1905, JM MSS, 29–30. See his notes there about the Thunders.

138. Mooney, *Sacred Formulas*, 341.

139. Ibid., 342.

140. Mooney and Olbrechts, *Swimmer Manuscript*, 24.

141. Ibid.

142. Ibid. Olbrechts said "white people." Personal communications, 1993–2007.

143. Mooney's fieldwork was done during the years 1887–1890; Witthoft's from 1944 to 1946 for the information quoted here.

144. Witthoft and Hadlock, "Cherokee-Iroquois Little People," 418. See Mooney, *Myths*, 438.

145. Witthoft and Hadlock, "Cherokee-Iroquois Little People," 418.

146. Ibid.

147. Fogelson, "Cherokee Little People Reconsidered," 92–97.

148. Ibid., 95.

149. Ibid.

150. Ibid., 94.

151. Ibid. 94. Fogelson referred to Mooney, *Myths*, 300–301, and to two other articles, but not to the Kilpatricks' work here. Review of this narrative shows that there was only one being aided, called by Mooney, "the Asga'ya Gi'gagei, the Red Man of the Lightning." Mooney, *Myths*, 300.

152. See Jack F. Kilpatrick and Anna G. Kilpatrick, *Friends of Thunder*, 51–56; Thunder Kills an UGH(A)DHE:N(A)," no. 8 in Jack F. Kilpatrick and Anna G. Kilpatrick, "Eastern Cherokee Folktales," 391–392. Thus Fogelson's conclusion hinges on two Eastern Cherokee narratives and several Western Cherokee narratives to place the Uktena and the Thunderers in such clear cosmic opposition.

153. See Jack F. and Anna G. Kilpatrick, *Friends of Thunder*, v; 135–36. I have written a document on the Thunders, which I hope will be a future project for publication, that treats this issue in more depth and contains additional supporting material for this contention.

154. Personal communications, 2000–2001.

155. Ibid.

156. Ibid.

157. Mooney and Olbrechts, *Swimmer Manuscript*, 24.

158. Ibid.

159. For a more detailed explanation, see, for example, Kelley, *Biblical Hebrew*, 32. Some Jewish people refrain from speaking or writing the English term as well, speaking one of the Hebrew terms or writing "G-d" instead.

160. In a published interview, an elderly Cherokee man, Solomon Bird, commented to this effect in answer to a question about what "medicine men" said to participants in the ball game. "I don't know, and nobody else knew either. In fact, they didn't speak out. They did it in their minds." Bird, "Solomon Bird Interview," 11. Also see Mooney and Olbrechts, *Swimmer Manuscript*, 155; Herndon, "The Cherokee Ballgame Cycle," 349.

161. Mooney, *Myths*, 294.

162. Ibid., 295.

163. Ibid.

164. Fogelson, "The Cherokee Ballgame Cycle," 335.

165. Ibid., 336.

166. Minutes of the Board of Commissioners of Indian Trade of South Carolina, 4 May 1714, *Journals of the Commissioners of the Indian Trade*, 53.

167. "Middle," "Upper" or "Overhill," and "Lower" are common designations given to groups of Cherokee settlements, and these refer to dialects of the Cherokee language. John Finger summarized this information as follows: "There were three general divisions among the Cherokees: the Lower towns along the upper Savannah River in South Carolina; the Middle towns occupying the upper Little Tennessee River and its tributaries in western North Carolina; and the Upper—or Overhill—Towns in eastern Tennessee and extreme western North Carolina. Some scholars divide the Middle Towns into a fourth division, the so-called Out Towns that lay to the north and east of the others." Finger, *Eastern Band of the Cherokees*, 3. As Finger noted of the Out Towns, "these remote villages were a Cherokee backwater. Yet one of them, Kituwha near present-day Bryson City, North Carolina, was apparently the 'mother town' of all three divisions. As progenitors of their people, the Out Towns would be a powerful force in preserving the Cherokee identity and homeland." Ibid. The present-day holdings of the Eastern Band on and around the Qualla Boundary incorporate much of this area, including the Kituwah mound site.

168. David H. Corkran, introduction, in Longe, "A Small Postscript," 3. Also see "Minutes," May 4, 1714, *Journals of the Commissioners*, 53.

169. Corkran, introduction, 3. There is disagreement on what towns were included. Corkran said it was Overhill warriors. Ibid. The account in the *Journals of the Commissioners* said they were from Middle towns. "Minutes," May 6, 1714, *Journals of the Commissioners*, 56. Also see Reid, "A Bare Board," 42. Reid said they were from Lower towns. Ibid. One final source said they were from the Middle towns, with the Lower being expressly excluded. Milling, *Red Carolinians*, 180–81.

170. Reid, *A Better Kind of Hatchet*, 44; "Minutes," May 4, 1714; May 5, 1714, in *Journals of the Commissioners*, 53, 55.

171. Reid, *A Better Kind of Hatchet*, 44. Given this explanation, it is unclear why there were some survivors.

172. Ibid.

173. Instructions to the Traders, August 3, 1711, *Indian Books*, 1:16, quoted in ibid., 43. Apparently a distinction was drawn in this case based on the incitement factor as to what constituted a war.

174. "Minutes," May 4, 1714, *Journals of the Commissioners*, 53.

175. The term was used throughout the minutes. See "Minutes," May 4–6, 1714, *Journals of the Commissioners*, 53–56. It also was used in other military contexts. For example, one author described a scene in which a commander, caught in an ambush, tried to maintain order among his troops: "Williamson was pressed to rally his men, who cried 'we shall be cut off!'" Badders, *Broken Path*, 45.

176. Malone, *Cherokees of the Old South*, 31.

177. Fogelson, "Cherokee Ball Game," 21.

178. Perdue, *Evolution of Cherokee Society*, 23. James Adair said, "the Indians are not fond of waging war with each other, unless prompted by some of the traders; when left to themselves, they consider with the greatest exactness and foresight, all the attending circumstances of war." Adair, *Adair's History*, 407; quoted in ibid., 23. One interesting point is there were "inter-tribal" or more properly, international games during this time. Fogelson also commented on this fact. Fogelson, "Cherokee Ball Game," 21.

179. The Yuchi did play ball, and also had Ball Game Dances the night before contests. See Speck, *Ethnology of the Yuchi Indians*, 86–89, pl. 16. This was Speck's doctoral dissertation at the University of Pennsylvania.

180. See note 87 above.

181. "Minutes," in *Journals of the Commissioners*, 53.

182. I will summarize these ritual activities in Chapter 3.

183. Adam Stephen to Henry Bouquet, November 7, 1763, Canada R.31, 552, Cherokee Documents in Foreign Archives, Microfilm Collection, Museum of the Cherokee Indian Archives, Cherokee, N.C. This transcription is my own. I wish to thank Joan W. Greene, former longtime archivist at the Museum of the Cherokee Indian, for bringing this reference, among others, to my attention.

184. Mooney, "Historical Sketch," in *Myths*, 45.

185. Ibid.

186. John Stuart to the Earl of Egremont, December 5, 1763, Part 2, Report after the Congress, Folio 69, Charleston C.O. 5/65, p. 4, Cherokee Documents in Foreign Archives, Microfilm Collection, Museum of the Cherokee Indian Archives, Cherokee, N.C.

Chapter 2

1. See "Reichel, Carl Gotthold," in "Appendix 2: Biographical List," in McClinton, *The Moravian Springplace Mission*, 2:498. McClinton stated that Reichel "served as bishop and president of the administrative board for Wachovia; returned to Europe in 1818." Ibid.

2. John and A. R. Gambold to Carl Gotthold Reichel, July 20, 1808, M 411:6:19, Moravian Archives, Winston-Salem, N.C., 42 (typescript pg. 2).

3. Perdue, *Cherokee Women*, 181.

4. Evarts was treasurer of the ABCFM from 1812 to 1821, and corresponding secretary from 1821 to 1831. He also edited the *Panoplist*, a religious journal, before helping to found the ABCFM in 1812. See Andrew, *From Revivals to Removal*.

5. Isaac Proctor to Jeremiah Evarts, December 11, 1827, Papers of the American Board of Commissioners for Foreign Missions, Missions on the American Continents and to the Islands of the Pacific, 1811–1919 (ABC 18–19) 1824–1831, Cherokee Mission (ABC 18.3.1) (hereafter ABCFM Papers), Microfilm Reel 739, Vol. 4, Cherokee Mission Letters, no. 189, 6.

6. Charles Long, "Silence and Signification," in *Signfications*, 61.

7. Irwin, "Cherokee Healing," 239.

8. Dowd, "Renewing Sacred Power in the South," in *A Spirited Resistance*, 173. McLoughlin, "Thomas Jefferson," quoted in ibid.

9. Irwin, "Cherokee Healing," 239. I agree with Irwin's point, though I would problematize the term "sacred."

10. Ibid.

11. Sensbach, *A Separate Canaan*, 288.

12. McLoughlin, *Cherokees and Missionaries*, 204.

13. William Holland, "Report on Candy's Creek Station," April 1828, ABCFM, quoted in ibid.

14. McLoughlin, *Cherokees and Missionaries*, 204.

15. Ibid.

16. Joel W. Martin, "Visions of Revitalization," 86.

17. Corman, review of *Writing Indians*, 742.

18. Ibid. Wyss, *Writing Indians*, 3; quoted in Corman, review of *Writing Indians*, 743.

Corman noted that Wyss cited Mary Louise Pratt's concept of "autoethnography" in support of her approach. Ibid.

19. Ibid., 745.
20. Ibid.
21. Hoxie, preface, in *Talking Back to Civilization*, viii.
22. Ibid.
23. Deloria, *Custer Died for Your Sins; We Talk, You Listen.*
24. Joel W. Martin, "Sioux Ghost Dance," 678. Italics in the original.
25. Ibid.
26. Joel W. Martin, "Visions of Revitalization," 85.
27. Perdue, *Cherokee Women*, 10.
28. Ibid.
29. Charles Long, "Silence and Signification," in *Significations*, 60. Wittgenstein quoted in ibid. This article and quotation spurred me to formulate a key aspect of my argument in this chapter. I do wish to acknowledge, however, that I employ their statements in such a way, removed from original context, that one might best describe them as disembodied.
30. Ibid., 59, 58.
31. Ibid., 58.
32. Ibid., 61.
33. Ibid.
34. For a critique of *Significations*, see McCutcheon, *Manufacturing Religion*, 33.
35. Such debates are ongoing in religious studies. Feminist scholars have debated similar issues regarding the silence of women in history. For a brief discussion, see Olson, "Feminist Perspectives on Religion," in *Theory and Method*, 477.
36. Joel W. Martin, "From 'Middle Ground' to 'Underground,'" 129.
37. Ibid.
38. Joel W. Martin, "Visions of Revitalization," 71. In the earlier work, noting that a large number of the elite were "métis," he referred to them as "metis mediators." Martin, "From 'Middle Ground' to 'Underground,'" 132.
39. Martin, "From 'Middle Ground' to 'Underground,'" 133.
40. McLoughlin, *Cherokees and Missionaries*, 185–86, with Martin's emphasis, quoted in Martin, "From 'Middle Ground' to 'Underground,'" 133.
41. Martin, "From 'Middle Ground' to 'Underground,'" 141.
42. Martin, "Visions of Revitalization," 86.
43. McClinton, introduction, in *Moravian Springplace Mission*, 1:18–20.
44. Mooney, "Historical Sketch," in *Myths*, 84.
45. McClinton, introduction, in *Moravian Springplace Mission*, 1:21.
46. This is the proper term to describe the town leaders, not "chief."
47. Mooney, "Historical Sketch," in *Myths*, 84. The town name is conventionally transliterated as "Oostenally."
48. Ibid.
49. Ibid. Mooney discussed earlier missionary activity on p. 83. He did not report any further particulars. Also see McLoughlin, *The Cherokees and Christianity*, 18–21.
50. Richard Peters, *The Case of the Cherokee Nation against the State of Georgia* (Philadelphia, 1831), 253, quoted in McLoughlin, *The Cherokee Ghost Dance*, 10.
51. Benjamin Hawkins, "Manuscript no. 5," *Treaty Commission, 1801* (Library of Georgia Historical Society), quoted in Mooney, "Historical Sketch," in *Myths*, 82–83.
52. Mooney, "Historical Sketch," in *Myths*, 83.

53. They were led by three influential individuals: John Watts, Doublehead, and Will. Ibid.

54. Finger, *Eastern Band of Cherokees*, 13.

55. Ibid. This opinion apparently was widespread, and some consultants have told me that the North Carolina territory was considered undesirable and its inhabitants unrefined, backwoods folks at that time. Ibid., and personal conversations, 1993–2007.

56. Henry Knox, Volume II, 54, in Walter Lowrie, Walter S. Franklin, and Matthew Clarke, eds., *American State Papers*, Class II, Indian Affairs, 2 vols., quoted in McLoughlin, *Cherokees and Missionaries*, 34.

57. McLoughlin, *Cherokees and Missionaries*, 150.

58. Ibid.

59. McClinton, introduction, in *Moravian Springplace Mission*, 1:31. McLoughlin, *Cherokees and Missionaries*, 60. Mooney, "Historical Sketch," in *Myths*, 84. Also see McLoughlin, *The Cherokees and Christianity*, 21–22. Samuel C. Williams, who edited Henry Timberlake's memoirs and other works, discovered the journal of the Rev. Dr. Samuel Davies, a Presbyterian minister who traveled around Cherokee settlements from 1757 to 1759. This is perhaps the oldest missionary account in existence. Davies said the people he met were "much given to conjuring & the conjurers have great Power over ym; they have these few days been preparing a Physick wc they say will drive away all their Disorders & the Man to whose care it was committed has ben every Night and Morning going round the Town House hollowing and crying and frequently in the Day to the great Man above for a blessing on the Physick, as they say." The next day, "Mon. 15," he had the following to say: "At Chotee; it being raining the men and boys ran naked to Suttico & back to run away the Rain, but they have not got fair weather by it." Samuel D. Williams, "Account of the Presbyterian Mission," 135.

60. McLoughlin, *Cherokees and Missionaries*, 60. Also see McClinton, *Moravian Springplace Mission*, 1:31.

61. McLoughlin, *Cherokees and Missionaries*, 63.

62. "Presbyterian Mission Difficulties," in ibid., 54–81; for the numbers of student see pages 57 and 60. Also see McClinton, introduction, in *Moravian Springplace Mission*, 1:31.

63. McClinton, introduction, in *Moravian Springplace Mission*, 1:22.

64. McLoughlin, *Cherokees and Missionaries*, 81.

65. McLoughlin, *Cherokees and Christianity*, 24. Charles Hicks was the son of white trader Nathan Hicks and a half-Cherokee woman (unnamed). He joined the Moravian Church in 1813. He was an interpreter for Return J. Meigs until he opposed Doublehead's plan to sell land. He was treasurer of the Cherokee Nation from 1813 to 1817, second principal chief under Principal Chief Pathkiller from 1817 to 1827, and principal chief in 1827; he died soon after taking office. Appendix 2, "Biographical List, Cherokee Visitors to Springplace," in McClinton, *Moravian Springplace Mission*, 2:463.

66. Edited and with an introduction by Rowena McClinton, this two-volume work provides scholars with a useful collection of the Springplace diary entries. The entries themselves provided detail about Cherokee activities as well as personal commentary by the Moravian authors. McClinton, *Moravian Springplace Mission*, 1:xv. Also see, for example, Sensbach, *A Separate Canaan*, xxi–xxiii.

67. McClinton, *Moravian Springplace Mission*, 1:xv–xvii.

68. John and A. R. Gambold to Reichel, July 20, 1808, Moravian Archives. The diary entry for March 2, 1809, stated that the boy was *"white"* (italics in source) and that his

father's name was Major Anderson. McClinton, *Moravian Springplace Mission*, 1:304. While it is unclear what initially led to the decision, apparently they felt it was the correct one; in December 1808 Anderson pushed another boy into a vat of wax when they were making candles for Christmas services. McClinton, *Moravian Springplace Mission*, 1:629n10.

69. John and A. R. Gambold to Reichel, July 20, 1808, Moravian Archives.

70. Ibid.

71. Ibid.

72. Ibid.

73. McClinton, *Moravian Springplace Mission*, 1:275. There are entries for July 10–19, 21, and 23–26. Perhaps no entry this day is due to the letter to Reichel.

74. "John Gambold to Reichel, July 20, 1808," Moravian Archives, Winston-Salem, N.C.; and Carl C. Mauleshagen, trans., "Diary of the Moravian Mission at Spring Place, 1801–1836," Georgia State Archives, Atlanta, Ga.], 71 (30 April 1808), paraphrased in McLoughlin, *The Cherokee Ghost Dance*, 49n22.

75. The document in the possession of the Georgia State Archives cited above has several smudged pages, including 71, so I have been as yet unable to access the April 30 diary entry that McLoughlin cited; McClinton, *Moravian Springplace Mission*, vol. 1, does not contain an entry for that date.

76. September 3, 1809, McClinton, in *Moravian Springplace Mission*, 1:329.

77. Carl F. Klinck, "Biographical Introduction," in Norton, *Journal of Major John Norton*, lxxx.

78. Norton, *Journal of Major John Norton*, 68.

79. Ibid., 69.

80. September 3, 1809, in McClinton, *Moravian Springplace Mission*, 1:329.

81. Klinck, in Norton, *Journal of Major John Norton*, xl–xli.

82. Fogelson, "Major John Norton as Ethno-ethnologist."

83. Raymond Fogelson's doctoral dissertation contains several of these passages.

84. Norton, *Journal of Major John Norton*, 54. There are few dates given in the *Journal*; one must go from a given date and count days to arrive at an estimate. I estimate this to have been sometime in July or August 1809.

85. Ibid., 54–55.

86. Ibid., 63. I estimate this to be about one week later.

87. Ibid., 63.

88. Ibid., 63–64. Quotation, 64.

89. Ibid., 65.

90. Ibid., 76, 78, 79.

91. Ibid., 79.

92. April 10, 1810, in McClinton, *Moravian Springplace Mission*, 1:1355; October 12, 1819; May 30, 1820, ibid., 2:319, 352.

93. Mooney, "Historical Sketch," in *Myths*, 88; also see Pesantubbee, "When the Earth Shakes," 301–17; McLoughlin, *Cherokees and Missionaries*, 82–101; and McLoughlin, *The Cherokee Ghost Dance*, 111–51. Walter H. Conser edited *The Cherokees and Christianity*, and he said in a brief preface that McLoughlin was close to completing this volume at the time of his death. He said his own contribution consisted of "clarifying minor discrepancies, eliminating repetition among essays, and incorporating Professor McLoughlin's most recent revisions into the text of various chapters." Conser, McLoughlin, preface, in *The Cherokees and Christianity*, n.p.

94. Pesantubbee, "When the Earth Shakes," 314.

95. Mooney, "Historical Sketch," in *Myths*, 88. Interestingly, he reported rejection by the mountain towns, historically the most conservative communities. Ibid. The occasion was a council at Oostenally on February 7, 1811. Pesantubbee, "When the Earth Shakes," 301.

96. February 10, 1811, in McClinton, *Moravian Springplace Mission*, 1:411–12.

97. Ibid., 411.

98. Ibid., 411, 412.

99. Dowd, *A Spirited Resistance*, 175.

100. McLoughlin, *Cherokees and Missionaries*, 83.

101. February 17, 1812, in McClinton, *Moravian Springplace Mission*, 1:474. Italics in the original.

102. Ibid.

103. February 23, 1812, in ibid., 475.

104. Ibid.

105. February 24, 1812, in ibid., 476.

106. March 1 and March 8, 1812, in ibid., 477, 479. Also see Pesantubbee, "When the Earth Shakes," 305–7; 309–10.

107. March 1, 1812, in McClinton, *Moravian Springplace Mission*, 1:477.

108. March 8, 1812, in ibid., 478–79.

109. October 11, 1811, in ibid., 452. Italics in the original.

110. Ibid., 453. The third sentence begins a new paragraph in the text.

111. McLoughlin, *The Cherokees and Christianity*, 26.

112. Pesantubbee, "When the Earth Shakes," 315, 314.

113. Mooney, "Historical Sketch," in *Myths*, 88–89.

114. McLoughlin, *The Cherokee Ghost Dance*, 11.

115. Ibid. McLoughlin did not cite any sources to support this general contention. While it certainly could have been the case, source material would have been appropriate here.

116. Ibid.

117. Return J. Meigs, "Some Reflections on Cherokee concerns, manners, state, etc.," March 19, 1812, National Archives RG 75, M208, "Records of the Cherokee Indian Agency in Tennessee, 1801–1835," reel 5, reprinted as Appendix F in McLoughlin, *The Cherokee Ghost Dance*, 148. The passage continued: "These ablutions are intended to show that their sins are washed away and that they are cleansed from all defilements." Ibid. The first portion of the passage also is quoted in McLoughlin, *The Cherokees and Christianity*, 26.

118. Dowd, *A Spirited Resistance*, 173. Return Jonathan Meigs, "Journal of Occurrences in the Cherokee Nation," n.d. in the Meigs Family Papers, United States Library of Congress, Manuscripts Division, Madison Building, Washington, D.C.; Meigs to General Smith, August 19, 1805, NA M208, roll 3, both cited in ibid., 173. Although there is no date given for the first document, Dowd says in the text it was from 1801.

119. Return Jonathan Meigs, "Journal of Occurrences in the Cherokee Nation," quoted in Dowd, *A Spirited Resistance*, 173.

120. Dowd, *A Spirited Resistance*, 174. He referred to McLoughlin's theory, as well as to the psychological interpretations of Anthony Wallace.

121. Ibid., 247n15; 173; 174.

122. Perdue, *Cherokee Women*, 9.

123. Ibid.

124. Duane Champagne, "Institutional and Cultural Order," 22.

125. April 30, 1820, in McClinton, *Moravian Springplace Mission*, 1:352.

126. Ibid., May 2, 1820, 352–53.

127. McClinton, *Moravian Springplace Mission*, 2:496–98.

128. Johann Renatus Schmidt, Diary entry, August 7, 1825, M 406 D, Springplace Diary, 1823–29, Diary of the Mission in Spring Place among the Cherokee Indians 1825, Moravian Archives, Winston-Salem, N.C., 18.

129. Johann Renatus Schmidt to Schulz, August 11, 1825, M413:24–27, Moravian Archives, Winston-Salem, N.C., 53.

130. Edmund Schwarze, *History of the Moravian Missions among Southern Indian Tribes of the United States*, Transactions of the Moravian Historical Society, Special Series, vol. 1 (Bethlehem, Pa.: Times Publishing Co., 1923), 203, quoted in Fogelson, "Cherokee Ball Game," 31. The parenthetical emendation is Fogelson's.

131. McLoughlin, *Cherokees and Missionaries*, 338. He did not cite this passage directly, but cited "Schwarze, *Moravian Missions*, pp. 203–04," a few sentences above. Also see Fogelson, "Cherokee Ball Game," 31, for citation of the same passage.

132. McLoughlin, *Cherokees and Missionaries*, 338.

133. Johann Renatus Schmidt, Diary entry, August 24, 1825, M 406 D, Springplace Diary, 1823–29, Diary of the Mission in Spring Place among the Cherokee Indians 1825, Moravian Archives, Winston-Salem, N.C., 18.

134. Ibid., 19; "October," October 1st, ibid.

135. McClinton, epilogue, in *Moravian Springplace Mission*, 2:443.

136. Ibid. New Springplace was a Moravian mission established in the Indian Territory in 1841. Ibid., 442.

137. Thorp, *The Moravian Community*, 178; quotations: Bethabara diary extracts, Fries et al., Records, 1: 470; Ettwein to die Conferenz in Bethlehem, Jan. 18, 1762, LC-MC, R.14. Ba.Nr.2c: 576–80 in ibid.

138. Thorp, *The Moravian Community*, 202; quotation: Benzien to Dobbs, March 12, 1757, MA-SP, Rowan County-Dobbs Parish Papers in ibid.

139. According to the society's website, "during DuPonceau's tenure as secretary, the Committee laid the foundation for the Society's development into one of the premier centers for the study of Native American Indian languages." "Background note," (http://www.amphilsoc.org/library/mole/d/duponceau.htm) (accessed July 2008).

140. John Gambold to Peter S. DuPonceau, July 20, 1818, 497.V85, American Indian Vocabulary Collection, American Philosophical Society, no. 39.

141. Ibid.

142. See "Paternalism," in Prucha, *The Indians in American Society*, 1–27.

143. John Gambold to Peter S. DuPonceau, December 16, 1818, 497.V85, American Indian Vocabulary Collection, American Philosophical Society, no. 40.

144. Ibid., 2.

145. McLoughlin, *The Cherokees and Christianity*, 22.

146. McLoughlin, *Cherokees and Missionaries*, 110–11. McLoughlin further stated that "under the Plan of Union between Congregationalists and Presbyterians in 1801, the two denominations had agreed to unite their efforts on the frontier." Ibid., 111.

147. Phillips and Phillips, *The Brainerd Journal*, 4.

148. Ibid.

149. Journal entry, July 5, 1822, in ibid., 285.

150. Journal entry, July 6, 1822, in ibid.

151. Ibid.

152. McLoughlin, *The Cherokees and Christianity*, 23.

153. Moody Hall to Jeremiah Evarts, August 20, 1825, ABCFM Papers, Microfilm Reel 738, Vol. 5, Cherokee Mission Letters, no. 338, 2.

154. Ibid., 3.

155. Ibid.

156. See Appendix I, "Catalog of Scholars at Springplace Mission School, 1805–1821," in McClinton, *Moravian Springplace Mission*, 2:448. McClinton noted that he was initially called "Buck" because his name was "represented a male deer"; McClinton included the English transliterations "Ooaty," for "Watie," and "Galagina" or "Kiakeena." Ibid.

157. D. S. Butrick and Moody Hall to J. Evarts, December 13, 1825, (ABC 18.3.1) Vol. 5, no. 386, 1. Boudinot attended an ABCFM boarding school in Cornwall, Conn.

158. Ibid.

159. Moody Hall, diary of July and August 1825, MP V, Papers of the American Board of Commissioners for Foreign Missions, Houghton Library, Harvard University, 338; cited in Starkey, *The Cherokee Nation*, 76. Many of Starkey's notes referenced these and other missionary source documents.

160. Hall, diary, quoted in Starkey, *The Cherokee Nation*, 76.

161. Starkey, *The Cherokee Nation*, 75. Starkey noted that "they had very ill success"; church members as well as "really model schoolboys" would go anyway. He gave a brief synopsis of some related activities, noting that the "conjure involved in preparing for a game was of the disciplinary sort." Ibid.

162. Ibid., 76.

163. McLoughlin, "Cherokee Anti-Mission Sentiment," 365.

164. "Chulioa and the other local Cherokee chiefs at Etowah to Charles R. Hicks and Path Killer, May 26, 1824" (letter written by Walter Adair), Box M 482 (1820–1827), "Cherokee Mission Papers," Moravian Archives, Winston-Salem, N.C., reprinted in Appendix to McLoughlin, "Cherokee Anti-Mission Sentiment," 368–69.

165. McLoughlin, "Cherokee Anti-Mission Sentiment," 366.

166. "Charles R. Hicks to Chulioa and the other Etowah chief, May 28, 1824," in Appendix to McLoughlin, "Cherokee Anti-Mission Sentiment," 369.

167. Ibid., 367.

168. Proctor to Evarts, December 11, 1827, 5–6.

169. Ibid., 6.

170. McLoughlin, *Cherokees and Missionaries*, 203.

171. Proctor to Evarts, December 11, 1827, 6.

172. Ibid., 9.

173. Andrew, *From Revivals to Removal*, 65.

174. Proctor to Evarts, December 11, 1827, 9.

175. Ibid.

176. Ibid., 9–10.

177. Isaac Proctor to Jeremiah Evarts, July 28, 1827, ABCFM Papers, Microfilm Reel 739, Vol. 4, Cherokee Mission Letters, no. 187, 3. This is reproduced as it appears in the original.

178. Ibid., 4. Again, this is reproduced as it appears in the original.

179. McLoughlin, "Cherokees and Methodists," 47.

180. McLoughlin, *Cherokees and Missionaries*, 165.

181. Ibid., 165, 169.

182. Isaac Proctor to Jeremiah Evarts, July 10, 1828, ABCFM, quoted in ibid.

183. McLoughlin, *Cherokees and Missionaries*, 175. In an earlier work, McLoughlin broke down the numbers: "In 1830 the two Moravian mission stations in the Georgia area of the nation reported only 45 Cherokee members; the Baptist mission in North Carolina reported 90; and the Presbyterians (who were strongest in eastern Tennessee and Georgia) reported 167." McLoughlin, "Cherokees and Methodists," 49.

184. McLoughlin, *Cherokees and Missionaries*, 175–76.

185. McLoughlin, "Cherokees and Methodists," 62.

186. McLoughlin, *The Cherokees and Christianity*, 26–27. There is some debate, however, among historians as to who the real leader might have been. Several names have been put forward. See, for example, McLoughlin, *Cherokees and Missionaries*, 224–25.

187. See "White Path's Rebellion and the Cherokee Constitution, 1827–1828," in McLoughlin, *Cherokees and Missionaries*, 213–38.

188. Ibid., 213, 214. Also see Russell Thornton, "Boundary Dissolution and Revitalization Movements."

189. McLoughlin, *Cherokees and Missionaries*, 226–29.

190. McLoughlin, *The Cherokees and Christianity*, 30; for more on Jones see ibid., 91–108, and Gardner, *Cherokees and Baptists in Georgia*.

191. Evan Jones, Journal, December 28, 1828, American Baptist Foreign Mission Society Correspondence (hereafter FM) 98/25, quoted in Gardner, *Cherokees and Baptists*, 12; Evan Jones to Lucius Bolles, April 28, 1830, FM 98/28, quoted in ibid., 17. Gardner also noted that "when speaking of the conjurer's functions, Jones was not always clear. They presided over 'sacrifices & Ceremonies,'" including dances, going to water, and other ceremonial activities. Gardner, *Cherokees and Baptists*, 14–15; and Evan Jones, Journal, 2 January 1829, FM 98/25, in ibid., 14.

192. Gardner, *Cherokees and Baptists in Georgia*, 18.

193. Evan Jones, "Evan Jones's journals, 1827–1828," "1828–1830," American Baptist Foreign Mission Societies, Records, 1817–1959, Reel FM 98, American Baptist Archives Center, Valley Forge, Pa. (photocopies, Baptist Missionary Records, MSS 93-11, Folders 13–14, Museum of the Cherokee Indian Archives, Cherokee, N.C.). There is no consistent pagination in this copy of the documents.

194. Jones journal entry, June 22, 1828. Robert Gardner noted that Jones did not consider himself to be in "Georgia" when he was in the Cherokee nation. Gardner, *Cherokees and Baptists in Georgia*, 18.

195. Jones journal, June 22, 1828.

196. Ibid., June 23, 1828.

197. Ibid., July 15, 1827.

198. Ibid., February 2, 1829.

199. Perdue, *Cherokee Women*, 171.

200. Ibid., 171. See ibid., 237n75 for Perdue's sources for the first figure; for the second, note 76, David Greene to Jeremiah Evarts, January 28, 1828, ABCFM.

201. John Howard Payne, "John Howard Payne Papers," 14 vols., manuscript and typescript, n.d., A. J. Ayer Collection, Newberry Library, Chicago. While original documents are part of the Ayer Collection, typescripts have been produced and are held by the Newberry Library and other institutions, including the Museum of the Cherokee Indian. The material in the Payne Papers is not indexed and is disorganized, though Irwin prepared a guide based on the Newberry Library typescript. "Appendix One, Reader's Guide to the Payne Papers," in Irwin, "Different Voices Together," 18–23. I have examined some of the documents at the Newberry Library; however most of my study of the Payne Papers was

done with the typescripts in the Museum of the Cherokee Indian Archives: John Howard Payne Papers (typescripts, MSS 87-04, 6 vols., Museum of the Cherokee Indian Archives, Cherokee, N.C.), hereafter cited as JHP TS. The Newberry Library typescript of the material, hereafter cited as JHP TS (NL), differs from the one in the Museum of the Cherokee Indian Archives in terms of pagination, the latter giving original manuscript page numbers for some volumes. The Museum of the Cherokee Indian Archives also has a microfilm copy of the manuscripts: John Howard Payne Papers (microfilm, DR.11, 2 rolls, Museum of the Cherokee Indian Archives, Cherokee, N.C.), hereafter cited as JHP MS, microfilm. As all of these sources were consulted, each will be cited individually. The Payne Papers collection has never been published in full, nor has an edited edition yet appeared, but various short portions have been published. In the past, many scholars, including Fogelson, often referred to them as the Payne-Butrick Manuscripts. Although letters in the collection bear dates, most of the other manuscripts do not; they were apparently collected for the most part between 1835 and 1840. A good summation of the material contained in the Payne Papers and the details of their authorship is in Irwin, "Different Voices Together."

202. Mooney, "Historical Sketch," in *Myths*, 122–23. Also see McLoughlin, *The Cherokees and Christianity*, 142.

203. Mooney, "Historical Sketch," in *Myths*, 122–23.

204. John Howard Payne, JHP TS 4:17–18 (A. J. Ayer Collection, Newberry Library, Chicago), quoted in Irwin, "Different Voices Together," 9. Irwin referenced the typescript made from the microfilm in the Museum of the Cherokee Indian Archives; he said the manuscript was no longer available for research. Ibid., 23nn2, 4, 18. There seems to be some confusion regarding the spelling of the missionary's last name. On the cover of Butrick's *Antiquities of the Cherokee Indians*, which was reproduced on the cover of the *Journal of Cherokee Studies* issue in which both Irwin's article and Butrick's publication appeared, it is spelled with two "t"s. However, most scholars, including Irwin, spell the name with one "t." See ibid., and the cover of *Journal of Cherokee Studies* 18 (1997).

205. McLoughlin, *The Cherokees and Christianity*, 142.

206. Daniel S. Butrick to John Howard Payne, December 29, 1840, Letter Number 4, JHP TS 4, pt. 1:7 (Museum of the Cherokee Indian Archives, Cherokee, N.C.).

207. Irwin, "Different Voices Together," 10.

208. McLoughlin, *The Cherokees and Christianity*, 142; Irwin, "Different Voices Together," 9.

209. JHP TS (NL) Catalog item entry, Newberry Library, Chicago. Also see Irwin, "Different Voices Together," 23n2.

210. McLoughlin, *The Cherokees and Christianity*, 28.

211. Ibid., 94, 104.

212. Buttrick, *Antiquities of the Cherokee Indians*. I quoted from one of these letters above and in the Introduction.

213. McLoughlin, *The Cherokees and Christianity*, 141.

214. Ibid., 142.

215. Ibid., 141–42.

216. Daniel S. Butrick, "Ball Play," JHP TS 4, pt. 1:50 (MS p. 78) (Museum of the Cherokee Indian Archives, Cherokee, N.C.). Also see Fogelson, "Cherokee Ball Game," 35.

217. Butrick, "Ball Play," 51–52 (MS pp. 79–81).

218. Butrick, JHP MSS 4:436 quoted in Fogelson, "Cherokee Ball Game," 37. The parenthetical emendations are Fogelson's.

219. Butrick, "Ball Play," 53–54 (MS 82). Also see Fogelson, "Cherokee Ball Game," 38.

220. Butrick, JHP MSS 4:439, quoted in Fogelson, "Cherokee Ball Game," 38.

221. J. P. Evans, "Ball Play," JHP TS 6:10. Also see Fogelson, "Cherokee Ball Game," 39.

222. Evans, "Ball Play," 10.

223. Ibid., 11.

224. Ibid., 11, 12, 14.

225. McLoughlin, *The Cherokees and Christianity*, 27; Mooney, "Historical Sketch," in *Myths*, 117.

226. Mooney, "Historical Sketch," in *Myths*, 117.

227. McLoughlin, *The Cherokees and Christianity*, 92.

228. See, for example, Wallace, *Jefferson and the Indians*.

229. Ibid., 71–72; Mooney, "Historical Sketch," in *Myths*, 119–20.

230. McLoughlin, *The Cherokees and Christianity*, 71–72; Jackson quote, Mooney, "Historical Sketch," in *Myths*, 120, see note 1 for his sources.

231. McLoughlin, *The Cherokees and Christianity*, 114.

232. McLoughlin, *Cherokees and Missionaries*, 289.

233. McLoughlin, *The Cherokees and Christianity*, 114–15.

234. Ibid., 43.

235. Ibid., 43–44.

236. *Raleigh Register and North Carolina Gazette*, August 21, 1837, Issue 42, col. D., "19th Century Newspapers," ⟨http://infotrac.galegroup.com⟩ (accessed July 2008).

237. Finger, *The Eastern Band of Cherokees*, 18–19.

238. Thornton, *The Cherokees*, 63–77; Perdue and Green, *The Cherokee Removal*; "Trail of Tears," in *Encyclopedia of North American Indians*, 639–40; Duane H. King, "Cherokee," in ibid., 106.

239. Starkey, *The Cherokee Nation*, 75.

240. Fogelson, "Cherokee Ball Game," 31.

241. Perdue, *Cherokee Women*, 181.

242. Ibid. I will carefully examine the relationship between anetso and warfare in Chapter 5.

243. McLoughlin, *Cherokees and Missionaries*, 208.

244. Ibid., 204. Strangely, he gave no footnote to support this quote; it may have come from the missionary William Holland, whom he quoted in the following footnote.

245. McLoughlin, *The Cherokees and Christianity*, 205.

Chapter 3

1. Fogelson, "Who Were the Aní:Kutání"; Gearing, *Priests and Warriors*, especially 23–28, 80–81, 102–4, Mooney, "The Massacre of the Aní'-Kuta'ni," in *Myths*, 392–93.

2. There were additional ceremonies held quarterly, monthly, weekly, and in one case, every seven years. Speck and Broom, *Cherokee Dance and Drama*, 7–8.

3. "Payne MS I, ll. 70–71," in ibid.

4. Longe, "A Small Postscript," 10.

5. David H. Corkran, introduction, in ibid., 4.

6. Mooney, "Massacre of the Aní'-Kuta'ni," in *Myths*, 392–93; Fogelson, "Who Were the Aní:Kutání," 255–63.

7. Norton, *Journal of Major John Norton*, 80.

8. Ibid.

9. Fogelson, "Who Were the *Aní:Kutání*"; Fogelson, "Ethnohistory of Events and Nonevents."

10. See the comments of James Adair, in Fogelson, "Who Were the *Aní:Kutání*," 260–61. Epidemics occurred in 1697, 1759–60, and 1780.

11. Ibid., 255–57, 259, 261.

12. Ibid., 256; and Charles Hicks quoted in ibid., 258.

13. Fogelson, "Ethnohistory of Events and Nonevents."

14. Ibid., 134.

15. Ibid., 134–35.

16. Ibid., 140. To this end, Fogelson endeavored to address "the applicability of the Annales approach and developments in historical anthropology to a possibly refashioned ethnohistory of the American Indian." Ibid., 138.

17. Ibid., 142.

18. Ibid., 143.

19. Fogelson, "Who Were the *Aní:Kutání*," 260; Fogelson, "Ethnohistory of Events and Nonevents," 143.

20. Norton, *Journal of Major John Norton*, 80. Interestingly, this account was preceded by a passage related by Norton in which he expressed his opinion to his host that the demeanor of participants was not especially reverent. The individual responded, "'It now appears only a matter of mutual congratulation and rejoicing, that the crops have so far ripened, as to become fit for food; but it is also certain that it has originated from a religious institution.'" Ibid., 79–80. Also see Fogelson, "Who Were the *Aní:Kutání*," 257, for his discussion of this source.

21. See Irwin, "Different Voices Together," 12, 25n49. Also see Gilbert, "Eastern Cherokees," 313–59.

22. Another possibility is that the designations of the different types of religio-medical specialists, conventionally called "conjurers," might account for the distinction in this account. See discussion below. They seem to be differentiated on the basis of the amount of power and how they use it. They all seem to be of the same professional class.

23. See Gearing, *Priests and Warriors*, 23–26; 103–8.

24. See above, Speck and Broom, *Cherokee Dance and Drama*, 7–8.

25. See, for example, Witthoft, *Green Corn Ceremonialism*; Hudson, *The Southeastern Indians*. Several other southeastern communities possessed similar ceremonial complexes related to the harvest of corn, as well as ball games. There is more detailed information on similar Muskogee or Creek activities, commonly referred to as "Busk" ceremonialism by scholars, than exists for the Cherokee. However, several key scholarly and historical accounts of Cherokee activities are available.

26. Witthoft, "The Cherokee Green Corn Medicine," 213.

27. Ibid., 214.

28. Ibid.

29. Ibid., 213–14, 215. Witthoft termed these the "Green Corn Feast" and the "Green Corn Medicine," respectively. Ibid., 213n2.

30. Mooney, 1914, quoted in ibid., 213.

31. Ibid.

32. Charles Hicks, "Manners and Customs of the Cherokees."

33. Ibid.

34. Wetmore, "The Green Corn Ceremony," 47–48.

35. Ibid., 49.

36. Mooney, *Myths*, 396.

37. Speck and Broom, *Cherokee Dance and Drama*, 53.

38. Ibid., 45. The authors said this name derived from a group of Cherokee people who "compressed their infants' heads laterally" and performed the dance "with great devotion." Ibid.

39. Ibid., 45.

40. Ibid., 52. Excluding the Booger, Bear, and Eagle Dances.

41. Ibid., 53.

42. Ibid., 53, 47, 51–52.

43. Personal communications, 1993–2007. See Witthoft, "The Cherokee Green Corn Medicine"; Wetmore, "The Green Corn Ceremony."

44. Attributed to Mollie Sequoyah in Witthoft, "The Cherokee Green Corn Medicine," 217.

45. Ibid. Sequoyah's version of the narrative had one son doing the killing, the other being born from the blood of Selu's severed neck.

46. Personal conversations, 1993–2007. Organizers said they learned the dances from Oklahoma relatives and brought it back to where it started. Ibid. Although I saw the arbor and talked with many participants, I have not had the opportunity to attend a dance. I have not inquired or heard any information about this activity since that time.

47. Mooney, *Sacred Formulas*, 318–19.

48. I will note selected details and sources and refer readers to additional scholarship.

49. See Fogelson, "Cherokee Ball Game," 54, for an explanation of "big match" games and "small" games.

50. Ibid., 50. At least one source stated that there were four conjurers. "Ritual of Ball Stick Game," in *Cherokee Progress and Challenge*, 71.

51. "Ritual of Ball Stick Game," 70.

52. Burt and Ferguson, *Indians of the Southeast*, 281.

53. Molly Sequoia, 2.4 "Morpheme List," in Ernest Bender, "Cherokee II," 226. Bender says Sequoia "dictated the text and translations." Ibid., 223. This is the same individual who furnished information to John Witthoft; Bender spelled her name differently.

54. Sequoia, 2.4 "Morpheme List," in Ernest Bender, "Cherokee II," 226. Bender put the Cherokee terms in roman type and italicized the English.

55. Mooney, "Cherokee Theory and Practice," 28.

56. Jack F. Kilpatrick and Anna G. Kilpatrick, *Walk in Your Soul*, 9. Anna Kilpatrick was a member of the Cherokee Nation of Oklahoma, as well as being fluent in the Cherokee language. Though in wide usage, the term "shaman" is of dubious utility. See Kehoe, "Eliade and Hultkrantz."

57. Alan E. Kilpatrick, "'Going to the Water,'" 50.

58. Molly Sequoia, 2.1 "Dance- and Ball-Games," in Ernest Bender, "Cherokee II," 225.

59. 2.4 "Morpheme List," in ibid., 226. The plural form in one narrative was "una-lhsdélhdo-di," translated as "they conjured"; he translated this as "conjure-men" as well. Ibid.

60. Fogelson, "Cherokee Ball Game," 50. His transliterations: "a.da.we.hi or a.do.ni.ski." Ibid.

61. See, for example, Fogelson, "Change, Persistence, and Accommodation"; Fogelson, "An Analysis of Cherokee Sorcery"; Fogelson, "Cherokee Notions of Power."

62. Irwin, "Cherokee Healing," 244–45.

63. Personal communications, 1993–2007. Also see, for example, Sequoia in Ernest Bender, "Cherokee II," examples quoted below; Callie Wachacha, in "Mose and Callie Wachacha interview" transcript, November 15, 1986, "Fading Voices," MSS 87-16, Museum of the Cherokee Indian Archives, Cherokee, N.C., 4–5.

64. Irwin, "Cherokee Healing," 246, 245.

65. Jack F. Kilpatrick and Anna G. Kilpatrick, *Walk in Your Soul*, 9.

66. See above. Teams have been known to hire more than one. Personal communications, 1993–2007.

67. Mooney, "The Cherokee Ball Play," 111.

68. Personal communications, 1993–2007.

69. Jack F. Kilpatrick and Anna G. Kilpatrick, *Walk in Your Soul*, 5.

70. Jack F. Kilpatrick and Anna G. Kilpatrick, "Cherokee Rituals," 24. Also see Alan E. Kilpatrick, "'Going to the Water,'" 56, 49.

71. Alan E. Kilpatrick, "On Translating Magical Texts," 24. He was discussing the Western Cherokee, but this is the case among the EBCI as well.

72. Jack F. Kilpatrick and Anna G. Kilpatrick, *Walk in Your Soul*, 5.

73. Ibid.

74. Bird, "Solomon Bird interview," 11.

75. Jack F. Kilpatrick and Anna G. Kilpatrick, *Walk in Your Soul*, 5.

76. Sequoia in Ernest Bender, "Cherokee II," 225.

77. Mooney, *Sacred Formulas*, 348; see 371n14 for Mooney, *Sacred Formulas* reference.

78. Ibid., 348.

79. Mooney, *Myths*, 431.

80. Jack F. Kilpatrick and Anna G. Kilpatrick, *Walk in Your Soul*, 5.

81. Fogelson has discussed this aspect of Cherokee conjuring in several articles. Alan Kilpatrick's *The Night Has a Naked Soul* deals with this issue as well, and in fact provides several examples of such malevolent formulas. Unfortunately, this aspect of conjuring seems to receive a great deal of attention from researchers, Cherokee and non-Cherokee, and amateur scholars alike. I think this reflects fascination with cultural conceptions of "witchcraft" and "magic"; as I stated above, it certainly is not an evenhanded representation of the range of activities, good and bad, that are part of this system.

82. Mooney, *Sacred Formulas*, 395–97. Also see Mooney, "Cherokee Ball Play," 127–28.

83. Mooney and Olbrechts, *Swimmer Manuscript*, 212.

84. Fogelson, "Cherokee Ball Game," 76–79 and 299–304; 84–89; 124–26; 129–31; 147–49; 161–64; 171–72; 240–42.

85. Ibid., 75, 124; personal communications, 1993–2007.

86. Fogelson, "Cherokee Ball Game." For the individual formulas, see page numbers given in note 84 above.

87. Ossie Crowe, Ledger books, 2 vols., Ossie Crowe Collection, MSS 99-03 (Museum of the Cherokee Indian Archives, Cherokee, N.C.).

88. Personal communication, 1998.

89. Hudson, *The Southeastern Indians*, 351–52.

90. Personal communications, 1993–2007.

91. Jack F. Kilpatrick and Anna G. Kilpatrick, *Notebook of a Cherokee Shaman*, 94. Also see Alan E. Kilpatrick, "'Going to Water,'" 49–58, 51. Kilpatrick seems to have adopted most, in not all, of his parents' transliterations. Their publications are valuable linguistic resources for Cherokee studies scholars.

92. Alan E. Kilpatrick, "Going to the Water," 51.

93. Mooney and Olbrechts, *Swimmer Manuscript*, 233.

94. Personal communications, 1993–2007.

95. Mooney, "The Cherokee River Cult," 2.

96. Lange, "A Small Postscript," 22.

97. Mooney, "The Cherokee Ball Play," 125; Mooney, *Myths*, 230.

98. Mooney, *Sacred Formulas*, 336.

99. Ibid.

100. Personal communications, 1993–2007.

101 Sequoia in Ernest Bender, "Cherokee II," 226.

102. "They are designated as official cultural ambassadors by the Tribal Council of the Eastern Band of Cherokee Indians and are sponsored by the Museum of the Cherokee Indian." ⟨http://www.cherokeemuseum.org/education-warriors.htm⟩ (accessed May 2009)

103. Bird, Solomon Bird interview, 16.

104. Personal communications, 1993–2007.

105. See Leonard Broom's discussion of Long, in "Foreword to the New Edition," Speck and Broom, *Cherokee Dance and Drama*, xvii–xx. Long's involvement was critical to the project, yet his name appears on the cover of the 1993 paperback edition of the book under the two other men's names, and in type that is roughly two font sizes smaller.

106. Fogelson, *The Cherokees*, 35.

107. Speck and Broom, *Cherokee Dance and Drama*, 2. Speck, who identified himself as the "senior author," first observed "Eastern Cherokee dances and ceremonials" in 1913 and made seven subsequent trips to the Qualla Boundary between 1922 and 1936, when he completed the second of two recording sessions of dance songs. A total of sixty-eight songs were recorded on rubber disks with a portable recording machine. Speck returned for several visits through 1944, while Broom visited in 1935, 1936, and 1940. Ibid., xxi–xxii.

108. Ibid., 6, 2, 4–5.

109. Ibid., 5, 3.

110. Ibid., 25.

111. See, for example, Fogelson and Walker, "Self and Other"; Fogelson and Bell, "Cherokee Booger Mask Tradition."

112. Speck and Brown, *Cherokee Dance and Drama*, 55.

113. Ibid.

114. Fogelson, "Cherokee Ball Game," 92.

115. Speck and Broom, *Cherokee Dance and Drama*, 59.

116. Sequoia in Ernest Bender, "Cherokee II," 225, first and last terms; Hamel and Chiltoskey, *Cherokee Plants and Their Uses*, 6; Callie Wachacha, "Mose and Callie Wachacha interview," 5; Personal communications, 1993–2007.

117. Hamel and Chiltoskey, *Cherokee Plants and Their Uses*. The authors noted that Amoneeta Sequoyah, son of Mollie and brother of Lloyd, told a newspaper reporter that he "knew six hundred forty two medicinal plants." The authors also stated that the "accumulated knowledge of several medicine men in a village might reach eight hundred or more plants." Ibid., 5.

118. She is singled out in the acknowledgements for *Cherokee Plants and Their Uses* as someone "who first showed Mary Chiltoskey this path." Ibid., 2. Also see Obituary, Hester Reagan Lambert, *Cherokee One Feather* (Cherokee, N.C.), July 9, 1986, 3.

119. Hester Reagan, Ethel McCoy et al., Fall Fair competition lists, "Plants," VF Culture File (typescripts, Museum of the Cherokee Indian, Cherokee, N.C., n.d.), compiled by Mary U. Chiltoskey, n.d., Museum of the Cherokee Indian Archives, Cherokee, N.C.

120. Mooney, *Sacred Formulas*, 323–29.

121. Ibid., 329.

122. Ibid.

123. Ibid., 329, 328. Frazer, *The Golden Bough*, 33, 14.

124. Frazer, *The Golden Bough*, 33. Here he either drew from Mooney, *Sacred Formulas*, 328, or Mooney, *Myths*, 425–26. In both passages Mooney noted that women used a decoction of the root to strengthen their hair, and that ballplayers used a decoction of the leaves; Frazer's passage noted both uses but did not make this distinction.

125. Mooney, "Cherokee Ball Play," 124.

126. Ibid.

127. Ibid., 131.

128. Olbrechts, "Some Cherokee Methods of Divination," 548; Mooney, *Sacred Formulas*, 393; Mooney, *Myths*, 516; Fogelson, "Cherokee Ball Game," 69.

129. Mooney, *Myths*, 459. For a brief survey of divinatory techniques, see Olbrechts, "Some Cherokee Methods of Divination," 547–52; he discussed the u:lunsu:ti on 548–49.

130. Mooney, *Sacred Formulas*, 393–94; Fogelson, "Cherokee Ball Game," 69, 83–86.

131. Mooney, *Myths*, 524; personal conversations, 1993–2007.

132. Mooney, *Myths*, 476; Mooney, *Sacred Formulas*, 335. The exception is glass, which is supposed to be a substitute for a flint arrowhead. Ibid. See, for example, Mooney and Olbrechts, *Swimmer Manuscript*, 68–71, 202–4, 212–13.

133. Fogelson, "Cherokee Ball Game," 67.

134. Ibid., 61.

135. August 26, 1808, in McClinton, *Moravian Springplace Mission*, 1: 276.

136. Mooney, "Cherokee Ball Play," 121–22.

137. Fogelson, "Cherokee Ball Game," 63–64.

138. Sequoyah, in ibid., 14.

139. Mooney, *Sacred Formulas*, 334–35.

140. Personal communications, 1993–2007.

141. Fogelson, "Cherokee Ball Game," 62.

142. Mooney, *Myths*, 518. He also used the terms "ceremonial tabu" and "tabu." Ibid., and Mooney, "Cherokee Ball Play," 110.

143. The prohibition against physical contact with women usually began twenty-eight days before the ball game, because, according to Mooney, it was the sum of four multiplied by seven, "sacred numbers" to the Cherokee. However, seven days was the minimum. Ibid., Mooney, "Cherokee Ball Play," 110.

144. Ibid., 110, 111.

145. Ibid. Anyone who has ever come upon a rabbit in the forest will attest to this fact. The animal typically freezes in its tracks, and then darts away.

146. Ibid.

147. Mooney, "Cherokee Theory and Practice," 27.

148. Fogelson, "Cherokee Ball Game," 58.

149. Ibid., 59–60.

150. Ibid., 59. Fogelson referenced the narrative and also cited an article in which Olbrechts stated, "'Eating the food a menstrual or pregnant woman has prepared; touching whatever object she has used, even walking along a trail by which she has travelled may cause a painful or obstinate malady.' Formerly such women were isolated in small low huts (osi)." Olbrechts, "Cherokee Belief and Practice," quoted in Fogelson, "Cherokee Ball Game," 59n1. The first half of the quote was Olbrechts's statement, and the second was Fogelson's. Also see Mooney, *Myths*, 469.

151. See "Nun'yunu'wi, the stone man," in Mooney, *Myths*, 319–20.

152. See Perdue, *Cherokee Women*, 29–37; and Churchill, "Purity and Pollution," 211–14; 223–25.

153. See Speck and Broom, *Cherokee Dance and Drama*, 13–18, including the reprinted Mooney version. The red paint is associated with the *A:ni:wo:di*, or Paint clan, and is an item used by religious and medical specialists. Marcelina Reed, *Seven Clans*, 5. Also see Mooney, *Myths*, 455, 469.

154. Fogelson, "Cherokee Ball Game," 58, 86.

155. Ibid., 58.

156. Ibid., note 1.

157. Ibid., 193–94.

158. Ibid., 60–61.

159. Zogry field notes, October 9, 1999.

160. Personal communications, 1998, 2000.

161. Personal communications, 1998, 1999.

162. Ibid., 119–21; Fogelson, "Cherokee Ball Game," 111–12.

163. Mooney, "Cherokee Ball Play," 120.

164. Ibid., 122.

165. Ibid.

166. Ibid., 125.

167. Ibid., 125–26. See also Mooney and Olbrechts, *Swimmer Manuscript*, 191–92.

168. Ibid., 126; Mooney, *Myths*, 518, 231. For further discussion of this concept, see Irwin, "Cherokee Healing," 240; Alan E. Kilpatrick, "Cherokee Theological Concepts," 394–95.

169. Ibid., 126.

170. Ibid., 131.

171. Fogelson, "Cherokee Ball Game," 68.

172. Ibid., 69.

173. Ibid., 72. The brackets enclosing the Cherokee terms are Fogelson's. He noted that a "period of fasting is required for the ritual to be effective." Ibid., 72n1. Interestingly, many of the same ingredients in the emetic are found in the scratching medicine. Ibid.

174. Ibid., 80.

175. Singer, "Cultural Pattern of Indian Civilization," 27. This statement was reworded a bit in his 1959 work *Traditional India: Structure and Change*, from which the quote typically is taken; the word "visitors" is replaced by "outsiders" in the latter work. See Singer, *Traditional India*, xii–xiii.

176. Personal communication, 1999.

177. Vennum, *American Indian Lacrosse*, xv.

178. Ibid.

179. Mooney, "The Cherokee Ball Play," 119.
180. Masuzawa, "Culture," 82.
181. Ibid.
182. Johnson, *Secrets, Gossip and Gods*; Urban, "The Torment of Secrecy"; Luther H. Martin, "Secrecy in Hellenistic Religious Communities"; Mathewes, "Religion and Secrecy"; Deloria, "Is Religion Possible?"; Barkun, "Religion and Secrecy After September 11"; Wax, "The Ethics of Research"; Brown, *Who Owns Native Culture?*
183. Deloria, "Is Religion Possible?" 265–66.
184. Brown, *Who Owns Native Culture?* 27.
185. Ibid., 27–28.
186. Wax, "The Ethics of Research," 452.
187. See, for example, McLoughlin, *The Cherokees and Christianity*; Irwin, "Different Voices Together"; Bloom, "Acculturation of the Eastern Cherokee"; Neely, *Snowbird Cherokees*; Albanese, "Exploring Regional Religion."
188. Kupferer, "The Principal People, 1960," 240.
189. French, "Missionaries among the Eastern Cherokees," 109.
190. "Cherokee, N.C. Fact Sheet," Museum of the Cherokee Indian, Cherokee, N.C., n.d., photocopy.
191. Fogelson, "Change, Persistence, and Accommodation," 219–20. Jack F. Kilpatrick and Anna G. Kilpatrick have said this "to a large extent holds true for the Oklahoma group." *Friends of Thunder*, 161.
192. Personal communications, 1993–2007.
193. Witthoft, "Cherokee Beliefs Concerning Death," 68. In the Museum of the Cherokee Indian archives there is a copy of the original handwritten document, and a handwritten notation in what appears to be another hand gives its author as Witthoft, the title as "Notes on Death," and the date of composition as July 1977. VF Culture File, "Death, Burial," MCI Archives.
194. Personal communications, 1993–2007.
195. Personal communication, 2000.
196. Catherine Albanese has added, "the conjurers were the acknowledged conservators of the past, the leaders of the spiritual force which opposed and balanced the force of Christianity. Yet for the leaders themselves . . . the two powers seemed not antagonistic but complementary." Albanese's conclusion is that what has resulted is a "regional religion"— "Cherokee Christianity." Albanese, "Exploring Regional Religion," 364. I think Albanese correctly identified one manifestation of the interaction, or one "position" on the religious "continuum" I described. Yet a subjugation of the "Cherokee" aspect to the "Christianity" element does not tell the whole story. As I have argued, there is a whole range of interaction of both elements, and such a construction plots but one position, albeit a popular one, among what is really a wide range of stances regarding belief and activity. Yet the incorporation and influence of Christianity were duly noted.
197. Calendars published by the North Carolina Cooperative Extension, 1997, 1998.
198. Ibid., 1997, 1998.
199. Ibid. The midway behind the boys' team picture in the 1997 calendar placed them at a previous fair, and their faces were painted, by the look of it perhaps to approximate a general tourist notion of "Indian" adornment. Some of them also had feathers in their hair. In contrast, the men's picture was in the middle of a field and the players had no such adornment.
200. Ibid., 1998.

201. Fogelson, "Cherokee Ball Game," 5.

202. I draw this conclusion primarily from the published work of Fogelson, who worked with Lloyd Sequoyah, and that of John Witthoft, who worked with Will West Long and Mollie Sequoyah (but also with Moses Owl of Birdtown).

203. Personal communications, 1993–2007.

204. Furthermore, it is likely some people believe in the same way, for example, as people who pray to a higher being or force when in danger, faced with hardship, or desirous of a particular result, such as professional athletes.

Chapter 4

1. Mooney, "Historical Sketch," in *Myths*, 181. I referenced this quotation in the Introduction.

2. Hymes, *In Vain*, 86.

3. Ibid., 84, 86.

4. He concluded this passage by stating, "Only the systematic study of performances can disclose the true structure." Ibid. While I am uneasy with his confidence in apprehending "true structure," I think one can use this description as a provisional definition and apply it in a focused sense to enter the dialogue regarding the concept of degeneration and its application to cultural practices.

5. Merrell, *The Indians' New World*, x.

6. Personal communications, 1993–2007.

7. Ibid.

8. Personal communication, 1997.

9. Sullivan, "American Religion is Naturally Comparative," 120. Sullivan cited Fabian for the second half of the formulation.

10. "Persistence," *Random House Webster's College Dictionary*.

11. Ibid.

12. Charles Long, introduction, in *Significations*, 2.

13. This conclusion is based on personal communications, 1993–2007.

14. Dilworth, *Imagining Indians in the Southwest*, 8; quoting Laura Chrisman and Patrick Williams, "Colonial Discourse and Post-Colonial Theory: An Introduction," in Williams and Chrisman, *Colonial Discourse and Post-Colonial Theory*, 16. Dilworth also said that Native American "utterances" were not "'authentic' or unmediated," and like all utterances she presented, were "part of a larger discourse about the formations of cultural authority and identity." Dilworth, *Imagining Indians in the Southwest*, 8. Dilworth recognized that she too was "implicated in the web of representations," and "there is no way for me to rise above a discourse that has a history of exploiting information about Native Americans." Ibid.

15. Dilworth, *Imagining Indians in the Southwest*, 7. She cited Debord, *Society of the Spectacle*, 4, for this statement.

16. Dilworth, *Imagining Indians in the Southwest*, 120.

17. Ibid., 121. She continued: "But ironically, the past (or simplicity or authenticity) that the primitive represents and that is so desired always slips from one's grasp: tourism constructs authenticity in such a way that it is never attainable. Sightseeing is doomed; the very presence of the observer spells the end of the authenticity of the observed. The same is true of the collector, whether ethnographer or tourist; in the act of collecting, the collectible disappears for the world of its origin and experience of collecting is no longer

available . . . tourism is a kind of pathology in that the touristic journey must be enacted time and time again." Ibid., 121.

18. Ibid., 141; quoting Stewart, *On Longing*, ix. Here and above Dilworth highlighted the silence of indigenous peoples in many narratives written about them. The actions of establishing subjectivity "in relation to an other," and creating narrative structure "that both invents and distances its object" and "inscribes . . . the gap between signifier and signified" also are evident in cultural presentations generated by the Eastern Band, as I discuss below. In a later section of this chapter, I include a statement by Michael Harkin regarding the Eastern Band's influence upon perceptions of First Nations peoples and potential culpability for stereotypes about "Indians." This viewpoint illustrates the need for careful interpretation of such cultural performances.

19. Dilworth, *Imagining Indians in the Southwest*, 120, 209.

20. Ibid., 9, 217; quoting Pratt, *Imperial Eyes*, 4; Riley, "Constituting the Southwest," 223.

21. For a discussion of "chiefing," see Finger, *Cherokee Americans*, 161–63, 184.

22. Personal communications, 1993–2007.

23. ⟨http://www.cherokee-nc.com⟩ (accessed May 2009).

24. See, for example, Sweet, *Dances of the Tewa Pueblo Indians*, 8, 37–42, 77–78; Szasz, "United States and New Mexico," 184. Also see Chamberlain, "Competition for the Native American Soul," 82, for a summary of different religious strategies employed by Native peoples. These include efforts to "syncretize" as well as "'compartmentalize'" aspects of different religious systems. Ibid.

25. Personal communications, Hopi Reservation, Arizona, 2000–2002.

26. Timberlake, *Lieutenant Henry Timberlake's Memoirs*, 102.

27. Ibid.

28. Ibid., "A Draught of the Cherokee Country, the West Side of the Twenty four Mountains, commonly called Over the Hills; Taken by Henry Timberlake, when he was in that Country, in March 1762. Likewise the Names of the Principal or Head men of each Town and what Number of Fighting Men they send to War."

29. Annotation to Samuel Cole Williams, "Tour of Duke of Orleans," 437n19. Williams said it was a tributary of the Tellico, but the creek is clearly marked as a tributary of the much larger "Tennessee river," the Little Tennessee River.

30. Alexander Cameron to John Stuart, April 12, 1774, Canada R. 44, p. 359, Cherokee Documents in Foreign Archives, Microfilm Collection, Museum of the Cherokee Indian Archives, Cherokee, N.C. This is my transcription, and all punctuation and spelling inconsistencies follow the original. Sugartown would be in August 1776 the site of a guerilla attack by Cherokees against the 2,400-strong army of North Carolinians sweeping across Cherokee territory. Seneca Town would see a conflict between Americans and a Cameron-led force of Native Americans and Tories. See Mooney, "Historical Sketch," in *Myths*, 49–50.

31. Mooney, "Historical Sketch," in *Myths*, 45.

32. Ibid., 69.

33. *American State Papers: Indian Affairs*, vol. 1 (Washington, 1832), 267–69, cited in Fogelson, "Cherokee Ball Game," 27–28.

34. Fogelson, "Cherokee Ball Game," 28.

35. John P. Brown, *Old Frontiers* (Kingsport, Tenn.: Southern Publishers, 1938), 333–34, quoted in Fogelson, "Cherokee Ball Game," 28. Fogelson quoted at length from this

summary of events, which included quotations from Governor Blount, and apparently constructed dialogue between the Governor and Eskaqua.

36. Ibid. Also see McLoughlin, *The Cherokee Ghost Dance*, 11.

37. Two accounts commonly cited in discussions of the Cherokee ball game from the last quarter of the eighteenth century are contained in the following: 1) James Adair, *The History of the American Indians* (1775); reprinted as *Adair's History of the American Indians*, edited by Samuel Cole Williams (Johnson City, Tenn.: Watauga Press, 1930). 2) William Bartram, *Travels Through North and South Carolina, Georgia, East and West Florida, the Cherokee Country, the Extensive Territories of the Muscogulges, or Creek Confederacy, and the Country of the Chactaws* [sic] (1791); reprinted as *Travels of William Bartram*, edited by Mark Van Doren (New York: Dover Publications, 1955). The Adair and Bartram accounts described ball games that are not clearly Cherokee events—they may have been descriptions of Choctaw and Creek events, respectively. See *Adair's History*, 428–30; *Travels of William Bartram*, 398–99. Bartram did provide an account of a ball play dance that was Cherokee. *Travels of William Bartram*, 298–99. Also see the Adair and Bartram accounts quoted in Fogelson and his comments regarding them in Fogelson, "Cherokee Ball Game," 22–27.

38. Louis-Philippe, *Diary of My Travels*, 71.

39. He continued by stating that "marriage is unknown among them (that is, in our meaning of the word)," but in an emendation he made to the comment that really took me by surprise: "I have learned since that there were ceremonies of marriage, varying with the tribe. These ceremonies consist of races, dances, or various games." While I am not sure to what he refers, it is an interesting comment that deserves further research. Ibid. The emendation is a footnote at the bottom of the page.

40. Williams, "Tour of Duke of Orleans," 437. Also cited in Fogelson, "Cherokee Ball Game," 29.

41. Louis-Philippe, *Diary of My Travels*, 83.

42. Ibid., 83, 91. I base the date on the caption of an illustration of Tokono that appears in this translation of the *Diary* that states the visit took place on May 1 and 2, 1797. Ibid., 87.

43. Ibid., 91, 92.

44. Ibid., 94. According to the duke they called for the ferry in vain and then canoed over with the empty hogsheads and "Little Turkey-Cock's belt and banner as credentials." Rebuffed, they calmly left and the next morning made no mention of the incident save to gesture in sign language that they had "drunk a bit too much the night before." Ibid.

45. McLoughlin, *The Cherokee Ghost Dance*, 11.

46. [Andrew] Barnard to Gov. Edward Dudley, April 6, 1840, GP 91, North Carolina Division of Archives and History, Raleigh, N.C., quoted in Finger, *Eastern Band of Cherokees*, 68.

47. [John] Mullay to CIA William Medill, December 14, 1848, M-234, 92/279–82 (Microcopy 234, Letters Received by the Office of Indian Affairs, 1824–1881, National Archives), quoted in ibid., 69. Mullay was appointed to take the Cherokee census in 1848, and his letter was to the Commissioner of Indian Affairs. Ibid., 48.

48. Charles Lanman, "Indian Ball . . . 1848 Version," *The State*, January 1, 1955, 16. The original is Charles Lanman, *Letters from the Alleghany Mountains* (New York: G. P. Putnam, 1849). Although I have not been able to access the original volume, I have located a book published in England with the same account. For the same quotation, also see Lanman, "Cherokee Customs," 172. Finger described Lanman as a "Whig journalist." Finger, *Eastern Band of Cherokees*, 69. He presented an idealized portrait of the Cherokee people and their

circumstances and published the "first widely read and popularized account of Tsali." Ibid., 70.

49. Lanman, "Indian Ball," 16; Lanman, "Cherokee Customs," 172.

50. Elizur Butler, Journal, July 7, 1851, ABCFM; quoted in McLoughlin, *The Cherokees and Christianity*, 204.

51. White, *Historical Collections of Georgia*, 670. Though this account certainly was written much earlier than its publication date, it was published soon after Lanman's account. This account probably was written before the Removal, though neither White nor Culin supplied further information. There were towns with these names in both Tennessee and Georgia, all of which presumably would have been destroyed or abandoned by 1855. See Mooney, "Tsatu´gi" (Chattooga) and "Tsikama´gi" (Chickamauga), in *Myths*, 536–37. This account is also quoted in Culin, *Games of the North American Indians*, 587–88.

52. White, *Historical Collections of Georgia*, 670.

53. Ibid.

54. As a boy Thomas was adopted by Yonaguska (Drowning-Bear), a well-known headman, and he worked in a local store. By 1831 he was legal counsel to what is known as the Quallatown band and owned a store; in 1840 he was appointed as a disbursing agent by the federal government. Finger, *Eastern Band of Cherokees*, 13, 31. Mooney, "Historical Sketch," in *Myths*, 160–61.

55. Finger, *Eastern Band of Cherokees*, 69.

56. Mooney, "Historical Sketch," in *Myths*, 161.

57. Finger, *Eastern Band of Cherokees*, 31: Duane H. King, "Cherokee," 107–8.

58. Godbold and Russell, *Confederate Colonel and Cherokee Chief*, 64.

59. Finger, *Eastern Band of Cherokees*, 80. Guests included Governor Charles Manly and the son of Senator John C. Calhoun. Ibid.

60. Daybook entry, August 23, 1860, *Day Book, Quallatown, Haywood County, 1858–63*, William Holland Thomas Papers, Rare Book, Manuscript, and Special Collections Library, Duke University, Durham, N.C. Sarah H. Hill cited what I believe to be this document, but gave the date as August 1859. Hill, *Weaving New Worlds*, 354n146.

61. Thomas Lenoir to brother, July 24, 1860, Thomas Lenoir Papers, Rare Book, Manuscript, and Special Collections Library, Duke University, Durham, N.C. John Finger cited what I believe to be this document, but incorrectly gave the month as June. Finger, *Eastern Band of Cherokees*, 198n46.

62. Census roll entry, "enrollment no. 1256, Tsaki, Jake," *Terrell Roll*, MSS 87–169, Cherokee Documents in Foreign Archives, Microfilm Collection, Museum of the Cherokee Indian Archives, Cherokee, N.C.

63. Finger, *Eastern Band of Cherokees*, 31; Duane H. King, "Cherokee," 107–8.

64. Godbold and Russell, *Confederate Colonel and Cherokee* Chief, 103.

65. Mooney, "Cherokee Ball Play," 106, 107. John Finger apparently accepted Mooney's account at face value. I have not located any other accounts of this incident, which appeared in an 1890 article. Finger, *Eastern Band of Cherokees*, 94.

66. Finger, *Eastern Band of Cherokees*, 98–102. The Cherokee people endured yet another smallpox epidemic that ended in 1866 and killed at least 125 people, including some prominent leaders. Some people believed the disease was retribution for foolishly participating in the Civil War.

67. William H. Thomas, notice, May 27, 1867, reprinted in Jack Frederick Kilpatrick, "Two Notices by Will Thomas," 27. The note is presented here as it was by Kilpatrick. He noted that Thomas's home was on the Tuckasegee River in Swain County, and the meeting

house may have been the Wolftown Townhouse. Ibid. Mooney said the settlement, which he cited as "Stikâ´yĭ," as well as "Stekoa," was on the river "at the old Thomas homestead just above the present Whittier, in Swain county, North Carolina." Mooney, *Myths*, 532.

68. "Cherokee's Gala-Day," [sic] *Raleigh (N.C.) News and Observer*, May 13, 1888, Issue 108, col. B.

69. "Cherokee Indians at the Fair," *Raleigh (N.C.) News and Observer*, October 1, 1889, Issue 90, col. A.

70. Sumner, "The State Fair," 149. *Raleigh (N.C.) News and Observer*, October 17, 1889, in ibid.

71. Spray, "Report of Superintendent," 307. As John Finger noted, the "federal agent's official title of superintendent of education and disbursing officer accurately reflected his duties." Finger, *Cherokee Americans*, 8.

72. Spray, "Report of Superintendent," 307.

73. Finger, *Cherokee Americans*, 9–10.

74. Ibid., 44–50, 106–7, 111–12.

75. Ibid., 57–58.

76. Photograph in the author's private collection.

77. Finger, *Cherokee Americans*, 58; and Kyselka to CIA, December 6, 1910, CA quoted in ibid.

78. Shepherd Photo Collection, MSS 99-04 (Museum of the Cherokee Indian Archives, Cherokee, N.C., 1921–1923). There are approximately thirty photographs in this collection, and they include shots of ball games at the Cherokee Fall Fair as well as in Asheville.

79. [no name given—Wadsworth or Henderson?], Narrative, Section 1, Law and Order, *Annual Report 1915, Cherokee Indian School, Cherokee, N.C.*, Superintendents' Annual Narrative and Statistical Reports from Field Jurisdictions of the Bureau of Indian Affairs, 1907–1938, National Archives Microfilm Publication M1011 (Washington, D.C.: National Archives, National Archives and Records Service General Services Administration, 1975), Roll 12, Cherokee Orphan Training School, 1912–24; Cherokee School, 1910–1928, 5–6 (microfilm 0575–0576).

80. [James Henderson, Supt.?], Narrative, Section 1: Law and Order, *Annual Report 1916, Cherokee Indian School, Cherokee, N.C.*, 6–7 (0610–0611).

81. James E. Henderson, Supt., Narrative, Section 1: Law and Order, *Annual Report 1917, Cherokee Indian School, Cherokee, N.C.*, 6 (0645).

82. James E. Henderson, Supt., Narrative, Section 1: Law and Order, *Annual Report 1918, Cherokee Indian School, Cherokee, N.C.*, 6 (0670). Caption for following pg.: "The 'Indian Ball' teams," ibid., 0688; picture, 0689.

83. James E. Henderson, Supt., Narrative, Section 1: Law and Order, *Annual Report 1920, Cherokee Indian School, Cherokee, N.C.*, 7 (0757).

84. James E. Henderson, Supt., Narrative, Section 1: Law and Order, *Annual Report 1923, Cherokee Indian School, Cherokee, N.C.*, 6 (1039).

85. C. W. Roberts, Secretary, Greensboro (N.C.) Chamber of Commerce to James E. Henderson, 19 November 1921, Record Group 75, Subject Numeric Correspondence Files, 06/14/1914–06/1926, NARA Southeast Region, Morrow, Georgia at ⟨http://www.archives.gov⟩ (accessed September 2004).

86. Henderson to Roberts, November 22, 1921, in ibid.

87. Roberts to Henderson, November 30, 1921, in ibid.

88. Finger, *Cherokee Americans*, 58.

89. Personal communication, 1998.

90. Finger, *Cherokee Americans*, 58, 60.

91. Anne D. Bryson, "Last Cherokees Of East Cling To Savage Beliefs In Spite Of Education: Medicine Man Still Invokes Spirits In Great Smokies And Colors Have Deep Meaning; Language in Spoken 'Shorthand,'" *Asheville (N.C.) Sunday Citizen*, Sunday Morning April 10, 1927, p. 6, section B, Manuscript 4600, Smithsonian Institution National Anthropological Archives, Box 22, Folder 117.

92. Ibid.

93. Majel Ivey, "Home of the Eastern Cherokees in Heart of Great Smokies," *Charlotte (N.C.) Observer*, September 30, 1928, sec. 3; 2, 4.

94. Ibid., 2, 4.

95. For example, "'Ah-woy-yea,'" "foul"; "'Tahl-do-gwah,'" "go to twelve"; "'hon-eh'" "here it is"; "'gacha-noola,'" "hurry up!" Ibid., 2, 4.

96. "Cherokee Indians Take Part in Atlanta Fair," *Asheville (N.C.) Citizen-Times*, Sunday, September 30, 1934.

97. Ibid., Associated Press photographs.

98. Ibid. I have located a photograph of the 1911 team, and a football held by one player reads "1911, Indians 18, Harvard 15." Photograph in the author's private collection and in the Museum of the Cherokee Indian.

99. Hemrick (no first name given), "Indians *Invade* Atlanta," *Atlanta Journal*, September 1934, 30; quoted in Hill, *Weaving New Worlds*, 292.

100. Hill, *Weaving New Worlds*, 292.

101. Ibid.

102. Dogwood Festival Committee minutes, September 23, 1932; October 25, 1932; Felix A. Grisette, Secretary, Dogwood Festival Committee to Daniel H. Clancy, November 1, 1932, Dogwood Festival Incorporated (Chapel Hill, N.C.) Records, 1932–1938, Collection no. 3654-z, Southern Historical Collection, Manuscripts Department, Wilson Library, University of North Carolina at Chapel Hill. The letter was addressed to Clancy, but Spalsbury responded. R. L. Spalsbury to Felix A. Grisette, November 7, 1932; Felix A. Grisette to Jarrett Blythe, November 11, 1932; Jarrett Blythe to Felix A. Grisette, December 6, 1932. Ibid.

103. Felix A. Grisette, Secretary, Dogwood Festival Committee to Harold Foght, February 25, 1935, RG 075, S. 6, O72, Box 31, "Feasts, Festivals, Fiestas," 1934–1939, National Archives Southeast Region, Morrow, Ga.

104. Harold Foght to Felix A. Grisette, February 27, 1935, Dogwood Festival Records, 1932–1938.

105. Foght to Grisette, March 21, 1935, in ibid.

106. Grisette to Foght, April 11, 1935, in ibid.

107. Foght to Grisette, April 19, 1935, in ibid.

108. Harold W. Foght to Carl Standingdeer, April 19, 1935, in "Feasts, Festivals, Fiestas," 1934–1939.

109. Ibid.

110. Foght to Grisette, April 20, 1935, Dogwood Festival Records, 1932–1938.

111. Program, Dogwood Festival, 1935, in ibid.

112. Financial Statement, Dogwood Festival, 1935, in ibid.

113. Will W. Long to Harold W. Foght, Ravensford, North Carolina, March 28, 1935, in "Feasts, Festivals, Fiestas," 1934–1939.

114. Publicity flyer, Second National Folk Festival, May 14th–18th, 1935, Memorial Auditorium, Chattanooga, Tenn., in ibid.

115. Harold W. Foght to Will W. Long, May 8, 1936, in ibid.

116. Foght to Long, May 14, 1936, in ibid.

117. "Golf at Asheville," Special to the *New York Times*, (1857–Current file), September 20, 1936, ProQuest Historical Newspapers, *New York Times* (1851–2003), pg. XX2 (accessed November 2008).

118. Holmes Bryson Jr. to Harold W. Foght, May 29, 1936, "Feasts, Festivals, Fiestas," 1934–1939.

119. Ibid.

120. Hill, *Weaving New Worlds*, 295.

121. Ibid., 295; and Blair to L. M. Glenn, August 15, 1939, RG 75, CA, Series 5, Box 31, FRCEP, in ibid.

122. Holmes Bryson Jr. to Clyde M. Blair, Asheville, N.C., May 23, 1938, "Feasts, Festivals, Fiestas," 1934–1939.

123. Jarrett Blythe to J. D. Chalk, March 20, 1941, "Feasts, Festivals, Fiestas," 1934–1939. Chalk, who was the Commissioner of the North Carolina Division of Game and Inland Fisheries, had been contacted by Eaton and had enclosed a letter from him. This likely was misplaced and should have been in the 1940–1952 folder.

124. F. W. LaRouche to C. M. Blair, Washington, D.C., May 12, 1941, "Feasts, Festivals, Fiestas," 1934–1939. This likely was misplaced as well.

125. Jack Eaton to Jarrett Blythe, New York, N.Y., April 17, 1941. RG 075, S. 6, O72, Box 31, "Feasts, Festivals, Fiestas," 1940–1952, National Archives Southeast Region, Morrow, Ga.

126. Blythe to Eaton, April 29, 1941, in ibid.

127. Joe Jennings to J. D. Brooks, May 19, 1948, in ibid.

128. Ibid.

129. Jarrett Blythe to Hugh Sloan, July 6, 1948, in ibid.

130. Gulick, "Eastern Cherokee Community Organization," 249–50. Gulick gave no citation to support this assertion.

131. Gulick, "Language and Passive Resistance," 64, 65. Again, he did not provide any evidence or a citation to support this assertion.

132. Gulick, *Cherokees at the Crossroads*, 113–14.

133. Hamel and Chiltoskey, *Cherokee Plants and Their Uses*, 11.

134. Fogelson, "Cherokee Ball Game," 185.

135. Ibid.

136. Personal communications, 1999–2001.

137. Photograph sheet no. 5914, bottom right, "Cherokee Ball Game, Cherokee, Swain County, 1946": Photograph sheet no. 8104, bottom and top left, top right, "Cherokee Fair, Cherokee, N.C. Swain County, Oct. 1949"; Photographs, 1937–1949, from Files of the North Carolina Department of Conservation and Development, Travel Information Division (North Carolina Division of Archives and History, Raleigh, N.C.). The photographs are arranged four on a sheet and are not individually numbered.

138. Photograph sheet no. 5928, bottom right, "Cherokee Ball Game, Cherokee, Swain County, 1946," Photographs, 1937–1949.

139. Fogelson, "Cherokee Ball Game," 2, 3, 64, 66, 128, 146, 151, 160, 184.

140. "Cherokee Stickball," *Life Magazine*, November 11, 1946, 91; A. Gould and E. C. Schurmacher, "Homicide: A Sport," *True Magazine*, February 1948, 3, quoted in Fogelson, "Cherokee Ball Game," 2–3.

141. "Cherokee Stickball," *Life Magazine*, 91.

142. Ibid. Two of these pictures were reproduced in Vennum, *American Indian Lacrosse*, 233, fig. 60; 40, fig. 11. See Finger's discussion of Noah Powell in *Cherokee Americans*, 155–56. For a list of Cherokee principal chiefs through the election of 1987, see Duane H. King, "Eastern Cherokee Government Since 1827," 13.

143. "Cherokee Stickball," *Life Magazine*, 92. A cropped version of the photograph appeared in *Life*; Vennum's book contained the full photograph. Ibid., and Vennum, *American Indian Lacrosse*, 40, fig. 11.

144. "Cherokee Stickball," *Life Magazine*, 92, 90. There are thirteen contact sheets of photographs from this shoot, which Dean's son Christopher kindly allowed me to review. The pictures constitute a small archive of their own in terms of documenting that year's fair.

145. *North Carolina: Variety Vactionland*, 16mm, Communication Center, University of North Carolina at Chapel Hill, for the North Carolina Department of Conservation and Development, 1951 (videotape, V.T. 46, North Carolina Department of Archives and History, Raleigh, N.C.).

146. Ibid.

147. Gulick, "Language and Passive Resistance," 80n14. Note to sentence 1 of the block quotation from p. 75.

148. Finger, *Cherokee Americans*, 115.

149. Gulick, *Cherokees at the Crossroads*, 117.

150. Ibid. He cited a personal communication from Harriet Kupferer for this last piece of information.

151. Warner Ogden, "The Cherokees: A Proud Race Tells Its Story," *New York Times* (1857–Current file), May 8, 1960, ProQuest Historical Newspapers, *New York Times* (1851–2003), pg. XX17.

152. Fogelson, "The Cherokee Ball Game," 194–95.

153. Gulick, "Language and Passive Resistance," 61.

154. Margaret Bender, *Signs of Cherokee Culture*, 1. The Cherokee language continues to be spoken by a portion of the population. I regularly have found myself in situations where it was being employed, though clearly the people who speak it are presently in the minority. Language classes have been reintroduced into the school system, and a new Head Start facility has begun to offer a regular schedule of adult language classes to complement classes that have been offered in the past elsewhere on the Qualla Boundary. In addition, several people have related to me how proud they are that a young relative can speak the language. Personal communications, 1993–2007.

155. This interaction occurred in November 1997.

156. ⟨http://www.cherokee-nc.com/events-detail.php?page_72⟩ (accessed November 2009).

157. ⟨http://www.cherokee-nc.com⟩.

158. Brochure, 95th Annual Cherokee Indian Fair, 2007.

159. Personal communications, 1993–2007.

160. Personal communication, October 2001.

161. Personal communications, 1993–2007.

162. Timberlake, *Lieutenant Henry Timberlake's Memoirs*, 102.

163. Fogelson, "Cherokee Ball Game," 22.

164. Ibid. He cited Olbrechts's unpublished field notes from 1926, comments by Will West Long's mother, Ayasta, the J. P. Evans account in the John Howard Payne Papers, and an account by William Bartram that may be describing another southeastern group. He

also noted an account of women playing among the Choctaw quoted by John Swanson. Ibid.

165. Fogelson, "Cherokee Ball Game," 48.
166. Ibid.
167. Ibid. But of course this does not mean that there were, or are, none.
168. Sider, *Lumbee Indian Histories*, xviii.

Chapter 5

1. Personal communication, October 2005.
2. Personal communications, 1993–2007.
3. Fogelson, "Cherokee Ball Game," 2.
4. Ibid., 17.
5. Ibid., 230.
6. Gilbert, "Eastern Cherokees," 357. All of his statements in this chapter regarding warfare are informed by the Payne Papers.
7. Gearing, *Priests and Warriors*, 27.
8. Fogelson, "Cherokee Ball Game," 17.
9. Ibid., 18.
10. Ibid., 19.
11. Robert K. Thomas, "Cherokee Values and World View," research paper, 1958, Papers Based on Research of the Cross-Cultural Laboratory of the Institute for Research in Social Science, North Carolina Collection, Wilson Library, University of North Carolina, Chapel Hill, 1.
12. Ibid.
13. Ibid., especially 1, 15–20.
14. See, for example, Finger, *Eastern Band of Cherokees*, 68, 100, 102; Finger, *Cherokee Americans*, 145. The term "harmony ethic" does not appear in Thomas's paper, though he does use the adjective "harmonious" and the noun "ethic" separately. Thomas, "Cherokee Values," 1–3. Apparently John Gulick coined this term in *Cherokees at the Crossroads*, his compilation of research done by his reasearch team.
15. See Loftin, "The 'Harmony Ethic'" for a good summation of this concept. A related concept, "*duyu:gh(o)dv*," meaning "right" and translated as "Principle," has not to my knowledge received much scholarly attention, save from Fogelson, as might be expected. Jack F. and Anna G. Kilpatrick referred to it as "that most hackneyed word in the Cherokee language" and quoted another work of theirs in which they repeated a common statement linking the concept to arguments over small items in estate disputes. Jack F. Kilpatrick and Anna G. Kilpatrick, *The Shadow of Sequoyah*, 9; and Jack F. Kilpatrick and Anna G. Kilpatrick, *Friends of Thunder*, 99, quoted in ibid.
16. Fogelson, "Cherokee Ball Game," 9–10.
17. Ibid., 10, 19.
18. Ibid., 18.
19. The gadugi, or free-labor groups, were community assistance organizations that performed a number of functions. They were widespread until at least the 1940s; since then many of their activities have been taken over by other community and church groups. See Fogelson and Kutsche, "Cherokee Economic Cooperatives," 83–124.
20. Fogelson, "Cherokee Ball Game," 230. Max Gluckman and Victor Turner saw patterns of social conflict as eufunctional, while Bernard J. Siegal and Alan R. Beals felt they were dysfunctional. Ibid.

21. Fogelson, "Cherokee Ball Game," 231.
22. Ibid., 232–33, 186.
23. Fogelson, "The Cherokee Ballgame Cycle," 330–31.
24. Kilpatrick, "'Going to the Water,'" 49.
25. Gilbert, "Eastern Cherokees," 359.
26. Ibid., 268.
27. Ibid., 304–5.
28. Gearing, *Priests and Warriors*, 61.
29. Gilbert, "Eastern Cherokees," 356. The first phase was "actual practical preparations of equipment and provisions as well as the divinations and magical rites of the priests." The second phase was "a series of stratagems and devices whereby the warriors, under the guidance of the priests and their magic, endeavored to outwit the enemy." The third phase was "ritual purification of the warriors for their return to the ranks of civilians." Ibid.
30. Mooney, *Sacred Formulas*, 388–91.
31. Ibid., 389. This reference is to the Cherokee soldiers who fought on the side of the Confederacy in the Civil War.
32. Ibid., 388. There are question marks in the text to mark paraphrases.
33. Ibid. This formula collected by Mooney contains references to specific supernatural beings, including the Red Bat (but not to members of the Thunder family). The Cherokee notion corresponding to "soul" has not to my knowledge received much scholarly attention. For discussion of this concept, see Witthoft, "Cherokee Beliefs Concerning Death." In this article Witthoft summarized information from Will West Long, who "explained a multiple-soul concept involving four souls and four stages in death." Ibid., 68. Long called all four "'Askina,'" and these were the "soul of conscious life," the soul of "physiological life," the soul of "circulation," and a fourth soul he discussed but did not name. Ibid., 68–70.
34. Mooney, *Sacred Formulas*, 390.
35. Ibid., 389.
36. Gilbert, "Eastern Cherokees," 351–52.
37. Ibid., 353.
38. Fogelson, "The Cherokee Ballgame Cycle," 334.
39. Ibid.
40. JHP, 202–3, 287, quoted in Vennum, *American Indian Lacrosse*, 216; see 336n7 (he gave no volume number).
41. Ibid., 215–16.
42. Fogelson, "The Cherokee Ball Game Cycle," 334. Gilbert, citing the Payne Papers, discussed "sacred arks" and said, "There were always two arks, one kept in the council house and the other used for war." Gilbert, "Eastern Cherokees," 353.
43. Fogelson, "The Cherokee Ball Game Cycle," 336.
44. Ibid. Gilbert noted based on his own research that "Curious linkages also occur of waterfalls with thunder and of snakes with lightning." Gilbert, "Eastern Cherokees," 183.
45. Fogelson, "The Cherokee Ball Game Cycle," 336.
46. Vennum, *American Indian Lacrosse*, 216.
47. Alexander Longe, quoted in ibid.,; see 336n8.
48. Fogelson, "Cherokee Ball Game," 201.
49. Gearing, *Priests and Warriors*, 61. I cited this statement about ancient priests in Chapter 2.
50. Gilbert, "Eastern Cherokees," 355.

51. Alexander Longe, quoted in Vennum, *American Indian Lacrosse*; see 336n8.
52. Vennum, *American Indian Lacrosse*, 216.
53. Ibid., 217.
54. Gilbert, "Eastern Cherokees," 357.
55. Ibid., 263.
56. Fogelson, "Cherokee Ball Game," 209.
57. Gilbert, "Eastern Cherokees," 357.
58. Ibid.
59. Mooney, *Myths*, 435.

60. John Witthoft, "Dolls, Games, Musical Instruments, Stone and Other Tools," audiocassette, 1968, John Witthoft Collection, MSS 87-171, Museum of the Cherokee Indian Archives, Cherokee, N.C., no. 11, side B.

61. See John Witthoft, "Cherokee Village Activities," typescript, 1951, John Witthoft Collection, MSS 87-171.1, Museum of the Cherokee Indian Archives, Cherokee, N.C., 1951. The Oconaluftee Indian Village is a project run by the Cherokee Historical Association and staffed by people in the community. Finely built replicas of 1760s buildings comprise the Village, including an osi, or sweathouse, a council house and a dance plaza with arbors. Cherokee artisans present traditional crafts, including basket making, carving, and blowgun construction.

62. Witthoft, "Dolls, Games, Musical Instruments," no. 11, side B.
63. Ibid.
64. Witthoft, "Ceremonies pt. 1," John Witthoft Collection, MSS 87-171, no. 4, side 2.
65. Witthoft, "Cherokee Beliefs Concerning Death," 70–71.
66. Mooney, "Cherokee Ball Play," 123–24.
67. Fogelson, "Cherokee Ball Game," 189–90; 98.

68. Ball game scarifier, item no. 180496, and catalog card, Smithsonian Institution's National Museum of the American Indian (NMAI) Cultural Resources Center (CRC), Suitland, Md.

69. Ibid.

70. Ball sticks, item no. 018993, NMAI CRC; two pair ball sticks, item no. E272976, Smithsonian National Museum of Natural History, Department of Anthropology, Ethnology Collections, Museum Support Center (MSC), Suitland, Md.; Ball sticks in the possession of the author.

71. One pair ball racket sticks, item no. E360223, MSC; ball rackets, item no. E151641, MSC.

72. Two pair ball sticks, item nos. E272975, E272976, MSC; author's ball sticks.
73. Fogelson, "Cherokee Ball Game," 135, 134.
74. Ball dress pants (four pairs), item no. E130487, MSC.

75. War dance mask representing human and rattlesnake, item no. 1805764, and collection card, NMAI CRC. In addition, a number of other objects related to the ball game are held in both museum collections, including a set of the sharpened sticks that were used at one time to keep score, a rattle belonging to the dance leader, head and belt ornaments and feathers, some with rattlesnake skin attached or accompanied by rattlesnake rattles.

76. Witthoft, *Green Corn Ceremonialism in the Eastern Woodlands*; "Eastern Woodland Community Typology."

77. For example, this is the case with Hudson, *The Southeastern Indians*. Though it does provide ample individual examples, as a whole the book is what is best called a synthesis of

elements of a number of religious systems in what is now the southeastern United States. Hudson relied heavily on Cherokee materials in chapters on belief system and ceremony. See "The Belief System," 120–83, and "Ceremony," 317–75, in ibid. Nevertheless, it is considered by some as a fair attempt of an overview of Cherokee religious traditions and for many years has been considered a standard source. A thoughtful critique of aspects of Hudson's approach is Churchill, "Purity and Pollution." Hudson's response, published in the *American Indian Quarterly*, as was Churchill's original article, continued the conversation with some interesting responses and other observations, albeit in a somewhat combative manner. Hudson, "Reply to Mary Churchill." Hudson's works still remain quite useful to scholars interested in nations and groups of what is now the southeastern United States. See, for example, Hudson, "North American Indians"; Hudson, *Four Centuries of Southern Indians*; Hudson, *Ethnology of the Southeastern Indians*.

78. Many works I discuss in this study support this view, including Nabokov, *Indian Running*; and Vennum, *American Indian Lacrosse*.

79. Culin, *Games of the North American Indians*.

80. See, for example, Green, Review of *Games of the North American Indians*. This is a review of an edition published by the University of Nebraska Press in 1992, split into two volumes and with an introduction by Dennis Tedlock.

81. Culin, *Games of the North American Indians*, 32.

82. Ibid.

83. Ibid., 34.

84. Ibid., 34, 35.

85. Ibid., 809. Culin divided his work into the following sections: "Games of chance," "Games of dexterity," "Minor amusements," "Unclassified games," and "Games derived from Europeans." Also included was a tabular index and an appendix on "Running races," and interspersed throughout the text were twenty-one plates and over a thousand illustrations. Ibid., 5, 6–28.

86. Interestingly, in the introduction he stated that the only evidence he had for such a divinatory function among First Nations peoples was from Cushing's work on the Zuni. Ibid., 35.

87. Culin, "Games," 484. Among other sources, it was quoted in Blanchard, "Sport and Ritual," 84.

88. Culin, "American Indian Games," 61.

89. What I also find interesting about the two versions of this statement is that the 1903 *American Anthropologist* article was published in the same year as *Games*. Given the staggered publication rate of BAE volumes Culin would likely have been in the midst of compiling *Games* when he wrote this article that appeared in 1903.

90. Culin, "American Indian Games," 63. He suggested a possible mythical origin for the racket but noted that it might simply be a "practical throwing contrivance." Ibid. This comment was repeated in his more comprehensive work, Culin, *Games of the North American Indians*, 562. He also made the following remark concerning the ball: "The ball was a sacred object not to be touched with the hand, and has been identified as symbolizing the earth, the sun, or the moon." Culin, "American Indian Games," 63n22.

91. Ibid., 63.

92. Lévi-Strauss, *The Savage Mind*, 30, 31.

93. Read, "Leadership and Consensus," 429; quoted in Lévi-Strauss, *The Savage Mind*, 30–31.

94. Read, "Leadership and Consensus," 429.

95. Lévi-Strauss, *The Savage Mind*, 31. Michelson, "Notes on Fox Mortuary Customs."
96. Michelson, "Notes on Fox Mortuary Customs," 385.
97. Lévi-Strauss, *The Savage Mind*, 31.
98. Ibid.
99. English paraphrase by Horace Poweshiek of Sam Peters, "This is the Story of What They Do and How They Pray when There is a Death," syllabary text, in Michelson, "Notes on Fox Mortuary Customs," 385. The Meskwaki terms are approximations of the renderings in the text.
100. Lévi-Strauss, *The Savage Mind*, 32.
101. Ibid., 32, 33. He noted after the first quoted clause that "we can therefore understand why competitive games should flourish in our industrial societies." Ibid., 32.
102. Goddard, "Linguistic Writings of Alfred Kiyana." Goddard termed the syllabary "the Meskwaki version of the Great Lakes Algonquian Syllabary." Ibid., 285.
103. Alfred Kiyana, "What They Do when an Adoption-Feast is Held, when the People Release Each Other," syllabary text, translated by Michelson, in Michelson, "Notes on Fox Mortuary Customs," 361. In this and the next quotations, the emendations in parentheses are Michelson's; the one in brackets is mine.
104. Ibid.
105. Ibid., 363.
106. Michelson, in ibid., 356. In the same section Michelson discussed the society of the "Religion Dance," noted that Sam Peters was a member, and said that the dance was introduced by Potawatomi people from Wisconsin. He also noted in a listing of his sources that Peters had some amount of Sauk heritage. Ibid., 378. Michelson said that "it should be mentioned" that Peters had "Sauk blood" on his father's side of the family, though both the father and grandfather had lived in the Fox community of Tama.
107. Jones (1871–1909) was born on the Sauk and Fox Reservation in Oklahoma and lived there until he was nine years old. Of mixed-race heritage, Jones had upon his death published little but left behind copious notes related to his extensive fieldwork with a variety of Algonquian nations. Like several works that bear Jones's name, this article was compiled and edited for publication, in this case by Franz Boas in 1911. This information is from the source listed below. According to this same source, Jones's father was born to "a Fox woman and a white man"; Jones's mother was English. See Margaret Welpley Fisher, preface, in Jones, *Ethnography of the Fox Indians*, vii–viii. The quotation is on pg. vii. The preface was dated 1934.
108. William Jones, "Notes on the Fox Indians," 221, 222. This earlier account did not specify that the team adopting the boys was the predetermined winner, though apparently that team did win. In the Cherokee context, as I discussed elsewhere in this book, the tradition of a team winning and inviting the opposing team to a Victory Dance was longstanding.
109. Ibid., 109–110.
110. Ibid., 109. The illustrations are on pp. 572–73.
111. Ibid., 92.
112. Michelson, introduction, in *The Owl Sacred Pack*, 11.
113. Fisher, preface, in Jones, *Ethnography of the Fox Indians*, 66. She cited Paul Radin's account in the *Thirty-Seventh Annual Report of the BAE*, 487.
114. Alice Beck Kehoe, introduction to Lesser, *Pawnee Ghost Dance Hand Game*, ix.
115. Blanchard, *The Anthropology of Sport*, 16.
116. Lesser, *Pawnee Ghost Dance Hand Game*, 309.

117. Ibid., 321.
118. Ibid., 321, 327.
119. Ibid., 61, 64, 324.
120. Ibid., 330, 331.
121. Ibid., 331.
122. Ibid., 327, 331.
123. Ibid., 156, 328.
124. Ibid., 332, 333.
125. Ibid., 330–31.
126. Ibid., 330, 333.
127. Ibid., 334–35; 331. Also see ibid., 309–37.
128. Ibid., 332–33.
129. Ibid., 337, 335.
130. Bloom, "Acculturation of the Eastern Cherokee," 123.
131. Ibid. Emphasis in original.
132. Speck and Broom, *Cherokee Dance and Drama*, 60–61.
133. For example, Guttman, *A Whole New Ball Game*, 14–22; Sansone, *Greek Athletics*, 54, 55, 60, 67; Salter, "Play in Ritual," 70–91; Blanchard, "Sport and Ritual," 83–98, 84; Vennum, *American Indian Lacrosse*, xv, 51. All are present notions that I think either can be traced to Culin or reflect the same interpretive scheme. Blanchard later altered his position on the issue.
134. Oxendine, *American Indian Sports Heritage*, 10. Oxendine, a Lumbee individual from North Carolina, served as chancellor of the University of North Carolina at Pembroke. He also played professional baseball. Ibid., back cover notes, 10. He cited Blanchard, "Play and Adaptation: Sport and Games in Native America," but did not give page numbers for the article or references for the statements.
135. Ibid.
136. Ibid.
137. Ibid.
138. MacAloon, "Games," 3266.
139. Ibid.; Culin, *Games of the North American Indians*, 34.
140. Turner, "Liminal to Liminoid," 159. Turner placed plays, symphonies, art exhibitions, and other performances in the same category as the Super Bowl. The flip side of this insight is that people do not typically struggle with feelings of guilt if they do not attend a sporting event, nor are they inclined to inflate their actual attendance rate if questioned.
141. One might argue that "wedding crashers" and people who serially attend funerals are fans; the same could be said about ethnographers.
142. Bell, *Ritual*, 154.
143. Ibid. Among the several scholars she cited were Kendall Blanchard and Allen Guttman. See ibid., 297nn56–64.
144. Ibid. Here and above Bell relied upon source material that included several works I discuss in this chapter, all with Victor Turner's interpretation of liminality as a backdrop. See ibid., 297nn56–64.
145. Ibid., 154.
146. See Girard, *Violence and the Sacred*; also see Hamerton-Kelly, *Violent Origins*.
147. Gluckman and Gluckman, "On Drama," 238–39.
148. Ibid., 239. They cited Long 1791 and Carver 1796, p. 564 in Culin.
149. Ibid.

150. Ibid., 239, 240.

151. Guttman, "From Ritual to Record," in *From Ritual to Record*, 15–55. Guttman noted this himself. Ibid., 165. See, for example, Scambler, *Sport and Society*, 25–28; Noel Dyck, "Games, Bodies, Celebrations and Boundaries: Anthropological Perspectives on Sport," and Susan Brownell, "Why Should an Anthropologist Study Sports in China?" in Dyck, *Games, Sports and Cultures*, 18–19, 44. The latter two authors also discussed the significance of John MacAloon: 16, 18; 44, 47–50.

152. Guttman, *From Ritual to Record*, 26.

153. Ibid.

154. Opler, "Jicarilla Apache Ceremonial Relay Race"; it also was a chapter in Opler, *Childhood and Youth*.

155. Opler, *Childhood and Youth*, 116.

156. Nabokov, Chapter 2, "Notes on Sources," in *Indian Running*, 199. The book is not an academic work, but it contains useful information and source endnotes account for most if not all references.

157. Nabokov, *Indian Running*, 9, 70.

158. Guttman, *From Ritual to Record*, 18.

159. Guttman, *A Whole New Ball Game*, 14–15.

160. Ibid., 16, 21, 22.

161. See Wittgenstein, *Philosophical Investigations*, point 67, 32e. Wittgenstein employed this term in a discussion of games. Wittgenstein argued that if one examines various types of games one finds "a complicated network of similarities overlapping and criss-crossing: sometimes overall similarities, sometimes similarities of detail. . . . I can think of no better expression to characterize these similarities than 'family resemblances.' . . . And I shall say: 'games' form a family." Ibid. He argued that the concept of game itself is unbounded: "For how is the concept of a game bounded? What still counts as a game and what no longer does? Can you give the boundary? No . . . We do not know the boundaries because none has been drawn." Ibid., points 68, 69, 33e.

162. See Turner, *The Ritual Process*.

163. Turner, "Liminal to Liminoid," 135.

164. Ibid., 155, 157, 158, 159.

165. Ibid., 159.

166. Ibid., 135. He did not give the Durkheim reference.

167. Ibid.

168. Geertz, "Deep Play: Notes on the Balinese Cockfight," in *The Interpretation of Cultures*, 437.

169. Ibid., 450.

170. Ibid., 448, 417.

171. See Barzun, "On Baseball"; Arens, "The Great American Football Ritual," 81; quoted in Blanchard, *The Anthropology of Sport*, 53.

172. Wiener, *Visible and Invisible Realms*, 113–14, 134, 10.

173. MacAloon, "The Theory of Spectacle," 15.

174. Ibid.

175. Ibid., 16.

176. Ibid.

177. Ibid., 19.

178. Ibid., 33n3. In the endnote to this sentence he chalked up his desire to explain the Olympics in terms of ritual because he was a former athlete (track and field).

179. Ibid., 19.
180. Ibid.
181. Ibid., 33–34n5.
182. "Wrestler who discarded medal expelled from Games," August 16, 2008, ⟨http://www.cnn.com/2008/WORLD/asiapcf/08/16/olympic.wrestler/index.html⟩ (accessed August 2008).
183. MacAloon, "The Theory of Spectacle," 33–34n5.

Conclusion

1. White, *Historical Collections of Georgia*, 670.
2. Several Cherokee people with whom I spoke had theories regarding the identity of the author, some intimating that he or she was a non-Cherokee longtime resident in the community; but to my knowledge the author's identity was never made public.
3. Personal communication, 1998.
4. Dr. I. M. Uneg, "Tracing Your Hysterical Roots," 1–4 (photocopy in the possession of the author).
5. Ibid., 1.
6. Ibid. Although when I first began my fieldwork I thought this was an exaggeration, my own experience confirmed it was not. I cannot count the number of times I have heard this last comment.
7. Ibid.
8. Ibid., 1–3.
9. Ibid., 4.
10. Personal communications, 1993–1998.
11. Linda Tuhiwai Smith, *Decolonizing Methodologies*, 1.
12. Ann T. Jordan, preface, in David Lewis Jr. and Ann T. Jordan, *Creek Indian Medicine Ways*, xx.
13. Personal communication, October 2007.
14. Ibid.
15. Blanchard, *The Mississippi Choctaws at Play*. For bibliographies of relevant works, see Vennum, *American Indian Lacrosse*; and Zogry, "Ballgames."
16. For a bibliography of relevant works, see Heather S. Orr, "Ballgames." Also see, for example, Harmon, "Religion and the Mesoamerican Ball Game"; Fash and Fash, "The Roles of Ballgames"; Fox et al., "Playing with Power"; Whittington, *Sport of Life and Death*.

Bibliography

Manuscript Sources
Cambridge, Mass.
   Houghton Library, Harvard University
      American Board of Commissioners for Foreign Missions Papers. Microfilm Reel 739, Missions on the American Continents and to the Islands of the Pacific, 1811–1919 (ABC 18–19) 1824–1831, Cherokee Mission (ABC 18.3.1), Vols. 4 and 5, Cherokee Mission Letters.
Chapel Hill, N.C.
   North Carolina Collection, University of North Carolina at Chapel Hill
      Hicks, Charles. "Manners & Customs of the Cherokees," *Raleigh Register and North Carolina Gazette*, Vol. 19, November 6, 1818, p. 1.
   Southern Historical Collection, Manuscripts Department, Wilson Library, University of North Carolina at Chapel Hill
      Dogwood Festival Incorporated (Chapel Hill, N.C.) Records, 1932–38, Collection No. 3654-z,
Cherokee, N.C.
   Museum of the Cherokee Indian Archives
      American Baptist Foreign Mission Society Correspondence, Baptist Missionary Records, MSS 93-11, Folders 13–14 (photocopies)
      Cherokee Documents in Foreign Archives. Microfilm Collection.
      "Fading Voices," MSS 87-16
      John Howard Payne Papers. Typescript volumes copied from microfilm, MSS 87-04, and microfilm of original manuscripts, 2 rolls, DR.11
      John Witthoft. "Cherokee Village Activities." Typescript of notes, 1951. John Witthoft Collection. MSS 87-171.1.
      Ossie Crowe Collection. Ledger books. 2 vols. MSS 99-03.
Durham, N.C.
   Rare Book, Manuscript, and Special Collections Library, Duke University
      Thomas Lenoir Papers
      William Holland Thomas Papers
Kansas City, Mo.
   National Archives, Central Plains Region
      Superintendents' Annual Narrative and Statistical Reports from Field Jurisdictions of the Bureau of Indian Affairs, 1907–1938. National Archives Microfilm Publication M1011, Roll 12. Cherokee Orphan Training School, 1912–24; Cherokee School, 1910–1928
Morrow, Ga.
   National Archives, Southeast Region
      Bureau of Indian Affairs. Record Group 75 (75.19.7). Records of the Cherokee Indian Agency, N.C. 1886–1952.

Philadelphia, Pa.
   American Philosophical Society
      Vocabularies and miscellaneous papers pertaining to Indian languages [1784–1828], manuscripts, 497.V85, part 1
Washington, D.C.
   Bureau of American Ethnology Catalogue of Manuscripts, National Anthropological Archives
      James Mooney. Original manuscripts of Cherokee stories published in the *Nineteenth Annual Report of the Bureau of American Ethnology, 1897–1898*, no. 1905.
Winston-Salem, N.C.
   Moravian Archives
      Diary of the Mission in Spring Place among the Cherokee Indians 1825, Springplace Diary, 1823–29, M 406 D
      Spring Place Correspondence 1808, M 411:6:19
      Spring Place Correspondence 1825, M 413:24–27

Published Primary Sources

Adair, James. *The History of the American Indians*. 1775. Reprinted as *Adair's History of the American Indians*, edited by Samuel Cole Williams. Johnson City, Tenn.: Watauga Press, 1930.

Bartram, William. *Travels through North and South Carolina, Georgia, East and West Florida, the Cherokee Country, the Extensive Territories of the Muscogulges, or Creek Confederacy, and the Country of the Chactaws* [sic]. 1791. Reprinted as *Travels of William Bartram*, edited by Mark Van Doren. New York: Dover Publications, 1955.

Board of Commissioners of Indian Trade of South Carolina. Minutes, May 4, 1714–May 6, 1714. *Journals of the Commissioners of the Indian Trade: September 20, 1710–August 29, 1718*, Colonial Records of South Carolina, edited by W. L. McDowell, 53–56. Columbia: South Carolina Archives Department, 1955.

Buttrick [Butrick], Daniel S. *Antiquities of the Cherokee Indians*. Vinita, Indian Territory: Indian Chieftain, 1884. Reprinted in *Journal of Cherokee Studies* 18 (1997): 27–51.

"A Catechism of the Ten Commandments in Cherokee & English." Cherokee and Asheville, N.C.: Big Cove Baptist Church and Global Bible Society, n.d.

Haywood, John. *The Natural and Aboriginal History of Tennessee* . . . . 1823. Reprint, edited by Mary U. Rothrock. Jackson, Tenn.: McCowat-Mercer, 1959.

Lanman, Charles. *Letters from the Alleghany Mountains*. New York, 1849.

———. "Cherokee Customs." Chapter 23 in *Adventures in the Wilds of North America*, edited by Charles Richard Weld, 172–76. London: Longman, Brown, Green and Longmans, 1854.

Longe, Alexander. "A Small Postscript on the ways and manners of the Indians called Cherokees, the contents of the whole so that you may find everything by the pages" (1725). Transcript of original manuscript from Library of Congress. Photostats and "modern version" edited, with an introduction, by David H. Corkran. *Southern Indian Studies* 21 (October 1969): 3–49.

Louis-Philippe, King of the French (1773–1850). *Diary of My Travels in America*. Translated from the French by Stephen Becker. New York: Delacorte Press, 1978.

Norton, John. *The Journal of Major John Norton (Teyoninhokarawen), 1816*. Edited by Carl F. Klinck and James J. Talmon. Toronto: Champlain Society, 1970.

Schneider, Martin. "Brother Martin Schneider's Report of His Journey to the Upper Cherokee Towns (1783–1784)." In *Early Travels in the Tennessee Country, 1540–1800*, edited, with introductions, annotations, and index by Samuel Cole Williams, 250–65. Johnson City, Tenn.: Watauga Press, 1928.

Spray, Henry W. "Report of Superintendent in Charge of Eastern Cherokee Agency, August 27, 1900." In *Annual Reports of the Department of the Interior for the Fiscal Year ended June 30, 1900, Indian Affairs, Report of Commissioner and Appendixes*, 306–8. Washington, D.C.: GPO, 1900.

Thomas, William H. Notice, May 27, 1867. Inoli Letters, no. 2241a, National Anthropological Archives, Washington, D.C. Reprinted in Jack Frederick Kilpatrick, "Two Notices by Will Thomas," *Southern Indian Studies* 14 (1962): 27–28; 27.

Timberlake, Henry. *Lieutenant Henry Timberlake's Memoirs, 1756–1765*. Edited by Samuel Cole Williams. Johnson City, Tenn.: n.p., 1927.

Uneg, Dr. I. M. "Tracing Your Hysterical Roots." N.p., [1998?].

White, George. *Historical Collections of Georgia*. New York: n.p., 1855.

Williams, Samuel C. "An Account of the Presbyterian Mission to the Cherokees, 1757–1759" [by Rev. Dr. Samuel Davies]. *Tennessee Historical Magazine*, 2nd ser., 1 (January 1931): 125–38.

Published Secondary Sources

Albanese, Catherine L. "Exploring Regional Religion: A Case Study of the Eastern Cherokee." *History of Religions* 23 (May 1984): 344–81.

Andrew, John A., III. *From Revivals to Removal: Jeremiah Evarts, The Cherokee Nation, and the Search for the Soul of America*. Athens: University of Georgia Press, 1992.

Anonymous. Review of "The Cherokee Ball Play" and "Cherokee Theory and Practice of Medicine." *American Journal of Psychology* 3, no. 2 (April 1890): 271.

Arneach, Lloyd. With illustrations by Lydia G. Halverson. *The Animals' Ballgame: A Cherokee Story from the Eastern Band*. N.p.: Lake Book Manufacturing, 1992. Children's book with audiocassette.

Asad, Talal. *Genealogies of Religion: Discipline and Reasons of Power in Christianity and Islam*. Baltimore: Johns Hopkins University Press, 1993.

Badders, Hurely E. *Broken Path: The Cherokee Campaign of 1776*. Pendleton, Ga.: Pendleton District Historical and Recreational Commission, 1976.

Baillou, Clemens de. "A Contribution to the Mythology and Conceptual World of the Cherokee Indians." *Ethnohistory* 8, no. 1 (Winter 1961): 93–102.

Barkun, Michael. "Religion and Secrecy After September 11." *Journal of the American Academy of Religion* 74, no. 2 (June 2006): 275–301.

Barzun, Jacques. "On Baseball." In *God's Country and Mine*, 159–65. Boston: Little, Brown, 1954.

Basso, Keith. *Wisdom Sits in Places: Landscape and Language among the Western Apache*. Albuquerque: University of New Mexico Press, 1996.

Bell, Catherine. *Ritual Theory, Ritual Practice*. New York: Oxford University Press, 1992.

———. *Ritual: Perspectives and Dimensions*. New York: Oxford University Press, 1997.

———. "Performance." In *Critical Terms for Religious Studies*, edited by Mark C. Taylor, 205–24. Chicago: University of Chicago Press, 1998.

Bender, Ernest. "Cherokee II." *International Journal of American Linguistics* 15, no. 4 (Oct. 1949): 223–28.

Bender, Margaret. *Signs of Cherokee Culture: Sequoyah's Syllabary in Eastern Cherokee Life.* Chapel Hill: University of North Carolina Press, 2002.

Bird, Solomon. "Solomon Bird Interview." *Journal of Cherokee Studies* 14 (Special Edition, 1989): 10–16.

Blanchard, Kendall. "Stick Ball and the American Southeast." In *Forms of Play of Native North Americans*, 1977 Proceedings of the American Ethnological Society, edited by Edward Norbeck and Claire Farrer, 189–207. St. Paul, Minn.: West Publishing Co., 1979.

———. "Sport and Ritual in Choctaw Society: Structure and Perspective." In *Play and Culture*, 1978 Proceedings of the Association for the Anthropological Study of Play, edited by Helen B. Schwartzman, 83–90. West Point, N.Y.: Leisure Press, 1980.

———. *The Mississippi Choctaws at Play: The Serious Side of Leisure.* Urbana: University of Illinois Press, 1981.

———. *The Anthropology of Sport: An Introduction—A Revised Edition.* Based upon a first edition by Kendall Blanchard and Alyce Cheska, with a foreword by Brian Sutton-Smith. Westport, Conn.: Bergin and Garvey, 1995.

Bourdieu, Pierre. *Outline of a Theory of Practice.* Translated by Richard Nice. Cambridge: Cambridge University Press, 1977.

———. "Programme for a Sociology of Sport." In *In Other Words: Essays Towards a Reflexive Sociology*, translated by Matthew Adamson, 156–67. Palo Alto, Calif.: Stanford University Press, 1990. Originally "Paper presented to the study group 'Physical life and games', CEMEA, in November 1980 and opening lecture to the Eighth Symposium of the ICSS, 'Sport, social classes and sub-culture,' Paris, July 1983."

Brown, Michael F. *Who Owns Native Culture?* Cambridge: Harvard University Press, 2003.

Bruchac, Joseph. "The Creator's Game." *Parabola* 21, no. 4 (Winter 1996): 84–86.

Burridge, Kenelm. *Mambu: A Melanesian Millennium.* 1960. Reprint, with a new preface by the author, Princeton: Princeton University Press, 1995.

Burt, Jesse, and Robert Ferguson. *Indians of the Southeast: Then and Now.* Nashville: Abingdon Press, 1973.

Callois, Roger. *Man, Play, and Games.* New York: Schocken Books, 1979. Originally published as *Les jeux et les hommes* (Paris: Librairie Gallimard, 1958).

———. "The Structure and Classification of Games." In *Sport, Culture, and Society*, edited by John Loy and Gerald Kenyon, 44–55. New York: Macmillan Publishing Company, 1969.

Campany, Robert Ford. "On the Very Idea of Religions (in the Modern West and in Early Medieval China)." *History of Religions* 42, no. 4 (2003): 287–319.

Chamberlain, Kathleen Egan. "Competition for the Native American Soul: The Search for Religious Freedom in Twentieth-Century New Mexico." In *Religion in Modern New Mexico*, edited by Ferenc M. Szasz and Richard W. Etulain, 81–99. Albuquerque: University of New Mexico Press, 1997.

Champagne, Duane. "Institutional and Cultural Order in Early Cherokee Society." *Journal of Cherokee Studies* 15 (1990): 3–23.

Cherokee Progress and Challenge. Cherokee, N.C.: Cherokee Tribal Government, 1972.

Chiltoskey, Mary Ulmer, ed. *Cherokee Fair and Festival: A History thru 1978.* Cherokee Indian Fall Festival Association, 1979.

Churchill, Mary C. "Purity and Pollution: Unearthing an Oppositional Paradigm in the

Study of Cherokee Religious Traditions." In *Native American Spirituality*, edited by Lee Irwin, 205–35. Lincoln: University of Nebraska Press, 2000. First published as "The Oppositional Paradigm of Purity versus Pollution in Charles Hudson's *The Southeastern Indians*," *American Indian Quarterly* 20 (Fall 1996): 563–93.

Corkran, David H. "A Cherokee Migration Fragment." *Southern Indian Studies* 4 (1952): 27–28.

Corman, Catherine A. Review of *Writing Indians: Literacy, Christianity, and Native Community in Early America*, by Hilary E. Wyss, and *The Brainerd Journal: A Mission to the Cherokees, 1817–1823*, by Joyce B. Phillips and Paul Gary Phillips. *William and Mary Quarterly* ser. 3, 58, no. 3 (July 2001): 742–45.

Culin, Stewart. "American Indian Games." *American Anthropologist* 5 (1903): 58–64.

———. *Games of the North American Indians*. In *Twenty-Fourth Annual Report of the Bureau of American Ethnology, 1902–1903*, 1–846. Washington, D.C.: GPO, 1907. Reprint, New York: Dover Publications, 1975 (page citations are to the reprint edition).

———. "Games." In *Handbook of American Indians North of Mexico*, edited by Frederick Webb Hodge, 483–84. Smithsonian Institution, Bureau of American Ethnology Bulletin 30, pt. 1. Washington, D.C.: GPO, 1907.

Debord, Guy. *Society of the Spectacle*. Detroit: Black and Red, 1983.

Deloria, Vine, Jr. *We Talk, You Listen: New Tribes, New Turf*. 1970. Reprint, Lincoln: University of Nebraska Press, 2007.

———. *Custer Died for Your Sins: An Indian Manifesto*. 1969. Reprint, Norman: University of Oklahoma Press, 1988.

———. "Is Religion Possible?: An Evaluation of Present Efforts to Revive Traditional Tribal Religions." In *For This Land: Writings on Religion in America*, 261–68. New York: Routledge, 1999.

Dilworth, Leah. *Imagining Indians in the Southwest: Persistent Visions of a Primitive Past*. Washington, D.C.: Smithsonian Institution Press, 1996.

Dowd, Gregory Evans. "Renewing Sacred Power in the South." In *A Spirited Resistance: The North American Struggle For Unity, 1745–1815*, 167–90. Baltimore: Johns Hopkins University Press, 1992.

Duncan, Barbara R., ed. *Living Stories of the Cherokee*. Chapel Hill: University of North Carolina Press, 1998.

Dyck, Noel, ed. *Games, Sports and Cultures*. Oxford, U.K.: Berg, 2000.

Eyman, Frances. "Lacrosse and the Cayuga Thunder Rite." *Expedition: The Bulletin of the Museum of the University of Pennsylvania* 6, no. 4 (Summer 1964): 15–19.

Fash, Barbara W., and William L. Fash. "The Roles of Ballgames in Mesoamerican Ritual Economy." In *Mesoamerican Ritual Economy: Archaeological and Ethnological Perspectives*, edited by Christian E. Wells and Karla L. Davis-Salazar, 267–84. Boulder: University Press of Colorado, 2007.

Faulkner, Charles H. "Origin and Evolution of the Cherokee Winter House." *Journal of Cherokee Studies* 3, no. 2 (1978): 87–93.

Fenton, William N. "Cherokee and Iroquois Connections Revisited." *Journal of Cherokee Studies* 3 (Fall 1978): 239–49.

Finger, John R. *The Eastern Band of the Cherokees, 1819–1900*. Knoxville: University of Tennessee Press, 1984.

———. *Cherokee Americans: The Eastern Band of Cherokees in the Twentieth Century*. Lincoln: University of Nebraska Press, 1991.

Fogelson, Raymond D. "Change, Persistence, and Accommodation in Cherokee Medico-Magical Beliefs." In *Symposium on Cherokee and Iroquois Culture*, edited by William N. Fenton and John Gulick, 213–26. Smithsonian Institution, Bureau of American Ethnology Bulletin 180. Washington, D.C.: GPO, 1961.

———. "An Analysis of Cherokee Sorcery and Witchcraft." In *Four Centuries of Southern Indians*, edited by Charles M. Hudson, 113–31. Athens: University of Georgia Press, 1975.

———. "Cherokee Notions of Power." In *The Anthropology of Power: Ethnographic Studies from Asia, Oceania, and the New World*, edited by Raymond D. Fogelson and Richard M. Adams, 185–94. New York: Academic Press, 1977.

———. *The Cherokees: A Critical Bibliography*. Newberry Library Center for the History of the American Indian Bibliographical Series. Bloomington: Indiana University Press for the Newberry Library, 1978.

———. "Major John Norton as Ethno-ethnologist." *Journal of Cherokee Studies* 3 (Fall 1978): 250–55.

———. "Cherokee Little People Reconsidered." *Journal of Cherokee Studies* 7 (Fall 1982): 92–97.

———. "Who Were the *Aní:Kutání*?: An Excursion into Cherokee Historical Thought." *Ethnohistory* 31, no. 4 (1984): 255–63.

———. "The Cherokee Ballgame Cycle: An Ethnographer's View." In *Ethnology of the Southeastern Indians: A Source Book*, edited by Charles M. Hudson, 327–38. New York: Garland Publishing, 1985. First published as "The Cherokee Ballgame Cycle: An Ethnographer's View," *Ethnomusicology* 15, no. 3 (Sept. 1971): 327–38.

———. "The Ethnohistory of Events and Nonevents." *Ethnohistory* 36, no. 2 (1989): 133–147.

Fogelson, Raymond D., and Paul Kutsche. "Cherokee Economic Cooperatives: the Gadugi." In *Symposium on Cherokee and Iroquois Culture*, edited by William N. Fenton and John Gulick, 83–124. Smithsonian Institution, Bureau of American Ethnology Bulletin 180. Washington, D.C.: GPO, 1961.

Fogelson, Raymond D., and Amelia B. Walker. "Self and Other in Cherokee Booger Masks." *Journal of Cherokee Studies* 5 (Fall 1980): 88–102.

Fogelson, Raymond D., and Amelia R. Bell. "Cherokee Booger Mask Tradition." In *The Power of Symbols: Masks and Masquerade in the Americas*, edited by N. Ross Crumrine and Marjorie Halpin, 48–69. Vancouver: University of British Columbia Press, 1983.

Fox, John G., et al. "Playing with Power: Ball Courts and Political Ritual in Southern Mesoamerica" [and Comments and Reply]. *Current Anthropology* 37 (1996): 483–509.

Frazer, James George. *The Golden Bough: A Study in Magic and Religion*. 1922. Abridged ed.; New York: Touchstone/Simon Schuster, 1996.

French, Laurence. "Missionaries among the Eastern Cherokees: Religion as a Means of Interethnic Communication." In *Interethnic Communication*, Southern Anthropological Society Proceedings, No. 12, edited by E. Lamar Ross, 100–112. Athens: University of Georgia Press, 1978.

Gardner, Robert G. *Cherokees and Baptists in Georgia*. Atlanta: Georgia Baptist Historical Society, 1989.

Gearing, Fred. *Priests and Warriors: Social Structures for Cherokee Politics in the 18th Century*. Memoir 93. Menasha, Wis.: American Anthropological Association, 1962.

Geertz, Clifford. *The Interpretation of Cultures*. New York: Basic Books, 1973.

Gilbert, William H., Jr. "Eastern Cherokee Social Organization." In *Social Organization of*

North American Tribes: Essays in Social Organization, Law and Religion, edited by Fred Eggan, 285–338. Chicago: University of Chicago Press, 1937.

———. "The Eastern Cherokees." Smithsonian Institution, Bureau of American Ethnology Bulletin 133, Anthropological Papers, no. 23, 169–413. Washington, D.C.: GPO, 1943. Reprinted as *The Eastern Cherokees* (New York: AMS Press, 1978). Page citations are to the reprint edition.

———. "The Cherokees of North Carolina: Living Memorials of the Past." In *Smithsonian Report for 1956*, 529–55. Washington, D.C.: Smithsonian Institution, 1957.

Gill, Sam D. "No Place to Stand: Jonathan Z. Smith as *Homo Ludens*, The Academic Study of Religion *Sub Specie Ludi*." *Journal of the American Academy of Religion* 66, no. 2 (1998): 283–312.

———. "Embodied Theology." In *Religious Studies, Theology, and the University: Conflicting Maps, Changing Terrain*, edited by Linell E. Cady and Delwin Brown, 81–92. Albany: State University of New York Press, 2002.

———. "Dancing Ritual, Ritual Dancing: Experiential Teaching." In *Teaching Ritual*, edited by Catherine Bell, 45–55. New York: Oxford University Press, 2007.

Girard, René. *Violence and the Sacred*. Translated by Patrick Gregory. Baltimore: Johns Hopkins University Press, 1977. Originally published as *La Violence et le sacré* (Paris: Librairie Plon, 1962).

Gluckman, Mary, and Max Gluckman. "On Drama, and Games and Athletic Contests." In *Secular Ritual*, edited by Sally F. Moore and Barbara G. Myerhoff, 227–43. Assen/Amsterdam, Netherlands: Van Gorcum, 1977.

Godbold, E. Stanley, Jr., and Mattie U. Russell. *Confederate Colonel and Cherokee Chief: The Life of William Holland Thomas*. Knoxville: University of Tennessee Press, 1990.

Goddard, Ives. "The Linguistic Writings of Alfred Kiyana on Fox (Meskwaki)." In *Anthropology, History, and American Indians: Essays in Honor of William Curtis Sturtevant*, edited by William L. Merrill and Ives Goddard, 285–93. Smithsonian Contributions to Anthropology 44. Washington, D.C.: Smithsonian Institution Press, 2002.

Green, Adriana Greci. Review of *Games of the North American Indians*, vols. 1 and 2, by Stewart Culin. *Ethnohistory* 41, no. 2 (Spring 1994): 333–35.

Grimes, Ronald L. "Defining Nascent Ritual." *Journal of the American Academy of Religion* 50, no. 4 (Dec. 1982): 539–55.

———. *Rite Out of Place: Ritual, Media, and the Arts*. New York: Oxford University Press, 2006.

Gulick, John. "The Acculturation of Eastern Cherokee Community Organization." *Social Forces* 36, no. 3 (March 1958): 246–50.

———. "Language and Passive Resistance among the Eastern Cherokee." *Ethnohistory* 5, no. 1 (Winter 1958): 60–81.

———. *Cherokees at the Crossroads*. Rev. ed., with an epilogue by Sharlotte Neely Williams. Chapel Hill: Institute of Research in Social Science, University of North Carolina, 1973.

Guttman, Allen. *A Whole New Ball Game: An Interpretation of American Sports*. Chapel Hill: University of North Carolina Press, 1988.

———. *From Ritual to Record: The Nature of Modern Sports*. 1978. Updated with a New Afterword. New York: Columbia University Press, 2004.

Hallowell, A. Irving. "Ojibwa Ontology, Behavior, and World View." In *Teachings from the*

American Earth: Indian Religion and Philosophy, edited by Dennis Tedlock and Barbara Tedlock. 141–78. New York: Liveright, 1975. Originally published in Stanley Diamond, ed., *Culture in History: Essays in Honor of Paul Radin* (New York: Columbia University Press, 1960).

Hamel, Paul B., and Mary U. Chiltoskey. *Cherokee Plants and Their Uses: A 400 Year History.* Sylva, N.C.: Herald Publishing, 1975.

Hamerton-Kelly, Robert G., ed. *Violent Origins: Walter Burkert, René Girard, and Jonathan Z. Smith on Ritual Killing and Cultural Formation.* With an introduction by Burton Mack and a commentary by Renato Rosaldo. Palo Alto: Stanford University Press, 1987.

Handelman, Don, and Galina Lindquist, eds. *Ritual in Its Own Right: Exploring the Dynamics of Transformation.* New York: Berghahn Books, 2005.

Harkin, Michael. "Staged Encounters: Postmodern Tourism and Aboriginal People." *Ethnohistory* 50, no. 3 (Summer 2003): 575–85.

Harmon, Marcel J. "Religion and the Mesoamerican Ball Game in the Casas Grandes Region of Northern Mexico." In *Religion in the Prehispanic Southwest,* edited by Christine S. Vanpool, Todd L. Vanpool, and David A. Phillips Jr., 185–217. Lanham, Md.: AltaMira Press, 2007.

Herndon, Marcia. "The Cherokee Ballgame Cycle: An Ethnomusicologist's View." In *Ethnology of the Southeastern Indians: A Source Book,* edited by Charles M. Hudson, 339–52. New York: Garland Publishing, 1985.

Hill, Sarah H. *Weaving New Worlds: Southeastern Cherokee Women and Their Basketry.* Chapel Hill: University of North Carolina Press, 1997.

Hiltebeitel, Alf. "Gambling." In vol. 5 of *The Encyclopedia of Religion,* 2nd ed., edited by Lindsey Jones, 3258–65. New York: Macmillan Reference USA, 2005.

Hoxie, Frederick, ed. *Talking Back to Civilization: Indian Voices from the Progressive Era.* Boston: Bedford/St. Martin's, 2001.

Hudson, Charles M. *The Southeastern Indians.* Knoxville: University of Tennessee Press, 1976.

———. "Uktena: A Cherokee Anomalous Monster." *Journal of Cherokee Studies* 3 (Spring 1978): 62–73.

———. "North American Indians: Indians of the Southeast Woodlands." In vol. 10 of *The Encyclopedia of Religion,* edited by Mircea Eliade, 485–90. New York: Macmillan Publishing, 1987.

———. "Reply to Mary Churchill." *American Indian Quarterly* 24 (Summer 2000): 494–502.

———, ed. *Four Centuries of Southern Indians.* Athens: University of Georgia Press, 1975.

———, ed. *Ethnology of the Southeastern Indians: A Source Book.* New York: Garland Publishing, 1985.

Huizinga, Johan. *Homo Ludens: A Study of the Play Element in Culture.* 1938. Translator not identified. Boston: Beacon Press, 1950.

Hymes, Dell H. *In Vain I Tried to Tell You: Essays in Native American Ethnopoetics.* Philadelphia: University of Pennsylvania Press, 1981.

Irwin, Lee. "Cherokee Healing: Myth Dreams, and Medicine." *American Indian Quarterly* 16 (Spring 1992): 237–57

———. "Different Voices Together: Preservation and Acculturation in Early 19th Century Cherokee Religion." *Journal of Cherokee Studies* 18 (1997): 3–26.

———, ed. *Native American Spirituality.* Lincoln: University of Nebraska Press, 2000.

Johnson, Paul C. *Secrets, Gossip and Gods: The Transformation of Brazilian Candomblé.* New York: Oxford University Press, 2002.

Jones, William. "Notes on the Fox Indians." *Journal of American Folklore* 24, no. 92 (Apr.–Jun. 1911): 209–37.

———. *Ethnography of the Fox Indians.* Smithsonian Institution, Bureau of American Ethnology Bulletin 125. Edited by Margaret Welpley Fisher. Washington, D.C.: GPO, 1939.

Kapferer, Bruce. "Ritual Dynamics and Virtual Practice: Beyond Representation and Meaning." In *Ritual in Its Own Right: Exploring the Dynamics of Transformation*, edited by Don Handelman and Galina Lindquist, 35–54. (New York: Berghahn Books, 2005).

Kehoe, Alice B. "Eliade and Hultkrantz: The European Primitivist Tradition." *American Indian Quarterly* 20, no. 3 (Summer 1996): 377–92.

Kelley, Page H. *Biblical Hebrew: An Introductory Grammar.* Grand Rapids, Mich.: William B. Eerdmans, 1992.

Kilpatrick, Alan E. "'Going to the Water': A Structural Analysis of Cherokee Purification Rituals." *American Indian Culture and Research Journal* 15, no. 4 (1991): 49–58.

———. "A Note on Cherokee Theological Concepts." *American Indian Quarterly* 19 (Summer 1995): 389–405.

———. *The Night Has a Naked Soul: Witchcraft and Sorcery among the Western Cherokee.* Syracuse: Syracuse University Press, 1997.

———. "On Translating Magical Texts." *Wicazo Sa Review* 14, no. 2 (Autumn 1999): 25–31.

Kilpatrick, Jack F., ed. "The Wahnenauhi Manuscript: Historical Sketches of the Cherokees, Together with Some of Their Customs, Traditions, and Superstitions." Smithsonian Institution, Bureau of American Ethnology Bulletin 196, Paper 77, 175–214. Washington, D.C.: GPO, 1966.

Kilpatrick, Jack F., and Anna G. Kilpatrick. *Friends of Thunder: Folktales of the Oklahoma Cherokees.* Dallas: Southern Methodist University Press, 1964.

———. "Cherokee Rituals Pertaining to Medicinal Roots." *Southern Indian Studies* 16 (1964): 24–28.

———. *Walk in Your Soul: Love Incantations of the Oklahoma Cherokees.* Dallas: Southern Methodist University Press, 1965.

———. "Chronicles of Wolftown: Social Documents of the North Carolina Cherokees, 1850–1862." Smithsonian Institution, Bureau of American Ethnology Bulletin 196, Paper 75, 1–111. Washington, D.C.: GPO, 1966.

———. "Eastern Cherokee Folktales: Reconstructed from the Field Notes of Frans M. Olbrechts." Smithsonian Institution, Bureau of American Ethnology Bulletin 196, Paper 80, 379–447. Washington, D.C.: GPO, 1966.

———, trans. and ed. *The Shadow of Sequoyah: Social Documents of the Cherokees, 1862–1964.* Norman: University of Oklahoma Press, 1965.

———. *Notebook of a Cherokee Shaman.* Smithsonian Contributions to Anthropology, Vol. 2, No. 6. Washington, D.C.: Smithsonian Institution Press, 1970.

Kimura, Takeshi. "Bearing the 'Bare Facts' of Ritual: A Critique of Jonathan Z. Smith's Study of the Bear Ceremony Based on a Study of the Ainu Iyomante." *Numen* 46, no. 1 (1999): 88–114.

King, Duane H. "The Origin of the Eastern Cherokees as a Social and Political Entity." In *The Cherokee Indian Nation: A Troubled History*, edited by Duane H. King, 164–80. Knoxville: University of Tennessee Press, 1979.

———. "Cherokee." In the *Encyclopedia of North American Indians*, edited by Frederick E. Hoxie, 105–8. New York: Houghton Mifflin Company, 1996.

———, compiler. "Eastern Cherokee Government Since 1827." In *Cherokee Heritage: Official Guidebook to the Museum of the Cherokee Indian*, 13. Cherokee, N.C.: Cherokee Communications, 1988.

King, Richard. *Orientalism and Religion: Postcolonial Theory, India, and "The Mystic East."* London: Routledge, 1999.

Kupferer, Harriet Jane. "The Principal People, 1960: A Study of Cultural and Social Groups of the Eastern Cherokee." Smithsonian Institution, Bureau of American Ethnology Bulletin 196, Anthropological Paper No. 78, 75–80. Washington, D.C.: GPO, 1966.

Lechte, John. *Fifty Key Contemporary Thinkers: From Structuralism to Post-Humanism.* 2nd ed. London: Routledge, 2008.

Lesser, Alexander. *The Pawnee Ghost Dance Hand Game: Ghost Dance Revival and Ethnic Identity.* 1933. Reprint, with an introduction by Alice Beck Kehoe, Lincoln: University of Nebraska Press, 1996.

Lévi-Strauss, Claude. *The Savage Mind.* Chicago: University of Chicago Press, 1966. Originally published in French as *La Pensée sauvage* (1962).

Lewis, David, Jr., and Ann T. Jordan. *Creek Indian Medicine Ways: The Enduring Power of Mvskoke Religion.* Albuquerque: University of New Mexico Press, 2002.

Lewis, T. M. N., and Madeline Kneberg. "The Cherokee 'Hothouse.'" *Tennessee Archaeologist* 9, no. 1 (1953): 224–27.

Loftin, John D. "The 'Harmony Ethic' of the Conservative Eastern Cherokees: A Religious Interpretation." *Journal of Cherokee Studies* 8 (Spring 1983): 40–45.

Long, Charles H. *Signfications: Signs, Symbols, and Images in the Interpretation of Religion.* Philadelphia: Fortress Press, 1986.

MacAloon, John J. *This Great Symbol: Pierre de Coubertin and the Rise of the Modern Olympic Games.* Chicago: University of Chicago Press, 1981.

———. "Olympic Games and the Theory of Spectacle in Modern Societies." In *Rite, Drama, Festival, Spectacle: Rehearsals toward a Theory of Cultural Performance*, edited by John J. MacAloon, 241–80. Philadelphia: Institute for the Study of Human Issues, 1984.

———. "Games." In vol. 5 of *The Encyclopedia of Religion*, 2nd ed., edited by Lindsey Jones, 3264–69. New York: Macmillan Reference USA, 2005.

———. "The Theory of Spectacle: Reviewing Olympic Ethnography." In *National Identity and Global Sports Events: Culture, Politics, and Spectacle in the Olympics and the Football World Cup*, edited by Alan Tomlinson and Christopher Young, 15–39. Albany: State University of New York Press, 2006.

MacAloon, John J., and Mihaly Czikszentmihalyi. "Deep Play and the Flow Experience in Rock Climbing." Excerpt from Mihaly Czikszentmihalyi, *Beyond Boredom and Anxiety* (San Francisco: Jossey-Bass, 1977), reprinted in *Play, Games and Sports in Cultural Contexts*, edited by Janet C. Harris and Roberta J. Park, 361–84. Champaign, Ill.: Human Kinetics Publishers, 1983.

Malone, Henry T. *Cherokees of the Old South: A People in Transition.* Athens: University of Georgia Press, 1976.

Martin, Joel W. "Before and Beyond the Sioux Ghost Dance." *Journal of the American Academy of Religion* 59 (Winter 1991): 677–701.

———. "From 'Middle Ground' to 'Underground': Southeastern Indians and the Early

Republic." In *Religion and American Culture: A Reader*, edited by David G. Hackett, 129–45. New York: Routledge, 1995.

———. "Visions of Revitalization in the Eastern Woodlands: Can a Middle-Aged Theory Stretch to Embrace the First Cherokee Converts?" In *Reassessing Revitalization Movements: Perspectives from North America and the Pacific Islands*, edited by Michael E. Harkin, 61–87. Lincoln: University of Nebraska Press, 2004.

Martin, Luther H. "Secrecy in Hellenistic Religious Communities." In *Secrecy and Concealment: Studies in the History of Mediterranean and Near Eastern Religions*, edited by Hans G. Kippenberg and Guy G. Stroumsa, 101–21. Leiden, Netherlands: E. J. Brill, 1995.

Masuzawa, Tomoko. "Culture." In *Critical Terms for Religious Studies*, edited by Mark C. Taylor, 70–93. Chicago: University of Chicago Press, 1998.

Mathewes, Charles. "Religion and Secrecy" (Editor's Introduction). *Journal of the American Academy of Religion* 74, no. 2 (June 2006): 273–74.

Mauss, Marcel. "The Notion of Body Techniques." In *Sociology and Psychology: Essays*. 1935. Translated by Ben Brewster. London: Routledge & Kegan Paul, 1979.

McClinton, Rowena, ed. *The Moravian Springplace Mission to the Cherokees*. 2 vols. With an introduction by Rowena McClinton. Lincoln: University of Nebraska Press, 2007.

McCutcheon, Russell. *Manufacturing Religion: The Discourse on Sui Generis Religion and the Politics of Nostalgia*. New York: Oxford University Press, 1997.

———. Review: "Relating Smith." *Journal of Religion* 86, no. 2 (April 2006): 287–97.

McLoughlin, William G. "Cherokee Anti-Mission Sentiment, 1824–1828." *Ethnohistory* 21, no. 4 (Fall 1974): 361–70.

———. "Thomas Jefferson and the Rise of Cherokee Nationalism, 1806–1809." *William and Mary Quarterly*, 3rd ser., 32 (1975): 77–78.

———. "Cherokees and Methodists, 1824–1834." *Church History* 50, no. 1 (March 1981): 44–63.

———. *The Cherokee Ghost Dance: Essays on the Southeastern Indians, 1789–1861*. Macon, Ga.: Mercer University Press, 1984.

———. *Cherokees and Missionaries, 1789–1839*. New Haven: Yale University Press, 1984.

———. *Cherokee Renascence in the New Republic*. Princeton: Princeton University Press, 1986.

———. "Ghost Dance Movements: Some Thoughts on Definition Based on Cherokee History." *Ethnohistory* 37 (Winter 1990): 25–44.

———. *The Cherokees and Christianity, 1794–1870: Essays on Acculturation and Cultural Persistence*. Edited by Walter H. Conser. Athens: University of Georgia Press, 1994.

Merrell, James H. *The Indians' New World: Catawbas and Their Neighbors from European Contact through the Era of Removal*. Chapel Hill: University of North Carolina Press, 1989.

Michelson, Truman. *The Owl Sacred Pack of the Fox Indians*. Smithsonian Institution, Bureau of American Ethnology Bulletin 72. Washington, D.C.: GPO, 1921.

———. "Notes on Fox Mortuary Customs and Beliefs." In *40th Annual Report, Bureau of American Ethnology, 1918–19*, 351–496. Washington, D.C.: G.P.O., 1925.

Milling, Chapman J. *Red Carolinians*. Chapel Hill: University of North Carolina Press, 1940.

Mooney, James. "Myths of the Cherokees." *Journal of American Folklore* 1, no. 2 (1888): 97–108.

———. "The Cherokee Ball Play." *American Anthropologist* 31 (1890): 105–32.

———. "Cherokee Theory and Practice of Medicine." *Journal of Cherokee Studies* 7 (Spring 1982): 25–29. Reprint of article first published in the *Journal of American Folkore* 3 (1890): 44–50.

———. *The Sacred Formulas of the Cherokees*. Seventh Annual Report of the Bureau of American Ethnology, 1885–1886, 301–97. Washington, D.C.: GPO, 1891. Reprinted in *Myths of the Cherokee and Sacred Formulas of the Cherokees* (Nashville: Charles and Randy Elder, 1982). Page citations are to the reprint edition.

———. *Myths of the Cherokee*. Nineteenth Annual Report of the Bureau of American Ethnology, 1897–1898, pt. 1, 3–576. Washington, D.C.: GPO, 1900. Reprinted in *Myths of the Cherokee and Sacred Formulas of the Cherokees* (Nashville: Charles and Randy Elder, 1982). Page citations are to the reprint edition.

———. "The Cherokee River Cult." *Journal of Cherokee Studies* 7, no. 1 (Spring 1982): 30–36. Reprint of article first published in *Journal of American Folklore* 13 (1900):1–10.

———. "The Cherokee Sacred Formulas: Statement of Mr. Mooney's Researches, Submitted Feb. 8, 1916." *Journal of Cherokee Studies* 7 (Spring 1982): 47–48.

Mooney, James, and Frans M. Olbrechts. *The Swimmer Manuscript: Cherokee Sacred Formulas and Medicinal Prescriptions*. Smithsonian Institution, Bureau of American Ethnology Bulletin 99. Washington, D.C.: GPO, 1932.

Muller, Jon. "The Southern Cult." In *The Southeastern Ceremonial Complex: Artifacts and Analysis*, The Cottonlandia Conference, edited by Patricia Galloway, 11–26. Lincoln: University of Nebraska Press, 1989.

Nabokov, Peter. *Indian Running: Native American History and Tradition*. Santa Fe, N.M.: Ancient City Press, 1981.

Neely, Sharlotte. *Snowbird Cherokees: People of Persistence*. Athens: University of Georgia Press, 1991.

The New Oxford Annotated Bible, New Revised Standard Version, with the Apocrypha. 3rd ed. New York: Oxford University Press, 2001.

Olbrechts, Frans M. "Some Cherokee Methods of Divination." International Congress of Americanists Proceedings 23 (1930), 547–52.

———. "Cherokee Belief and Practice with Regard to Childbirth," *Anthropos* 26 (1931): 17–33.

Olson, Carl. *Theory and Method in the Study of Religion: A Selection of Critical Readings*. Belmont, Calif.: Wadsworth, 2003.

Opler, Morris Edward. "The Jicarilla Apache Ceremonial Relay Race and its Relation to Pueblo Counterparts." *American Anthropologist* 46 (1944): 75–97.

———. *Childhood and Youth in Jicarilla Apache Society*. 1946. Los Angeles: Southwest Museum, 1964.

Orr, Heather S. "Ballgames: Mesoamerican Ballgames." In vol. 5 of *The Encyclopedia of Religion*, 2nd ed., edited by Lindsey Jones, 749–52. New York: Macmillan Reference USA, 2005.

Orr, Joan Greene, and Lois Calonehuskie. "Fading Voices Project Introduction." *Journal of Cherokee Studies* 14 (Special Edition, 1989): 5–6.

Oxendine, Joseph B. *American Indian Sports Heritage*. 1988. Reprint, with a new afterword by the author, Lincoln: University of Nebraska Press, 1995.

The Oxford American Desk Dictionary and Thesaurus. 2nd ed. New York: Berkley Books, 2001.

Parris, John. *The Cherokee Story*. Asheville, N.C.: Stephens Press, 1950.

Penner, Hans H. "Language, Ritual and Meaning." *Numen* 32, fasc. 1 (July 1985): 1–16.

Perdue, Theda. *Slavery and the Evolution of Cherokee Society: 1540–1866.* Knoxville: University of Tennessee Press, 1979.

———. *Cherokee Women: Gender and Culture Change, 1700–1835.* Lincoln: University of Nebraska Press, 1998.

Perdue, Theda, and Michael D. Green, eds. *The Cherokee Removal: A Brief History with Documents.* Boston: Bedford Books of St. Martin's Press, 1995.

Pesantubbee, Michelene. "When the Earth Shakes: The Cherokee Prophecies of 1811–12." *American Indian Quarterly* 17, no. 3 (Summer 1993): 301–17.

Phillips, Joyce B., and Paul Gary Phillips, eds. *The Brainerd Journal: A Mission to the Cherokees, 1817–1823.* Lincoln: University of Nebraska Press, 1998.

Pratt, Mary Louise. *Imperial Eyes: Travel Writing and Transculturation.* London: Routledge, 1992.

Prucha, Francis Paul. *The Indians in American Society from the Revolutionary War to the Present.* Berkeley: University of California Press, 1985.

———. *The Great Father: The United States Government and the American Indians.* Abr. ed. Lincoln: University of Nebraska Press, 1986.

Random House Webster's College Dictionary. New York: Random House, 1992.

Ray, Benjamin C. "The Koyukon Bear Party and the 'Bare Facts of Ritual.'" *Numen* 38, fasc. 2 (December 1991): 151–76.

Read, K. E. "Leadership and Consensus in a New Guinea Society." *American Anthropologist* 61, no. 3 (1959): 425–36.

Reed, Marcelina. *Seven Clans of the Cherokee Society.* Cherokee, N.C.: Cherokee Publications, 1993.

Reed, Mark. "Reflections on Cherokee Stickball." *Journal of Cherokee Studies* 2 (Winter 1977): 195–200.

Reid, John Phillip. "A Bare Board: The Failure of Law." Chapter 5 in *A Better Kind of Hatchet: Law, Trade, and Diplomacy in the Cherokee Nation during the Early Years of European Contact.* University Park: Pennsylvania State University Press, 1976.

Riley, Michael J. "Constituting the Southwest, Contesting the Southwest, Re-Inventing the Southwest." *Journal of the Southwest* 36 (Autumn 1994): 221–41.

Roberts, Tyler. "All Work and No Play: Chaos, Incongruity and *Différance* in The Study of Religion." *Journal of the American Academy of Religion* 77, no. 1 (March 2009): 81–104.

Rozema, Vicki. *Footsteps of the Cherokees: A Guide to the Eastern Homelands of the Cherokee Nation.* Winston-Salem, N.C.: John F. Blair, 1995.

Salter, Michael A. "Meteorological Play-Forms of the Eastern Woodlands." In *Studies in the Anthropology of Play: Papers in Memory of B. Allan Tindall,* edited by Phillips Stevens Jr., 16–28. Cornwall, N.Y.: Leisure Press, 1978.

———. "Play in Ritual: An Ethnohistorical Overview of Native North America." In *Play and Culture,* 1978 Proceedings of the Association for the Anthropological Study of Play, edited by Helen B. Schwartzman, 70–91. West Point, N.Y.: Leisure Press, 1980.

Sansone, David. *Greek Athletics and the Genesis of Sport.* Berkeley: University of California Press, 1988.

Scambler, Graham. *Sport and Society: History, Power and Culture.* Berkshire: Open University Press, 2005.

Searle, John R. *Speech Acts: An Essay in the Philosophy of Language.* Cambridge: Cambridge University Press, 1969.

Sensbach, Jon F. *A Separate Canaan: The Making of an Afro-Moravian World in North Carolina, 1763–1840.* Chapel Hill: Published for the Omohundro Institute of Early

American History and Culture, Williamsburg, Virginia, by the University of North Carolina Press, 1998.

Sider, Gerald M. *Lumbee Indian Histories: Race, Ethnicity, and Indian Identity in the Southern United States*. Cambridge: Cambridge University Press, 1993.

Singer, Milton. "The Cultural Pattern of Indian Civilization: A Preliminary Report of a Methodological Field Study." *Far Eastern Quarterly* 15, no. 1. (Nov. 1955): 23–36.

———. *Traditional India: Structure and Change*. Philadelphia: American Folklore Society, 1959.

Smith, Linda Tuhiwai. *Decolonizing Methodologies: Research and Indigenous Peoples*. London and Dunedin: Zed Books and University of Otago Press, 1999.

Smith, Jonathan Z. "Religion, Religions, Religious." In *Critical Terms for Religious Studies*, edited by Mark C. Taylor, 269–84. Chicago: University of Chicago Press, 1998.

Speck, Frank G. *Ethnology of the Yuchi Indians*. Anthropological Publications of the University Museum, vol. 1, no. 1. Philadelphia: University of Pennsylvania Museum, 1909.

Speck, Frank G., and Leonard Broom, in collaboration with Will West Long. *Cherokee Dance and Drama*. 1951. Reprint, with a foreword by Leonard Broom, Norman: University of Oklahoma Press, 1983.

Staal, Frits. "The Meaninglessness of Ritual." *Numen* 26, fasc. 1. (June 1979): 2–22.

———. *Rules Without Meaning: Ritual, Mantras and the Human Sciences*. New York: Peter Lang, 1989.

Starkey, Marion L. *The Cherokee Nation*. 1946. Reprint, New York: Russell and Russell, 1972.

Starr, Emmet. *Early History of the Cherokees*. N.p., 1917.

———. *History of the Cherokee Indians and Their Legends and Folk Lore*. Oklahoma City: Warden Company, 1922.

Stewart, Susan. *On Longing: Narratives of the Miniature, the Gigantic, the Souvenir, the Collection*. Baltimore: Johns Hopkins University Press, 1984.

Strickland, Rennard. "Summary of Early Laws of the Cherokees." In *Fire and the Spirits: Cherokee Law from Clan to Court*, 211–26. Norman: University of Oklahoma Press, 1975.

———. "Emmet Starr." In *Encyclopedia of North American Indians*, edited by Frederick E. Hoxie, 609–10. New York: Houghton Mifflin Company, 1996.

Sullivan, Winnifred Fallers. "American Religion is Naturally Comparative." In *A Magic Still Dwells: Comparative Religion in the Postmodern Age*, edited by Kimberly C. Patton and Benjamin C. Ray, 117–30. Berkeley: University of California Press, 2000.

Sumner, Jim L. "The State Fair and the Development of Modern Sports in Late Nineteenth Century North Carolina." *Journal of Sport History* 15, no. 2 (Summer 1988): 138–50.

Sweet, Jill D. *Dances of the Tewa Pueblo Indians*. Santa Fe, N.M.: School of American Research Press, 1985.

Szasz, Ferenc M. "The United States and New Mexico: A Twentieth-Century Comparative Religious History." In
Religion in Modern New Mexico, edited by Ferenc M. Szasz and Richard W. Etulain, 171–96. Albuquerque: University of New Mexico Press, 1997.

Tambiah, Stanley J. *Buddhism and the Spirit Cults in North-East Thailand*. Cambridge: Cambridge University Press, 1970.

Thornton, Russell, with the assistance of C. Matthew Snipp and Nancy Breen. *The Cherokees: A Population History.* Lincoln: University of Nebraska Press, 1990.

———. "Boundary Dissolution and Revitalization Movements: The Case of the Nineteenth-Century Cherokees." *Ethnohistory* 40, no. 3 (Summer 1993): 359–83.

Thorp, Daniel B. *The Moravian Community in Colonial North Carolina: Pluralism on the Southern Frontier.* Knoxville: University of Tennessee Press, 1989.

"Trail of Tears." In the *Encyclopedia of North American Indians*, edited by Frederick E. Hoxie, 639–40. New York: Houghton Mifflin Company, 1996.

Turner, Victor. *The Ritual Process: Structure and Anti-Structure.* Ithaca, N.Y.: Cornell University Press, 1969.

———. "Liminal to Liminoid, in Play, Flow, and Ritual: An Essay in Comparative Symbology." In *Play, Games and Sports in Cultural Contexts*, edited by Janet C. Harris and Roberta J. Park, 123–64. Champaign, Ill.: Human Kinetics Publishers, 1983. First published in *Rice University Studies* 60, no. 3 (Summer 1974): 53–92.

Urban, Hugh. "The Torment of Secrecy: Ethical and Epistemological Problems in the Study of Esoteric Traditions." *History of Religions* 37, no. 3 (Feb. 1998): 209–48.

Vennum, Thomas, Jr. *American Indian Lacrosse: Little Brother of War.* Washington, D.C.: Smithsonian Institution Press, 1994.

Walker, James R. *Lakota Belief and Ritual.* Edited by Raymond J. DeMaille and Elaine A. Jahner. 1980. Lincoln: University of Nebraska Press, 1991.

———. *Lakota Myth.* Edited by Elaine A. Jahner. Lincoln: University of Nebraska Press, 1983.

———. Wallace, Anthony F. C. *Jefferson and the Indians: The Tragic Fate of the First Americans.* Cambridge: Belknap Press of Harvard University Press, 1999.

Wax, Murray L. "The Ethics of Research in American Indian Communities." *American Indian Quarterly* 15, no. 2 (1991): 431–56.

Wetmore, Ruth. "The Green Corn Ceremony of the Eastern Cherokees." *Journal of Cherokee Studies* 8, no. 1 (Spring 1983): 46–56.

Whittington, E. Michael, ed. *The Sport of Life and Death: The Mesoamerican Ballgame.* New York: Thames & Hudson, 2001.

Wiener, Margaret. *Visible and Invisible Realms: Power, Magic, and Colonial Conquest in Bali.* Chicago: University of Chicago Press, 1995.

Patrick Williams and Laura Chrisman, eds. *Colonial Discourse and Post-Colonial Theory: A Reader.* New York: Columbia Press, 1994.

Williams, Samuel Cole, ed. "The Tour of Duke of Orleans, Later Louis Philippe, King of the French (1797)." In *Early Travels in the Tennessee Country, 1549–1800*, with introductions, annotations, and index by the editor, 433–41. Johnson City, Tenn.: Watauga Press, 1928.

Wittgenstein, Ludwig. *Philosophical Investigations.* Translated from the German by G. E. M. Anscombe. 3rd ed. New York: Macmillan Publishing Company, 1958.

Witthoft, John. "The Cherokee Green Corn Medicine and the Green Corn Festival." *Journal of the Washington Academy of Sciences* 36, no. 7 (1946): 213–19.

———. "Notes on a Cherokee Migration Story." *Journal of the Washington Academy of Sciences* 37, no. 9 (1947): 304–5.

———. "Will West Long, Cherokee Informant." *American Anthropologist* 50, no. 2 (April–June 1948): 355–59.

———. *Green Corn Ceremonialism in the Eastern Woodlands*. Occasional Contributions from the Museum of Anthropology of the University of Michigan. Ann Arbor: University of Michigan Press, 1949.

———. "Eastern Woodland Community Typology and Acculturation." In *Symposium on Cherokee and Iroquois Culture*, edited by William N. Fenton and John Gulick, 67–76. Smithsonian Institution, Bureau of American Ethnology Bulletin 180. Washington, D.C.: GPO, 1961.

———. "Cherokee Beliefs Concerning Death." *Journal of Cherokee Studies* 8 (Fall 1983): 68–72.

Witthoft, John, and Wendell S. Hadlock. "Cherokee-Iroquois Little People." *Journal of American Folklore* 59 (1946): 413–22.

Wyss, Hilary E. *Writing Indians: Literacy, Christianity, and Native Community in Early America*. Amherst: University of Massachusetts Press, 2000.

Zogry, Michael J. "Ballgames: North American Indian Ballgames." In vol. 2 of *The Encyclopedia of Religion*, 2nd ed., edited by Lindsey Jones, 752–56. New York: Macmillan Reference USA, 2005.

Dissertations, Theses, and Other Unpublished Works

Bloom, Leonard. "The Acculturation of the Eastern Cherokee." Ph.D. diss., Duke University, 1937.

"Cherokee, N.C. Fact Sheet." Museum of the Cherokee Indian, Cherokee, N.C., n.d. Photocopy.

Fogelson, Raymond D. "A Study of the Conjuror in Eastern Cherokee Society." Master's thesis, University of Pennsylvania, 1958.

———. "The Cherokee Ball Game: A Study in Southeastern Ethnology." Ph.D. diss., University of Pennsylvania, 1962.

King, Duane Harold. "A Grammar and Dictionary of the Cherokee Language." Ph.D. diss., University of Georgia, 1975.

Owl, W. David. "The Big Ball Game." In "Stories from a Wise Old Owl: As Told by Rev. W. David Owl of the Great Smoky Mountain Eastern Band of Cherokees," 6–8. Versailles, N.Y.: W. David Owl and Jean Owl Huff, 1972. Museum of the Cherokee Indian Archives.

Reagan, Hester, Ethel McCoy et al. Fall Fair competition lists. "Plants," VF Culture File. Typescripts, Museum of the Cherokee Indian, Cherokee, N.C., n.d., compiled by Mary U. Chiltoskey, n.d., Museum of the Cherokee Indian Archives, Cherokee, N.C.

Thomas, Robert K. "Cherokee Values and World View." Research paper. Papers Based on Research of the Cross-Cultural Laboratory of the Institute for Research in Social Science. North Carolina Collection, Wilson Library, University of North Carolina, Chapel Hill, 1958.

Witthoft, John. "Notes on Death." Typescript, July 1977. VF Culture File, "Death, Burial," Museum of the Cherokee Indian Archives, Cherokee, N.C.

Nonbook Materials

Calendars published by the North Carolina Cooperative Extension, 1997, 1998.

Enduring Voices Collection. Interviews, 1997–1998. MSS 99-11. Museum of the Cherokee Indian Archives, Cherokee, N.C. Videocassettes and transcriptions.

Howard, Gregg, and Rick Eby, eds., with Marie Junaluska, speaker. "A Cherokee

Language Sampler: 'Kituwah Dialect.'" N.p.: VIP Publishing Company, 1995. Audiocassette and pamphlet.

North Carolina: Variety Vactionland. 16mm. Communication Center, University of North Carolina at Chapel Hill, for the North Carolina Department of Conservation and Development, 1951. V.T. 46, North Carolina Department of Archives and History, Raleigh, N.C. Videotape.

Objects. Item no. 180496 (ball game scarifier) and collection card; item no. 018993 (ball sticks); item no. 1805764 (war dance mask representing human and rattlesnake) and collection card. Smithsonian Institution's National Museum of the American Indian Cultural Resources Center, Suitland, Md.

Objects. Item no. E272976 (two pair ball sticks); item no. E360223 (one pair ball racket sticks); item no. E151641 (ball rackets); item nos. E272975 and E272976 (two pair ball sticks); item no. E130487 (four pairs ball dress pants). Smithsonian National Museum of Natural History, Department of Anthropology, Ethnology Collections, Museum Support Center, Suitland, Md.

Photographs, 1937–1949. Files of the North Carolina Department of Conservation and Development, Travel Information Division. North Carolina Division of Archives and History, Raleigh, N.C.

Royce, Charles C. "Map of the Former Territorial Limits of the Cherokee 'Nation of' Indians," 1884. In *Fifth Annual Report of the Bureau of American Ethnology, 1888.* Reprint of map, Museum of the Cherokee Indian, 1977.

Shepherd Photo Collection. Photographs, 1921–1923. MSS 99-04. Museum of the Cherokee Indian Archives, Cherokee, N.C.

Witthoft, John. "Ceremonies, pt. 1." Audiotape of remarks. John Witthoft Collection, 87–171. Museum of the Cherokee Indian Archives, Cherokee, N.C., 1968. Audiocassette no. 4, side 2 (cassette no. 5 in original master).

———. "Dolls, Games, Musical Instruments, Stone and Other Tools." Audiotape of remarks. John Witthoft Collection, 87–171. Museum of the Cherokee Indian Archives, Cherokee, N.C., 1968. Audiocassette no. 11, side B.

"Wolftown 1939 Ball Team Photograph." Ph 482. Museum of the Cherokee Indian Archives, Cherokee, N.C., 1939.

Zogry, Michael J. Photographs in the author's private collection.

———. Videocassettes in the author's private collection. Cherokee Indian Fair, 1997–2007.

Zogry, Michael J., interviewer. Michael J. Zogry Collection (#20339). Interviews, 1997–1998. Southern Folklife Collection, Wilson Library, University of North Carolina at Chapel Hill, Chapel Hill, N.C. Videocassettes and transcriptions (same materials as the Enduring Voices Collection).

Newspapers and Popular Magazines

Asheville (N.C.) Citizen-Times, September 30, 1934; September 4, 1977; September 18, 1977; September 22, 1988; October 8, 1998.

Asheville (N.C.) Sunday Citizen, April 10, 1927.

Charlotte (N.C.) Observer, September 30, 1928.

Cherokee (N.C.) One Feather, February 16, 1968; April 22, 1970; September 30, 1970; July 13, 1977; July 9, 1986; October 5, 1988; October 4, 2000.

Knoxville (Tenn.) Journal, September 29, 1988.

Life Magazine, November 11, 1946.

New York Times, September 20, 1936; May 8, 1960.
Raleigh, (N.C.) News and Observer, May 13, 1888; October 1, 1889; October 17, 1889; November 16, 2000.
Raleigh Register and North Carolina Gazette, August 21, 1837
State, 1 January 1955.

Websites
⟨www.amphilsoc.org/library/mole/d/duponceau.htm⟩
⟨www.census.gov⟩
⟨www.cherokeemuseum.org/education-warriors.htm⟩
⟨www.citizen-times.com⟩
⟨www.cnn.com⟩
⟨www.nc-cherokee.com⟩
⟨http://infotrac.galegroup.com⟩
⟨www.nature.nps.gov⟩
⟨www.proquest.com/products_pq/descriptions/pq-hist-news.shtml⟩
⟨www.wbir.com⟩

Index

Page numbers in italics refer to illustrations.

A-lhsdelhdo-di ("conjure-man"), 114. *See also* Conjurer
Abrahamian, Ara, 224
Adair, James, 38, 62, 126, 272 (n. 37)
Ada'nunwisgi, 114. *See also* Conjurer
Adawehi, 115. *See also* Conjurer
Adáwisgi ("conjure-man"), 114. *See also* Conjurer
Adela diktati, adélâ diktă:tĭ (examining with the beads). *See* Sunikta diktati
Adonisgi ("conjure-man"), 114. *See also* Conjurer
A. J. Ayer Collection, 99
Alcohol consumption during ball game training and games, 83, 84, 86, 130, 131, 158, 159, 160
Amayi didadzun:stisgi (the one who takes them to water), 114. *See also* Conjurer; Amohi atsvsdi
American Board of Commissioners for Foreign Missions (ABCFM), 67, 76, 89, 94; mission school, 68, 90
American Philosophical Society, Historical and Literary Committee, 88
American Philosophical Society Library, 88
Amohi atsvsdi, amó:hi atsv´:sdi (going, being taken to water), 3, 30, 36, 107; defined and described, 3, 13, 15–16, 119–21; component of narrative transmission, 37–38, 43; nineteenth-century reports, 84, 100–101, 260 (n. 191); component of green corn ceremonialism, 111; igawesdi (formula) for, 117, 118; accounts of, 117, 144, 170, 214; distinction between going and being taken to water, 119–20; earliest written account, 120; as part of medicinal activity, 125; consequences of not performing activity, 132; historical comparative description, Mooney / Fogelson / Zogry, 132–37; demonstrated for the camera, *135*, *177*; distinction between final occasion after contest and previous occasions during course of complex, 136–37; and issues of cultural propriety, 137–39; as part of tourist presentation, 179; address of team manager before, 185–86; as component of war ceremonialism, 191, 193
Anăda´dûñtăskĭ (Roasters), 44
Ana-dóni-ha (they conjure now, conjuring), 114. *See also* Conjurers, Conjuring
A-nahnezóʌsgi (ball game). *See* Anetso
Anderson, Rufus King, 77
Andrew, John, III, 104
Anetso, a:ne:tso, a-nahnezóʌsgi (Cherokee ball game): as public performance, 1, 152, 160, 168, 172, 174, 176; meaning of term, 2; as analogue to ball games in Popol Vuh, 2; basic description of game and complex, 11–14; as autotelic activity, 11, 21, 24, 211, 219, 226; as figure of speech, 44, 60, 63–64, 103, 186, 194; earliest non-Cherokee written reference to, 60–63; as stratagem in warfare, 62; as analogue of warfare, 104, 187; key elements of, 113–32; women playing, 144, 145, 155, 157, 182–84; rendering of term, 159; revival of as stratagem in struggle for voting rights, 164; participants' belief in activities of the complex, 169, 179, 184; supposed suppression of by Cherokee Indian Agency, 175–76; as part of tourist presentation, 179; as a surrogate of war, 187, 189, 192; as a mechanism for managing aggression and maintaining social cohesion, 189;

relationship between warfare and ball game, 189; similarities between ball game and warfare ceremonialism, 190–94, 214–15; as ritual focused on Little Men, 195–96; role in preserving other Cherokee cultural elements, 214. *See also* Match games; Women

Anetso ceremonial complex: key elements of, 3, 113–32; change in, 4, 30, 107, 144, 148, 152, 184, 213, 232; women's roles in, 9, 132

Anida'wehĭ (supernaturals), 60

Anigilohi, 108

Ani'-Hyûñ'tikwălâ'skĭ (Thunders), 41. *See also* Thunders *and associated cross-references*

Anikutani, Aní:Kutánî (priestly caste), 107–10

Animals: in Cherokee narratives, 36, 243–44 (n. 22); relationships of with plants, humans, and other beings as compared with Jewish and Christian biblical traditions, 45

Anisga'ya Tsunsdi'ga (Little Men), 57. *See also* Thunders *and associated cross-references*

Anisgaya Tsvsdi, Anisga'ya Tsunsdĭ' (Little Men), 45, 57, 194; as distinct from Yûñwĭ Tsunsdi' (Little People), 57. *See also* Thunders *and associated cross-references*

Anitsalagi (Tsalagi, Cherokee) people, 5

Aniyvwiya (Principal People, Real People), 5

Arens, William, 222

Asga'ya Gi'găgeĭ (Red Man of the Lightning), 251 (n. 151). *See also* Lightning; Little Red Men; Red Man

Asheville, N.C., 165, 175

Asheville (N.C.) Citizen-Times, 170

Asheville (N.C.) Sunday Citizen, 169

Âsĭ, 37. *See also* Osi

Assimilation program, 75–76

A.su.lo'. *See* Pants, ball players'

Atlanta, Ga., 170

Atlanta Journal, 170–71

Atsi'la gălûñkw'ti'yu (honored fire), 111

Attakullakulla (Little Carpenter), 74

Atûnka (lamb's-quarter), 129

Autotelic activity, 21, 240 (n. 59)

Ax. *See* Ităgû'năhĭ

A'yûñ'inĭ (Swimmer), 246 (n. 60)

Bakhtin, Mikhail, 11

Ball (a-lhsgalhdi), 2

Ball game, Cherokee. *See* Anetso

Ball game, Choctaw, 235

Ball game of the birds and animals, Cherokee narrative of, 47–48, 127, 191, 233

Ball games, First Nations, 201, 235, 272 (n. 37), 285 (n. 15). *See also* Anetso; Ball game, Choctaw; Lacrosse

Ball games, Mesoamerican, 217, 221

Ball play. *See* Anetso

Ball Play Creek, 155, 156

Ball used in anetso, 12, 58

Baptist mission, 76, 97

Barnard, Andrew, 160

Barzun, Jacques, 222

Basso, Keith, 34

Bathing, Ceremonial, 3, 9, 37, 43, 119, 125, 191. *See also* Amohi atsvsdi

Bat in Cherokee narrative, 47; appearance and behavior of bats explained by, 48. *See also* Tla'mehă

Bell, Catherine, 11, 18, 22–24, 217–18

Bender, Ernest, 114

Bender, Margaret, 180

Big Bear, 81

Big Cove, 5, 173, 175; cultural consultants from, 57, 58, 112–13, 114, 118, 121, 122, 127, 144, 145; Big Cove ball team, 127, 129, 176

Big Sawney, 157

Bird, Solomon, 117, 121

Birdtown, 5, 169, 173

Blackburn, Gideon, 76

Black Fog, 134

Black Man, 57

Black Rattlesnake, 134

Black Spider, 134

Blair, C. M., 174

Blanchard, Kendall, 211, 215, 235

Bloom, Leonard. *See* Broom (Bloom), Leonard

Blount, William, 157–58

Blue Ridge Parkway, 6

Blythe, Jarrett, 171, 174–75
Board of Indian Trade, 60–61
Booger Dance (Tsu `nigādu`lĭ), 121, 122–23
Boudinot, Elias (Buck Watie), 91, 92
Bouquet, Henry (Col.), 63
Bourdieu, Pierre, 11, 16, 17, 67, 68
Bowl Game, Iroquois, 215
Brainerd Mission, 89, 90
Broom (Bloom), Leonard, 201, 211, 214–15; and Frank Speck, 111, 112, 121, 122, 123, 193
Brown, Michael F., 138
"Brown face," European American actors appearing in, 154
Bryson, Anne. D., 169
Bryson, Holmes, Jr., 173, 174
Bureau of Indian Affairs, 6, 164, 233
Burridge, Kenelm, 53, 188
Butler, Elizur, 102, 161
Butrick (Buttrick), Daniel S., 91, 93, 95, 99–101, 193
Buzzard in Cherokee narrative, 41
Byhan, Gottlieb, 75

Caesar (Cherokee headman), 61
Callois, Roger, 25
Cameron, Alexander, 157
Campany, Robert Ford, 19
Cardinal directions, and corresponding colors, Cherokee, 117–18
Carlisle Indian School football teams, 170
Catawba Nation, 149
Catawgwatihih, 79
Ceremonial complex, defined, 1, 2, 237 (n. 4). *See also* Anetso ceremonial complex; Ritual complex
Ceremonial cycle. *See* Ceremonial complex
Ceremonial Grounds, Cherokee, 5–7
Ceremonial round of festivals, 108
Champagne, Duane, 85
Charlie, 81, 82
Charlotte Observer, 169
Chattanooga, Tenn., 173
Chattooga (Cherokee town), 161
Cherokee, N.C. (Elowadi, Yellowhill), 173; description of, 5–7
Cherokee Boys Club, 142

Cherokee High School, 182, 183
Cherokee Historical Association, 178–79
Cherokee Indian Agency, 28, 75, 164, 166, 175, 178; records of, 166–68
Cherokee Indian Fair (Fall Festival), 5, 31, 111, 123, 169, 171, 173, 179, 181, 182; anetso as feature event of, 1, 28, 113–14, 129, 131, 135–36, 143, 147, 151–52, 165, 173, 174, 176, 178, 179, 227; Cherokee dancing as event of, 121; women's games as events of, 183
Cherokee language, 179–80, 277 (n. 154). *See also* Syllabary, Sequoyan
Cherokee Nation of Oklahoma, 29, 187
Cherokee One Feather (newspaper), 228, 238 (n. 11), 248 (n. 90), 267 (n. 118),
Cherokee Phoenix (newspaper), 91
Cherokee religious system, 5, 26, 235; scholarship regarding of some vintage, 9, 200; as a construction and heuristic device, 19, 29, 33, 107, 113, 115; interface with Christianity, 27, 54, 56, 90, 91, 96, 98–99, 104, 147; privatization of/shift in, 30, 97, 107–10, 234; cultural narratives in, 34–53 passim; peoples' rejection of in favor of Christianity, 53, 98, 115, 140, 143; other-than-human persons in, 53–60, 194–96, 198, 200; peoples' maintenance of and nonacceptance of Christianity, 69, 70, 75, 98, 140, 141, 142; rituals of, 107–45 passim; no systematic or comprehensive scholarly treatment of, 113; plotted on spectrum of Cherokee people's beliefs, 141; blended with elements of Christianity, 142; public/private dichotomy in, 132, 136, 139, 144. *See also* Anikutani; Conjurers; Conjuring
Cherokee Tribal Police, 183
Cherokee Voices (oral history project and yearly event), 181
Chestowe (Yuchi town), 27, 60–63
Chickamauga (Chicamauga) Creek Mission, Tenn., 79, 80, 89, 161
"Chief Koychezetel," 81
"Chiefing," Cherokee, 154
Chiltoskey, Mary, 123, 176
Christianities, 239 (n. 39)

Christianity, 149; notions of the body from informing scholarly discourse, 16; acceptance of by Cherokee people, 53, 98, 115, 140, 143; nonacceptance of by Cherokee people, 69, 70, 98, 140, 141, 142; Cherokee converts to, 70, 98; Butrick's primary sources converts to, 99, 100; negative characterization of contrasted with that of conjuring, 115; as largest contemporary religious system on the Qualla Boundary, 139; plotted on spectrum of Cherokee people's beliefs, 141; blended with elements of Cherokee religious system, 142; recourse to herbal medicine and, 142; and traditional practices of New Mexico and Arizona First Nations peoples, 154–55; and doctrine of the Ghost Dance, 212, 213; possible influence in privatization of Cherokee religious system, 234; notions of sacrifice in Cherokee cultural narratives, 246–47 (n. 73); as regional religion, "Cherokee Christianity," 269 (n. 196)

Churches, contemporary, on the Qualla Boundary, 139–40

Clan revenge, 188

Clans, Cherokee: revenge killing, sanctioned by, as basic theme in Cherokee narratives, 35; among animals in Cherokee narratives, 36; possible survival of Anikutani as Anigilohi, 108; structure of dance arbor and, 112, 143; number of as sacred number, 117; red paint found in ashes of Nvyanvwi associated with Paint Clan, 130, 268 (n. 153); matrilineal nature of, 185; anetso as expression of clan identity, 186, 188; as mechanism for managing aggression among, 189; male members of pitted against each other in anetso, 190; members of Bird Clan responsible for preparation of bird feathers worn by warriors and ball players, 191

Clea, 27, 61, 62, 63

Cockfight, Balinese, 222

Cold-run (village), 79

Collier, John, 170

Congregationalists, 89, 91, 99, 102

Conjure-men, 114, 115, 234. *See also* Conjurers

Conjurers (conjurors): descriptions of in primary documents, 79, 95, 101, 111, 157, 161, 164; distinguished from doctors, 97; distinguished from "priests," 100, 109–10; religious and medicinal specialists, 107, 110, 114–19, 120, 121, 132, 140–41, 220, 234; who combine elements of Cherokee religious system with Christianity, 115, 140; who advocate Christianity, 140; who reject Christianity, 140, 141. *See also* Ada'nunwisgi; Adawehi; Adáwisgi; Adonisgi; A-lhsdelhdo-di; Amayi didadzun:stisgi; Conjure-men; Conjure-women; Conjuring; Dida:hnese:sg(i); Didanvwisgi; GosΛsgi náwohdi; Tsikili

Conjure-women, 115, 234. *See also* Conjurers

Conjuring, 3, 114–16, 169, 170, 214, 265 (n. 81); negative characterization of contrasted with that of Christianity, 115; as consistent with Christian doctrine, 140; as inconsistent with Christianity, 143; two types, 195. *See also* Conjurers

Coosawatte, 86

Corman, Catherine, 71

Corn and Game, origin of in Cherokee narrative, 37, 39, 42–45

"Cosmogonic Myths," Cherokee. *See* Cultural narratives, Cherokee

Creator, Cherokee. *See* Unehlanvhi

Creek War of 1812, 82

Culin, Stewart, 11, 200–201, 202–5, 210, 212; critique of, 215, 216, 218, 225

Cullowhee, N.C., 31

Cultural change and continuity, Cherokee, 147–51, 169, 184

Cultural consultation, author's. *See* Fieldwork, author's

Cultural decline, Cherokee: concept of among scholars, 83–85, 151, 158, 160. *See also* Degeneration

Cultural narratives, Cherokee: classifica-

tion of, 34–36, 40–41; relationship with Cherokee ritual action, 36; transmission of and concomitant ritual, 36–40; discussion of, 40–53; definition of term, 242 (n. 1)
Cultural narratives, Zuni, 203
Cultural performance, 10, 135, 181, 223
Cultural underground, 74, 105, 151, 153
Cushing, Frank Hamilton, 202
Czikszentmihalyi, Mihaly, 21

Da.na.waḣ u'sdi' ("little brother of war"), term, 186. *See also* Anetso
Dance, 7, 16
Dance, Ballplayers' (Dā`tselā`nūni:", Dane `ksi:natani), Ball Play Dance, ball dance, 9, 79, 94, 100, 123, 166, 167, 168; last one held, 175–76, 214–15. *See also* Dancing, Cherokee; Dancing, Hopi
Dancing, Cherokee (Analhsgi), 3, 36, 121–23, 161, 173, 175, 179, 181, 191. *See also* Dance, Ballplayers'; Green Corn Dance
Dancing, Hopi, 155
Dane `ksi:natani:". *See* Ballplayers' Dance
Darkening Land (Usûñhi´yĭ), 43, 45, 46–47, 49, 57, 58, 134
Dā`tselā`nūni. *See* Ballplayers' Dance
Daughter of the Sun, 46–47
Davies, Samuel, 255 (n. 59)
Dâyuni`sĭ (water beetle), 41
Dean, Loomis, 176–77
Death, origin of, 46–47
Debord, Guy, 153, 223
Degeneration, cultural: concept in study of Cherokee and other First Nations cultural practices, 147–49, 201, 202, 203, 204, 205, 214
Deloria, Vine, Jr., 72, 137–38; on fieldwork, 31
De Schweinitz, Christian Frederic, 74
De´tsinuga´skû. *See* Scratching
Dida:hnese:sg(i), 115. *See also* Conjurers; Tsikili
Didanvwisgi (dida:hnvwi:sg(i), dida'nunwiski), 114–15, 125. *See also* Conjurers

Dilworth, Leah, 152, 153
Disease and Medicine, origin of in Cherokee narrative, 45–46
Di.tsu.hi.sti.ski (team manager), 13, 113, 116, 136, 186
Divination, 3, 25, 133, 170, 191, 193, 267 (n. 129). *See also* Sunikta diktati
Doctor: profession synonymous with that of conjurer, 114–15; verbal form of term, 114, 119
Dogwood Festival (Chapel Hill, N.C.), 171; ball game during, 172–73
Dowd, Gregory, 69, 81, 84
Duke of Orleans. *See* Louis-Philippe (king of France)
DuPonceau, Peter S., 88, 89
Dutch Reformed Calvinists, 89
Duyu:gh(o)dv (Principle), 278 (n. 15)

Eagle in Cherokee narrative, 47
Eagle Dance, 94, 121, 193
Earl of Egremont, 63–64
Eastern Band of Cherokee Indians (EBCI), 5, 104; name change, 238 (n. 19)
Eastern Band of Cherokee Nation (EBCN): name change, 238 (n. 19)
Elowadi (Yellowhill). *See* Cherokee, N.C
Emerson Field (Chapel Hill, N.C.), 172
Emetic, 111, 134
Enduring Voices Collection (oral history project), 10, 32, 148, 180, 182, 228, 238–39 (n. 19)
Eskaqua, 158
Ethnotourism, 138
Etowah (Hightower), 92
Evans, J. P., 101
Evarts, Jeremiah, 68, 91

Fabian, Johannes, 150
Fading Voices (oral history project), 5, 121, 238 (n. 19)
Fair Grounds, Cherokee Indian. *See* Cherokee Ceremonial Grounds
Fairs. *See* Cherokee Indian Fair; North Carolina State Fair
Fall Festival, Cherokee. *See* Cherokee Indian Fair

Index 309

Fasting, 132, 214
Feast-day dances, "Pueblo," 154–55
Field mouse in Cherokee narrative, 47
Fieldwork, author's: methodology and detail, 30–32
Finger, John, 75, 160, 169, 179
Fire: origin of in Cherokee narrative, 41–42; in anetso and warfare ceremonialism, 192
Fisher, Margaret Welpley, 209–10
Flint (Cherokee headman), 61, 62, 63
Flying Squirrel in Cherokee narrative, 47
Fogelson, Raymond, dissertation by, 7, 9; interpretation of anetso and the ceremonial complex, 11, 144, 179, 188–89, 201, 209, 217, 222; influence of scholarship, 29, 200; ethnographic fieldwork, 30; Cherokee narratives recorded by, 47; and interpretations of anetso, 53, 62; on "Cherokee pantheon" and constituent beings, 53, 58–59, 60; interpretations of missionary accounts, 86–87, 104; on the Anikutani, 108–9, 110; on conjuring, 114, 140; ball game formulas collected by, 118, 119; on *Cherokee Dance and Drama*, 121; on aspects of the ceremonial complex, 123–34 passim; request for a ball game to be played, 151; on match games, 176; on women's games, 183, 184–85; on relationship between anetso and warfare, 186–87, 190, 191, 192, 193; on objects associated with anetso, 196, 198
Foght, Harold W., 171–72
Football (soccer), 236. *See also* World Cup
Footracing, First Nations, 235–36. *See also* Running
Formulas (igawesdi, i:gawé:sdi: to say, one; plural: idigawesdi, idi:gawé:sdi), 3, 59, 69, 114, 121, 122, 126; content linked to Cherokee "myths," 35, 36, 43; related to the Thunders, 56, 57, 58, 60, 192; critique of English term, 118; described, 116–19; for taking people to water, 120, 134; taught to Cherokee people by Nvyanvwi (Stone Coat), 130; for examining the beads, 133–34,
170, for preparing people for warfare, 190–91
Formulas for Coca-Cola Classic and Kentucky Fried Chicken, 139
Frazer, James George, 125
French, Laurence, 139

Gadugi (free labor and community aid groups), 142, 189, 278 (n. 19)
Gahuka-Gama, 201, 205–6, 209, 210
Gaktvda , gaktuñ´ta, gaktûnta (prohibition), 79, 100, 129–32, 191, 214
Galvladi, Gâlûñ´lătĭ, galvlati, Gûlkwâ´gine Di´gălûñ´lătiyûñ´ (world above, above, seventh heaven), 41, 46, 117, 133–34, 244 (n. 22), 245 (n. 47)
Gambling: on outcome of anetso, 3, 25–26, 79, 80, 86, 87, 95, 100, 157, 158, 167, 193, 215; in First Nations narratives, 202
Gambold, Anna Rosina (A. R.), 67, 76–78, 80, 81, 82, 85, 126–27
Gambold, John, 67, 76–78, 80, 85, 88, 89
Game and ritual, theoretical perspectives regarding relationships between, 200–226
Games, First Nations, 4, 11, 200, 201, 202–5
Games, Hopi, 204
Games, theoretical perspectives regarding, 24–25
Games, Zuni (sholiwe), 203
Ganges River, 95
Gardner, Robert C., 97
Gatayûstĭ (gambling game), 49
Gatlinburg, Tenn., 6
Gearing, Fred, 110, 190, 195
Geertz, Clifford, 11, 19, 222
Genesis, 34
Ghost Dance hand game, Pawnee, 211–14
Gilbert, William H., 187, 189, 190, 193; on Cherokee "myths," 35, 36
Gill, Sam, 11, 16, 20
Girard, René, 218
Gluckman, Mary and Max, 218–19
"Gluckman-Turner position," 189
God, covenant name of and ritual concerning, 59

Going to Water. *See* Amohi atsvsdi
GosʌSgi náwohdi (he-made medicine), 114, 125. *See also* Conjurers
Great Smoky Mountains, 82
Great Smoky Mountains National Park, 6, 169, 174
Green, Gardiner, 87
Green Corn ceremonialism, 263 (n. 25); Cherokee, 63, 107, 110–13, 126–27
Green Corn Ceremony, Cherokee, 84, 109, 120, 121, 142, 194
Green Corn Dance, Cherokee (akɔhādĭ), 38, 83, 84, 110, 111–12, 113, 121, 166
Green Corn medicine, Cherokee, 111, 112
Greensboro, N.C., Chamber of Commerce, 168
Grimes, Ronald, 11, 21–22
Grisette, Felix A., 171
Gulick, John, 175, 178, 179–80, 187
Guttman, Alan, 219–20

Habitus, 16–17
Hall, Moody, 91, 92
Hallowell, A. Irving
Handelman, Don, 11, 21
Harkin, Michael, 178
Harmony ethic, 187–88, 190
Harrah's Cherokee Casino, 6
Harrison, Jane E., 215
Haudenausaunee (Iroquois)-Cherokee cultural affinities, 198–99
Henderson, James, 167, 168, 169
Henderson purchase, 157
Hicks, Charles R., 92, 109, 111
Hill, Sarah H., 170–71, 174
Holland, William, 69–70
Holsten River, 162
Hoxie, Frederick, 72
Hudson, Charles, 119, 280–81 (n. 77)
Huizinga, Johan, 24–25, 216, 223–24
Humans, propagation of described in narrative, 41
Hunter, Kermit, 154
Hymes, Dell, 149

Identity, Cherokee, 11, 71–72, 85, 96–97, 184, 218, 228, 230; anetso as symbol of, 1, 3, 4, 227, 250 (n. 129); performance of as text, 11; as vehicle for expression of: in nineteenth century, 28, 29, 67–70, 72, 90, 93, 105, 233; in twentieth century, 28, 143, 152, 164–65, 186, 233; anetso as vehicle for presentation of, 30; author not arbiter of, 71–72; cultural underground reinforcing, 74, 153; Christianity and, 139; anetso and community identity, 175; and language, 179, 180; physical hardship or violence linked with, 218; anetso and, 232
Igawesdi, i:gawé:sdi (to say, one; plural: idigawesdi, idi:gawé:sdi). *See* Formulas
Igv´:n(e)dhi (to do, one), 117. *See also* Formulas
I´năge-utăsûñ´hĭ (Wild Boy), 42
Indian Removal Act, 102
International Olympic Committee, 224–25
Irwin, Lee, 114
Ităgû´năhĭ (John Ax), 37, 246 (n. 60)
Ivey, Majel, 169–70

Jackson, Andrew, 102
Jacob wrestling with God (in Book of Genesis, Hebrew Bible), 34
Jennings, Joe, 175
Jones, Evan, 97–99, 102, 161
Jones, William, 208, 209, 210
Jordan, Ann T., 231–32

Kănăane´skĭ Amai´yĕhĭ (Water Spider), 42
Kanati, Kana´tĭ, 10, 50, 53, 57, 58, 63, 194, 202. *See also* Thunders *and associated cross-references*
Kanati (Kana´tĭ) and Selu, narrative of, 27, 37, 39, 40, 42–45, 49, 50, 52, 57, 194, 233, 245 (n. 53), 246 (n. 65)
Kanuga ("scratcher," scarifier), 127, 196
Kapferer, Bruce, 19, 20
Kayelli, Clokeske, 80
Kehoe, Alice Beck, 211
Kīckō moiety (Kĭ'ckō'agki'), 206–10
Kilpatrick, Alan, 114, 189
Kilpatrick, Jack, and Anna G. Kilpatrick, 114, 115, 116–17

Index 311

King, Richard, 52–53
Kituwah, Gaduwa (mother town), 252 (n. 167)
Kiyana, Alfred, 207–8, 209
Knox, Henry, 76
Kupferer, Harriet, 139
Kyselka, Frank, 165–66

Lacrosse, 1–2, 170, 173, 215, 235
—Chippewa, 218
—Haudenausaunee (Iroquois), 198, as healing activity, 215
—Meskwaki (Fox), 206, 207, 208, 209–10
Lanman, Charles, 161–62
"Laughing Molly," 82
Lenoir, Thomas, 162
Lesser, Alexander, 201, 211–14
Lévi-Strauss, Claude: distinction between games and ritual, 4, 18, 200–201, 205–11(esp. 207), 219, 224; critique of distinction, 209–11, 225, 235
Lewis, David, Jr., 231
Life (magazine), 176–77
Lightning: in Cherokee narratives, 41, 44, 50, 51, 55; beliefs regarding, 57, 58–59; association with snakes, 60, 190; ritual significance in war and ball game preparations, 190, 192, 195–96. *See also* Thunders *and associated cross-references*
Linguistic device (prefatory statement) in Cherokee narratives, 38–40
Literary Digest, 176
Little Men (Thunder Boys, Thunders, Little Red Men, Sons of Thunder, Twin Gods): in Cherokee narratives, 10, 45, 46–47, 202; beliefs regarding, 57, 194, 194–95; association with snakes, 60. *See also* Thunders *and associated cross-references*
Little Red Men, 53, 58, 59, 60, 192. *See also* Thunders *and associated cross-references*
Long, Charles H., 69, 73, 105, 152, 153
Long, Will West, 57–58, 111, 121, 122, 123, 173, 201
Longe, Alexander: on thunder and lightning, 56; involvement in incident at Chestowe, 61, 63; on the Anikutani, 108; on going to water, 120; on "red condition" of warriors, 192
Long Man, 56, 133
Louis-Philippe (king of France): account of ball games, 158–60
Lumbee, 184
Lyons, Oren, 215

MacAloon, John, 11, 21, 24–25, 215–16, 222, 223–26
Marching, 3, 132, 179, 191
Marshall, John, 102
Martin, Joel W., 71, 72, 74, 105, 151, 153
Masks, 192
Masuzawa, Tomoko, 137
Match games, 174, 175, 179, 189–90, 194, 264 (n. 49); distinguished from exhibition games, 113–14, 152, 169; preparations for, 129, 137, 172; locations of, 133; cessation of, 147, 148; ban or formal action by agency superintendent, 152, 175; superintendents' opinions of, 166–68; last real match game, 175, 176
Matsuri, 236
McClinton, Rowena, 76, 87–88
McCoy, Ethel, 123
McLoughlin, William G., 70, 76, 78, 86, 87, 93, 99, 102; cultural divisions in Cherokee society, 69, 74, 82, 90, 96; theory of Cherokee anomie and renaissance, 83, 84, 104, 158, 160; critique of theory of Cherokee anomie and renaissance, 85
McNair, David, 82
Medicine, Cherokee. *See* Nvwoti
Medicine, Green Corn, 111, 112
Medicine Man. *See* Conjurers
Meigs, Return Jonathan, 84
Menstruation, 130, 132, 192, 244 (n. 32), 268 (n. 150). *See also* Women
Merrell, James, 149
Meskwaki adoption rituals, 206–11. *See also* Sac and Fox Nation
Methodist mission, 76, 95–96
MGM News of the Day, 174
Michelson, Truman, 206, 207, 208, 210

Migration narrative, Cherokee, 35
Missionaries, Christian, 29, 65
Missionary accounts, published, 70–71
Mooney, James, duration of fieldwork, 7, 9; influence of scholarship, 9, 29, 200; interpretation of anetso and the ceremonial complex, 11, 28, 147, 164, 186, ; ethnographic fieldwork, 30, 140, 144; classification of Cherokee narratives, 33, 34–36; transmission of narratives, 36–39; Cherokee narratives recorded by, 37, 41–60 passim, 188; on Green Corn ceremonialism, 39, 111; on constituent beings of Cherokee religious system, 41–60 passim, 75; on religious revival of 1811–12, 81, 82; on Anikutani, 108; on Cherokee religious system, 113; on conjuring, 114, 116; on formulas, 117, 118; ball game formulas collected by, 118; on going to water, 120; on plants, 123, 125; on aspects of the ceremonial complex, 126, 127, 129, 130, 132, 133, 134, 137, 162; on relationship between anetso and warfare, 190; on objects associated with anetso, 195, 198
Moon in Cherokee narratives, 48
Moore, David, 95
Moravian Archives, Winston-Salem, N.C., 76, 85–86
Moravian mission, 74–76
Moravian missionary diaries, 70–71, 76–77
Murphy, N.C., 163
Museum of the Cherokee Indian, 5, 10, 119, 140, 180, 181, 228
Museum of the Cherokee Indian archives, 123, 166, 194
Myth, myths. *See* Cultural narratives
Myth-Dream, 53, 188

Nabakov, Peter, 219
Narratives, cultural. *See* Cultural narratives
Narrativization of First Nations histories, 150
National Anthropological Archives, 34, 44

National Folk Festival, 173
National Museum of Natural History, 196
National Museum of the American Indian, 196
National Park Ranger Station, Cherokee, N.C., 176
National Park Service, 6
Nayɔhi unehí. *See* Thunders
Neely, Richard, 95
New Echota, Ga., 91, 94
New Testament, 97, 98
New York Times, 173, 179
Nighthawk Keetoowah, 250 (n. 129)
Nonevents, concept of, 109
North Carolina Arts Council, 181
North Carolina Cooperative Extension Service calendars, 143–44
North Carolina State Fair, 163–64
Norton, John, 78–80, 101, 108, 109
Numbers, Cherokee sacred, 117
Nv:wo:dhi digo:hwé:li (medicine books), 116, 119
Nvwoti, Nv:wo:ti, Náwohdi, Nah wa ti, Nv wo ti (medicine), 3, 38, 40, 46, 54, 81, 117, 123, 125–26. *See also* Green Corn medicine
Nvyanvwi, Nûñ´yunu´wĭ, Nun´yunu´wi (Stonecoat): narrative of, 39, 130, 245 (n. 43), 246–47 (n. 73), 268 (n. 151)

Oconaluftee River, 5–6, 13, 121, 136, 185
Oconaluftee Village, 112, 178, 179, 194, 280 (n. 61)
Olbrechts, Frans, 38, 120
Old Zacharias, 95
Olympic Games, contemporary, 223, 224, 225, 236
Olympic Games, Greek, 11, 217, 236
Oostenally (Ustanali), Ga., 81
Oothcaloga Mission, 85
Opler, Morris, 219
Organic metaphor: as facet of definition of religion, 147, 239 (n. 39)
Origin Narratives, Cherokee, 35, 243 (n. 16)
Orthography, Cherokee: system used in this book, 237 (n. 1)

Osi (multifunction structure serving as sweathouse, meeting place, and sleeping house), 37–38, 112, 120, 244 (n. 32), 268 (n. 150)
Other-than-human persons, Cherokee, 29, 33, 36, 41, 50, 52, 53–60, 242 (n. 2); relationships of with animals, plants, humans as compared with Jewish and Christian biblical traditions, 45. *See also* Aní-Hyûñ´tikwălâ´skĭ; Anisga´ya Tsunsdi´ga; Anisgaya Tsvsdi; Asga´ya Gi´găgeĭ; Kanati; Lightning; Little Men; Little Red Men; Long Man; Nvyanvwi; Red Man; Selu; Sons of Thunder; Thunder Beings; Thunder Boys; Thunderers; Thunder Family; Thunders; Twin Gods; Uktena; Unehlanvhi; Ûñtsaiyĭ; U'tlun´ta; Yûñwĭ Tsunsdi´; Yûwĭ Gûnahi´ta; *individual names of animals*
Oxendine, Joseph, 201, 215
Owl, Moses, 50–51

Painttown, 5, 173
Pants, ball players' (A.su.lo´), 12, 198
Partridge (Cherokee headman), 62
Pawnee Nation, 201
Payne, John Howard, 99, 101
Payne Papers (John Howard Payne Papers, Payne-Butrick Manuscripts), 99–102, 108, 109–10, 187, 192–93, 195, 260–61 (n. 201)
Penner, Hans, 21
Perdue, Theda, 67, 72, 85, 98, 104
Performance, 4, 7, 149, 223
Performance forms (types, genres), 11, 223, 226
Perseverance, cultural: concept of, 150–51
Persistence, cultural: concept of, 151
Pesantubbee, Michelene, 81, 82
Peters, Sam, 206, 207, 208
Plants in Cherokee narratives, 45–46; locating, 46; medicinal uses and properties, 119, 123, 125, 126, 266 (n. 117); relationships of with animals, humans, and other beings as compared with Jewish and Christian biblical traditions, 45

Play: theoretical considerations, 22–25; war as social analogue, 218
Popol Vuh, 2
Powell, Ben, 170
Powell, Noah, 177
Pratt, Mary Louise, 154
Prayer, and propitiation, in Christianity and Cherokee religious system, 220–21
Preliminary Green Corn Feast, 111
Presbyterian Mission, 89
Priests: leading prayers in locker rooms, 220; contrasted with Cherokee conjurers, 220–21
Princesses, Cherokee, 228
Privacy/secrecy distinction, cultural, 132, 137–38, 139
Proctor, Isaac, 27, 68, 92, 93, 94, 95, 97
Progressive Era, 164
Prohibitions. *See* Gaktvda
Protestant Ethic, 187–88
Protestant Reformation, 149
Prucha, Francis Paul, 88

Qualla (Cherokee town), 173
Qualla Boundary, 30, 31, 32, 38, 110, 139, 140; constituent communities of, 5; description of, 5–7
Qualla Boundary Cooperative, 181
Quallatown Indians, 103

Rackets, ball. *See* Sticks (rackets)
Radin, Paul, 210
Raleigh News and Observer, 163, 238 (n. 11), 274 (nn. 68–70)
Raleigh Register and North Carolina Gazette, 103, 111
Rattlesnakes (Utsa´nătĭ, sing.) 60; in Cherokee narratives, 46, 49, 50–52; as design motif, 192, 196–98
Read, K. E., 206, 209
Reading people back into history, concept of, 70–72
Reagan, Hester Lambert, 123
Red Bat, 133
Redbird in Cherokee narrative, 47
"Red condition," 192
Red Deer, 133

Red Hawk, 133
Red Man, 53, 55, 56, 57, 59, 250 (n. 153). *See also* Thunders *and associated cross-references*
Red Rattlesnake, 133
Reichel, Carl Gotthold, 77
Reid, John Phillip, 61
Relay Race, Jicarilla Apache, 219, 220
Religion, etymology of, 52–53
Religion, Cherokee. *See* Cherokee religious system
Religious landscape, contemporary, 139–44
Religious Revival of 1811–12, 81, 82
Religious system, Cherokee. *See* Cherokee religious system
Religious system, definition of, 19–20, 239 (n. 39)
Removal policy, 96. *See also* Trail of Tears
Revitalization, concept of, 150–51
Rhododendron Festival (Asheville, N.C.), 173
Rice, Grantland. *See* Sportlight
Riley, Michael J., 154
Riley, Richard, 95
Ripe Green Corn Feast, 111
Ritual: and game and sport, 16–18; distinguished from ceremonial, 2; problem of definition, 18–24; definition of, 19–20
Ritual complex, 2, 237 (n. 4)
Ritual drama, 53; anetso as, 189
Ritualization, 21–23
Ross, John, 97, 99
Running, 219. *See also* Footracing

Sac and Fox Nation, 201, 206
Salter, Michael, 201
Scalp Dance, 193
"Scalp Dance and Harvest Feast" (Greensboro, N.C.), 168
Scarification. *See* Scratching
Scarifier. *See* Kanuga
Schmidt, Gertraud, 85
Schmidt, Johann Renatus, 85–86, 87, 91, 92
Schneider, Martin, 74

Schwarze, Edward, 86–87
Scratcher. *See* Kanuga
Scratching, scarification, (de´tsinuga´skû), 3, 38, 100, 118, 126–29, 128, 132, 144, 170, 179, 214
Second Great Awakening, 94
Selu, 10, 81, 112, 194, 202, 246 (n. 65). *See also* Kanati (Kana´tĭ) and Selu, narrative of; Thunder Family
Seneca (Cherokee town), 157
Sensbach, Jon, 69
Sequoyah, Lloyd Runningwolf: narrative provided by, 47–48, 118, 127, 176, 188
Sequoyah, Molly (Sequoia, Mollie), 57–58, 112, 114, 118
Shenandoah National Park, 6
Shriner's Convention (Washington, D.C.), 169
Shrovetide football, 215, 235
Sider, Gerald M., 184
"Siegel-Beals position," 189
Signification, 152–53, 154
Silence, 69, 73, 105, 153, 154
Singer, Milton, 135, 223
"Sitting up," 142
Sixty-ninth North Carolina Infantry. *See* Thomas Legion
Slavery, 75
Smallpox, 108
Smith, Jonathan Z., 13, 18, 22, 26, 225
Smith, Linda Tuhiwai, 230–31
Snakes, various: in Cherokee narratives, 46, 49; in anetso and warfare symbolism, 192. *See also* Rattlesnakes
Snowbird, 5
Soccer. *See* Football; Soccer teams, Zulu; World Cup
Soccer teams, Zulu, 219
Sons of Thunder, 60, 192. *See also* Thunders *and associated cross-references*
Sorcerer. *See* Dida:hnese:sg(i)
Soul, Cherokee notion of, 279 (n. 33)
South Carolina, Indian trade in, 27
Southeastern Fair (Atlanta, Ga.), 170, 173
Spalsbury, R. L., 171
Speck, Frank, 196, 201; and Leonard Broom, 111, 112, 121, 122, 123, 193

Index 315

Sport: theoretical considerations, 17–18; war as social analogue, 218;
Sportlight, 174
Spray, Henry W., 164
Springplace Mission, Ga., 75, 80, 85–86
Springplace Mission diaries, 76–77, 87–88
Squirrel in Cherokee narratives, 47
Staal, Frits: "meaninglessness" of ritual, 20–21, 25
Standingdeer, Carl, 171, 172
Starkey, Marion, 91, 92, 104
Starr, Emmet, 55–56
Steiner, Abraham, 74, 75
Stephen, Adam (Col.), 63
Stewart, Susan, 153
Sticks (rackets), ball players', Cherokee, 12, 13, 181, 182, 191; in Cherokee narratives, 51; formula for preparing, 118, 119; gaktvda regarding, 130; use of when going to water, 133, 134, 135, 177; design motifs of, 196–98, 197
Sticks, ball players', Meskwaki, 207, 208
Stika'yi, Stekoa (Cherokee town), 274 (n. 67)
Stone Coat. See Nvyanvwi
Strawberry Plains, Tenn., 162–63
Structural poses, red and white, 110, 191, 192–93, 195
Stuart, John (Capt.), 63–64, 155, 157
Sugar Town, 157
Sullivan, Winnifred, 150
Sumo, 215, 235
Sunikta diktati, sû'nĭkta diktă:tĭ, Adela diktati (examining with the beads), 3, 126, 133, 191; demonstrated for the camera, 177
Sun in Cherokee narratives, 41, 46–47, 48; as creator being, 54, 55, 57, 58
Super Bowl, 216, 221
Sweat baths, 112, 120. See also Osi
Swimmer. See A'yûñ'inĭ
Syllabary, Sequoyan, 74, 97, 180. See also Cherokee language
Syracuse University, 215

Talala (woodpecker, team position), 123, 132, 159, 191

Talking back to American society, 72
Taloney (Carmel), Ga., 93
Tambiah, Stanley, 2
Tellico River, 155
Tewa (Flying Squirrel) in Cherokee narratives, 47–48
3200–Acre Tract, 5
Thomas, Robert K., 187, 188
Thomas, William H., 161–62, 163
Thomas Legion (Sixty-ninth North Carolina Infantry), 162–63, 190
Thorp, Daniel B., 88, 89
Thorpe, Jim, 170
Thunder, 49–50. See also Kanati
Thunder Beings, 53, 56, 57, 59, 195, 198. See also Thunders *and associated cross-references*
Thunder Boys, 45, 50, 57, 58, 59. See also Thunders *and associated cross-references*
Thunderers, 58, 59, 250–51 (n. 136), 251 (n. 152); as distinct from Yûñwĭ Tsunsdi' (Little People), 57. See also Thunders *and associated cross-references*
Thunder Family, 50, 57, 144, 145, 251 (n. 137). Thunder Boys, 45, 50, 57, 58, 59. See also Thunders *and associated cross-references*
Thunders, 41–52 passim, 56–60, 112, 119, 198, 200; in Cherokee narratives, 41–45, 50–52; earliest written account of, 56. See also Ani'-Hyûñ'tikwălâ'skĭ; Anisga'ya Tsunsdi'ga; Anisgaya Tsvsdi; Kanati; Lightning; Little Men; Little Red Men; Other-than-human persons, Cherokee; Red Man; Selu; Sons of Thunder; Thunder Beings; Thunder Boys; Thunderers; Thunder Family; Twin Gods
Timberlake, Henry, 155, 156, 157, 181, 183, 193
Tla'mehă, Tsameha (the Bat), 47–48
Tō'kān moiety, Tō'kānagki', Tokans (Tō'kănna, sing.), 206–10
Tokono (Cherokee town), 159
Tommotley (Cherokee town), 155
Toqua (Cherokee town), 155
Tourism on the Qualla Boundary, 174, 176, 178, 180, 181

Tourist narrative, 153–54
Towns, Cherokee: Middle, Upper/Overhill, Lower, 252 (n. 167)
"Tracing Your Hysterical Roots," 228–30
Trail of Tears, 29, 65, 97, 99, 103–4; traditional activities in wake of, 160–61
Travel Information Division, North Carolina Department of Conservation and Development, 176, 178
Treaty of New Echota, 91
Treaty of 1791, 75, 83, 157–58
Tribal Council, Eastern Band of Cherokee Indians, 10, 30–31, 171
True Magazine, 176
Trunks, ball players'. See Pants, ball players'
Tsaki, Jake, 162
Tsameha (Bat). See Tla´mehă
Tsikili (horned owl, name for class of conjurer), 115. See also Dida:hnese:sg(i); Conjurers
Tsûsginâ´ĭ (Ghost country), 46–47
Tsuskwănûñ´năawa´tă (Wafford), 246 (n. 60)
Tug of War, 215
Turner, Victor, 11, 21, 123, 221
Tu´sti (Water Spider's bowl) in Cherokee narrative, 42
Twin Gods, 194, 195. See also Thunders and associated cross-references

Uktena in Cherokee narratives, 46, 58, 59
Ulvsvti, Ulûñ-sû´tĭ, u:lunsu:ti, Ulun-su ti (divination tool), 126, 130, 190, 191
Unehlanvhi, une:hlanv':hi, Une.lanu.hi (Creator, Provider, Apportioner), 54–56
Uneg, Dr., 228–30
Unega (European American, white person), 228
Universe, Cherokee: contours of described in narrative, 41
Unser Tisch, concept of, 88, 89
Unto These Hills, 154, 178, 181
Ûñtsaiyĭ, Vtsayi (Brass, the Gambler), 51, 60; Cherokee narrative of, 49–50
Usûñhi´yĭ. See Darkening Land
U-ta-la'-wa-shu-hi' ("red" or "bloody" condition), 192

U'tlun´ta (Spearfinger), 245 (n. 43)
Utsa´nătĭ. See Rattlesnake

Valley River, 160
Van Gennep, Arnold, 123, 221
Vann, James, 76, 77, 78
Vann, Margaret Scott, 76, 82
Vennum, Thomas, Jr., 137, 192
Victory Dance, 48, 123, 130, 134, 144, 193, 214
Voting rights, Cherokee, 164
Vtsayi (Brass, the Gambler). See Ûñtsaiyĭ

Wachovia, settlement of, 74
Wafford. See Tsuskwănûñ´năawa´tă
Wahnenauhi manuscript, 43
Walker, James R., 34
Warfare: vis-á-vis ball game, 189; similarities between ball game and warfare ceremonialism, 190–94; affinities with ritual, 218
Warner, Glenn "Pop," 170
Warrior, Robert Allen, 72
Warrior code, Cherokee, 185
Warriors of AniKituhwa, 121, 181
Washington, D.C., 169
Washington, George, 75
Wax, Murray L., 139
Weber, Max, 187–88
Western Carolina University, 31
Wetmore, Ruth, 111
White, George, 161, 227
White Path's Rebellion, 29, 96–97
Wiener, Margaret, 222
Wiggan, Eleazer, 61, 63
Witch. See Dida:hnese:sg(i)
Wittgenstein, Ludwig, 73
Witthoft, John, 50–51, 110–11, 112, 118; theory of anetso as ritual, 194–95, 198, 200,
Wolf people, Wolves, 44
Wolftown, 5, 129, 131, 144, 145;
Wolftown ball team, 8, 13, 14, 16, 129, 131, 144–45, 176–77, 177, 185; women's team, 145, 183
Women: as conservators and transmitters of cultural traditions, 38, 244 (n. 32); apocalyptic prophecies related by, 82;

Index 317

rape of by Anikutani cited in narratives, 108; separate osi constructed for, 112; role in capture of Nvyanvwi, 130; playing anetso, 144, 145, 155, 157; Choctaw women playing a ball game, 278 (n. 164). *See also* Anetso; Menstruation
Worchester, Samuel A., 102
World Cup, football (soccer), 224
Wovoka, 212

Wrestling, Jacob with God. *See* Jacob wrestling with God

Yellowhill (Yellow Hill). *See* Cherokee, N.C
Yellowhill ball team, 176
Yuchi, 61–63
Yûñwĭ Tsunsdi´ (Little People), 57. *See also* Anisgaya Tsvsdi
Yûwĭ Gûnahi´ta (Long Man), 133. *See also* Long Man

Made in the USA
Monee, IL
26 March 2026

46900249R00192